HUMAN RIGHTS
E:

THE EFFECTS OF THE CONVENTION ON THE UNITED KINGDOM AND IRELAND

AUSTRALIA
LBC Information Services—Sydney

CANADA AND USA
Carswell—Toronto

NEW ZEALAND
Brooker's—Auckland

SINGAPORE AND MALAYSIA
Thomson Information (S.E. Asia)—Singapore

HUMAN RIGHTS AND THE EUROPEAN CONVENTION

THE EFFECTS OF THE CONVENTION ON THE UNITED KINGDOM AND IRELAND

BRICE DICKSON

General Editor

LONDON
SWEET & MAXWELL
1997

Published in 1997 by
Sweet & Maxwell Ltd of
100 Avenue Road,
London NW3 3PF
Computerset by Wyvern 21 Ltd, Bristol
Printed in Great Britain by Clays Ltd, St Ives plc

No natural forests were destroyed to make this product;
only farmed timber was used and replanted

A CIP catalogue record for this book is available from the British Library

ISBN 0 421 531 606

PREFACE

There is now no shortage of books in English on the European Convention on Human Rights, many of which are excellent. The rationale for producing yet another is two-fold. First, none of the books currently available focuses on the impact of the Convention on the distinct common law jurisdictions of these islands. If they do try to integrate discussion of the Convention into, say, a treatment of the law concerning civil liberties in England and Wales, they tend to ignore the role of the Convention in other areas of law as well as in the neighbouring jurisdictions of Scotland, Northern Ireland and the Republic of Ireland. Nor do they consider the significance of the Convention within European Union law. It is those gaps which the current book seeks to plug. Second, existing books do not, for the most part, pay much attention to the role played by the European Convention within the domestic courts of the common law jurisdictions in these islands. That role is becoming ever more important, especially as British judges have been aware for some time that the policy of the Labour Party is to bring about the incorporation of the Convention into United Kingdom law before the end of the century. Each of the main chapters in this book therefore devotes several pages to the ways in which the domestic courts in all of the jurisdictions have interacted with the Convention up to now. Consideration is also given to likely developments in the future, though the details of the incorporation plans of the new Labour Government could not be discussed because they had not yet been announced.

The book is primarily aimed at students on undergraduate and postgraduate courses on human rights and civil liberties. It should also be of use to the busy practictioner and to members of advice centres and pressure groups who want to weigh up their chances of achieving reform of the law through reliance upon the Convention either locally or in Strasbourg.

Thanks are due not only to the individuals who have contributed chapters to the book but also to the publishing and editorial staff at Sweet & Maxwell who have been most supportive throughout the longer than expected production period. An acknowledgement is also due to the publishers for arranging for the compilation of the Tables and Index.

Contributors have sought to ensure that the law as stated is up to date as of June 1, 1997.

Brice Dickson
University of Ulster
July 1997

NOTES ON CONTRIBUTORS

Noreen Burrows is Professor of European Law at the University of Glasgow.

Alpha Connelly is a member of the Equality Studies Centre and Lecturer in Law at University College Dublin.

Brice Dickson is Professor of Law at the University of Ulster at Jordanstown.

Piers Gardner is Director of the Brithsh Institute of International and Comparative Law in London.

Jim Murdoch is Senior Lecturer in Public Law and Head of the School of Law at the University of Glasgow.

Chanaka Wickremasinghe is Senior Research Officer at the British Institute of International and Comparative Law in London.

CONTENTS

TABLE OF CASES

CASES BEFORE THE
EUROPEAN COURT OF HUMAN RIGHTS

CASES BEFORE THE EUROPEAN COMMISSION OF HUMAN RIGHTS (NOT REPORTED IN *DECISIONS AND REPORTS*)

CASES BEFORE THE EUROPEAN COMMISSION OF HUMAN RIGHTS (REPORTED IN *DECISIONS AND REPORTS*)

CASES BEFORE UNITED KINGDOM COURTS

CASES BEFORE THE EUROPEAN COURT OF JUSTICE AND THE COURT OF FIRST INSTANCE

TABLE OF LEGISLATION

TREATIES AND CONVENTIONS

LEGISLATION APPLICABLE IN PARTS OF THE UNITED KINGDOM

STATUTES

STATUTORY INSTRUMENTS

TABLE OF IRISH LEGISLATION

CHAPTER 1

THE COUNCIL OF EUROPE AND THE EUROPEAN CONVENTION

The European Convention for the Protection of Human Rights and Fundamental Freedoms, though in many respects still a flawed document, is without doubt the most successful human rights instrument in the world today. Its impact continues to grow not just within Europe but throughout the world. People who are impressed by the Convention's reputation, and who feel that it may be able to help them pursue a grievance, need to be clear as to its exact scope and the procedures that have to be followed if they are to take full advantage of it. The purpose of this opening chapter, therefore, is to explain the institutional setting and present workings of the Convention with a view to providing background material for the more detailed expositions contained in subsequent chapters.

The Council of Europe and Human Rights

One of the commonest misconceptions shared by persons new to the European Convention is that it is a creature of the European Economic Community—now the European Union. In fact the Convention is the offspring not of that intergovernmental body but of an older and larger one, the Council of Europe. It has nothing whatsoever to do with the European Union's organs in Brussels or Luxembourg. The Council of Europe was formed in 1949 with the general aim of enhancing the cultural, social and political life of Europe, which had, of course, been devastated during the Second World War. The Treaty establishing the Council was signed in London on May 5, 1949. Today the Council of Europe lists its aims under the following five headings:

1. To protect human rights and pluralist democracy

2. To promote awareness of a European cultural identity and encourage its development

3. To seek solutions to problems facing European society (minorities, xenophobia, intolerance, environmental protection, bioethics, AIDS, drugs, etc.)

4. To develop a political partnership with Europe's new democracies

1

5. To assist central and eastern European countries with their political, legislative and constitutional reforms

The fact that the protection of human rights is stated as the Council's first aim is itself an indication of the success of the European Convention on Human Rights in raising the profile of human rights across the Continent. It should not be forgotten, though, that fulfilment of the other four aims can also serve, directly or indirectly, to protect the rights of people living in Europe. This is particularly so as regards the fourth and fifth aims: the fall of Communism in the late 1980s and early 1990s has helped to shift the focus of the Council of Europe's activities and concerns, the hope being that long-standing democracies in the West can give guidance to emerging new Republics. To that end the Demosthenes programme has been set up, whereby expertise and information garnered in the West can be channelled systematically to states in the East.[1]

There were 10 original signatories to the Treaty of London in 1949. They were Belgium, Denmark, France, Ireland, Italy, Luxembourg, the Netherlands, Norway, Sweden and the United Kingdom. Greece and Turkey signed later that same year. Since then a further 28 countries (as of February 1, 1997) have joined the Council: Germany and Iceland (1950), Austria (1956), Cyprus (1961), Switzerland (1963), Malta (1965), Portugal (1976), Spain (1977), Liechtenstein (1978), San Marino (1988), Finland (1989), Hungary (1990), Poland (1991), Bulgaria (1992), the Czech Republic, Estonia, Lithuania, Romania, Slovakia and Slovenia (1993), Andorra (1994), Albania, Latvia, the former Yugoslav Republic of Macedonia, Moldova and Ukraine (1995), and Russia and Croatia (1996). Belarus has also lodged an application for membership and is awaiting a decision on its acceptability. The only European countries not, then, members of the Council of Europe will be Bosnia, Serbia and other former Republics of the USSR (such as Armenia and Azerbaijan).

The Council of Europe's Decision-making Organs[2]

The Council of Europe is run by three main organs. They are the Committee of Ministers, the Parliamentary Assembly and the Congress of Local and Regional Authorities of Europe. The most important is the Committee of Ministers, composed of the Ministers for Foreign Affairs of all the member states. It meets at least twice a year, in Strasbourg, though the occasions are usually low-key affairs and do not often attract press coverage. More frequent meetings—at least twice a month—are held for the so-called Permanent Representatives of each member state of the Council of Europe. These are government-appointed diplomats who have the same decision-

---

[1] A joint Council of Europe and European Union initiative operates on the North–South axis: the European Public Campaign on North–South Interdependence and Solidarity, created in 1988, promotes public awareness of the need for solidarity between so-called developed and under-developed nations and for respect for human rights. A European Centre for Global Interdependence and Solidarity has been established in Lisbon.

[2] Much of the material for this section is taken from a publication of the Directorate of Information of the Council of Europe entitled *The Council of Europe: Achievements and Activities* (November 1995).

making powers as the Ministers for Foreign Affairs. The chairing of meetings is rotated among the member states on a six-monthly cycle.

Like the executive organ of other inter-governmental organisations, the Committee of Ministers, or of Permanent Representatives, issues its decision in the form of treaties, declarations, resolutions and recommendations.[3] Generally speaking it is enough if a decision is taken by a two-thirds majority of the votes cast, though if recommendations are to be addressed to governments they have to be taken unanimously. To date more than 150 treaties have been drawn up by the Committee, most of them given the title "Convention"; the actual drafting is usually undertaken by a committee of governmental experts. The European Convention on Human Rights and Fundamental Freedoms is simply the first and best known of these treaties; others include the European Convention on Extradition (1957), the European Convention for the Suppression of Terrorism (1977), the European Convention on Recognition and Enforcement of Decisions Concerning Custody of Children (1980),[4] the European Convention on the Transfer of Sentenced Prisoners (1983), the European Convention on the Prevention of Torture (1987), the European Convention on Laundering, Search, Seizure and Confiscation of the Proceeds from Crime (1990)[5] and the European Framework Convention on the Protection of National Minorities (1994).[6] Two important treaties have been given the title "Charter"—the European Social Charter (1961)[7] and the European Charter for Regional or Minority Languages (1992). Most of these treaties are "closed", in the sense that they can be ratified only by member states of the Council of Europe, but some are "open", meaning that the Committee of Ministers may invite non-member states to accede to them. The European Convention on Human Rights is a closed treaty, but it could be made into an open one, as occurred in 1993 with the European Convention on the Prevention of Torture, by the addition of a Protocol to that effect. However, such a Protocol would become operative only when all the existing Convention states had ratified it.

As far as the United Kingdom and Ireland are concerned, of course, these inter-governmental treaties become binding in domestic law only if they have been formally incorporated into that law by, respectively, an Act of Parliament or an Act of the Oireachtas. Mere ratification of the treaties at an international level does not suffice to make these treaties part of domestic law.[8] Neither the United Kingdom nor Ireland has incorporated the European Convention on Human Rights into domestic law, although it is the policy of the British Labour Party to do so in the Parliamentary

---

[3] See F. E. Dowrick, "Juristic Activity in the Council of Europe—25th Year" (1974) 23 I.C.L.Q. 610; "Council of Europe Juristic Activity 1974–86" (1987) 36 I.C.L.Q. 633 and 878. A chapter carrying information on the activities of the Council of Europe is included in the *Yearbook of European Law*, published annually by Clarendon Press, Oxford: see *e.g.* (1993) 13 Ybk Eur. L. 527, (1992) 12 Ybk Eur. L. 675, (1991) 11 Ybk Eur. L. 533.

[4] Jones, (1981) 30 I.C.L.Q. 467.

[5] (1990) 10 Ybk Eur. L. 495.

[6] On this last Convention, see H. Klebes, (1995) 16 HRLJ 92 and G. Gilbert, "The Council of Europe and Minority Rights" (1996) 18 HRQ 160.

[7] A Revised European Social Charter, designed progressively to replace the original Charter, was agreed in Strasbourg on May 3, 1996.

[8] In this sense the United Kingdom and Ireland are "dualist" countries; many other countries, such as France and Germany, are "monist", which means that ratification at the international level does automatically make the treaty part of domestic law without further ado.

session 1997–98. Both countries have, however, incorporated a number of other Council of Europe Conventions. United Kingdom Acts in this category include the State Immunity Act 1978,[9] the Suppression of Terrorism Act 1978,[10] the Data Protection Act 1984,[11] the Repatriation of Prisoners Act 1984,[12] the Child Abduction and Custody Act 1985[13] and the Sporting Events (Control of Alcohol Etc.) Act 1985.[14] Irish legislation based on Council of Europe Conventions includes the Extradition (European Convention on the Suppression of Terrorism) Act 1987, the Data Protection Act 1988, the Child Abduction and Enforcement of Custody Orders Act 1991 and the Transfer of Sentenced Prisoners Act 1995.

The Committee of Ministers' declarations, resolutions and recommendations cover a vast range of issues. For present purposes it suffices to note that one category of resolutions is those taken after consideration has been given to reports from the European Commission of Human Rights.[15] This consideration occurs when the case has not been referred to the European Court of Human Rights. As we shall see, the role of the Committee of Ministers in making these resolutions is a controversial one. Less so is its role as superviser of the execution of the judgments of the Court.[16] This role too is explained below.

In its work in the human rights field the Committee of Ministers is assisted by a Steering Committee for Human Rights, which in turn receives reports from various Committees of Experts. These committees should not be confused with those which serve the Parliamentary Assembly, explained next. In particular, the Committee of Experts for the Development of Human Rights must be distinguished from the Assembly's Committee on Legal Affairs and Human Rights.

The second important organ of the Council of Europe is the Parliamentary Assembly. This body deliberates rather than takes decisions. It is not directly elected in the way that the Parliament of the European Union is, but rather is composed of groups of representatives from the national Parliaments of the Council of Europe's member states. In February 1997 it had 286 members, the size of the national delegation depending approximately on the population of the member state concerned. The largest states had 18 seats (France, Germany, Italy, the United Kingdom), the next largest 12 seats (Poland, Spain, Turkey, Ukraine) and the rest a variety of seats (*e.g.* Ireland had four). Obviously, additional places will need to be made available for the representatives of any further new member states. At present, special "guest" status has been conferred on Armenia, Azerbaijan, Belarus, Bosnia and Georgia; this allows them to make contacts with established Parliamentarians and thus to foster democratic ideals. Israel has observer status and Canada is seeking it.

[9] Based on the European Convention on State Immunity, Cmnd. 7742 (1972).
[10] Based on the European Convention for the Suppression of Terrorism, Cmnd. 7031 (1977).
[11] Based on the European Convention for the Protection of Individuals with regard to Automatic Processing of Personal Data, Cmnd. 8341 (1981), reprinted at (1981) 3 EHRR 440.
[12] Based on the European Convention on the Transfer of Sentenced Prisoners, Cmnd. 9049 (1983).
[13] Based on the European Convention for the Recognition and Enforcement of Decisions Concerning Custody of Children, Cmnd. 8155 (1980).
[14] Based on the European Convention on Spectator Violence and Misbehaviour at Sports Events, Cmnd. 9649 (1985).
[15] Art. 32. For more details see the section on the Committee of Ministers below.
[16] Art. 54.

The Parliamentary Assembly sits in public for a week four times a year in Strasbourg and for a fifth week each Spring in one of the member states. It chooses its own agenda, rather than being given topics for debate by the Committee of Ministers, and in theory the discussions taking place within the Assembly have an influence on the activities of the Committee of Ministers. Party politics do not have the significance they would have within national Parliaments, although at present five broad political groupings have been formed out of the various representatives—the Socialists, the Group of the Unified European Left, the Liberal, Democratic and Reformers Group, the European People's Party, and the European Democratic Group. The Assembly members elect their own President, usually for three one-year terms, and a number of Vice-Presidents. Perhaps more importantly the Assembly also has the function of electing the Secretary-General of the Council of Europe, the Clerk of the Assembly and the judges of the European Court of Human Rights.

Obviously the Assembly is too unwieldy a body to deal effectively with issues as a collectivity. It therefore appoints a series of specialist committees, comparable to the Select Committees of the United Kingdom Parliament, to work on a number of different areas. These areas currently include legal affairs and human rights, migration and refugees, and political affairs. Some of the committees can be observed by representatives from non-governmental organisations and often the Assembly organises discussions with other intergovernmental organisations such as the Organisation for Economic Co-operation and Development, the European Bank for Reconstruction and Development and UNESCO. The Assembly's committees report back to the Assembly and the Assembly in turn may adopt a text drafted by the committees; this is how the Convention on Human Rights and Fundamental Freedoms, and some of the Protocols thereto, first saw the light of day.

The least well known of the decision-making organs of the Council of Europe is the Congress of Local and Regional Authorities of Europe. This was created as recently as 1994, although there was a predecessor body with a similar remit (the Standing Conference of Local and Regional Authorities). Like the Parliamentary Assembly, the Congress currently has 286 members (with the same number of deputies), all of whom are local or regional authority representatives or officials in their home country. The members are divided between two Chambers, one for Local Authorities and the other for Regions. Each of these elects a President and bureau for a two-year period, with a standing committee carrying on the work in the periods between the annual sessions of the Congress. Three important initiatives of the Congress, or of the Standing Conference it replaced, deserve to be mentioned because of their human rights dimension. The first is the Charter of Local Self-Government (1985), which sets out the principles which ought to govern the allocation of powers to, and the control of functions by, local authorities. The second is the Charter for Regional or Minority Languages (1992), which seeks to enhance protective mechanisms for threatened tongues. The third is the Convention on the Participation of Foreigners in Public Life at Local Level (1992),[17] the purpose of which is to enable foreign residents to acquire full civil and political rights in the district where they live. The Congress issues a newsletter six times a year as well as an ad hoc series of studies and texts.

---

[17] See (1992) 12 Ybk Eur. L. 685.

The Scope of the Convention on Human Rights

The achievements of the Council of Europe during its 48 years of existence are many and varied. They are widely documented, especially in the Council's own publications. But the activity which has been most successful in terms of bringing about real changes to the lives of residents of Europe has been the norm-setting activity carried out through the promotion of international conventions. The best known of these Conventions are probably the Convention on Human Rights (1950), the Convention on Data Protection (1981), the Convention on the Suppression of Terrorism (1977) and the Convention on the Prevention of Torture (1987). The Human Rights Convention, however, has had far and away the most significant influence.

The history of the drafting of the Convention has been told elsewhere.[18] It is clear that officials from the United Kingdom played an important part in that process.[19] A first draft was transmitted to the Committee of Ministers within two months of the Council of Europe's formation; as this was in turn just six months after the adoption of the Universal Declaration of Human Rights by the General Assembly of the United Nations in December 1948, it is natural that the draft European document should have borrowed heavily from that. The Committee of Ministers insisted that some of the provisions should be toned down, in particular through the inclusion of exceptions and qualifications. The United Kingdom was implacably opposed to the creation of the Commission and Court of Human Rights and succeeded in persuading the Committee of Ministers that acceptance of the jurisdiction of these bodies should be a matter left to the discretion of each member state.

The Convention was opened for signature in Rome on November 4, 1950 and was to come into force for those nations which had ratified it when the Council of Europe received the 10th instrument of ratification. The United Kingdom was the first country to ratify, on March 8, 1951 and the 10th ratification occurred on September 3, 1953. That is therefore the official birthday of the Convention. Since that year the number of nations wishing to adhere to the Convention has grown enormously, the latest surge coming with the fall of the Berlin Wall and the collapse of communism in Eastern Europe.[20] Although a state can join the Council of Europe without having first ratified the Convention on Human Rights, a condition of membership is that ratification must take place as soon as possible thereafter. By February 1997, 33 countries had already ratified the Convention while seven more were in line to do so.[21] Each country, of course, has its own procedures for ratifying international treaties.

---

[18] See, e.g. A. H. Robertson and J. G. Merrills, "Human Rights in Europe" (3rd ed., 1993), chap. 1. This also helpfully explains the origins of the first 10 Protocols to the Convention.

[19] A. Lester, "Fundamental Rights: The United Kingdom Isolated?" [1984] P.L. 46; G. Marston, "The UK's Part in the Preparation of the European Convention on Human Rights" (1993) 42 I.C.L.Q. 796.

[20] The order in which ratifications have occurred is as follows: the United Kingdom (1951), Germany, Norway and Sweden (1952), Denmark, Iceland, Ireland and Luxembourg (1953), the Netherlands and Turkey (1954), Belgium and Italy (1955), Austria (1958), Cyprus (1962), Malta (1967), France, Greece and Switzerland (1974), Portugal (1978), Spain (1979), Liechtenstein (1982), San Marino (1989), Finland (1990), Bulgaria, the Czech Republic, Hungary and Slovakia (1992), Poland (1993), Romania and Slovenia (1994), Lithuania (1995), Andorra and Estonia (1996).

[21] The seven Council of Europe member states which are not yet Convention states are Albania, Croatia, Latvia, the former Yugoslav Republic of Macedonia, Moldova, Russia and Ukraine. For a handy overview of the state of play concerning ratifications of the Convention and its Protocols as of July 31, 1996, see (1996) 17 HRLJ 234–235.

Along with an increase in the number of states adhering to the Convention, the Convention itself has grown in size. This has occurred through the adoption of numerous Protocols—11 so far—some of which have added to the rights protected by the Convention, others of which have altered the procedural aspects of the Convention's operation. We shall see later in this chapter that two of the most recent Protocols—numbers 9 and 11—have very profound consequences for the way in which the Convention will operate in future.

It may now be helpful to set out in summary fashion the rights protected by the Convention and Protocols. For the full text of these documents, readers are referred to Appendices A and B.

Article 1:   Parties to the Convention must secure for everyone within their jurisdiction the rights and freedoms provided for in the Convention

Article 2:   The right to life

Article 3:   The right to freedom from torture or inhuman and degrading treatment or punishment

Article 4:   The right to freedom from slavery, servitude or forced or compulsory labour

Article 5:   The right to liberty and security of the person

Article 6:   The right to a fair trial

Article 7:   The right to freedom from retroactive criminal offences and punishments

Article 8:   The right to respect for private and family life, home and correspondence

Article 9:   The right to freedom of thought, conscience and religion

Article 10:   The right to freedom of expression

Article 11:   The right to freedom of assembly and association

Article 12:   The right to marry and to found a family

Article 13:   The right to an effective remedy

Article 14:   The right to freedom from discrimination in respect of protected rights

Protocol No. 1 (1952)   (ratified by the United Kingdom and Ireland)

Article 1:   Protection of property

Article 2:   The right to education

Article 3:   The right to free elections

Protocol No. 4 (1963)   (signed but not ratified by the United Kingdom; ratified by Ireland)

Article 1: Prohibition of imprisonment for debt

Article 2: Freedom of movement

Article 3: Prohibition of expulsion of nationals

Article 4: Prohibition of collective expulsion of aliens

Protocol No. 6 (1983)   (neither signed nor ratified by the United Kingdom; ratified by Ireland)

Article 1: Abolition of the death penalty

Protocol No. 7 (1984)   (neither signed nor ratified by the United Kingdom; signed but not ratified by Ireland)

Article 1: Procedural safeguards relating to expulsion of aliens

Article 2: The right of appeal in criminal matters

Article 3: Compensation for wrongful conviction

Article 4: The right not to be tried or punished twice

Article 5: Equality between spouses

A list of rights is only as good as the mechanisms in place for enforcing those rights. While the Convention and its Protocols may not, taken together, represent the most progressive list of human rights to be found in the world today (various social and economic rights and the rights to a clean environment and to peaceful co-existence, for instance, are not mentioned), its mechanisms for enforcing the rights which are listed are the best available.

Enforcing the Convention[22]

Provided the state complained against has declared that it recognises the competence of the Commission to receive such petitions under Article 25,[23] any person who feels that he or she has a grievance which might be remedied by the European Convention

---

[22] See also S. Farran, *The U.K. Before the European Court of Human Rights* (1996), pp. 5–18 and 384–388; D. Gomien, D. Harris and L. Zwaak, *Law and Practice of the European Convention on Human Rights and the European Social Charter* (1996), pp. 31–92; F. G. Jacobs and R. C. A. White, *The European Convention on Human Rights*, chaps. 23–27; D. J. Harris, M. O'Boyle and C. Warbrick, *Law of the European Convention on Human Rights* (1995), chaps. 22–26; M. Janis, R. Kay and A. Bradley, *European Human Rights Law* (1995), chaps. 2–3; L. Clements, *European Human Rights: Taking a Case under the Convention* (1994); A. H. Robertson and J. G. Merrills, *Human Rights in Europe* (3rd ed., 1993), chaps. 7–9; R. Beddard, *Human Rights and Europe* (3rd ed., 1993), chaps. 3 & 9; H. Hannum (ed.), *Guide to International Human Rights Practice* (2nd ed., 1990), pp. 135–151 (K. Boyle); P. van Dijk and G. J. H. van Hoof, *Theory and Practice of the European Convention on Human Rights* (2nd ed., 1990), chaps. 2–3.

[23] As of July 31, 1996, all 33 states that had ratified the Convention had also granted such recognition: see (1996) 17 HRLJ 234–235.

Table 1: Applications Registered 1990–96[28]

	1990	1991	1992	1993	1994	1995	1996
United Kingdom	236	202	222	205	236	413	471
Ireland	13	7	9	5	18	20	18
All	1657	1648	1861	2037	2944	3481	4758

can write, or get a representative to write on his or her behalf, to the Secretary of the European Commission of Human Rights in Strasbourg.[24] Ireland has recognised the competence of the Commission since the day of its ratification of the Convention (February 25, 1953), and has done so indefinitely. The United Kingdom recognised the right of individual petition only on January 13, 1966, and only for a five-year period;[25] although it has renewed this recognition quinquenially ever since,[26] there has occasionally been speculation that, because it did not like some of the judgments against it emanating from Strasbourg, the government would not issue a renewal notice.

Those petitions received by the Secretary to the Commission are placed in a "provisional file" and are initially screened. The Secretary's office may have to write back to the petitioner seeking further details of the rights allegedly infringed, the remedies that have already been sought domestically and the decisions rendered in those proceedings. In 1995 a total of 10,201 provisional files were opened, including 1,249 against the United Kingdom and 36 against Ireland.[27] If the Secretary's office believes that the complaint is one that can be registered, a form will be sent to the petitioner allowing this to be done.

Even after a petition is registered, however, it may very quickly fall out of consideration. This is because once officials look at it in more detail they may come to the realisation that the Commission has no power to consider the application. The reason might be that the application is exactly the same as one that has already been considered or that the right in question is not one that is mentioned in the Convention or Protocols at all. Therefore, not all applications which are registered are dealt with by the Commission itself—some are screened out by officials. Despite this screening, as Table 1 demonstrates, the number of applications registered in Strasbourg has risen steadily in the last few years, although the number registered against the United Kingdom remained fairly constant until 1995. In 1996 the only countries against which

---

[24] The address is simply the Council of Europe, F-67075 Strasbourg.
[25] Time-limited recognitions are permissible under Art. 25(2).
[26] The latest notice dates from January 1996; see *Hansard*, H.L. Vol. 567, col. 117 (December 14, 1995).
[27] "Survey of Activities and Statistics of the European Commission of Human Rights 1995" (Council of Europe, 1996), pp. 27–28.

9

a greater number of applications was registered than against the United Kingdom were Italy (729), France (600) and Turkey (562).[28]

States as well as individuals may refer alleged breaches of the Convention by other Convention states to the Secretary-General.[29] These are not conditional upon the state complained against having first recognised the competence of the Commission, but as virtually every Convention state has now done this the point is largely of theoretical interest. Contrary to the surge in individual petitions, however, the number of state-sponsored petitions has remained at a very low level: by the end of 1995 only 12 different applications had been lodged since 1956.[30]

The European Commission of Human Rights

Presuming that the application is not screened out, it will, as procedures currently stand, be considered by a selection of members from the European Commission of Human Rights. This body is provided for by Section III (Articles 20–37) of the Convention. It consists of one member for each state which has ratified the Convention; members are elected by the Committee of Ministers of the Council of Europe, on a majority vote basis, from a list of names drawn up by the Bureau of the Parliamentary Assembly.[31] The candidates must be of "high moral character" and must either have the qualifications required for high judicial office or be persons "of recognised competence in national or international law".[32] Those elected hold office for six years but may be re-elected;[33] once replaced they continue to deal with such cases as they already have under consideration.[34] Commissioners sit in their individual capacity, not as a representative of their own state, and while serving on the Commission they must not hold "any position which is incompatible with their independence and impartiality as members of the Commission."[35] The Commission was first appointed in 1954 but did not begin to exercise its jurisdiction over individual applications until July 5, 1955, when the sixth declaration of competence under Article 25 was deposited. The persons from the United Kingdom and Ireland who have served as Commissioners are listed in Table 2.

Because there are now so many petitions being lodged with the Commission, and so many Commissioners, not all petitions can be considered by all Commissioners. The Commission therefore operates mainly in Chambers of at least seven Commissioners, with the Commissioner elected in respect of the state against which a petition

[28] Source: the Council of Europe's annual "Survey of Activities and Statistics of the European Commission of Human Rights" (1991–96).
[29] Art. 24.
[30] These comprise five against Turkey (four by Cyprus and one jointly by Denmark, France, the Netherlands, Norway and Sweden), four against the United Kingdom (two by Greece and two by Ireland), two against Greece (jointly by Denmark, Norway, Sweden and the Netherlands) and one against Italy (by Austria).
[31] Art. 21(1).
[32] Art. 21(3).
[33] Art. 22(1).
[34] Art. 22(6).
[35] Art. 23.

Table 2: British and Irish Members of the European Commission of Human Rights 1954–97

Commissioners from United Kingdom	Commissioners from Ireland
Sir Humphrey Waldock, 1954–62	William Black, 1954–57
Sir James Fawcett, 1962–84	James Crosbie, 1956–61
Alexander Anton, 1984–85	Martin Maguire, 1961–62
Sir Basil Hall, 1985–93	Conor Maguire, 1962–65
Nicolas Bratza, 1993–	Philip O'Donoghue, 1965–71
	Kevin Mangan, 1971–75
	Brendan Kiernan, 1975–87
	Jane Liddy,[37] 1987–

has been lodged having the right to sit in the Chamber where that petition is being dealt with.[36] A Chamber can exercise all the powers conferred on the Commission by the Convention, except that cases which cannot be dealt with on the basis of established case law or which raise a serious question affecting the interpretation or application of the Convention must be dealt with by the plenary Commission.[38] Moreover only the plenary can examine inter-state applications submitted under Article 24 or refer cases to the Court of Human Rights under Article 48.[39] The Commission can also sit in the form of committees of three or more Commissioners. These can declare petitions inadmissible, or strike them off the list, only if the Commissioners are unanimous and if the decision can be taken "without further examination".[40]

The Commission, and its Chambers and committees, do not sit all year round: Commissioners serve in a part-time capacity, sitting in Strasbourg for two weeks at a time on about eight occasions in the year. Regardless of how many Commissioners sit to hear a case, the proceedings are always *in camera*.[41] The Commission has drawn up Rules of Procedure, which are regularly amended. The current set date from June 28, 1993.[42]

The chief function of the European Commission is to decide whether registered petitions should be declared admissible. It therefore acts as a filter which sifts out those petitions which do not deserve to run the full course of the Strasbourg process.

[36] Art. 20(2).
[37] Mrs Liddy is one of only two women on the Commission.
[38] *ibid*. This is the result of an amendment to the Convention introduced by Protocol No. 8 in 1980.
[39] Art. 20(5). This too results from Protocol No. 8.
[40] Art. 20(3).
[41] Art. 33.
[42] An extract from the Rules dated from January 7, 1992 is included in Appendix 3 of L. Clements, *European Human Rights: Taking a Case under the Convention* (1994).

Table 3: Decisions on Admissibility 1990–96

		1990	1991	1992	1993	1994	1995	1996
Applications declared inadmissible		991	1371	1441	1452	1700	2093	2712
Applications struck off the list		74	70	74	95	90	89	64
Applications declared admissible	U.K.	7	38	12	10	16	24	26
	Ireland	2	0	1	0	1	0	1
	All	151	217	189	218	582	807	624

This system stands in place of one which would allow all applications to be given the full treatment and then some of them to be looked at again on appeal; it is less protracted and cheaper than such a system would be. As Table 3 shows, at present approximately one-quarter of all applications registered with the Commission are declared admissible by the Commission. Only one or two a year are declared admissible against Ireland; the average annual number declared admissible against the United Kingdom over the past seven years is 19.

Before it reaches a conclusion on that point the Commission will often give notice of the application to the state concerned and seek the government's written observations on it. During this period the Commission may be asked by the applicant to ensure that interim measures are taken to protect him or her against an on-going or potential abuse of human rights. Article 25(1) of the Convention states that countries which have declared that they recognise the competence of the Commission to receive petitions "undertake not to hinder in any way the effective exercise of this right". Moreover the Commission's Rules of Procedure allow the Commission to "indicate to the parties any interim measure the adoption of which seems desirable in the interest of the parties or the proper conduct of the proceedings before it".[43] The leading case on the extent to which member states are constrained by this Rule is *Cruz Varas v. Sweden*[44] where, despite a request from the Commission not to do so until the Commission had had a chance to consider the case, Sweden deported a man to Chile, the country of which he was a national. By 10 votes to 9[45] the European Court of Human Rights held that this action had not violated Article 25(1). Since the Convention itself did not provide the Commission (or the Court) with a specific power to order interim measures to protect the rights of parties in pending proceedings, Rule 36 could not be seen as giving rise to a binding obligation on states. Compliance with it was therefore a matter of goodwill. The Court added that no assistance could be derived from general principles of international law, since "the question whether interim measures indicated

---

[43] Rule 36.
[44] Series A, No. 201; (1992) 14 EHRR 1.
[45] Judge Walsh was one of the dissenters.

by international tribunals are binding is a controversial one and no uniform legal rule exists''.[46]

There are nine grounds upon which the Commission may declare an application to be inadmissible:

1. That the applicant was not a victim, nor the next-of-kin of a victim who has died (Article 25(1));

2. That the right allegedly violated is not one set out in the Convention (Article 25(1));

3. That all domestic remedies have not yet been exhausted within the state complained against (Article 26);

4. That more than six months have elapsed since the date on which the final decision in the state complained against was taken (Article 26);

5. That it is anonymous (Article 27(1)(a));

6. That it is substantially the same as a matter which has already been examined by the Commission or has already been submitted to another procedure of international investigation or settlement and it contains no relevant new information (Article 27(1)(b));

7. That it is incompatible with the provisions of the Convention (Article 27(2));

8. That it is manifestly ill-founded (Article 27(2));

9. That it is an abuse of the right of petition (Article 27(2)).

As far as applications by states are concerned, under Article 24, there is in effect no ground upon which they can be declared inadmissible. However, states, like individuals, must not sit on their applications and neglect to keep them active.

At any stage, even after a petition has been declared admissible, the Commission may decide ''to strike a petition out of its list of cases'' where it has concluded that the applicant does not intend to pursue his or her petition, that the matter has been resolved (provided it is on the basis of respect for human rights as defined in the Convention), or that for any other reason it would no longer be justified in continuing to examine the petition.[47] If the decision to strike a case out is reached after the petition has already been declared admissible, the Commission must draw up a report stating the facts, the decision and the reasons for the decision. This must be sent to the parties concerned and to the Committee of Ministers, but the Commission retains a discretion whether or not to publish it.[48] A Commission decision to admit a petition is not, in

---

[46] (1992) 14 EHRR 1, 42, para. 101. The decision in *Cruz Varas v. Sweden* is criticised by Robertson and Merrills, *Human Rights in Europe* (1993), pp. 260 and 281. See also J. G. Merrills, "Interim Measures of Protection in the Recent Jurisprudence of the International Court of Justice" (1995) 44 I.C.L.Q. 90.

[47] Art. 30(1).

[48] Art. 30(2). In 1994 the Commission adopted three reports under this provision; in 1995 there was only one. The Commission's striking off power was governed by the Commission's Rules of Procedure until Protocol No. 8 inserted them directly into Art. 30 in 1990.

any event, binding on the European Court of Human Rights should the case get that far: a state can still argue in that forum that, for example, an applicant has not exhausted his or her domestic remedies and the Court can reverse the Commission's admissibility decision if it is convinced by such an argument.[49] To date, however, this has never happened.

Once the Commission has decided that a petition is admissible it must then examine it more closely with a view to ascertaining the facts.[50] It will, if necessary, conduct an investigation into the case after exchanging views with the state concerned, and this state must "furnish all necessary facilities" for the effective conduct of the investigation.[51] The investigation can include site inspections, oral hearings and the calling of expert witnesses. In 1994 and 1995, for example, there were 29 and 21 oral hearings respectively; all of these were devoted not just to a consideration of the admissibility issue but also to the merits of each case. The Commission does not, though, have the power to compel someone to attend the oral hearing as a witness. If during the course of the examination the Commission finds that the petition is, after all, inadmissible under the grounds mentioned in Article 27 (grounds 5 to 9 above), it can decide to reject it at that point, provided a two-thirds majority is in favour of so doing.[52]

At the same time as it is undertaking its further examination of the petition the Commission must "place itself at the disposal of the parties concerned with a view to securing a friendly settlement of the matter on the basis of respect for human rights as defined in this Convention".[53] If a friendly settlement is arrived at the Commission then draws up a report and sends it to the state concerned, the Committee of Ministers and the Secretary-General of the Council of Europe for publication. The report is confined, however, to a brief statement of the facts and of the solution reached.[54] The Commission's obligation to try to secure a friendly settlement highlights that the primary purpose of the Convention is not to condemn states for violating human rights but rather to vindicate petitioners who claim that a violation has occurred. Although lawyers might sometimes prefer cases not to be settled, because they would otherwise lead to a Commission opinion on the merits and possibly to a Court judgment, thereby clarifying the law for the future, from the applicants' point of view it is an important element in their claim that they be given quick and just satisfaction for their grievances. If this can be facilitated by the Commission, always on the condition that the Convention's standards of human rights are maintained, so much the better. A settlement can often lead to immediate administrative changes which benefit not only the

---

[49] See *De Wilde, Ooms and Versyp v. Belgium (No. 1)* (the vagrancy case), Series A, vol. 12; (1979–80) 1 EHRR 373.

[50] Art. 28(1)(a). See also "Standards of Proof in Proceedings Under the ECHR," Chap. 7 in L. G. Loucaides (ed.), *Essays on the Developing Law of Human Rights* (1995).

[51] *ibid.* Robertson and Merrills (1993), at pp. 275–280, give descriptions of several investigations conducted by the Commission, including that in the case brought by Ireland against the United Kingdom.

[52] Art. 29. The main part of this provision was inserted into the Convention by Protocol No. 3 in 1963; Protocol No. 8 (effective in 1990) reduced the voting requirement from unanimity to two-thirds. The power conferred by Art. 29 has not yet been exercised and its very existence has been criticised: see Robertson and Merrills (1993), p. 287.

[53] Art. 28(1)(b).

[54] Art. 28(2).

current applicant but other potential applicants waiting in the wings. Today, greater use is being made of the friendly settlement procedure than in the past: in 1995 there were 807 individual applications declared admissible and 67 of these were settled, a ratio of nearly 1:12; in 1996 the figures were 624 and 46, a ratio of 1:13.

If a petition has been declared admissible and no friendly settlement has been reached the Commission eventually draws up a report on its examination of the facts and states its opinion—not its decision—on whether the facts found disclose a breach by the state concerned of its obligations under the Convention.[55] This report (on the merits of the case) is transmitted to the state concerned and to the Committee of Ministers,[56] and may be accompanied by such proposals as the Commission may think fit to make,[57] though only if it considers that there has been a violation of the Convention. The Commission is not otherwise entitled to make recommendations or suggestions as to how, for example, the state concerned could take steps to avoid having such petitions brought against it in future. The Commission's report may also contain separate concurring or dissenting opinions. It is important to realise that although the Commission's actual opinion on the merits is made public at this stage, the report itself is not. However, although there is nothing in the Convention to authorise communication of the Commission's report to the applicant, the Commission has asserted its entitlement to do so in its Rules of Procedure and this was upheld as legitimate in the first case ever to reach the Court of Human Rights, *Lawless v. Ireland*.[58] The applicant is still barred from publishing the report to someone else.

The Commission having given its opinion on the merits, responsibility for processing the applicant's petition passes to the Committee of Ministers. The Committee is a political, not a judicial, body and so it may allow political considerations to influence its further actions in the matter. During the three-month period following transmission of the report to the Committee the Commission can pre-empt any such political moves by itself referring the case to the European Court of Human Rights. So can any state involved in the case. Whether or not the applicant can do so depends on whether the state against which the application has been brought is one which has ratified Protocol No. 9 to the European Convention.[59] This Protocol was drawn up by a Committee of Experts and adopted by the Committee of Ministers in 1990. Unlike earlier Protocols on procedure, which required unanimity, this one came into force whenever the 10th ratification took place, which occurred on October 1, 1994. Ireland has ratified the Protocol but the United Kingdom has not even signed it. This means that there is now a divergence between the two countries concerning the rights of individual applicants in Strasbourg.[60] Whereas an applicant against the United Kingdom has no right to receive a copy of the Commission's Report (though this will be automatic if the Commission or the United Kingdom itself refers the case to the

---

[55] Art. 31(1).
[56] Art. 31(2).
[57] Art. 31(3).
[58] Series A, No. 1; (1979–80) 1 EHRR 1.
[59] See (1991) 12 HRLJ 51.
[60] There are two sets of Court Rules of Procedure in use: Rules "A" apply to states that have not ratified Protocol No. 9, while Rules B apply to those that have done so.

Table 4: Friendly Settlements (FS) and Reports on Merits (RM) 1990–96[61]

	1990	1991	1992	1993	1994	1995	1996
United Kingdom							
FS	1	1	3	2	1	0	1
RM	12	32	8	12	11	12	18
Ireland							
FS	0	0	0	0	0	0	1
RM	1	2	0	1	0	0	0
All states							
FS	12	32	35	20	32	67	46
RM	75	144	173	179	348	564	552

Court), an applicant from Ireland does have this right;[62] he or she then has the additional right, under the amended version of Article 44 of the Convention, to refer the case to the Court. A new Article 48(2) provides that such references to the Court must first be examined by a panel of three judges, including the judge elected in respect of the state against which the application has been lodged, who sits *ex officio* on the panel.[63] If the panel decides that the case "does not raise a serious question affecting the interpretation or application of the Convention and does not for any other reason warrant consideration by the Court" it may, by a unanimous vote, not consider it.[64] This procedure kicks in only after the three-month period for referrals to the Court by the Commission or by the state concerned has elapsed. The consequence is that if the panel decides not to consider the case, that is the end of the judicial road for the applicant. The Committee of Ministers is then the only body that can decide, under Article 32 of the Convention, whether there has been a violation of the Convention. In 1995, the first full year of the operation of Protocol No. 9, 44 cases were referred to the Court by applicants (compared with 60 by the Commission and nine by the state concerned). In the event, only three of these references were accepted by the Court, the panel of judges having considered all the others to be inappropriate for a full hearing.

---

[61] Source: the Council of Europe's annual "Survey of Activities and Statistics of the European Commission of Human Rights" (1991–96). The figures given here relate to "cases", not to applications; since a case can involve more than one application they cannot be set alongside the figures supplied in Tables 1 and 3. The figures for referrals to the Court per member state are not available.
[62] Art. 31(2) of the Convention, as amended by Art. 2 of Protocol No. 9.
[63] If the application is against more than one state the panel's size must be increased accordingly.
[64] It remains uncertain what documents or observations the panel can rely upon when determining these issues.

The European Court of Human Rights

Whatever the route by which a case may be referred to the Court, it can deal with it only if the state concerned has already accepted the jurisdiction of the Court under Article 46 of the Convention. All of the Convention states have now done this;[65] unlike with the right of individual petition, there is no express provision allowing the Court's jurisdiction to be accepted for a limited period only, but the Secretary-General of the Council of Europe appears not to object to time-limited acceptances of between two and five years.

The composition and powers of the European Court are governed by Section IV of the European Convention (Articles 38–56). It comprises one judge for each member state of the Council of Europe, whether or not that state has already ratified the Convention. The judges are not elected directly by the Committee of Ministers but by the Parliamentary Assembly of the Council of Europe from a list of nominees put forward by the Committee of Ministers. The qualifications required for candidates are slightly different from those required for Commissioners: both must be of high moral character, but whereas Commissioners can either possess the qualifications required for high judicial office or "be persons of recognised competence in national or international law", judges on the Court can either possess the qualifications required for high judicial office or "be jurisconsults of recognised competence".[66] Like Commissioners, they are entitled to immunity from legal process in respect of words spoken or written and all acts done in their official capacity.[67] The judges are elected for periods of nine years and may be re-elected, there being no specified retirement age;[68] after having been replaced they continue to deal with cases they already have under consideration.[69] Of course, the judges sit in an individual, not representative, capacity and during their term of office they must not hold any position that is incompatible with their independence and impartiality as judges of the Court. They remain, however, part-time.[70] The Court elects its own President and one or two Vice-Presidents for periods of up to three years, and the persons chosen may be re-elected.[71] The judges from the United Kingdom and Ireland who have sat in the Court since its inception are indicated in Table 5.[72]

Despite the fact that each judge is not on the Court as a representative of his or her own state, Article 43 of the Convention provides that the judge who is a national of the state concerned in a case must sit *ex officio* as a judge in that case. Alternatively

---

[65] See the Table in (1996) 17 HRLJ 234–235. For a U.K. conspectus, see C. Gearty, "The European Court of Human Rights and the Protection of Civil Liberties: An Overview" (1993) 52 C.L.J. 89, and A. Bradley, "The United Kingdom before the Strasbourg Court 1975–1990," in Finnie, Himsworth and Walker (eds.), *Edinburgh Essays in Public Law* (1991), p. 185.

[66] Art. 39(3).

[67] Art. 59 (and Art. 40 of the Council of Europe's Statute).

[68] Art. 40(1).

[69] Art. 40(6).

[70] Art. 40(7).

[71] Art. 41. Mr Rolv Rysdaal, the judge from Norway, is the current President. He is well into his 80s.

[72] Although the Court became competent on September 3, 1958 the first judges were not elected until 1959.

Table 5: British and Irish Judges of the European Court of Human Rights, 1959–97

Judges from United Kingdom	Judges from Ireland
Lord McNair, 1959–66	Richard McGonigal, 1959–64
Sir Humphrey Waldock, 1966–74	Conor Maguire, 1965–71
Sir Gerald Fitzmaurice, 1974–80	Philip O'Donoghue, 1971–80
Sir Vincent Evans, 1980–91	Brian Walsh, 1980–
Sir John Freeland, 1991–	

an ad hoc judge from the state in question can be appointed just for that case.[73] At the time of writing there appears to be no published survey systematically analysing the voting record of the judges, but it is no secret that very often they will vote in favour of the position adopted by the government of the state from which they come and against the position adopted by the government of the state with which the former state has troubled relations. Cases are usually heard by a Chamber composed of nine judges,[74] but exceptionally—where a case raises one or more serious questions affecting the interpretation of the Convention—they will be dealt with by a Grand Chamber consisting of 19 judges[75] or even by a plenary Court.[76] The plenary Court *must* be invoked where the resolution of the questions at issue might have a result inconsistent with a judgment previously delivered by a Chamber or the plenary Court. This indicates that although the Court does not follow the common law doctrine of precedent, it normally expects to follow its own previous decisions and will only not do so if very careful consideration has been given to the case. The Court's current Rules of Procedure date from February 1, 1994.

As with many Supreme Courts and Constitutional Courts around the world (but in contrast with the House of Lords in the United Kingdom and with the Supreme Court in Ireland), the proceedings in the European Court of Human Rights are predominantly written, with oral submissions kept to a minimum. Once the judges have considered all the documents the President will appoint a date for an oral hearing, which will take place in Strasbourg. This will be the first occasion on which any part of the proceedings in the case will have taken place in front of the public, and even television

---

[73] *E.g.* Professor R. Y. Jennings, Q.C. was appointed an ad hoc judge by the U.K. government to hear *X v. United Kingdom* (1982) 4 EHRR 188. Between 1959 and 1994 there were 25 such cases; they are listed in the European Court's "Survey: 35 Years of Activity 1959–94", p. 92.

[74] Art. 43.

[75] From 1959 to 1994 a Chamber relinquished jurisdiction to a Grand Chamber in just five cases (including *Margaret Murray v. United Kingdom* (1995) 19 EHRR 193 and *McCann v. United Kingdom* (1996) 21 EHRR 97).

[76] From 1959 to 1994 a Chamber relinquished jurisdiction to the plenary Court in 87 cases (out of a total of 506). These are listed in the "Survey", note 73 above, pp. 92–94.

and radio broadcasts are permitted, but the hearing can be *in camera* in sensitive cases.[77] The Court will be addressed by representatives of the state concerned, by representatives of the applicant (or by the applicant in person)[78] and, if needs be, by representatives of the Commission, which participates in the proceedings as a sort of defender of the public interest.[79] The President may invite other interested parties to submit *amici curiae* briefs to help the Court in its deliberations, and several non-governmental organisations have done just this in cases brought against the United Kingdom.[80] No-one can be compelled to appear before the Court and the applicant can insist upon anonymity if he or she wishes.[81] Proceedings are in English or French, but the President can authorise the use of another language, both in documents and at hearings.

In its first 10 years of operation the European Court delivered only 10 judgments; thereafter its output has increased exponentially. By the end of June 1996, a total of 671 cases had been referred to the Court and 608 judgments had been issued.[82] As Table 6 indicates, about half a dozen judgments are issued in cases involving the United Kingdom each year.

Under Article 53 of the Convention all Convention states undertake "to abide by the decision of the Court in any case to which they are parties" and under Article 54 the judgment of the Court "shall be transmitted to the Committee of Ministers which shall supervise its execution". Together these provisions mean that the Strasbourg organs cannot themselves order the state concerned to take particular remedial measures in compliance with the judgment. The general purpose of the Convention remains the identification and rectification of a particular human rights violation that has occurred in the past; it is not to "punish" a state for committing this violation or to guarantee that such a violation cannot occur in the future. A delicate balance has to be struck here between enhancing the international legitimacy of the European Convention and preserving the freedom of action of member states of the Council of Europe. The furthest the Court can go in "remedying" a violation is through ordering just satisfaction to be made to the injured party. Usually the Court will hold that its decision upholding the applicant's view of the merits of the case is enough satisfaction for his or her loss, but where the applicant is able to prove that financial loss has been a direct consequence of the violation then the Court is prepared to order the state to

---

[77] *E.g. W v. United Kingdom* (1988) 10 EHRR 29.

[78] But only since a change to the Court's Rules in 1982.

[79] Rule 29 of the Court's Rules states: "the Commission shall delegate one or more of its members to take part in the consideratoin of a case before the Court. The Delegates may be assisted by other persons".

[80] The cases where such briefs have been permitted are listed in the European Court's "Survey", note 73 above, pp. 95–96.

[81] From 1959 to 1994, applicants in 27 of the 506 cases referred to the Court preserved their anonymity: *ibid.* p. 20.

[82] A small part of the explanation for the rise in the number of judgments has been the Court's willingness to consider whether to afford just satisfaction to the injured party under Article 50 of the Convention. In recent years several cases have been before the Court twice—once on the merits and again on the just satisfaction point: see, *e.g. Brogan v. United Kingdom No. 1* (1989) 11 EHRR 117 and *No. 2* (1991) 13 EHRR 439; *Fox, Campbell and Hartley v. United Kingdom No. 1* (1991) 13 EHRR 157 and *No. 2* (1992) 14 EHRR 108; *Airey v. Ireland No. 1* (1979–80) 2 EHRR 305 and *No. 2* (1981) 3 EHRR 592; *Pine Valley Developments Ltd v. Ireland No. 1* (1992) 14 EHRR 319 and *No. 2* (1994) 16 EHRR 379.

Table 6: The European Court's Workload 1990–96

	1990	1991	1992	1993	1994	1995	1996	1959–96
Cases referred to the Court								
United Kingdom	4	3	5	8	12	11	7	87
Ireland	1	1	0	1	1	1	0	8
All states	61	93	50	52	59	113	165	784
Judgments issued by the Court								
United Kingdom	6	4	3	6	7	8	11	75
Ireland	0	1	1	1	1	0	0	8
All states	30	72	81	60	50	87	126	711

pay compensation.[83] Successful applicants will also normally be awarded their reasonably incurred legal costs and expenses.

The Committee of Ministers

For the sake of completeness it should be noted that the European Court of Human Rights, under Protocol No. 2 (1963), also has the power to give advisory opinions on legal questions concerning the interpretation of the Convention and its Protocols, if asked to do so by a two-thirds vote of the Committee of Ministers. This power has never been exercised. Its mention at this point allows us to look at other ways in which the Committee of Ministers might be involved in the processing of an application under the Convention. In all the Committee can be said to have nine other important functions with regard to the Convention:

1. It elects the members of the Commission (Article 21(1));

2. It presents to the Parliamentary Assembly of the Council of Europe a list of nominees for the Court (Article 39(1));

3. It receives reports from the Commission on the friendly settlements which the latter has succeeded in effecting (Article 28(2));

[83] As in *Pine Valley Developments Ltd v. Ireland* (1993) 16 EHRR 379.

4. It receives reports from the Commission explaining why the latter has struck out a petition after having accepted it (Article 30(2));

5. It receives reports from the Commission stating the latter's opinion as to whether a petition discloses a breach by a state of its obligations under the Convention (Article 31(1));

6. If the case has not been referred to the Court, within three months of the transmission of the report, the Committee of Ministers must decide, by a two-thirds vote, whether there has been a violation of the Convention (Article 32(1));

7. If the Committee decides that there has been a violation it must prescribe a period during which the state concerned must take required measures, and this is binding on the state (Article 32(2) and (4));

8. If the state concerned has not taken satisfactory measures within the prescribed period the Committee of Ministers must decide, by a two-thirds vote, what effect shall be given to its original decision and must publish the Commission's report (Article 32(3));

9. The Committee receives the Court's judgments and must supervise their execution (Article 54).

There are at least three difficulties with these functions. First, crucial decisions by the Committee on whether a violation of the Convention has occurred and what effect must be given to these decisions can be taken only by a two-thirds vote. Though this is less demanding than the requirement of unanimity which the Council of Europe's governing Statute lays down for recommendations made by the Committee to member states, it means that if it is not possible to secure such a majority the questions remain undecided and no further action on the case can be instigated. This is what happened in the East African Asians case.[84] That the Committee was given this function at all in the first place is due to the fact that when the European Convention was being drafted some governments (including the United Kingdom's) made it clear that they would not be prepared to accept the compulsory jurisdiction of a European Court. The compromise solution was to confer the power to take decisions about Commission reports to the Committee. Now that practically all Convention states accept the compulsory jurisdiction of the Court, the time for relieving the Committee of this function is overdue. In the meantime Protocol No. 10 to the Convention, opened for signature in 1992, amends Article 32(1) of the Convention so as to allow decisions to be taken by a simple majority of the members of the Committee; unfortunately, the Protocol requires ratification by all Convention states before coming into force and by the end of June 1996 only 23 Convention states had ratified it (including the United Kingdom and Ireland).

Second, it is clear that the Committee of Ministers has the power to amend or even

---

[84] *East African Asians v. United Kingdom* (1981) 3 EHRR 76; the Commission's report in this case was not even ordered to be published until March 21, 1994, although extracts were included in the EHRR. See now (1994) 15 HRLJ 215.

reverse the opinion of the Commission if it so wishes, yet it is under no obligation to seek the applicant's views on the Commission's report (which, if the case has not been referred to the Court, will be released to the applicant only in exceptional circumstances). The Committee can even carry out its own investigation into a case, although to date it has not done so. The Committee is also prepared to rubber-stamp a settlement between the parties, which is not the same thing as a "friendly settlement" brokered by the Commission under the terms of Article 28. It will then decide that no further action is called for and ignore its obligation under Article 32(1) to take a decision on whether a violation has occurred.

On the other hand, the Committee of Ministers has given itself the power to make non-binding recommendations to member states and it takes these into account when assessing whether the states have taken the satisfactory measures required by the Committee. It has even begun to recommend that states pay the costs and expenses incurred by applicants and, where appropriate, compensation.[85] In 1995, moreover, the Committee began to adopt "interim" resolutions in Article 32 cases, thereby allowing its decision on whether a violation has occurred—and the Commission's report—to be made public straightaway. "Final" resolutions are reserved for those cases where the Committee has satisfied itself that all the measures required to be taken after a violation has been found (including perhaps compensation to the applicant) have in fact been executed.[86]

Third, the Committee of Ministers has failed to take a proactive stance when fulfilling its supervisory duty under Article 54. Not only does it not press the state concerned to supply it with information as to whether the Court's judgment has been properly executed, but when it does receive such information its usual practice is merely to "take note" of it, not to assess whether the steps taken do indeed properly execute the judgment. The Committee does not at present have the resources or powers to conduct such an assessment.

Proposed Reforms to the Enforcement Procedures

For many years the Commission and Court of Human Rights worked out of cramped conditions in the old *Palais des Droits de l'Homme* in Strasbourg. In 1991 work was begun on a new Human Rights Building—somewhat ironically, given the United Kingdom's poor record before the Commission and Court, the design chosen was that

---

[85] The decisions and recommendations of the Committee are published as Resolutions. A list of those issued under Articles 32 and 54 is given in the bi-annual Information Sheets issued by the Directorate of Human Rights at the Council of Europe and they are published collectively in the Yearbook of the European Convention on Human Rights (Martinus Nijhoff Publishers). The Committee's recommendations on other matters are published by the Council of Europe in a bound volume each year; in 1983 a volume of all the recommendations issued since 1964 in the fields of civil, commercial, public and international law was published, and a second volume, covering 1983–1994 was published in 1995.

[86] There were 108 interim resolutions in 1995. In the first six months of 1996 there were 174 interim resolutions (mostly concerning the length of civil proceedings in Italy) and 19 final resolutions: Information Sheet No. 38, pp. 96–101. The Sheet has now become an Information Bulletin, No. 39 covering the period July 1996 to February 1997. In that time there appear to have been 207 interim resolutions and 44 final resolutions.

of the British architect Sir Richard Rogers—and the building was officially opened in 1995. In tandem with the physical renewal has been a movement geared towards procedural renewal of the institutions. This is encapsulated in Protocol No. 11, by far the most important of all the procedural protocols added to the Convention to date.[87] When it comes into force, which unfortunately will not be until one year after all Convention states have ratified it, and so probably not until the turn of the millenium,[88] it will radically alter the Convention's enforcement machinery.

Recognising that the present machinery is cumbersome and wasteful—with both a Commission and a Court, each working with part-time decision-makers—the new Protocol will establish a single permanent Court, with one judge per Convention state.[89] The judges will be elected, as at present, by the Parliamentary Assembly of the Council of Europe, but only for six, not nine, years, and subject to a retiring age of 70. The Court will continue to operate through committees and Chambers, but the largest Court will be the Grand Chamber, comprising 17 judges. This will hear the most important cases, including all interstate applications, and it will even have an appellate function for cases decided by a Chamber which raise a serious question on interpretation or application of the Convention.[90] The Committee of Ministers will lose its function as a body taking decisions on applications under Article 32, but will keep its supervisory role over the execution of judgments under Article 54.

Sources of Information

When considering where to look for further information about the European Convention on Human Rights it is instructive to distinguish between material which is produced in Strasbourg by the organs themselves and that which is commercially available through other outlets.

Council of Europe Sources

The Secretary of the European Commission of Human Rights issues an Information Note every few weeks summarising the activities of the Commission at its most recent sessions[91] and every year the Commission publishes a "Survey of Activities and

---

[87] See A. Drzemczewski, "The Need for a Radical Overhaul" (1993) 143 New L.J. 126 and A. Drzemczewski and J. Meyer-Ladewig, "Principal Characteristics of the New ECHR Control Mechanism as Established by Protocol No. 11" (1994) 15 HRLJ 81; H. Schermers, "The European Court of Human Rights after the Merger" (1993) 18 E.L.Rev. 493 and "Adaptation of the 11th Protocol to the European Convention on Human Rights" (1995) 20 E.L.Rev. 559; A. Mowbray, "Reform of the Control System of the European Convention on Human Rights" [1993] P.L. 419 and "A New European Court of Human Rights" [1994] P.L. 540; John Hedigan, *Revolution in Strasbourg* (1997), p. 6.

[88] And the old Commission and Court will probably have to continue to sit for a year or two in order to finish dealing with applications lodged prior to the establishment of the new Court.

[89] At present the Court has one judge per member state of the Council of Europe, whether that state is yet a party to the Convention or not.

[90] This is the proposed new Article 43 of the Convention, substituted by Protocol No. 11.

[91] *E.g.* Information Note No. 138 deals with the 266th session of the European Commission of Human Rights which took place from Monday November 25, 1996 to Friday December 6, 1996.

Statistics''. The Registrar of the Court of Human Rights provides press releases once there has been a noteworthy development in particular cases (*e.g.* if a case has recently been referred to the Court or if there is to be an oral hearing). Every few weeks these press releases are consolidated and sent to addressees on the Court's mailing list. The press releases only summarise Court judgments and cannot be relied upon to give the full flavour of the decision in question, but the full text is now available on-line at http://www.dhcour.coe.fr.

The Council of Europe's Directorate of Human Rights also produces a six-monthly Human Rights Information Bulletin (often running to 200 pages).[92] Not only does this summarise the activities of the Commission, the Court and the Committee of Ministers, but it also outlines what has been done by the Parliamentary Assembly in the field of human rights and by the Directorate of Human Rights itself. Recent issues have also included sections on human rights activities by the European Union, the United Nations, the Organisation for Security and Co-operation in Europe and the Organisation of American States. The Sheet helpfully contains a list of the Council of Europe's currently available publications dealing with human rights, both those for sale and those that are free.

In 1995 the Court of Human Rights issued a "Survey: 35 Years of Activity 1959–94". This booklet lists all the references to the Court and judgments by the Court and contains useful additional information such as the time taken for each case to be processed by the Court and the effects each judgment had within the domestic law of the state concerned.

Two books have recently been published by the Council of Europe Press that are extremely useful to any student of the Convention. One is *Judgments of the European Court of Human Rights: Reference Charts* by Donna Gomien (1995). This provides details, in tabular form, of all the judgments so far issued by the Court: it lists the date of the judgment, the date on which the application in the case was first lodged, the main issues examined, the Articles of the Convention considered by the Commission and the Court, the Articles found by either of those bodies to have been violated, the damages or costs ordered to be paid by the state in question and the implementation measure, if any, taken by that state as a result of the judgment. The other book is a textbook, by Donna Gomien, David Harris and Leo Zwaak, *Law and Practice of the European Convention on Human Rights and the European Social Charter* (1996).

Other Sources

The *Reports of Judgments and Decisions* are officially published by the Carl Heymanns publishing firm in Germany.[93] The *European Human Rights Reports*, published by Sweet & Maxwell, appears 12 times a year and contains the full judgments in all Court decisions. A supplement is published every six months containing selected decisions and reports of the Commission. The *Human Rights Case Digest*, published jointly by Sweet & Maxwell and the British Institute of Human Rights, is issued 11

---

[92] No. 39 covers the period July 1996–February 1997.
[93] Carl Heymanns Verlag KG, Luxemburger Strasse 449, Cologne 50939, Germany. The volumes in Series A contain the Court judgments; those in Series B contain the pleadings, the arguments put at the oral hearings, and other documents.

times a year. It contains extensive summaries of the Court's judgments, analyses of the Commission's decisions and explanations of the Committee of Ministers' Resolutions. There are at least two other privately published digests of Convention jurisprudence[94] and recent developments are regularly noted in *Current Law* and *European Current Law* under the heading "Human Rights".

The *European Law Review* now publishes an annual Human Rights Survey as a separate issue of the journal (the pages are numbered HRC/1, etc., referring to Human Rights Checklist). As well as containing articles on substantive human rights issues the 1996 Survey, for example, provides information on the extent to which states have ratified the Convention (as well as the European Social Charter, the Convention for the Prevention of Torture and the Framework Convention on National Minorities) and reviews of the decisions and reports of the Commission of Human Rights, the judgments of the Court of Human Rights and the Resolutions of the Committee of Ministers under Articles 32 and 54 of the Convention on Human Rights. A further annual review of European Convention case-law, though one that tends to appear considerably *ex post facto*, is that written by J. G. Merrills for the *British Yearbook of International Law*. Annual analyses of the case law of the Court of Human Rights have also been published since 1992 by the journal *Juridical Review*, all of them so far compiled by Wilson Finnie,[95] and in the *Yearbook of European Law*, compiled by Colin Warbrick.[96] A *Yearbook of the European Convention on Human Rights* is published annually by Martinus Nijhoff (The Hague): the latest is volume 34, covering the year 1994. These are bilingual tomes, stretching to more than 600 pages in both English and French; they provide summaries of some Commission opinions, all the Court judgments, activities of the Committee of Ministers and the Council of Europe in general on human rights matters and brief surveys of the impact of the Convention within the Parliaments and courts of some of the Council's member states.

Journals dealing with the European Convention include the *European Human Rights Law Review* (new in 1996), which appears six times per year, the *Human Rights Law Journal*, the *Human Rights Quarterly*, the *Harvard Human Rights Journal* and the *Columbia Human Rights Law Review*. Journals otherwise specialising in public international or comparative law also publish articles on the international protection of human rights, so students should regularly check the *International and Comparative Law Quarterly*, the *American Journal of International Law* and the *American Journal of Comparative Law*. Of course, mainstream British and Irish law journals will occasionally carry articles impinging upon the European Convention.[97]

A welter of textbooks and monographs now exist on the European Convention, many of them appearing in the last year or two. They include *European Civil Liberties*

---

[94] Vincent Berger, *Case Law of the European Court of Human Rights* (1995) Vol. 3: 1991–93, and Peter Kempees (ed.), *A Systematic Guide to the Case Law of the European Court of Human Rights* (1995).
[95] [1992] J.R. 287–322; [1993] J.R. 192–211; [1994] J.R. 328–358.
[96] But for some reason not in (1993) 13 Ybk Eur. L.
[97] *E.g.* Sir Thomas Bingham, 'The European Convention on Human Rights: Time To Incorporate" (1993) 109 L.Q.R. 390; C. Osborne, "Hearsay and the European Convention on Human Rights" [1993] Crim.L.R. 255; T. Jones, "The Devaluation of Human Rights under the European Convention" [1995] P.L. 430; S. Marks, "Civil Liberties at the Margin: the United Kingdom Derogation and the European Court of Human Rights" (1995) 15 O.J.L.S. 69; F. Boland, "Insanity, the Irish Constitution and the European Convention on Human Rights" (1996) 47 N.I.L.Q. 260.

and the European Convention on Human Rights, edited by Conor Gearty (1997), *The European Convention on Human Rights* by Francis Jacobs and Robin White (2nd ed., 1996), *Law of the European Convention on Human Rights* by David Harris, Michael O'Boyle and Colin Warbrick (1995), *European Human Rights Law* by Mark Janis, Richard Kay and Anthony Bradley (1995), *Human Rights in Europe* (3rd ed., 1993) by A. H. Robertson and J. G. Merrills, *Human Rights and Europe* (3rd ed., 1993) by Ralph fiBeddard, *European Human Rights: Taking a Case under the Convention* by Luke Clements (1994), *The European System for the Protection of Human Rights* by R. St. J. Macdonald, E. Matscher and H. Petzold (1993) and *The U.K. Before the European Court of Human Rights: Case Law and Commentary* by Sue Farran (1996). See also the extensive treatment of the Convention in *Civil Liberties: Cases and Materials* (4th ed., 1995) by S. H. Bailey, D. J. Harris and B. L. Jones. There are, of course, textbooks in other languages besides English. The best book in French is probably *La Convention Européenne des Droits de l'Homme* by L.-E. Pettiti, E. Décaux and P.-H. Imbert (1995) and the two best foreign journals are *Revue universelle des droits de l'homme* and *Europäische Grundrechte-Zeitschrift*.[98]

---

[98] For these journals' reports of European Court judgments, see the list of references in (1994) 15 HRLJ 125 and 131.

CHAPTER 2

THE EUROPEAN UNION AND THE EUROPEAN CONVENTION

Introduction

The European Convention on Human Rights now plays an important role within the European Union. This contrasts with the situation in the 1950s, when the European Coal and Steel Community Treaty and the European Economic Community and EURATOM Treaties were adopted (1951 and 1957 respectively). There was no mention in these constituent Treaties of any concept or conception of human rights. The European Union, in contrast, proclaims amongst its common provisions that "The Union shall respect fundamental rights, as guaranteed by the European Convention for the Protection of Human Rights and Fundamental Freedoms signed in Rome on 4 November 1950 and as they result from the constitutional traditions common to the Member States, as general principles of Community Law."[1]

The inclusion of human rights in the Treaty on European Union takes the Community back full circle to the early 1950s, when the initial proposals for a European Political Community and for a European Defence Community were made. Commentators have pointed to the inclusion of references to human rights in these early proposals.[2] Twomey explains that the Treaty for the EPC "proposed the incorporation of Section 1 of the Convention on Human Rights . . . as well as the First Protocol".[3] The explanation for their absence in the Treaties of Paris and Rome is perhaps found in the absence of any concept of citizenship in these Treaties. It is significant that the earlier draft treaties on EPC and EDC used the terminology of citizenship (now resurrected in the Treaty on European Union), whereas the Treaty of Rome used the terminology of the peoples of Europe. There was to be an "ever closer union" of the peoples. It is tempting to discern here a distinction in rights terminology between individual and collective rights. This is probably not a helpful distinction, but nonetheless the difference must be explained. In the earlier Treaties there was a clear understanding that a move towards greater political integration would require a shift in the

---

[1] Article F, Treaty on European Union. This Treaty is also known as the Maastricht Treaty.

[2] A. Charlesworth and H. Cullen, *European Community Law* (1994), Chap. 6; D. Wyatt and A. Dashwood, *European Community Law* (3rd ed., 1993), Chap. 4.

[3] P. M. Twomey, "The European Union: Three Pillars Without a Human Rights Foundation" in D. O'Keefe and P. Twomey (eds.) *Legal Issues of the Maastricht Treaty* (1994), p. 121.

level at which protection of human rights should be provided. A European "state" would require European level protection. The Treaty of Rome compromises on the nature of the political union and puts the ever closer union into a secondary position *vis à vis* economic integration, *i.e.* the creation of the customs union and the common market. Under these circumstances, without the shift of political focus, the nation state was to remain the correct focus as protector of human rights. "The peoples" collectively, in this political scenario, owe the protection of their rights to the nation of which they are part.

Human Rights in the Early Case Law of the Court of Justice

If this interpretation is the correct one, then the early case law of the European Court of Justice can more readily be understood. Commentators have accused the Court of, at best, being reluctant to take on board issues of human rights. Hartley, for example, states that "it is probably fair to say that the conversion of the European Court to a specific doctrine of human rights has been as much a matter of expediency as conviction".[4] Mancini attributes the Court's "discovery" of human rights to a "well-founded fear that in Germany and Italy the constitutional courts would assume power to test Community laws for compliance with the fundamental rights enshrined in their own constitutions".[5]

It might be argued that these views have been expressed with the benefit of hindsight and in fact read into the development of Community law by the Court of Justice some kind of early game plan as to the nature of rights within the Community legal order. It is easy to quote early cases in which rights arguments could have been advanced but were not and contend that the Court ought to have raised issues which were not argued by the parties at the time in order to install a system of protection of human rights within the Community at the earliest possible date. However, this ignores two very simple and fundamental legal facts of life in the Community legal order. The first is that the Community legal order is a new one; it is not a fully fledged constitutional order comparable to those of the member states. It is a legal order "*en train de se faire*". The second point is that the Community Court, by default, was required to install the parameters of this new legal order as and when it could as cases were brought before it.

Bearing these factors in mind, is it true to say, as Hartley has done (amongst others), that the Court was "unsympathetic" to arguments based on human rights in the 1950s and 1960s? He cites as evidence two cases brought to the Court under the terms of the Coal and Steel Community Treaty in which decisions of the High Authority were challenged.[6] Before discussing these cases, it is worth bearing in mind that they were decided before the two later landmark cases of *Van Gend en Loos v. Nederlandse*

---

[4] T. Hartley, *The Foundations of European Community Law* (3rd ed., 1994), p. 139.
[5] G. F. Mancini and D. T. Keeling, "Democracy and the European Court of Justice" (1994) 57 *Modern Law Review* 175 at 187.
[6] Case 1/58 *Stork v. High Authority* [1959] ECR 17 and joined cases 16–17/59 *Geitling v. High Authority* [1959] ECR 17.

Administraitie der Belastingen[7] and *Costa v. E.N.E.L.*[8] in which the Court of Justice laid down the two fundamental tenets of Community law that the Community Treaties created a new legal order of international law which created rights and obligations for Member States and individuals and that Community law was supreme over existing national law. These tenets of Community law simply did not exist at the time of the High Authority cases. They are later judicial constructions. At the time of deciding these cases, therefore, it is true to say that there was no overlap between the legal orders of the Communities on the one side and the Member States on the other. There was a separation of legal orders which was broken down by *Van Gend en Loos* and *Costa*.

Both *Stork v. High Authority* and *Geitling v. High Authority* related to the organisation of coal selling agencies in the Ruhr and were challenges to decisions adopted by the High Authority, which was attempting to prevent cartelisation by mining companies. *Stork* related to the right of an undertaking to challenge decisions of the High Authority. In this case the Court, in discussing admissibility, gave a wide interpretation to Article 65 ECSC which provided for the right of undertakings to challenge the validity of such decisions. On the merits, *Stork* had argued that the High Authority, in making decisions, ought to have regard to provisions of German constitutional law. The Court did not accept this view. It drew the distinction between the law governing the decision-making powers of the High Authority and provisions of national constitutional law:

"Under Article 8 of the Treaty the High Authority is only required to apply Community law. It is not competent to apply the national law of the Member States. Similarly, under Article 31 the Court is only required to ensure that in the interpretation and application of the Treaty, and of rules laid down for implementation thereof, the law is observed. It is not normally required to rule on provisions of national law. . . . An agreement which is valid under national law may well run counter to the prohibition in Article 65(1). In such a case it is void under Community law."[9]

Geitling similarly concerned a challenge to the validity of provisions adopted by the High Authority. One of the grounds of challenge was that the decisions of the High Authority contravened Article 14 of the Basic Law of the Federal Republic of Germany, which guarantees the right to private property. In this case the Court quite firmly laid out the limits of its own jurisdiction:

"It is not for the Court, whose function is to judge the legality of decisions adopted by the High Authority . . . to ensure that rules of internal law, even constitutional rules, enforced in one or other of the Member States are respected. . . . Therefore the Court may neither interpret nor apply Article 14 of the German

---

[7] Case 26/62 *Van Gend en Loos v. Nederlandse Administraitie der Belastingen* [1963] ECR 1; [1963] CMLR 105.
[8] Case 6/64 *Costa v. E.N.E.L.* [1964] ECR 585; [1964] CMLR 425.
[9] *Stork* at p. 29.

Basic Law in examining the legality of a decision of the High Authority. . . . Moreover Community law, as it arises under the ECSC Treaty, does not contain any general principle, express or otherwise, guaranteeing the maintenance of vested rights.''[10]

These cases must be read in their context and the time at which they were decided. The respective jurisdictions of the Community court and the courts of the Member States was still to some extent open to speculation. The judgment of the Court was given in July 1960. In December of the same year, the Court was asked to annul a provision of Belgian law which, it was alleged, was contrary to Community law. The Court returned to the subject of its own jurisdiction.[11] Here the applicant attempted to argue that a provision of Belgian law should be overruled by the European Court on the grounds that it conflicted with Community law. The Court rejected this argument:

"The Court has no jurisdiction to annul legislative or administrative measures of one of the Member States. . . . The ECSC Treaty is based on the principle of a strict separation of the powers of the Community institutions and those of the authorities of the Member States. . . . Community law does not grant to the institutions of the Community the right to annul legislative or administrative measures adopted by a Member State.''[12]

Taking these three cases together, it can be seen that the Court was not refusing to accept a doctrine of rights as part of Community law but was concerned with delimiting its own jurisdiction. Clearly the Court could not apply the Basic Law of the Federal Republic. That was not its remit. The same answer would today be given by the Court of Justice. Neither could the Court declare invalid national legislation. The control of legality of national acts was within the purview of national authorities— either the national courts or the national parliaments. It is tempting to say that the Court here was applying some concept of legal subsidiarity. In fact, what the Court was doing, as is well known in most civil law systems, was to define its own functions *vis à vis* other court structures. In these cases the Court could do nothing else.

This argument is strengthened by an examination of the role of rights in the Community order at that date. As stated above, the member states had explicitly rejected the inclusion of rights in the (what was then) new Treaty of Rome adopted in 1957. If the Court in 1959 had embarked on a spree of judicial activism at that time it would have been in danger of overstepping its judicial function. This argument is particularly pertinent in relation to the ECSC Treaty which, unlike the Treaty of Rome, lays down detailed rules, agreed by the Member States, on the operation of the free trade area in coal and steel.[13] However, the Court did give a hint as to how rights based arguments

---

[10] *Geitling* at p. 439.
[11] Case 6/60 *Humblet v. Belgium* [1960] ECR 559.
[12] *ibid.* at p. 568.
[13] When the Court does embark on a spree of judicial activism, it may become the subject of extensive criticism. See H. Rasmussen, *On Law and Policy in the European Court of Justice* (1986). See also the arguments of the Eurosceptic wing of the Tory Party in the United Kingdom, which wishes to "emasculate" an over-zealous European Court of Justice.

could be introduced into the new Community legal order. This hint is given in the extract from *Geitling* quoted above. The Court stated that "Community law does not contain any general principle, express or otherwise, guaranteeing the maintenance of vested rights". In this case, the Court referred to the ECSC Treaty. It used a technique which is now familiar to students of European Community law, that of developing the law by a series of decisions, one building upon the other, in order to develop a *jurisprudence constante*. *Geitling* could be read, not as a refusal to develop human rights as part of the Community legal order, but as an indication that human rights could form part of the general principles of the law which the Court was entrusted to uphold.

Acceptance of Human Rights as Part of the Community Legal Order

An explanation of how and why the Court of Justice came to accept the place of human rights as part of the Community legal order and, in particular, the principles enshrined in the European Convention on Human Rights, necessitates a brief summary of legal and political developments within Europe in the 1960s and 70s. There were at least four distinct developments which showed both the need for the recognition of human rights within the Community legal order and a solution to the method of incorporation of such protection. These developments can be summarised as follows.

The Development of Conceptions of Human Rights Outside the Community Legal Order

The European Convention on Human Rights had been elaborated in the aftermath of the second world war and contained what might be regarded as a traditional view of the nature of civil and political rights. The meaning of the Convention itself was gradually being interpreted by the Commission and the Court of Human Rights. By 1974, with French ratification, the European Convention on Human Rights achieved considerable status as the most important internationally agreed standard of human rights for Europe. It could be argued, however, that the Bill of Rights as provided by the European Convention was not an appropriate model for the European Community, whose remit was primarily economic and social. The kind of rights which were to be enshrined in the United Nations' International Covenant on Economic, Social and Cultural Rights of 1966 were more likely to be those that would be involved within the Community legal order. The 1960s and 1970s were the decades of international human rights development, and the Community could not be immune from these developments. In particular, it became apparent with the adoption of the International Covenants in the mid 1960s that there was a diversity in concepts of human rights and that rights could exist in both the economic and political spheres. It seemed that economic rights would be appropriate within the Community.

31

The Creation Within the Community Legal Order of Enforceable Community Rights Particular to that Legal Order and Derived from It

The Treaty of Rome widened the scope of operation of Community law to cover whole sections of economic activity. The Court of Justice placed the individual at the heart of this system in 1962 with its decision in *Van Gend en Loos*, which related to the rights of traders in respect of tariffs and taxation.[14] In this case the Court established that the Treaty of Rome was intended to create rights which were to be protected by the national courts by virtue of the doctrine of direct effects. In developing this doctrine, the Court was careful to delineate the respective functions of the national courts and the Community court. It was a matter of Community law to determine those provisions of Community law which could create direct effects, this being a question of interpretation of the Treaty and secondary provisions, but the task of upholding and enforcing Community rights was a matter of national law. A dilemma such as that facing the national court in *Humblet* was to be decided by the national courts. The European Court assisted the national courts in clarifying what they should do in case of conflict between what is known as a directly effective provision of Community law and a provision of national law. In these circumstances, the national court must accept the supremacy of Community law[15] and set aside any legislation that might conflict with the Community provision.[16]

Having determined that the Treaty of Rome created specific rights, the Court developed its jurisprudence and enumerated those rights which were derived from the Community legal order. Some of these, such as the right to equal pay for equal work, were contained in the Treaty text. Others related to the principles of sex and nationality discrimination. Very significant were the Treaty provisions relating to the rights of workers and traders within the common market. In all these areas the Treaty came to be supplemented by new Community secondary legislation in the form of regulations and directives and the meaning of the Treaty text was interpreted in an expansive way by the Court of Justice. At the same time and equally important the basic principles of law which governed the institutions and the Member States in the development and operation of Community law were evolved by the Court.

The Resolution by the European Court of Justice of the Problem of the Interaction of Legal Orders,

It was in the 1960s that the European Court of Justice developed key principles governing the relationship between the new legal order of European law and the domestic laws of the member states. As stated above, the Court developed the idea of direct effects of Community provisions, immediately raising the question of a potential clash between those provisions and provisions of national law. The European Court insisted

---

[14] Case 26/62 *Van Gend en Loos v. Nederlandse Administraitie der Belastingen* [1963] ECR 1; [1963] CMLR 105.

[15] Case 6/64 *Costa v. E.N.E.L.* [1964] ECR 585; [1964] CMLR 425.

[16] Case 106/77 *Amministrazione delle Finanze dello Stato v. Simmenthal* [1978] ECR 629; [1978] CMLR 263.

that Community law was supreme, even as against provisions of national constitutional law. In two cases which were brought in preliminary references from Germany, the European Court of Justice reiterated the supremacy of Community law and, at the same time, reassured the German courts that the fear that human rights were insufficiently protected at the Community level were unfounded. The Court did this by taking up the theme of general principles which it had first hinted at in *Geitling*.

The case brought by Mr Stauder is fairly well known.[17] In this case, the European Court rejected an argument brought by a German national that a Community provision relating to the distribution of surplus butter stocks infringed "the fundamental human rights enshrined in the general principles of Community law and protected by the Court".[18] The importance of the case lies in this recognition that fundamental human rights did indeed form part of the general principles of Community law and that the European Court itself took on the role of protector of individual rights.

The principles of *Stauder* were reiterated in *Internationale Handelsgesellschaft*.[19] Here the European Court specifically reassured the German court on the place of human rights within the Community legal order, holding that "respect for fundamental human rights forms an integral part of the general principles of law protected by the Court of Justice". However, as the Court had done in the earlier German cases under the Coal and Steel Treaty, it rejected the notion that it could apply German constitutional provisions. Instead it could apply only those provisions common to the member states and developed "within the framework of the structure and objectives of the Community".

The motivation of the Court in reaching these judgments has been questioned. Many commentators see the Court attempting to preserve the specific and autonomous nature of the Community legal order which might otherwise be threatened if the courts of the member states were to fail to accept the development of that order. Others see the Court as cynically accepting the role of protector of human rights in principle but as denying individual protection in practice. Whatever the motivation, the Court was left with a dilemma. Where was it to find provisions common to the Member States that could be developed within the framework and objectives of the Community? One possible source was the European Convention on Human Rights and other international treaties. In fact the Court has turned for inspiration in the enumeration of the fundamental rights which it is willing to protect to these sources, but, in the case of the European Convention on Human Rights, it did so only after ratification by all the Member States (1974).

In 1974, 11 days after France had ratified the European Convention on Human Rights,[20] the Court in *Nold* accepted that "international treaties for the protection of human rights on which the member states have collaborated or of which they are signatories, can supply guidelines which should be followed within the framework of Community law."[21] In *Nold*, the applicant had argued that a decision of the Commis-

---

[17] Case 29/69 *Stauder v. Ulm* [1969] ECR 419; [1970] CMLR 112.
[18] *ibid.* [1969] ECR at p. 425.
[19] Case 11/70 *Internationale Handelsgesellschaft* [1970] ECR 1125; [1972] CMLR 255.
[20] As pointed out by H. G. Schermers and D. Waelbroeck, *Judicial Protection in the European Communities* (5th ed., 1992), p. 39.
[21] Case 4/73 *Nold v. Commission* [1974] ECR 491 at 507; [1974] 2 CMLR 338.

sion had violated his property rights as protected by the German Constitution and the European Convention. The Court rejected his argument but accepted that rights of ownership and rights to practise a profession could form part of the Community legal order, stating that such rights must be seen in the light of their social function. In other words, property rights must always be subject to limitations in the public interest. In a Community context, public interest is equated to Community objectives.

In subsequent cases, discussed below, the Court of Justice has used the European Convention as a guideline in the way suggested in *Nold*, but it has also drawn direct inspiration from the European Convention as a source of general principles. Either way, the European Convention became part of that area of Community law which is known as the general principles of Community law. However it must be stressed that the jurisdiction of the Court of Justice does not extend to assessing the compatibility of national measures with the standards of human rights which are enshrined in the European Convention of Human Rights and which are accepted by the European Court of Justice as general principles of law where those measures come within an area of concern which is within the remit of the national legislator.[22] The Court of Justice has made it clear that when national authorities implement Community rules they must observe those fundamental rights which flow from the Community legal order and that the function of the European Court where the national court requests a preliminary ruling in these cases is to provide the "criteria of interpretation needed by the national court to determine whether those rules are compatible with the fundamental rights whose observance the Court ensures".[23]

The Recognition by the Political Institutions of the Need to Incorporate Conceptions of Human Rights at the Community Level

The case law of the Court of Justice had a significant impact on the thinking of the political institutions of the European Community. In 1977, a Joint Declaration was adopted by the European Parliament, the Council and the Commission which cited the case law of the European Court of Justice to the effect that European Community law embodies fundamental rights and recognises that all the member states are Contracting Parties to the European Convention on Human Rights. The Declaration stressed the importance placed on human rights by the Member States and the Communities, who pledged to continue to respect fundamental rights.[24] In 1979, the Commission and Council circulated a memorandum raising the question of whether the European Community could accede to the European Convention on Human Rights, thereby closing the gap identified by the Commission in the protection of human rights within the Community legal order. Both the Economic and Social Council and the

---

[22] Cases 60–61/84 *Cinéthèque SA and Others v. Fédération nationale des cinémas français* [1985] ECR 2605; [1986] 1 CMLR 365. The Court held (at p. 2627) that "although it is true that it is the duty of this Court to ensure observance of fundamental rights in the field of Community law, it has no power to examine the compatibility with the European Convention of national legislation which concerns, as in this case, an area which falls within the jurisdiction of the national legislator".

[23] Case C-2/92 *R v. MAFF, ex p. Dennis Clifford Bostock* [1994] ECR I-955 at 983; [1994] 3 CMLR 547.

[24] For text see O.J. No. C103/1 (1977).

European Parliament endorsed the view at that time that the Community should accede to the European Convention.[25]

The Commission gave several reasons in favour of accession to the European Convention on Human Rights. The first is that the institutions are not subject to an external control mechanism, unlike the Member States themselves whose activities are subject both to the European Court of Justice and to the Convention authorities. Secondly, the Single European Act and the Maastricht Treaty commit the Member States and the Community to respect for the rights enshrined in the European Convention. The third reason is that the Community, in entering agreements with third states, emphasises the importance for those states of respect for human rights. Anyone who has read the European Agreements with the states of Eastern Europe will see that this is a fundamental aspect of those agreements and, it could be argued, the Community could be seen to be rather hypocritical in approach if it demanded greater commitment from others than it is willing to give itself.

The issue of ratification of the European Convention on Human Rights was most recently discussed in an Opinion given by the European Court of Justice on the question of whether the European Community has the competence, or legal authority, to ratify the Convention.[26] The Court held that there was no legal base in the Treaties which would allow for the ratification of the Convention by the Community. The Court stated that there was no legal power, either a specific enumerated power or any implied power, which would allow the Community to accede. None of the references to the Convention in the Single European Act or in the preamble to the Treaty on European Union, neither the concept of European citizenship nor yet the general power contained in Article 235 of the Treaty which allows the Community to take action to attain one of the objectives of the Treaty, could, according to the Court, provide a legal basis for Community accession. The effect of this Opinion is to require an amendment to the Treaty structure should the Community wish to accede. In fact, the European Parliament, following Opinion 2/94, has called on the Intergovernmental Conference for such an amendment.[27] The political institutions and the member states must, therefore, determine whether accession is to be achieved.

The Adoption of General Principles of Human Rights by the Court of Justice

Charlesworth and Cullen provide a list of Articles in the European Convention of Human Rights which have been borrowed by the Court of Justice and which have led to what they describe as a "curious Community Bill of Rights".[28] They identify the

---

[25] All these issues and projects are discussed in the Commission Communication on Community Accession to the European Convention for the Protection of Human Rights and Fundamental Freedoms and some of its Protocols, SEC(90) 2087 final of November 19, 1990.

[26] Opinion 2/94 of the European Court of Justice relating to Accession by the Community to the European Convention for the Protection of Human Rights and Fundamental Freedoms, [1996] E.C.R. I-1759; [1996] 2 C.M.L.R. 265.

[27] "It [the European Parliament] calls on the IGC to amend the Treaty to allow the Union to accede to the ECHR", *Agence Europe*, September 19, 1996.

[28] Charlesworth and Cullen, *European Community Law* (1994), p. 103.

right to a fair hearing, the right to privacy, the right to family life, freedom of religion, freedom of expression, trade union rights, and the right to own property or to pursue a trade. To this list can also be added the general principle of non-retroactivity of penal law.

In the act of referring to the European Convention, it is clear that the Court of Justice is not applying the Convention because it, the Convention, is binding on the Community. The Court is not bound by any rule of public international law or Community law to apply the Convention provisions. In turning to the Convention, as it turns to the constitutional traditions of the member states, the Court is refining and defining the general principles of law that are part of the Community's own legal order. The Convention is a useful source of inspiration given that it has been ratified by all of the Member States. However, it must be stressed that the Community is not bound by the Convention as such; the general principles applied by the Court are the constitutional principles particular to the Community legal order. This legal order is not subject to the Convention. The significance of the debate on ratification is that ratification would subject the Community legal order to the whole Convention and the Convention authorities, the European Commission of Human Rights and the Court of Human Rights. This is a very different matter from the European Court of Justice accepting the principles of the Convention as some sort of self-denying ordinance. These points were argued by several Member States before the Court in Opinion 2/94.

The cases in which the Court has used the European Convention are discussed below. These are not, of course, the only cases relating to human rights. The Court also has relied on the constitutional provisions common to the Member States in cases relating to human rights. Whilst these cases are interesting, they are not relevant for the purposes of this chapter.

The Right to a Fair Hearing

Cases have been argued before the European Court of Justice concerning both the procedures of the Community institutions themselves and the procedures adopted by the Member States in their implementation of Community law.

Article 6 of the European Convention has formed the basis of a challenge to the competence of the European Commission in its enforcement of the Community rules on competition. The European Court of Justice has held that the Commission is not a "tribunal" in the meaning of Article 6[29] and has rejected the argument as irrelevant that the Commission combines the function of judge and prosecutor in the application of Treaty articles relating to competition. The Court draws a distinction between an administrative body which is bound to observe the procedural safeguards provided by Community law and a "tribunal" within the meaning of Article 6 ECHR.[30]

The same article was raised in a case brought by a French woman, alleged to be a

---

[29] Cases 209 to 215 and 218/78 *van Landewyck v. Commission* [1980] ECR 3125; [1981] 3 CMLR 134.
[30] Cases 100–103 *Musique Diffusion Française v. Commission* [1983] ECR 1825. In this case the Court held that the rules of Community law guaranteed the existence of the right to a fair hearing (at p. 1881).

prostitute, against the Belgian authorities who wished to deport her on the grounds of public morality.[31] Mrs Pecastaing relied on a Community directive on free movement of persons to challenge the validity of the Belgian deportation measure and also argued that her right to bring a claim in the Belgian courts would be negated if she were to be deported pending a hearing of her case. This, she alleged, was contrary to Article 6 of the ECHR. The Court of Justice held that the provisions of the directive fulfilled the requirement of a "fair hearing" and that a fair hearing did not require the presence of an individual in a particular country in the time leading up to that hearing. In its judgment, the European Court made no reference to any decisions of the European human rights authorities.

Mrs Johnston was luckier in her case brought against the Royal Ulster Constabulary in respect of her argument that Article 53(2) of the Sex Discrimination Order deprived her of the right to an effective judicial hearing since that Article gave to the national authorities the power to determine the conditions for derogating from the principle of equal treatment. The Court underlined the importance of effective judicial control which is provided for in the Community directive on equal treatment by stating that this is a general principle of law underlying the constitutional provisions of the member states. The Court specifically made reference to Articles 6 and 13 of the ECHR and stated that the principles upon which the Convention is based must be taken into consideration in Community law.[31a]

Most recently, Article 6 has been argued in a staff case where the Court of First Instance rejected the argument that it should apply to internal disciplinary proceedings against a member of staff of the Community institutions.[32]

From these cases it can be seen that the European Court, including the Court of First Instance, has accepted that European law contains general principles relating to the right to a hearing. However, it has only upheld those principles as against an individual's challenge against a Member State. It has not, as yet, accepted Article 6 as a basis of challenge against Community procedures.

The Right to Privacy

The right to privacy was in issue in the case of *Stauder*, which is discussed above. In that case the Court of Justice made reference to general principles of law but stated that the case turned on the question of interpretation of a Community provision which had, in effect, been interpreted wrongly by a Member State. The Court said nothing more about privacy. However, in a case in 1980 the Court discussed the extent of Article 8 of the European Convention on Human Rights. *National Panasonic*[33] con-cerned the powers of the Commission to investigate alleged breaches of the com-petition rules. The applicant argued that by failing to inform it of the decision to commence an investigation against it and to give it advance notice, the Commission

---

[31] Case 98/79 *Pecastaing v. Belgium* [1980] ECR 691; [1980] 3 CMLR 685.
[31a] [1987] Q.B. 129.
[32] Case T-26/89 *De Compte v. European Parliament* [1991] ECR II-781.
[33] Case 136/79 *National Panasonic v. Commission* [1980] ECR 2033; [1980] 3 CMLR 169.

had breached Article 8 of the ECHR, which relates to the obligation of public authorities to respect the private and home life of individuals and his or her home and correspondence. The European Court examined the provisions of Community law and held that there was a public interest in preventing the distortion of competition and noted that Article 8(2) acknowledges the right of public authorities to interfere with the privacy of legal persons (insofar as their rights are protected by Article 8) where such a public interest is at stake.

The fundamental right of the inviolability of the home was raised in 1989 as a basis for challenging the power of the Commission to seek information about allegations relating to the breach of competition law.[34] In this case, the European Court agreed that the fundamental right to the inviolability of the home did form part of the general principles of Community law as regards the private dwellings of natural persons but held that it did not apply in respect of business premises. The Court argued that there was not a common approach in the Member States to this issue and that no inference could be drawn from Article 8 of the ECHR to that effect, particularly as there is no case law of the European Court of Human Rights on this matter.

An area where there has been case law of the European Court of Human Rights is in the testing for AIDS. This issue arose also before the Court of First Instance in a staff case brought by Mr A, who applied for a post as administrator with the European Commission and was turned down on the grounds of his being HIV positive.[35] Mr A had volunteered information about his medical condition and had voluntarily submitted to testing. He argued that the Commission had violated its own code on AIDS in the workplace,[36] and his trade union argued that the contested decision constituted an infringement of the right to respect for family life and Article 8 of the European Convention. The union argued that medical screening was solely in the interest of the institution in order to protect its financial position, and that this objective was incompatible with Article 8 of the ECHR. Furthermore, the mere fact that the test had been carried out was in itself an infringement of the right to family life, since the test was superfluous as Mr A had volunteered information about his condition.

This case is the first in which the Court referred to Article F of the Treaty on European Union, but to no avail as far as Mr A was concerned. The Court said that the requirement to undergo a medical examination was "in no way" a violation of Article 8 of the ECHR. The objective of the examination was to avoid the appointment of unsuitable candidates in terms of the duties to be assigned to them. That objective is compatible with Article 8 of the ECHR. The Court also rejected the view that the examination was superfluous, since medical tests necessarily included clinical testing. The requirement for a potential employee to submit to a medical test has been accepted by the European Court of Justice in the past, which has restricted judicial review to ascertaining whether procedures were conducted in a fair manner.[37] The compatibility of employment-related tests has not been assessed by the human rights institutions,

---

[34] Case 85/87 *Dow Benelux v. Commission* [1989] ECR 3137.

[35] Case T-10/93 *A v. Commission* [1994] ECR II-179; [1994] 3 CMLR 242.

[36] The Council code on AIDS in the workplace specifies that HIV positive employees, who do not show any symptoms of the disease, "should be looked on and treated as normal employees, fit for work". See 89/C 28/02, O.J. No. C28.2.

[37] Case 189/82 *Seiler v. Council* [1984] ECR 229.

although the compatibility of medical tests carried out on suspects has been referred under the ECHR where the Commission has held that such tests may be both compatible and desirable.[38] Any claims against compulsory medical testing would be subject to a two-stage investigation. Compulsory testing would be presumed to be contrary to Article 8(1) of the Convention and would therefore have to be justified under the second paragraph of that Article.

The Right to Family Life

The right to family life was raised in the case discussed above and dismissed as irrelevant by the Court. It is surprising that it has not appeared to present a large number of difficulties for individuals given that the Community has adopted a wide variety of legal instruments in relation to migration of workers. It may be that the Community provisions, by and large, do reflect the tenor of the ECHR in these matters. The issue of the right to family life was considered in *Demirel*, a case concerning the rights of Turkish workers.[39] Here the German court raised the issue of the rights of Turkish workers under the Association Agreement between Turkey and the Community. The Court of Justice held that the Association Agreement did not give rise to rights which Turkish workers could claim in the German courts and that it is not within the jurisdiction of the European Court "to examine the compatibility with the European Convention of Human Rights of national legislation lying outside the scope of Community law".[40] It would seem to follow from this that it is within the jurisdiction of the European Court to examine such compatibility in matters lying within the scope of Community law. This is in fact what the Court did in the case of *Commission v. Germany*,[41] which related to the rights of workers. Here, the Commission challenged the validity of German legislation which refused renewal of residence permits to Community migrant workers if their living conditions were deemed inappropriate. The Court examined the legality of this legislation in the light of Community provisions and stressed that the Community regulation must be interpreted in the light of the right to family life. The Court held that "that requirement is one of the fundamental rights which, according to the Court's settled case law, restated in the Preamble to the Single European Act, are recognised by Community law."[42]

Non-retroactivity of Penal Law

Captain Kirk boldly argued that Community provisions should be subject to Article 7 of the European Convention on Human Rights in a case which came to the Court of Justice as a preliminary reference from the Crown Court at Newcastle.[43] Captain Kirk

---

[38] See discussion in P. van Dijk and G. J. H. van Hoof, *Theory and Practice of the European Convention on Human Rights* (2nd ed., 1990), pp. 372–373.
[39] Case 12/86 *Demirel v. Stadt Schwabisch Gmund* [1987] ECR 3719; [1989] 1 CMLR 421.
[40] *ibid.* [1987] ECR at 3754.
[41] Case 249/86 *Commission v. Germany* [1989] ECR 1263; [1990] 3 CMLR 540.
[42] *ibid.* [1989] ECR at 1290.
[43] Case 63/83 *R v. Kirk* [1984] ECR 2689; [1984] 3 CMLR 522.

was charged with a criminal offence of fishing in United Kingdom waters contrary to the Sea Fish Order 1982. From a human rights point of view, the case turned on the issue of whether a Community measure could validate *ex post facto* national measures of a penal nature imposing penalties for an act which was not punishable at the time it was committed. The Court stated that the principle that penal provisions may not have a retroactive effect takes its place among the general principles of law whose observance is assured by the Court. In this case the national measure was not authorised by Community law.

The non-retroactivity of criminal provisions also arose in a case brought against a Dutch bar owner who was charged with selling mineral water that did not meet national and European standards.[44] Students of European Community law will remember this case for the way in which the European Court placed an obligation on national courts to interpret national law in the light of the wording and purposes of directives regardless of the date of implementation contained in the directive itself. However, the Court attached a rider to this statement saying that this obligation is limited by the principles of legal certainty and non-retroactivity. Directives themselves cannot independently of member states legislation "have the effect of determining or aggravating the liability in criminal law" of individuals who act in contravention of a directive.[45] The European Convention was not argued in this case but it is worth noting that certain principles of Community law are common to the European Convention. As noted above, the European Convention can be one source of obligation, as was the case with Kirk, but an alternative source may be the general principles of law common to the Member States.

Freedom of Religion

Article 9 of the European Convention on Human Rights was argued in support of a woman who applied for a post with the European Commission and who was unable to attend for aptitude tests because they fell on a Jewish holiday.[46] Ms Prais argued that the Commission ought to have informed itself of a potential clash of dates of this kind, but the European Court rejected this view. The Court held that the Commission would have been obliged to choose an alternative date for the tests had any applicant informed them of the fact that a particular date was unsuitable. There was no general obligation, either in Article 9 of the European Convention, or in the Staff Regulations, which obliged the Commission to inform itself of the dates of religious holidays and to fix tests accordingly.

Freedom of Expression

Article 10 of the European Convention on Human Rights formed part of an argument put forward by certain Dutch and Belgian publishers in defence of an agreement held by the Commission to be incompatible with the Community provisions on competi-

---

[44] Case 80/86 *Criminal Proceedings against Kolpinghuis Nijmegen BV* [1987] ECR 3969; [1989] 2 CMLR 18.
[45] *ibid.* p. 3986. The Court did not make reference to the European Convention in this case.
[46] Case 130/75 *Prais v. Commission* [1976] ECR 1589; [1976] 2 CMLR 708.

tion.[47] The publishers argued that the small scale of the market for published materials in Flemish necessitated the retention of a system of resale price maintenance and that the Commission's attempt to abolish such a system contravened Article 10 of the ECHR. The Court rejected the argument, stating that the applicants had failed to establish a link between the Commission's decision and the provisions relating to freedom of expression, even supposing that "it might be possible to interpret Article 10 in such a way as to include guarantees regarding the possibility of publishing books in economically profitable conditions."

The relationship between Article 10 and the competition rules was also raised in a case relating to radio and television broadcasting in Greece.[48] In addition, the case involved questions relating to the freedom to provide services, the free movement of goods and the principle of non-discrimination. The facts concerned a Greek law that gave an exclusive franchise to a Greek television station for any activity that contributed to the information, culture and entertainment of the Hellenic People. The Court held that the grant of such a monopoly was not in itself contrary to Community law. However, the national court had to determine whether the way in which the monopoly was organised might infringe the Community rules relating to the free movement of goods and services and also whether the monopoly constituted an infringement of Article 10 of the ECHR. In relation to the latter point, the Court held that the national court must examine the Greek law to ensure that the provisions of Article 10 are not infringed. It is the function of the national court to apply the general principles of Community law (as embodied in Article 10) to matters of national law where such national law (as in the present case) falls within the scope of Community law.

Article 10 of the European Convention was raised in proceedings relating to the freedom to provide information in relation to abortion services offered in the United Kingdom.[49] A student organisation in Ireland wished to distribute information in relation to these services. SPUC, an organisation whose purpose is to prevent decriminalisation of abortion in Ireland, brought proceedings against the students in an attempt to prevent them publishing details about abortion clinics. The Irish High Court referred the case to the European Court of Justice, and the issue of freedom of expression was raised by the students. They argued that the prohibition contained in Irish law against providing information about abortion was contrary to Article 10 of the European Convention and that this prohibition prevented the legitimate exercise of Community rights of the freedom to receive and provide services.

The European Court accepted that abortion services were "services" for the purpose of Community law but found that the students' organisations were not themselves the providers of these services and therefore that it is not contrary for a Member State to prohibit such organisations from distributing information. The Court went on to say that when requested to give a preliminary ruling it was its

---

[47] Cases 43 & 63/82 *VBVB and VBBB v. Commission* [1984] ECR 19. The discussion by the Court is at p. 62.

[48] Case C-260/89 *Elliniki Radiophonia Tileorassi AE v. Dimotiki Etairia Pliforissis and Sotirios Kouvelas* [1991] ECR-I 2925; [1994] 4 CMLR 540.

[49] Case C-159/90 *Society for the Protection of Unborn Children v. Grogan* [1991] ECR-I 4685; [1991] 3 CMLR 849.

function to provide the necessary guidelines for the national court in order to allow the national court to assess the compatibility of national legislation with Community law but only in matters relating to Community law. This was not the case here.[50]

The Right to Own Property or Pursue a Trade

The right to dispose of property was discussed in the case of *Internationale Handelsgesellschaft*, which is discussed above. However, in this case, no specific reference was made to the European Convention provisions. The case of *Nold*, also discussed above, did raise the issue of the ECHR, but the argument was dismissed by the Court. Article 1 of the First Protocol to the European Convention for the Protection of Human Rights was discussed at some length by the Court of Justice in the case of *Hauer*.[51] The Court stated unequivocally that the right to property is guaranteed in the Community legal order. However, the court analysed the provisions of Article 1 of the First Protocol and the provisions in force in the Member States with respect to property rights and held that there may be legitimate restrictions placed on the use of private property where these are necessary for the general interest. In order to determine whether Community measures are necessary and in the general interest, the Court examined the scheme in place for the common organisation of the wine market and held that the measures adopted did not impose any undue limitations upon the exercise of the right of private property.

A rather more complex case in relation to property rights arose in 1980.[52] It concerned an application for the annulment of a decision taken by the Commission at a time of manifest crisis in the steel industry and related to pricing of steel. Amongst other arguments put forward by the applicants, all Italian steel manufacturers, was that the Commission decision would deprive them of their businesses as they would become unprofitable. The Court gave this argument short shrift and held that the right to private property, recognised as a general principle of Community law, did not extend to a guarantee of commercial interests, "the uncertainties of which are part of the very essence of economic activity".[53]

Mr Wachauf did not find a great deal of support from the Court of Justice in his argument that the Community rules relating to the common organisation of the milk sector were contrary to the First Protocol. In this case the Court held that

---

[50] Following this ruling, the matter returned to the Irish High Court, which upheld the prohibition against the students. See *Society for the Protection of the Unborn Child v. Grogan* [1993] 1 CMLR 197. In a case relating to the right of an individual to travel to England to obtain an abortion, the Irish High Court decided that the right to travel was protected by Community law but that Irish public policy was sufficient to derogate from the rights created under Article 59 EEC. On appeal the Supreme Court dealt with this case on other grounds, namely the balance of probabilities that the child in question might commit suicide if she were forced to continue with her unwanted pregnancy. See *Attorney General v. X and Others* [1992] 2 CMLR 277. On the wider issue of abortion rights, see C. Forder, "Abortion: a Constitutional Problem in a European Perspective" [1994] *Maastricht Journal of European and Comparative Law* 1.

[51] Case 44/79 *Hauer v. Land Rheinland-Pfalz* [1979] ECR 3727; [1980] 3 CMLR 42.

[52] Cases 154, 205, 206, 226 to 228, 263 and 264/78, 39, 31, 83 and 85/79 *Valsabbia and Others v. Commission* [1980] ECR 907; [1981] 1 CMLR 613.

[53] *ibid.* p. 1011.

the fundamental rights which formed part of Community law must be examined in the context of their social function and that restrictions may be imposed on the exercise of property rights by the rules relating to the common organisation of a particular market provided that such restrictions do not provide a disproportionate and intolerable interference in the exercise of those rights. If the Community had adopted rules which would have deprived a lessee, without compensation, of the fruits of his or her labour then those rules would be contrary to the fundamental rights protected by the Court. However, in this case the Community rules did allow for compensation and it was the national rules which prevented Mr Wachauf from receiving compensation. In these circumstances, the Member States, when they implement such Community rules, are bound by the provisions relating to fundamental rights. The Community law, however, was not at fault.[54]

Conclusions

From this survey of the cases which have arisen before the European Court of Justice and the Court of First Instance, it is apparent that an individual may attempt to argue that specific Articles of the European Convention should be applied in determining the outcome of his or her case. Such arguments can be led in one of four circumstances. First, an aggrieved member of staff of or potential applicant for a post with one of the European institutions may attempt to rely on the Convention. This happened in the case of Mr A, Ms Prais and Mr de Compte discussed above. It is significant that no one has ever successfully argued his or her case in this way and the European institutions have never been found to have violated the European Convention. It may be that the Community institutions do genuinely attempt to adopt procedures which are in conformity with the Convention but this argument might be strengthened if the Community judiciary was more willing to explore Convention arguments and case law in the judgments given.

Alternatively, an individual may wish to challenge the validity of Community legislation as against the standards laid out in the Convention. This might happen in a case brought for judicial review before the European Court of Justice and has happened several times in relation to competition matters. The cases discussed under the heading of the right to a fair hearing or the right to privacy are examples of this type of action. It should be noted that these cases are now brought before the Court of First Instance, which has adopted the case law of the European Court of Justice and will apply the same principles. However, there are no examples where the Court has allowed a successful challenge to Community procedures.

The validity of European legislation might also be raised in a case before a national court which could refer the matter to the European Court of Justice for

---

[54] These issues were again raised in case C-2/92 *R v. MAFF, ex p. Dennis Clifford Bostock*, [1994] ECR I-955, [1994] 3 CMLR 547, discussed above, a case referred to the European Court of Justice from the English High Court. The European Convention was not specifically referred to in this case, but instead the following formula was used: "requirements flowing from the protection of fundamental rights in the Community legal order are also binding on Member States when they implement Community rules", *ibid.* [1994] ECR I at 983.

a preliminary ruling. Several of the cases discussed above have come to the European Court in this way. Again, there have been no successful challenges to the validity of European legislation on Convention issues.

More successful have been cases challenging national procedures. This is likely to be a growth area in the future as Community law expands into areas which were previously within the ambit of the national legislator. Where the Member State is acting on behalf of the Community there has been some limited success in challenging national rules. The cases of *Kirk* and *Johnston*, discussed above, are examples of such challenges. Here the European Court is quite clearly saying to national courts that they must apply the general principles of the Community legal order when they are dealing with areas which are within the Community competence. The European Court has stressed that such general principles can be discerned from the European Convention. However, this is not a back door incorporation of the Convention into national law since the European Court has been keen to state that the national court can use these general principles of Community law only in matters where Community law is at issue. These general principles cannot be applied to matters which fall solely within the ambit of the national legislator although the Convention itself might apply, given that all the member states have individually ratified the Convention and are, therefore, bound by it.

It is surprising in reading the cases that there is an almost total lack of reference by the European Court of Justice to the jurisprudence of the European Court or Commission of Human Rights. In some of the cases discussed above, this is understandable since there is little jurisprudence to go on. However, there are several areas which have been examined both by the European Court of Justice and by the European Court of Human Rights where it might be expected that the European Court of Justice might have cited as persuasive or binding authority the judgments of its sister institution. The example of Mr A and AIDS testing is a good example of this absence of reference to European Convention decisions. On reading the cases, the impression is given of the European Court interpreting the Convention in a way which suits the Community but which is not necessarily consistent with the jurisprudence of the Convention authorities. In particular, the Court of Justice is ready to place Community objectives, the Community public interest, over and above the protection of human rights.

This approach is explicable given the way in which Convention issues have been brought into play in Community law. The Community is not a party to the European Convention and the political institutions have refused to take the lead in order to bring the Community into the Convention scheme. The absence of action cannot be laid at the feet of the European Court of Justice, which has accepted in principle that it, together with the entire Community, might be subject to a judicial system which is capable of giving judgments binding on the Court of Justice itself. The Opinion of the Court of Justice relating to the European Economic Area Treaty lays down the way in which this can be achieved[55] and nothing

---

[55] Opinion 1/91 on the draft agreement between the Community and the countries of EFTA relating to the creation of the European Economic Area. The Court stated:

"Where, however, an international agreement provides for its own system of courts, including a court

44

in Opinion 2/94 would indicate that the Court would argue against acceptance of the authority of the Convention authorities were the Treaty to be amended. However, accession is a question for the political institutions and the Member States to solve.

with jurisdiction to settle disputes between the Contracting Parties to the agreement, and, as a result to interpret its provisions . . . an international agreement providing for such a system of courts is in principle compatible with Community law. The Community's competence in the field of international relations and its capacity to conclude international agreements necessarily entails the power to submit to the decisions of a court which is created or designated by such an agreement as regards the interpretation and application of its provisions''.

CHAPTER 3

ENGLAND AND WALES AND THE EUROPEAN CONVENTION

Introduction

This chapter sets out to review the European Convention on Human Rights in England and Wales. In so doing it deals first with a review of some of the principal cases which have been examined by the Commission and the Court which have originated from this jurisdiction. Secondly, the chapter considers the reciprocal position—the extent to which the Convention and its interpretation have been taken into account by the courts and the legislature within England and Wales.

The review of cases is prefaced by some observations about the operation of the Convention system and the allocation of responsibility between the Commission and the Court. This section is intended to provide a framework to answer the frequent question why there are "so many" cases against the United Kingdom and concerning England and Wales in particular.[1] The number of cases that there have been means that the review of cases decided by the Commission and the Court is obviously selective. Reference to the Commission's decisions is limited for reasons of space to certain cases that illustrate the inter-relationship either of the Commission and the Court or of the Convention system to English law.

The Convention system is litigant-driven, and this creates a further "selection". A case arises only if an individual lodges an application, not merely because there is "a problem" of conformity between English law and practice and the Convention.[2] However, as the Convention as interpreted does not treat all the rights it contains as of equal importance,[3] the review of the case law of the Strasbourg institutions seeks to reflect the precedence of rights under the Convention. As a result, the Articles from

---

[1] On a per capita basis, 40 judgments before the European Court of Human Rights concerning England and Wales in 29 years is in fact not very many compared with, say, Sweden (31) or Belgium (28). France had 42 within the first ten years of its accepting the right of individual petition.

[2] Hence the statistics are affected by whether various individuals affected by a given provision complain to the Commission. The Court has dealt with over 100 cases against Italy, but many concern the same issue—length of proceedings. Although prisoners' cases have caused copycat applications in England and Wales, *e.g. Silver v. United Kingdom*, March 25, 1983, Series A, No. 61; 13 EHRR 582, why did not more parents complain in circumstances similar to *O., H., W., B., R. v. United Kingdom*, July 8, 1987, Series A, No. 120/121; (1988) 10 EHRR 29?

[3] Formally all the rights in section 1 are of equal weight, but contrast Article 1 with the prevention of Article 3 treatment and the protection of fair trials in *Soering v. United Kingdom*, Series A, No. 161; (1989) 11 EHRR 439.

which no derogation can be made are dealt with first.[4] This chapter then deals with derogable rights and thirdly with those whose terms are qualified, before considering the position of the Convention in English law.

Since this part of the analysis relates to the position in England and Wales, it is fortunately not necessary to consider the application and interpretation of Article 2 of the Convention, which protects the right to life, or Article 4, which prohibits slavery and forced labour, as there have been no substantial cases in which these rights have been invoked before the Commission and none before the Court. This apparently banal statement is not without importance: first, recognition must be given to the factual situation in a legal system in which the rights under Articles 2 and 4 of the Convention are not seriously at issue. This is a characteristic shared with virtually all the population of the member states of the Council of Europe. It is an important indicator of the basic prerequisites of social stability and personal safety upon which the system of protection of human rights established under the European Convention is based. This social stability has been a major factor in determining the way in which the Commission and the Court operate in examining applications. It is an important distinction between the scope of their work and the scope and manner of the work of other international agencies and judicial bodies whose responsibility is the protection of human rights in other areas of the world.[5]

The work of the Commission and the Court is quite different for another, related, reason: the voluntary nature of the procedure. The Commission has accepted a judicial function rather than an inquisitorial one. It has no power to initiate an investigation or to reach an opinion without a complaint being lodged with it. It is responsible, and responds, only when proceedings are initiated.[6] The Commission is in this respect closely constrained by the limits that it has itself imposed and developed on the scope of its jurisdiction arising from individual complaints and a small number of interstate cases. The victim requirement in Article 25(1) of the Convention has introduced an important prerequisite for *locus standi* before the Commission and hence limited the cases that may ultimately be examined by the Court.[7] A similar function has been played by the Commission's extensive interpretation of the criteria for rejecting applications as inadmissible. This arises particularly from the extensive development of the term "manifestly ill-founded" to describe applications that the Commission rejects as not arguable and so inadmissible under Article 27(2) of the Convention.[8]

As a result of this role, the Commission has developed an extensive case law of its own. This case law defines the threshold of seriousness that constitutes an arguable case of a violation of one of the rights protected in section 1 of the Convention. In this way the Commission has underlined the importance of its role as the preliminary

---

[4] See Art. 15(2).
[5] Prominent amongst these is the work of the Inter-American Commission of Human Rights with its proactive response in investigating allegations of large-scale disappearances or unlawful killings.
[6] On one occasion the Commission carried out an on-the-spot investigation to establish whether an application was in fact intended to be lodged: *Sands v. United Kingdom*, Application No. 9338/81, unreported (1981).
[7] *e.g.*, *Vijayanatham and Pushparajah v. France*, Series A, No. 241-B; (1993) 15 EHRR 62.
[8] *e.g.* the reasoning in *McFeeley and Others v. United Kingdom*, 20 DR 44; (1981) 3 EHRR 161 which runs to 58 pages, concluding "manifestly ill-founded".

investigator of fact and law in relation to all applications made under the Convention.[9]

It has been widely recognised[10] that the process of admissibility by the Commission, including the examination of legal arguments as well as allegations of fact, followed by a further separate examination of questions of law by the Court in cases referred to it under Article 46 of the Convention, is duplicative as well as unnecessarily elaborate. These considerations have underlain the adoption of Protocol No. 11 to the Convention under which a new single institution, the European Court of Human Rights, is established. Individuals will have direct access to it in a way that is similar to the current direct (though optional) access to the Commission.[11] It is, however, noticeable that Protocol No. 11 provides little detail on the task ascribed to the three-member committee of the Court whose job it will be to determine whether or not applications are admissible.

Non-derogable Rights

One product of the elaborate case law of the Commission interpreting the threshold of arguability is the gap between the number of cases in which the most fundamental rights in the Convention are invoked and the number in which significant argument and discussion are devoted to the interpretation of these provisions by the Commission and ultimately the Court. As has been noted above, there is no substantial case arising from England and Wales involving the interpretation of Article 2. However, the right to life is frequently invoked by applicants who are unfamiliar with the interpretation which has been given to this provision by the Commission and the Court or with the threshold of seriousness established by the Commission in its interpretation of the requirements of admissibility. This is particularly true of cases brought by applicants in person, which still represent the majority of cases.

A similar issue arises in relation to reliance on Article 3. The Convention sets out in Article 1 the obligation that all states shall secure to everyone within the jurisdiction the rights and freedoms defined in Section 1. Although these rights are not accorded any formal precedence, the most important in the case law of the Commission and the Court is Article 3, which provides: "No-one shall be subjected to torture, or to inhuman or degrading treatment or punishment." Some degree of precedence is afforded to this Article (together with Articles 2, 4 and 7) by the terms of Article 15 and particularly Article 15(2). Article 15 provides for the possibility that parties to the Convention may take measures derogating from the Convention obligations in exceptional circumstances. However, Article 15(2) prohibits any derogation at all in respect of Article 3.

Interpreting Article 3 is difficult because the actual text is not couched in legal

---

[9] The extent of this role is often belittled as the Commission being a "mere filter" and not infrequently criticised because of the length of time which a detailed investigation of the prima facie arguability of allegations of a breach of the Convention takes. See, however, *Ribitisch v. Austria*, Series A, No. 336; (1996) 21 EHRR 573.

[10] Explanatory Memorandum of the Council of Europe accompanying the text of Protocol No. 11 to the Convention.

[11] Art. 25(1).

terms but refers to factual circumstances. "Inhuman" or "degrading" are not words that are subject to existing legal definition in domestic law any more than "treatment" or "punishment", and "torture" has acquired a statutory definition only by virtue of the enactment of domestic legislation to reflect international obligations.[12]

Interpretation of Article 3 in Cases Concerning England and Wales

The interpretation of Article 3 of the Convention is unique in that the Court has identified the threshold of seriousness sufficient to constitute a breach of Article 3 as part of the substantive right rather than as merely a procedural obstacle to establishing a violation. Thus, in relation to Article 3, the Court has said that any treatment complained of must "attain a minimum level of severity" if it is to amount to inhuman treatment contrary to Article 3.[13] This approach applies a threshold of arguability which is similar to that which the Commission has operated in relation to all individual applications brought under Article 25. The special seriousness of an allegation under Article 3 means that there is a minimum severity of treatment which must be established for a violation of this particular provision to be found.

The assessment of the seriousness of any particular treatment is relative and must reflect the severity of its effects on the particular recipient. Thus it is relevant to take into account the sex, age and other circumstances of the recipient of the treatment in question.[14] Under Article 1 of the Convention there must be state responsibility for the matters about which an individual complains: some state action, therefore, or conceivably state inaction, will be required.[15] The general terms of this text raise a central question about the scope of protection under the Convention: does Article 3 protect against degrading punishment imposed by private persons rather than officials? What is the role of consent?[16] Importantly, however, in *Ireland v. United Kingdom* the Court left largely undetermined whether Article 3 protects an applicant from the inevitable consequences of generalised circumstances or only protects an applicant against a deliberate act.[17] The cases concerning England and Wales in which Article 3 has been analysed illustrate these difficult issues, which will be considered below under three principal headings: cases of deliberate punishment, cases relating to conditions of treatment or punishment, and cases relating to the removal of individuals from the jurisdiction.

[12] Criminal Justice Act 1988, ss. 134–138.
[13] *Ireland v. United Kingdom*, Series A, No. 25; (1979–80) 2 EHRR 25.
[14] *ibid.*, para. 162.
[15] Article 1 provides: "The High Contracting Parties shall secure to everyone within their jurisdiction the rights and freedoms defined in Section 1 of the Convention".
[16] *Cf. R. v. Brown* [1993] 2 All E.R. 75 (in this respect see the Court's findings in *CR v. United Kingdom* and *SW v. United Kingdom*, discussed in relation to Article 7 below); also *Laskey, Jaggard and Brown v. United Kingdom*, judgment of February 19, 1997, where the Court found there to have been no violation of Article 8.
[17] The Commission based its finding of a violation of Article 3 arising from the use of the five techniques on the fact that these actions had been deliberate. Report 25.1.76; extensive extracts are published at (1976) 19 Ybk ECHR 512–913.

Deliberate Punishment

Where the act complained of by an applicant is a formal punishment, the deliberateness of the act is not at issue. An example is the case of *Tyrer*,[18] which concerned the operation of judicially imposed corporal punishment in the Isle of Man. The United Kingdom exercises responsibility for the external affairs of the Isle of Man and at the time of the *Tyrer* application the scope of the Convention was extended to the Isle of Man by the United Kingdom under Article 63 of the Convention.

In 1972 Mr. Tyrer, then aged 15 and of good character, pleaded guilty before the local juvenile court to unlawful assault on one of the senior boys at his school. Apparently that boy had reported Mr. Tyrer and others for taking beer into the school, as a result of which Mr. Tyrer and the other boys concerned had been caned as a school punishment. The applicant complained not about his caning at the school,[19] but the sentence imposed on him for the assault,[20] which was three strokes of the birch.

The heart of the Court's judgment directed itself not merely at the particular circumstances of the individual applicant but in fact at the institution of state-inflicted corporal punishment itself. The Court held:[21]

> "The very nature of judicial corporal punishment is that it involves one human being inflicting physical violence on another human being. Furthermore, it is institutionalised violence: that is, in the present case, violence committed by the law, ordered by the judicial authorities of the State, and carried out by the police authorities of the State. Thus, although the applicant did not suffer any severe or long-lasting physical effects, his punishment—whereby he was treated as an object in the power of the authorities—constituted an assault on precisely that which it is one of the main purposes of Article 3 to protect, namely a person's dignity and physical integrity."[22]

[18] *Tyrer* case, Series A, No. 26; (1979–80) 2 EHRR 1.

[19] Compare the cases of *Warwick v. United Kingdom, Y. v. United Kingdom* and *Costello Roberts v. United Kingdom* discussed below. As with judicial birching in the Isle of Man, the exercise of formalised corporal punishment over children is an anachronistic feature of English education viewed with incomprehension in most of continental Europe, where it has either never been practised or has been formally prohibited for more than a century. The law in England has also now been reformed. Section 47 of the Education (No. 2) Act 1986 (together with S.I. 1987 No. 1987 and S.I. 1989 No. 1825) abolished corporal punishment in state schools and for state-funded pupils at independent schools; s.293 of the Act extends the ban to corporal punishment in independent schools in so far as it amounts to inhuman or degrading punishment.

[20] The sentence was administered under the provisions of the Petty Sessions and Summary Jurisdictions Act 1927 (as amended).

[21] *Tyrer* at para. 33.

[22] This dogmatic approach to the interpretation of the Convention was criticised by Judge Sir Gerald Fitzmaurice in his separate opinion, but the majority of the Court stated that they had taken due account of the inevitable degrading or humiliating aspect of all punishment. More surprising are some of the procedural features of the case, which included the applicant's request, made in 1976 before the Commission had completed its examination of the application, that the case be withdrawn. The Court continued in the face of this position and the fact that the acceptance of the compulsory jurisdiction of the Court under Art. 46 of the Convention had lapsed in respect of the Isle of Man at the time that the case was referred to the Court. Both facts show the Court's determination not to relinquish its grip on an application once put before it. This approach is perhaps characteristic of the Court in the early years of its operation at a time when the number of cases pending before it seldom exceeded four in any year. The radical change in the number of cases proceeding through the Convention system in the intervening

Mr. Tyrer did not complain about the caning that he had received at his school. From such little material as is available from the case reports and supporting documentation, this appears to have been considerably less serious than the judicial birching to which he was exposed and about which he did complain.[23] Subsequently, however, the Commission has been faced with three cases, one of which was ultimately determined by the Court, in which the corporal punishment of children at school was alleged to violate Article 3. These cases illustrate some of the difficulties of an incomplete Convention, *i.e.* a Convention setting out only a limited number of rights. It appears that the Commission found itself faced with a practice which was regarded generally as incompatible with the common European standard but which was difficult to categorise as a breach of such a fundamental provision of the Convention as Article 3.

The Commission relied on an extensive interpretation of Article 8 to fill this gap,[24] derived from a comparative analysis of constitutional remedies protecting personal physical integrity. On this basis the Commission considered that Article 8, which protects the right to respect for private life,[25] was at issue in cases which did not attain the degree of severity and seriousness envisaged by Article 3. The cases had also been argued as raising issues in relation to the respect for philosophical convictions in the provision of education, a right separately protected under Article 2 of Protocol No. 1 of the Convention.[26] However, that right has been interpreted essentially as a right of the parents rather than of the child.

The result has been a group of three cases which would be difficult for a conservative English observer to accept. They reflect an important theme in the Court's case law, namely that the Convention must be interpreted as a living instrument. This analogy means that the rights protected by the Convention are not limited strictly to the interpretation of the words adopted (in the English and French texts) at the time when the Convention was drawn up in the early 1950s or when it was initially ratified.[27] Instead the Court has held that "the Convention is a living instrument which ... must be interpreted in the light of present-day conditions."[28]

There have been a large number of other examples of this dynamic or living interpretation of the Convention, such as the interpretation of Article 8 to address and protect the situation of transsexuals[29] or the development of extraterritorial jurisdiction

---

period of some twenty years makes both of these decisions and the dogmatic attitude of the Court in relation to judicial corporal punishment seem out of step with the current attitude of the Court.

[23] The Tynwald (the Isle of Man's parliament) voted to retain judicial corporal punishment despite the Court's judgment. The right of individual petition and the compulsory jurisdiction of the Court have not subsequently been extended to the Isle of Man.

[24] *Warwick v. United Kingdom*, No. 9471/81, 60 DR 5; *Y. v. United Kingdom*, Series A, No. 247A; (1994) 17 EHRR 238, to which the Commission Report is annexed.

[25] Art. 8(1): "Everyone has the right to respect for his private and family life, his home and his correspondence".

[26] Art. 2, Protocol No. 1: "No person shall be denied the right to education. In the exercise of any functions which it assumes in relation to education and to teaching, the State shall respect the right of parents to ensure such education and teaching in conformity with their own religions and philosophical convictions."

[27] Ratified by the United Kingdom in 1953.

[28] *Tyrer* case, judgment of April 25, 1978, Series A, No. 26, at para. 31; (1979–80) 2 EHRR 1.

[29] *Cossey v. United Kingdom*, Series A, No. 184; (1991) 13 EHRR 622.

to protect persons facing removal from one of the Convention member states to a third state where human rights are not protected.[30] The criticism may certainly be made that the interpretation of a fixed and unchanged text by a court with an international composition is an inefficient way to adapt all but the most basic laws to rapid social change. However, it appears from the cases that in the opinion of the Commission and the Court the social change required to prevent corporal punishment of children at school was not rapid but rather should have already been concluded in all the member states of the Council of Europe.

These difficulties are reflected in the outcome of the three English cases concerned. *Warwick v. United Kingdom*[31-32] concerned the complaint of a sixteen-year-old girl who was given one stroke of the cane by a male headmaster. The Commission was of the opinion in its Report under Article 31 of the Convention that these facts constituted a breach of Article 3 of the Convention. However, the case was not referred to the European Court of Human Rights and the final decision on this question was therefore left to the Committee of Ministers of the Council of Europe. The Committee did not follow the Commission's opinion.[33] The second case[34] resulted in a settlement of the proceedings before the Court when the applicant withdrew the application on receipt of an *ex gratia* payment from the United Kingdom Government. The third case of *Costello Roberts v. United Kingdom*[35] is the most surprising. The complaint related to the corporal punishment of a child at a private fee-paying school. The child, a boy of seven years, was punished with a gym shoe on his bottom. The Court was heavily split[36] as to whether this constituted degrading punishment contrary to Article 3, but the majority considered that the fact that the boy was much younger than Mr. Tyrer was one reason why the punishment was not degrading. For the minority the young age of the child underlined his vulnerability.

Conditions of Punishment and Treatment

The second main area of complaints concerning England and Wales invoking Article 3 of the Convention relates to the conditions in which treatment or punishment has been imposed rather than the actual punishment itself. These cases, concerning largely prisoners and those detained in mental hospitals, have been far more numerous than the cases of punishments referred to above and underline some of the difficulties mentioned at the beginning of this section of identifying the degree of deliberateness which is necessary for a breach of Article 3 of the Convention to be established.

A transition case which illustrates the distinction between these two issues is *Reed v. United Kingdom*.[37] The applicant was detained as a Category A (high security) prisoner as a result of his conviction for crimes of violence. He was detained at Hull

---

[30] *Soering v. United Kingdom*, Series A, No. 161; (1989) 11 EHRR 439.
[31-32] 60 DR 5.
[33] It failed to reach the requisite two-thirds majority to establish its opinion as to whether or not the facts found constituted a breach of the Convention at all. Resolution CM Res DH (89)5.
[34] *Y. v. United Kingdom*, Series A, No. 247-A; (1994) 17 EHRR 238.
[35] *Costello-Roberts v. United Kingdom*, Series A, No. 247-C; (1995) 19 EHRR 112.
[36] The vote was five to four for no breach; *ibid.*
[37] Application No. 7360/76, 19 DR 113.

Prison at the time of a major riot, lasting four days, in the summer of 1976. After the riot was brought under control, Reed alleged that he was attacked repeatedly by groups of officers who kicked and punched him on various occasions, knocking him out at least once. He also complained of the conditions of his detention in what he contended was solitary confinement for a period of some three months after his transfer to Winchester Prison.

The two sets of allegations were clearly distinguished by the Commission. The first was very serious, especially bearing in mind that the applicant was held in detention at the time of the assaults. There is an obvious risk of a cover-up where the system of discipline collapses. The difficult problems of proof have subsequently been dealt with by the Court, in a way placing a heavy responsibility on the authorities to justify injury to detainees.[38] These considerations did not arise in Reed's case because before the Commission the United Kingdom Government admitted that several prisoners, including the applicant, had been attacked by members of the prison staff who had subsequently been put on trial and some of whom had been convicted of offences of assault.[39]

Whereas the applicant's complaints concerning the assaults were declared admissible by the Commission,[40] the complaints concerning solitary confinement were carefully analysed and rejected as manifestly ill-founded. They did not attain the threshold of seriousness which the Court had established as necessary to constitute a breach of Article 3. This conclusion was reached notwithstanding the fact that Reed's conditions of detention in Winchester were undoubtedly severe, partly as a result of the strict regime of segregation from other prisoners under rule 43 of the Prison Rules 1968, and partly because of the dilapidation of Winchester Prison at that time, which was by admission an old building without adequate sanitation and with serious cockroach infestation. Furthermore, Reed had been subject to physical violence at the hands of the prison officers in Hull and so was recovering both physically and to some extent mentally from that ordeal. He was a long-term prisoner on a sentence of life imprisonment for whom the sparse furnishings and severe regime would have been a particular burden.

The rejection of his complaints concerning the conditions of his detention in Winchester may have been intended partly to highlight the significance of the allegations declared admissible by the Commission, which were later the subject of a friendly settlement under Article 30 of the Convention. The distinction in question is one which has underlain a significant number of decisions of the Commission where cases have been rejected as inadmissible and thus not raising an arguable issue, even though the detailed examination of the factual allegations and of the relevant interpretation of the Convention has consumed considerable quantities of legal argument.[41]

Extreme examples of cases relating to the conditions of detention of long-term

---

[38] *Tomasi*, Series A, No. 241-A; (1993) 15 EHRR 1; also *Ribitisch v. Austria*, Series A, No. 336; (1996) 21 EHRR 573.

[39] Application No. 7630/76, Dec. Comm. December 6, 1979, 19 DR 113 at 120, para. 28.

[40] Together with other complaints concerning interference with correspondence and access to legal advice and the courts, see para. 54 at p. 142.

[41] *McFeeley*, 8317/78, 20 DR 44.

prisoners in English prisons include W^{42} and $M.^{43}$ Both were Category A prisoners convicted of murders and accordingly detained in the most stringent conditions in English prisons. Because of their long-term prison sentences, it was to be expected that these strict conditions of confinement would continue indefinitely.

In the first case, the applicant, W, had been convicted of murder and sentenced to life imprisonment in 1974; he subsequently attacked a prison officer, was charged with attempted murder and given two further five-year sentences in 1976. He was also an inmate at Hull Prison in August 1976 at the time of the riot there; he was thereafter transferred to Durham Prison where he was kept in a small four-celled unit known as "the cage" isolated from the rest of the prison. Subsequently, he was transferred to Parkhurst Prison where, in September 1978, he killed another prisoner and was given a further life sentence in April 1979.

At the time of his application the applicant was detained in Long Lartin Prison and segregated under rule 43 of the Prison Rules. His complaint concerned the overall duration of his detention in close confinement and segregation from other prisoners under rule 43, which measures were obviously taken as a response to the risk that the applicant was considered to represent to prison officers and other inmates. Those conditions involved great restrictions on his access to other parts of the prison for security reasons, the exclusion of contact with other prisoners, and his confinement in his cell, in effect for 23 hours each day with one hour's exercise. The application was referred to the United Kingdom Government shortly after it was lodged in January 1982, but by the end of the year the respondent Government was able to provide information relating to a considerable relaxation of the regime to which the applicant was subjected. In March 1983 the applicant wrote to the Commission requesting that his application be withdrawn and ascribing his stable and more social behaviour to the time that he had spent removed from association. The Commission accordingly decided to strike the application off its list of cases.[44]

The factual background of the M case was even more severe, as a result of the extraordinary danger which the prison authorities considered M to represent. He had pleaded guilty to manslaughter with diminished responsibility in 1974 and severe violent incidents had ensued during his detention in Broadmoor, when he had attacked other prisoners and killed one other inmate, which resulted in his further conviction for murder in 1977. A year later the applicant killed two fellow prisoners, was again charged with murder and convicted in 1979 and was sentenced to further terms of life imprisonment.

From the time of those murders the applicant was detained in a special unit in Wakefield Prison, removed from association, in what he described as "a cage" since it was a special cell with a cage-like door made of steel mesh as a second layer of protection apart from the normal external cell door. The cell measured approximately two metres by four, with a window some two metres from the ground with frosted glass and a small ventilation gap through which one corner of the sky was visible. In

---

[42] Application No. 9348/81, 32 DR 190.

[43] Application No. 9907/82, 35 DR 130.

[44] A defect in the text of the Convention was the absence of a power to strike out a case; this was initially covered by the Commission's Rules of Procedure and now by amendment to the Convention, Art. 30.

view of the extreme risk which the applicant represented, his movements around the prison were severely limited and were undertaken in the company of five prison officers. His contact with other prisoners was excluded on security grounds. The applicant complained both about the extreme severity of the conditions of his detention and the absence of any adequate psychiatric review, notwithstanding the recommendation of the judge on his conviction in 1977 that consideration be given to his detention in a special hospital.

Once again, in the course of the proceedings the respondent Government informed the Commission of proposed amendments to the regime of detention applicable to M.[45] These included the provision of a different cell with substantially more room and integral sanitation, and it was anticipated that some limited association with other prisoners might also be permitted. However, in part by reference to these developments and in part by reference to the risk which the applicant demonstrably represented, the Commission rejected his complaints that his conditions of detention amounted to a breach of Article 3 as manifestly ill-founded.

It is open to question whether the applications made to the Commission by these two applicants contributed directly or indirectly to an amelioration of the circumstances of their detention. It is obvious that dangerous prisoners must be dealt with in a manner which protects other inmates and prison officers from the risks which they represent. At the same time the Commission has repeatedly emphasised the duty on the detaining authority to take account of the requirements of the Convention, and in particular Article 3, even in the face of serious risks of this kind.[46] At the very least, the numerous cases brought by long-term prisoners complaining about their conditions of confinement in English prisons, including especially the absence of adequate sanitation, the problems of overcrowding and restrictions on association, exercise and correspondence, as well as limited access to lawyers and to the courts, may well have contributed to accelerating a process of review and reform of these conditions.

The hallmark of the Commission's examination of complaints in such cases has been an evaluation of the proportionality of the steps taken by the prison authorities in relation to the risk imposed by dangerous prisoners. These considerations were not wholly appropriate to considering the unusual case of *T v. United Kingdom*,[47] where a prisoner was refusing to wear prison clothes and regarded himself as a political prisoner. The prisoner insisted on being detained naked, although he was provided with blankets by the prison authorities. His recalcitrant attitude resulted in his foregoing remission for good behaviour and in his serving almost the entirety of his two-year sentence arising from a trivial offence of criminal damage which was ascribed by the applicant to his longstanding dispute with Cambridge University and the Establishment.

The applicant's refusal to dress meant that he could not move around the prison or associate with other prisoners. As a result he was segregated for a considerable period in conditions made stringent by his own strict insistence that his conviction and detention were improper.

---

[45] Application No. 35 DR 130, at 133.
[46] *McFeeley*, 20 DR 44, at para. 46.
[47] Application No. 8231/78, 28 DR 5.

The applicant ascribed his refusal to wear prison clothes or co-operate with the prison administration to the requirements of his philosophical and religious convictions and beliefs. Nevertheless, the Commission recognised that the opportunity rested with the applicant to ameliorate the inevitably severe conditions of his detention which resulted from those decisions, and that the authorities were at all times prepared to provide him with prison uniform and to allow his association with other prisoners if he would conform to normal prison discipline. Whether or not the facts actually illustrate circumstances of choice in relation to the conditions of detention in view of the personal convictions to which the applicant referred, the case is authority for the view that treatment contrary to Article 3 arises only where that treatment is involuntary.

The fact that the majority of cases referred to concern the interpretation of Article 3 by the Commission, and not the Court, reflects the high threshold which has been imposed before a claim under this provision is regarded as arguable. The position has been slightly different in relation to more vulnerable groups, as illustrated by the cases of the corporal punishment of children referred to above, and a similar pattern emerges in relation to the cases concerning persons detained in psychiatric institutions. The principal case in this category, *B v. United Kingdom*,[48] gave rise to one of the Commission's rare on-the-spot investigations into the secure psychiatric hospital at Broadmoor.

B complained of three major factors. First, of his incarceration in Broadmoor following his diagnosis as suffering from a schizophrenic personality disorder. He was detained in Broadmoor for a period of three and a half years at a time when the physical conditions in the hospital were very poor as a result of serious overcrowding and lack of adequate sanitation or any satisfactory privacy for the detainees. Second, he complained that during this period he received no adequate medical treatment for his psychiatric condition, if any, as a result of a stalemate between him and the senior psychiatrist responsible for his case. He and his family disputed the need for any medication, and on his ultimate transfer from Broadmoor the applicant's condition significantly improved. Third, the applicant complained that his detention was unlawful since he was not a person of unsound mind and that he was unable to challenge his detention before a court as required by the provisions of Article 5(4) of the Convention.

Having conducted an on-the-spot investigation, the Commission proceeded to conclude that the applicant's complaints concerning the conditions of detention in Broadmoor and the circumstances of the stalemate over his refusal of treatment did not constitute a breach of Article 3 of the Convention. The conditions at Broadmoor had clearly been very unsatisfactory at the time of the original application, but the Commission was able to note certain improvements that had subsequently been introduced. Of greater concern in the light of those improvements were the applicant's complaints concerning the absence of any realistic treatment for the psychiatric condition from which the doctors at Broadmoor considered he suffered and his contention that he needed no treatment. The Commission noted a surprising length of time during which the deadlock between the responsible medical officer and the applicant continued, and during which there was no possibility of administering any specific treatment. Given

---

[48] Application No. 6870/75, 10 DR 37 and 32 DR 5.

that the applicant received general care and attention from other members of the medical team, the Commission deferred to the expert clinical judgment of the psychiatric staff in concluding that the evidence did not establish that the applicant's treatment could amount to a violation of Article 3 of the Convention. An alternative view would have required a greater positive obligation on the state to treat a patient detained in a psychiatric hospital and possibly even to achieve successful results in so doing.[49]

A review of these cases relating to detention and the conditions of detention for individuals underscores the open-textured nature of Article 3. The text refers objectively to the fact that nobody shall be subjected to the treatment that it prohibits. On its face the text would seem to imply that no deliberate harmful act need be shown by an applicant in order to establish a breach of Article 3. It is, however, a considerable step from that position to derive an obligation on the state to cure a detained patient of psychiatric illness within a particular time-frame. It is also difficult for an international tribunal, even one that had in this case exceptionally taken the step of an on-the-spot investigation, to form its own view *ex post facto* on appropriate psychiatric treatment which should have been given to a particular patient. The Commission's finding of a violation of Article 5(4) of the Convention, in the absence of a procedure whereby B's detention in a psychiatric hospital could be periodically reviewed by the domestic courts, is therefore perhaps of greater significance for the protection of such inmates than the attempt to review the psychiatric treatment which was afforded to the particular applicant.

Compulsory Removal from the Jurisdiction

The final category of cases concerning England and Wales in which Article 3 has been invoked are cases where applicants complained about their compulsory removal from the jurisdiction.

The first and in many ways most important of these applications concerned 31 citizens of the United Kingdom and Colonies or British Protected Persons who were all holders of United Kingdom passports and originally resident in Kenya or Uganda.[50] Being Asian and not citizens of Kenya or Uganda, their continued residence there became increasingly difficult and in certain cases illegal as a result of the post-independence "Africanisation" policy, and they therefore sought to settle in Britain. Under the terms of the Commonwealth Immigrants Act 1968 they were refused admission to the United Kingdom, or if admitted were not granted permission to remain permanently. Six of the applicants whose applications were adjourned had attempted to enter Britain indirectly through other European countries and had been stranded in the process. Others sought to enter the United Kingdom in Dover, were refused admission to the United Kingdom and detained for two weeks in Canterbury Prison before being put on board ship to return to France. On arrival at Calais they were refused

---

[49] This view is implicit in certain of the dissenting opinions of two members of the Commission, Messrs Opsahl and Melchior, who did not support the majority finding. By contrast Mr Kiernan based his dissent on the inflexibility of the approach of the staff at Broadmoor to the stalemate between patient and psychiatrist.

[50] 78A DR 5.

admission to France and were sent straight back to Dover and once again detained in Canterbury Prison and released six weeks later on temporary leave to remain in the United Kingdom.

The Commission concluded that the amendment to the immigration regime that had been introduced by the 1968 Act was racially motivated and that the exclusion of the East African Asians in the circumstances of international ping-pong between the United Kingdom and other adjacent jurisdictions, coupled with the attendant publicity and the implicit status of second-class citizen, together constituted treatment contrary to Article 3 of the Convention.[51] The case was not referred to the European Court of Human Rights and resulted in a resolution of the Committee of Ministers that no further action was required (and hence no finding of compliance or violation of the Convention was established) when the Committee of Ministers was informed that the 25 applicants in question had ultimately been granted leave to remain in the United Kingdom.[52]

Cases where an individual facing removal from the jurisdiction also faces the prospect of treatment contrary to the Convention in the country of destination, have raised important questions as to the scope of the protection in Article 1 of the Convention.[53] In a number of cases with a dramatic factual content, the Commission has been confronted with the argument that an individual who was to be removed from England and Wales would face treatment contrary to Article 3 in the country to which he or she was being sent. Obviously, the primary responsibility for that treatment arose in the foreign country, but the responsibility for exposing the individual to the risk of that treatment resulted from the decision of the authorities in England and Wales to order their removal. As the case law under the Convention has developed, it has established that where the authorities knew or should have known of a real risk of very serious harm in the country of destination, the decision to remove the individual to face that risk may itself breach Article 3 of the Convention.

This interpretation of the Convention is a broad one, but it reflects the historical background that underlies the Convention's original drafting. In the aftermath of the Holocaust and the atrocities of World War Two, the Convention was designed as a long-stop against failures in the protection of fundamental human rights by the domestic authorities. It is not, therefore, surprising that the Commission and the Court should be wary of allowing the domestic authorities to assert that they did not know or need not consider the foreseeable consequences of a decision to remove an individual from his or her jurisdiction into imminent danger.

If the principle is straightforward, its application to facts has caused great difficulty.[54] Although the Commission and ultimately the Court have confirmed that the risk of treatment contrary to Article 3 is effectively a protection against removal, this has involved both institutions, and especially the Commission, in reviewing large numbers of complaints by individuals alleging fearful risks to them if removed in circumstances where the accuracy of the allegations cannot easily be evaluated.

---

[51] *ibid.*, p. 62.
[52] Res Comm Min, CM DH (77)2.
[53] See introduction to this chapter and note 15 above.
[54] *Cruz Varas*, Series A, No. 201; (1992) 14 EHRR 1; see also *Vilvarajah and Others*, Series A, No. 215; (1992) 14 EHRR 248.

By their nature, cases of this type are not suitable for examination by a procedure as cumbersome and long as those under the Convention. For many years the majority of such complaints were dealt with by the Commission alone since the urgency with which they arose and the possible severity of the treatment in the destination countries necessitated a rapid evaluation of the decision-making procedure which had been applied by the domestic authorities and the risk that that procedure had failed to take account of treatment contrary to Article 3 in the country of destination. As a result, the Commission developed an extensive practice of urgent response to emergency cases, including the use of interim measures under rule 36 of its Rules of Procedure.[55]

The majority of such cases were resolved either by a rapid decision by the Commission that the complaints raised by the individual concerned were unsubstantiated, quickly resulting in that person's removal from the jurisdiction, or through a preliminary review by the Commission resulting in a change of mind by the State Party to the Convention and a revocation of a decision to remove the individual concerned. As a result, very few cases which gave rise to findings of a violation of Article 3 have been examined in any detail by the Commission and only a handful by the Court.[56]

The first of these was the Court's judgment in the *Soering* case; this is also the case that has most rapidly passed through the Commission and the Court, taking a total of 364 days from being lodged until the Court's conclusion. The applicant's extradition was sought by the United States from the United Kingdom on the basis of his alleged responsibility for two brutal murders. Under the law of the state of Virginia and under U.S. federal law, anyone convicted of murder and sentenced to capital punishment in Virginia would be likely to endure a period of six or more years on death row under the threat of execution, whilst a long series of appeals are considered.

The United Kingdom obtained an assurance from the United States authorities that representations would be made on its behalf to the Governor of the state of Virginia to the effect that, if the applicant were sentenced to death and appeals did not change that conclusion, the United Kingdom Government would wish his sentence to be commuted to life imprisonment. That assurance would only operate, however, after the appeals process had been concluded and the applicant contended that, for political and legal reasons, an assurance would not necessarily be effective. He complained that the decision to order his extradition to the United States would result in exposing him to the risk of treatment contrary to Article 3 in the form of the severe conditions of detention coupled with the anxiety and pressure of a prolonged detention on death row.

---

[55] The Rule provides: "The Commission, or when it is not in session, the President may indicate to the parties any interim measure the adoption of which seems desirable in the interest of the parties or the proper conduct of the proceedings before it". It has been applied in serious cases to prevent an irreversible consequence from arising which would undermine the effective examination of a case, which in turn is protected by Art. 25(1), third sentence: "Those of the High Contracting Parties who have made such a declaration [recognising the competence of the Commission] undertake not to hinder in any way the effective exercise of this right".

[56] The Court's unfamiliarity with the operation of rule 36 (which it applied in only one case concerning England and Wales) in the *Soering* case (Series A, No. 161) may explain in part its limited ruling in the *Cruz Varas* case (Series A, No. 215) in which it held that rule 36 of the Rules of Procedure was not a binding obligation on states.

The Court found unanimously[57] that a decision to implement the applicant's extradition to the United States would breach Article 3 of the Convention, thus vindicating the Commission's established extraterritorial application of the Convention in holding that allegations that these provisions might be breached in the destination country were a basis for a finding that removal of the individual to that country could breach the Convention. The applicant had argued for a wider interpretation of this provision, namely that surrender could be authorised only where the destination country respected all the rights contained in the Convention. It remains to be determined whether protection is effectively provided only in respect of Article 3 and Article 6 or whether other provisions, including notably Article 2, the right to life, Article 4, the prohibition of slavery, and Article 5, the right to liberty and security of person, are equally areas in which extraterritorial protection of the Convention is provided.

The difficulty of evaluating the risk of ill-treatment is illustrated by the case of *Vilvarajah*[58] concerning the deportation from England of young male Tamils to Sri Lanka in circumstances where they contended that they ran the risk of torture, ill-treatment or death in Sri Lanka as a result of the communal troubles there. The case focused in particular on the scope and adequacy of the remedies available to the applicants to challenge the decision for their removal and in particular the adequacy of the issues which could be examined in judicial review, a remedy which normally addresses the procedural form of decisions rather than their correctness on the merits.

The applicants argued that the situation in Sri Lanka was sufficiently serious to justify their allegations but the Court held that they must be able to show that they were at special risk of severe treatment. By the time the case came before the Court, there was evidence that three of the five applicants (all of whom had been deported to Sri Lanka) had in fact been subjected to ill-treatment, but the Court nevertheless held that there had been no basis upon which the United Kingdom should have been able to anticipate this specific treatment for these particular individuals at the time of their removal.

In the case of *Chahal*, the Court and Commission were faced with an applicant who was still in the United Kingdom but who was under imminent threat of deportation to India. The applicant was a well known advocate of Sikh separatism, and was due to be deported for reasons of national security and the international fight against terrorism. The applicant was still in the United Kingdom because the Government had complied with a request from the Commission under rule 36[59] that it should take no action to deport the applicant during the currency of the Strasbourg proceedings.

In a strong judgment on Article 3[60] the Court stressed the absolute nature of Article 3 and rejected the Government's submission that in cases of national security there was an implied limitation to Article 3, on the basis of the danger posed by the person in question to the security of the host nation. It then carried out a "rigorous" review of the evidence before it as to the existence of a real risk of ill-treatment should the applicant be deported, and in doing so made clear that it reserved the right to call

[57] See judgment at p. 50. The Commission had found against the applicant under Art. 3 by a majority of six to five (annexed to judgment at p. 17).
[58] Series A, No. 215; (1992) 14 EHRR 248.
[59] See above.
[60] For the court's findings on Articles 5 and 13 see below.

other evidence *proprio motu*, if necessary. The Court found that there was a real risk to the applicant, basing itself on information before it as to (i) the general situation on violations of human rights by members of the Indian security forces, and (ii) the special situation of the applicant due to his high profile in the Sikh separatist movement and the Indian Government's accusations of his involvement in terrorism.[61]

However, the Court devoted by far the majority of its findings to those on the general situation, and very much less to the special situation of the applicant. Given the evidential difficulties which may arise from too high a threshold for an applicant being set by virtue of the "special risk" requirement, the Court's judgment in *Chahal* may indicate an important procedural development in the Court's case law since *Vilvarajah*, in favour of the applicant in such circumstances.

Conclusion in Relation to Article 3

It is appropriate to review briefly at this juncture some of the consequences which may be drawn from the operation and interpretation of Article 3 in cases concerning England and Wales.

First and most importantly, there is some evidence that applying to the Commission has had a beneficial effect, not only on the individuals concerned but also on the general position which their cases have illustrated. Thus the *East African Asians* cases contributed to a resolution of one particular aspect of the difficulties experienced in England and Wales in relation to the imposition of restrictions on coloured immigration from former dependencies and Commonwealth countries. Similarly, the cases concerning prison conditions may have contributed in part to the increased awareness of the acute problems of prison overcrowding and the lack of adequate sanitation and, within a narrower frame, renovation and improvement of conditions in a psychiatric hospital. It is quite clear that these problems were not solved by the Convention procedure, nor were they first identified there. The involvement of applications to Strasbourg may nevertheless have contributed to bringing these issues higher up the agenda of domestic policy-making.

Second, certain of the cases have contributed to a direct solution of the particular complaint of the applicant. It is perhaps surprising that it should be necessary for complaint to be made to an international tribunal in order to resolve the circumstances involved in a case such as *Reed*, especially where the factual basis for the applicant's allegations were not disputed by the United Kingdom Government and where the applicant had in fact given evidence for the prosecution of the prison officers accused of ill-treating him. The *ad hoc* solution achieved for Mr Reed in the friendly settlement has *not* contributed to an amendment of the law relating to the position of victims of criminal assaults.

The law has, however, been amended in relation to corporal punishment of children, and it is hard to avoid the conclusion that this is significantly due to the applications brought under the Convention in relation to this issue. In this area as in all others,

---

[61] It is notable also that the Court found the assurances offered by the Indian Government, that the applicant would not face ill-treatment if returned, to be insufficient guarantee of his safety.

however, it is essential to recall that the initiative for bringing applications before the Commission lies with the persons concerned. The Commission has no power of initiative of its own and it is therefore the responsibility of individuals or voluntary organisations and others to seek to achieve the change of domestic law at least in those areas where it is out of step with the basic European common standards. In relation to a value as fundamental as that protected by Article 3 of the Convention, the number of such cases is unlikely to be large.

Interpretation of Article 7 in Cases Concerning England and Wales

In its implementation of the prohibition on retrospective criminal offences and punishments contained in Article 7,[62] the Court has similarly shown a willingness to apply substantive protection of rights. In the case of *Welch v. United Kingdom*,[63] the Court, unlike the Commission, was not persuaded that confiscation orders made against the proceeds of drug trafficking, under the Drug Trafficking Offences Act 1986, did not amount to a punishment on the basis that they were confiscatory or preventive measures. It found that "to render the protection offered by Article 7 effective, the Court must remain free to go behind appearances and assess for itself whether a particular measure amounts in substance to a 'penalty' within the meaning of this provision."[64] The fact that in reality the applicant faced more far-reaching detriments as a result of the order than that to which he was exposed at the time of the commission of the offences for which he was convicted, led to the finding of a violation of Article 7.

The Court showed a similarly robust approach in the cases of *SW v. United Kingdom*[65] and *CR v. United Kingdom*,[66] where it rejected a claim of violations of Article 7 by men who had been convicted of rape of their wives as result of the House of Lords, final dismantling of the marital immunity for the crime of rape.[67] The Court found that the House of Lords' decision was the final stage of the gradual judicial recognition of an absence of marital immunity and that it was reasonably foreseeable. It then went on to make the following comments:

"The essentially debasing character of rape is so manifest that the result of the decisions of the Court of Appeal and House of Lords—that the applicant could be convicted of attempted rape, irrespective of his relationship with the victim—cannot be said to be at variance with the object and purpose of Article 7 of

---

[62] Article 7 states:
  "1. No one shall be held guilty of any criminal offence on account of any act or omission which did not constitute a criminal offence under national or international law at the time when it was committed. Nor shall a heavier penalty be imposed than the one that was applicable at the time the criminal offence was committed.
  2. This article shall not prejudice the trial and punishment of any person for any act or omission which, at the time when it was committed, was criminal according to the general principles of law recognized by civilized nations."
[63] Series A, No. 307-A; (1995) 20 EHRR 247.
[64] *ibid.*, para. 27.
[65] Series A, No. 335-B; (1996) 21 EHRR 363.
[66] Series A, No. 335-C; (1996) 21 EHRR 363.
[67] *R. v. R.* [1992] 1 A.C. 599.

the Convention, namely to ensure that no one should be subjected to arbitrary prosecution, conviction or punishment. What is more, the abandonment of the unacceptable idea of a husband being immune against prosecution for rape of his wife was in conformity not only with a civilised concept of marriage but also, and above all, with the fundamental objectives of the Convention, the very essence of which is respect for human dignity and human freedom."[68]

Derogable Rights

Interpretation of Article 5 in Cases Concerning England and Wales

Article 5 protects two closely related and central rights: the right to liberty and the right to security of person.[69] These rights may be subject to interference only for one of the specified exceptions listed at Article 5(1)(a) to (f) and only then when the requirements of lawfulness imposed both by domestic law and by the Convention itself have been respected.

The cases concerning England and Wales in which Article 5 has been at issue may be divided into three separate categories: first, cases in which detention has been judged to be unlawful and contrary to Article 5(1) because it has not fallen within one of the exceptions specified in sub-paragraphs (a) to (f); second, cases of excessive length of detention prior to trial contrary to Article 5(3) of the Convention; and, third, cases concerning inadequate review of the lawfulness of detention, mainly by reference to Article 5(4).[70]

Unlawful Detention

Clearly the review of the lawfulness of detention, and hence of allegations that detention does not comply with Article 5(1) of the Convention, involves the Commission and the Court in a close examination of the operation of domestic law. The question arises to what extent and on what basis could the Court find detention unlawful which a domestic court had found lawful. By contrast, if the domestic court had found detention unlawful as a matter of domestic law, how would the applicant have had a basis to claim to be a victim under the terms of Article 25(1) of the Convention of a violation of Article 5(1)? As a result of this dilemma, the Court has developed an interpretation of the requirement of lawfulness which goes beyond mere compliance with domestic law. Compliance with domestic law is a necessary prerequisite but it is

---

[68] Series A, No. 335-C, s.43.
[69] See Appendix A for the text of Article 5.
[70] It is a matter of some irony that Article 5(4) appears to have been drafted primarily to reflect the operation of habeas corpus in common law jurisdictions and to extend its guarantees to the whole sphere of operation of the Convention. This has not prevented the Commission and the Court from considering various cases attacking the narrowness and alleged ineffectiveness of habeas corpus as a remedy to comply with Article 5(4) (*e.g. Zamir v. United Kingdom*, 40 DR 42).

not sufficient. That law and its operation in practice must also comply with the requirements of the Convention.[71]

One example of this dilemma arose in the case of *Monell and Morris v. United Kingdom*.[72] The applicants were both convicted in criminal proceedings and each sought leave to appeal against sentence and conviction. Each application was considered by a single judge and rejected under a written procedure. Both applicants sought to renew their applications for leave to appeal against sentence and conviction to the full Court of Appeal. In so doing they completed forms which warned them that the Court had power under section 29(1) of the Criminal Appeal Act 1968 to discount from service of their sentence some of the period spent subsequent to their conviction at trial and up to the date of the determination of their application for leave to appeal, if the Court judged their applications to be without merit. Such orders were made, with the result that 28 days spent by Mr Monell in custody pending the hearing of his application was not counted towards his sentence and an equivalent order amounting to 56 days was made in the case of Mr Morris.

The applicants complained both that there was no authority under the Convention for these periods of deprivation of liberty and that the fact that they had not been present in the Court of Appeal when these determinations were made was unfair, contrary to Article 6 of the Convention. This involved first an interpretation of Article 5(1)(a), which permits the "lawful detention of a person *after* conviction by a competent court", and second a determination whether the requirements of Article 6(1), protecting fair trial, and Article 6(3)(c), which guarantees the right "to defend oneself in person", had been respected.

The Court concluded, in a judgment which reflects a balance of policy considerations in an area of obvious difficulty, that the applicants' complaints did not amount to a violation of the Convention. It held, first, that there was a requirement in Article 5(1)(a) of a close connection between the order of the Court imposing detention and the detention itself. Thus the word "after" in this provision did not merely mean after in time (which would have deprived the provision of any significant benefit for the individual). The Court was clearly mindful of the policy behind loss of time orders in cases of unmeritorious applications for leave to appeal. That was to expedite the examination of cases that might have genuine merit on appeal and to avoid overburdening the courts. The Court also declined to consider whether the applicants' requests to reopen their applications for leave to appeal were really hopeless or frivolous, as this was a matter for the English courts applying English law. Nevertheless, the Court carefully confirmed that it was "not disputed that the relevant rules and procedures under English law were properly observed by the English courts."[73] The Court concluded that the actual sentence to be served by an individual convicted by the English courts was subject to an adjustment which could be imposed by the Court of Appeal,

---

[71] *Winterwerp* case, Series A, No. 33, para. 45 at p. 19; (1979–80) 2 EHRR 387. The Court has not explained how the courts of a legal system which incorporates the Convention into domestic law can carry out a review which goes beyond the test of conformity of detention with the requirements of domestic law.

[72] Series A, No. 115; (1988) 10 EHRR 205.

[73] *ibid.*, p. 20, para. 50.

including the possibility of a loss of time order under section 29(1) of the Criminal Appeal Act 1968.

The complaint under Articles 6(1) and 6(3)(c) of the Convention may seem somewhat farfetched to those familiar with the procedure of applications for leave to appeal, but it reflects a principle developed in the case law of the Court that as a general rule "paragraph 1 of Article 6 requires that a person charged with a criminal offence be entitled to take part in the trial hearing."[74] The Court had also held[75] that the applicant's involvement was necessary as well in appeal proceedings where the potential consequences for him were adverse, at least to the extent that personal evaluation might be of relevance to the Court's decision. The Court concluded, after a careful review of the procedures available to the applicants, that it was not necessary for the fairness of the proceedings to be maintained for the applicants to have done more than be able to make submissions as fully as they wished in writing.

The celebrated case of *Benham v. United Kingdom*[76] arose from the imposition of a period of imprisonment for failure to pay the community charge (or poll tax) contributions. The applicant complained that his detention for failure to pay the community charge constituted breach of Article 5(1) of the Convention and that he had been unable to bring an action for damages in respect of that detention contrary to Article 5(5). The Commission adopted its report on November 29, 1994, expressing the opinion (by a majority) that there had been violations of both of these provisions.

The Court[77] however found the applicant's detention fell within Article 5(1)(b). Further, although the order of the magistrates had later been overturned by the Divisional Court, this in itself did not mean that the detention order was unlawful, and so there was no violation of Article 5(1). It then followed that there having been no violation of Article 5(1), the basis of the complaint under Article 5(5) also fell away. The Court did however find that the failure to grant the applicant free legal representation was a breach of Article 6(3)(c). Notwithstanding that these were for the purposes of English "civil" proceedings, the fact that the applicant faced a deprivation of his liberty, coupled with the relatively complicated nature of the law which the magistrates were applying, meant that it was in the interests of justice for the applicant to receive free legal representation. Thus the Court maintained a high threshold for violations of Article 5(1), but placed emphasis on the need for procedural guarantees for the individual faced with a lawful deprivation of liberty.

Length of Detention

Few cases have arisen concerning England and Wales relating to the length of detention pending trial, reflecting to some extent the different legal traditions in the common law and civilian jurisdictions, all of which contribute to establishing the appropriate bases for the interpretation of these guarantees under Article 5(3) of the Convention.[78]

---

[74] *Colozza v. Italy*, Series A, No. 89, at p. 14, para. 27; (1985) 7 EHRR 516.
[75] In the *Pakelli* case, Series A, No. 64; (1984) 6 EHRR 1.
[76] (1996) 22 EHRR 293.
[77] In a judgment of June 10, 1996.
[78] See, *e.g. W. v. Switzerland*, Series A, No. 254; (1994) 17 EHRR 60.

Nevertheless, two cases concerning delay in the removal of a person from the United Kingdom merit mention. The first, *O v. United Kingdom*, resulted in a decision of the Commission.[79] The applicant, whose extradition was requested by Hong Kong, was detained pending extradition for a period in excess of five years while repeated challenges to the propriety of the extradition request against him were considered by the English courts.[80] The Commission took account of the exceptional circumstances of the case and in particular the repeated applications for habeas corpus, four of which had been rejected by the time of the Commission's examination of the admissibility of the application. The last of these applications was rejected as an abuse of the judicial process, and the Commission concluded that on the particular facts of the case the applicant could not complain that proceedings which he himself had initiated on a timetable which he had done little to accelerate had been unduly lengthy, especially where they appeared to have been pursued in part in order to secure the applicant's continued presence in the United Kingdom and maintain his resistance to extradition.

In the case of *Chahal v. United Kingdom*,[81] the applicant was subject to a decision by the Home Secretary in August 1990 to deport him on the grounds of national security and the international fight against terrorism. He was detained on August 16, 1990 and remained in custody until the judgment of the European Court of Human Rights in November 1996. His detention was maintained during a period in which the initial deportation order was quashed, but then replaced with an identical subsequent order which was similarly challenged, though the challenge was ultimately rejected by the House of Lords in March 1994. The Commission adopted its report expressing the opinion, *inter alia*, that Article 5(1) had been violated by reason of the length of the applicant's detention.

The Court, however, took a different view on the basis of a narrower interpretation of Article 5(1)(f), finding that all that is required is that "action is being taken with a view to deportation". As such, detention would be permissible during the currency of deportation proceedings, and provided that the proceedings were prosecuted with "due diligence". The Court considered that during the period from 1990 until the refusal of leave to appeal by the House of Lords in March 1994, the proceedings had been carried out with due diligence, and thus there was no violation of Article 5(1) in that respect.[82] As to whether the detention was "lawful" for the purposes of Article 5(1)(f), regard had to be had not only to compliance with the safeguards of domestic law, but also to compliance with the policy underlying Article 5, *i.e.* to protect the individual from arbitrariness. In this respect, although the English court could not effectively control the detention (the decision having been made on grounds of national security, so that all of the evidence was not before the court), the Advisory Panel procedure

---

[79] Application No. 15399/89, Dec. Comm. January 14, 1991.

[80] See [1990] 1 W.L.R. 277; [1988] 3 All E.R. 173; [1990] 1 W.L.R. 878; [1991] 1 W.L.R. 284; [1992] 1 W.L.R. 36; and [1992] 1 All E.R. 579.

[81] (1997) 23 EHRR 413. In relation to the Court's findings in Article 3, see above, p. 61 and in relation to Article 13 see below, p. 76.

[82] Curiously, the Court did not consider the period of detention from March 1994 onwards when by its own findings the applicant was no longer under threat of deportation, the United Kingdom having agreed to comply with the Commission rule 36 request not to take any action towards the applicant's deportation.

was able to provide an important safeguard against arbitrariness. There was thus no violation of Article 5(1)(f).

The Court did, however, find that there had been a violation of Article 5(4), as the applicant did not have the right to go before a court to determine the lawfulness of his detention. Whilst the Advisory Panel (as the only forum to which all of the evidence for the Home Secretary's decision was available) provided the safeguards against arbitrariness, implicit in the word "lawful" in Article 5(1)(f), it fell short of the Article 5(4) requirement for review by a court.[83] Thus the European Court, whilst expressing concern as to the length of the applicant's detention, found Article 5 had been violated only insofar as the applicant did not enjoy the full procedural guarantees required under Article 5(4).

Review of Detention

A series of cases concerning England and Wales have developed the scope of the protection provided by Article 5(4) of the Convention. This Article protects the right to take proceedings to test the lawfulness of detention and guarantees that that decision will be taken speedily and by accord. The principal issue that the English cases have explored is whether this right applies only at the beginning of detention, or whether it also provides the opportunity where detention continues for a prolonged period for the detained person to challenge the propriety of that continuing detention.

The first context in which this issue arose was in relation to the detention of a person of unsound mind who was committed to a psychiatric hospital for an indefinite period after a conviction. He was released on licence but three years later ordered to return to hospital under sections 60(1) and 65(1) of the Mental Health Act 1959. The issue before the Court was therefore whether Article 5(4) provides a second opportunity of court review of a period of detention in which new issues provide the primary justification for the detention.[84] The Court examined carefully the implications of detention of persons of unsound mind, recognising in particular the way in which mental illness may change and develop and in particular regress over time. Although Article 5(4) guarantees only the right to review the "lawfulness" of the detention, the Court interpreted this provision to mean that a person confined in a psychiatric institution for a lengthy period is entitled to take proceedings at reasonable intervals to check the propriety of his or her detention, even where his or her original detention derived from a court order.[85]

Having established this principle, the Court reviewed whether habeas corpus pro-

---

[83] The Advisory Panel procedure was established under the Immigration Act 1971, as the review mechanism in place of the usual appeals procedure, in cases of deportation of persons who are not British citizens where the Secretary of State deems this to be conducive to the public good in the interests of national security or on political grounds. The person threatened with deportation is entitled to appear before, or make written statements to, the Panel (which includes judicial figures in its composition) but is not entitled to legal representation. It is for the Home Secretary to decide how much information about his decision is given to the person concerned. The decision of the Panel is not binding upon the Home Secretary.

[84] *X. v. United Kingdom*, Series A, No. 46; (1982) 4 EHRR 188. The Court revisited this issue in *Ashingdane v. United Kingdom*, Series A, No. 93; (1985) 7 EHRR 528.

[85] *X. v. United Kingdom*, at para. 52.

vides a sufficient review of the substance of the decision to detain. The limitations on judicial review, testing merely the technical lawfulness in English law, were found wanting for this purpose, on the basis that "once it was established that X was a patient who had been conditionally discharged while subject to a Restriction Order, the statutory requirements for recall by warrant under section 66(3) of the 1959 Mental Health Act were satisfied. This being so, it was then effectively up to X to show, within the limits permitted by English law, some reason why the apparently legal detention was unlawful. The evidence adduced by X did not disclose any such reason and the Divisional Court had no option but to dismiss the Application".[86]

The Court's conclusion was therefore that X had the right to go to a court to test the lawfulness of his detention, but although lawfulness was the test required under the terms of Article 5(4), a more thorough review than mere compliance with the specific letter of the law was required and habeas corpus proceedings failed to provide that review. Once again, the central feature of this decision is the emphasis placed on the requirement of lawfulness and the development of an independent interpretation of what that word means under the Convention rather than under domestic law.[87]

The Court was faced with similar circumstances in the *Weeks*[88] case, which involved the revocation of the licence upon which Mr Weeks had been released from custody after serving ten years of a life imprisonment sentence. The sentence had been imposed in 1966 when the applicant, then aged 17, pleading guilty to armed robbery, assaulting a police officer and being in unlawful possession of a firearm in circumstances where he had entered a pet shop with a starting pistol loaded with blank cartridges, pointed it at the owner and told her to hand over the till. The sum of 35 pence was stolen, an amount later found on the shop floor. In an ensuing struggle after the applicant had telephoned the police, voluntarily surrendering himself, the starting pistol went off. The applicant told the police that he had committed the robbery because he wanted to pay back £3.00 to his mother, who had that morning told him to find lodgings elsewhere. The Secretary of State ordered Weeks' re-detention in revoking the licence upon which he had been released in March 1976, and the United Kingdom Government argued that the lawfulness of the Home Secretary's action in recalling Weeks derived from the fact of his conviction and sentence in 1966. They submitted in short that this was in itself sufficient to justify his re-detention and submitted that no new issue of lawfulness was capable of arising in relation to his recall to prison.

Once again, the European Court of Human Rights held that Article 5(4) required that Weeks should be entitled to a court hearing, which was capable of determining whether his deprivation of liberty had become unlawful in the changed circumstances. The Court held that neither the Parole Board, whose decision was not binding, nor the opportunity for judicial review of the decision of the Secretary of State, which was insufficiently wide in scope, could satisfy the requirements of Article 5(4), which were therefore found to have been violated.

This line of authority developed further in the judgment of the Court in the cases

---

[86] Series A, No. 46, at para. 56.
[87] The Mental Health (Amendment) Act 1982 enabled Mental Health Review Tribunals to discharge persons subject to restriction orders and discharge directions (now contained in Part V of the Mental Health Act 1983, notably s. 73).
[88] Series A, No. 114; (1988) 10 EHRR 293.

of *Thynne, Wilson and Gunnell v. United Kingdom.*[89] These cases related to the operation of discretionary life sentences imposed for more serious offences; the characteristic therefore of these applicants' detention was the imposition of indeterminate life sentences. The practice in respect of life sentences distinguishes between a punitive element, or "tariff", which reflects the need for retribution and deterrence in the sentence, and a subsequent security element. This security element constitutes a discretionary period during which the question of release must be weighed against the necessity of protecting the public from mentally unstable or dangerous offenders.

Although the cases differ from the *Weeks* case referred to above, the Court held that the same principles were applicable in recognising in particular that "life imprisonment was judged to be the most appropriate sentence in the circumstances, since it enabled the Secretary of State to assess their progress and to act accordingly".[90] The Court noted that in each of the three cases the punitive period had clearly expired and the applicant's detention was therefore within the discretionary zone, reflecting the potential risk which they represented to the community if released. As a result it held the applicant's right under Article 5(4) had been violated and seemingly their rights under Article 5(5), which protects everyone who has been the victim of arrest or detention in contravention of the provisions of Article 5, by granting them an enforceable right to compensation.[91]

However, the principle established in *Thynne, Wilson and Gunnell* was affirmed in relation to those convicted of serious offences before reaching the age of majority in the judgment of the Court in *Hussain* and *Singh*.[92]

The final case in this series was the judgment in the *Wynne* case,[93] in which the applicant had been convicted and sentenced to life imprisonment for murder in 1964 and released on licence in 1980. In the following year, the applicant killed again and pleaded guilty to manslaughter on the grounds of diminished responsibility. The English court imposed a discretionary life sentence and at the same time revoked his life licence under section 62(7) of the Criminal Justice Act 1967. Before the European Commission and Court, the applicant contended that he was entitled to a review of the lawfulness of his detention once the punitive period of the original discretionary life sentence had expired. The Court rejected this contention on the basis that the applicant's detention continued to be lawful as a result of his first mandatory life sentence in respect of which no right or review arose under Article 5.

---

[89] Series A, No. 190; (1991) 13 EHRR 666.
[90] *ibid.* at para. 72.
[91] Following the case of *Thynne, Wilson and Gunnell*, a new review procedure was introduced in respect of discretionary life prisoners under the Criminal Justice Act 1991 (in particular s. 34). The new legislation enables a discretionary life prisoner to require the Home Secretary to refer his case to the Parole Board, which may then make a direction to the Home Secretary that continued detention of the prisoner is no longer necessary for the protection of the public. Where such a direction is made the Home Secretary is under a duty to release the prisoner. If a direction is not made the prisoner may make further requirements of the Home Secretary to refer his case at two yearly periods. These provisions appear to satisfy the requirements of the Court's judgment in *Weeks* and *Thynne*, but as to concerns in relation to other aspects of preventative detention under s. 2(2)(b) of the 1991 Act, see E. Fitzgerald, "The Criminal Justice Act 1991: Preventative Detention of the Dangerous Offender" [1995] EHRLR 39.
[92] Series A, No. 294-A; (1995) 19 EHRR 333.
[93] (1996) 22 EHRR 1.

Interpretation of Article 6 in Cases Concerning England and Wales

The guarantees of fair trial contained in Article 6[94] are central to the scheme of the Convention. The Court has repeatedly held that guarantee of fair trial is one of the "fundamental principles of any democratic society within the meaning of the Convention",[95] and it is a commonplace that Article 6 is the most litigated of all of the Convention rights. It is, therefore, all the more interesting that the United Kingdom has been found in violation of Article 6 on comparatively few occasions, and in relation to an even smaller number of issues. The common law traditions and adversarial nature of criminal procedure in the United Kingdom and the unified jurisdiction of the non-criminal courts have ensured that many of the issues which have been most difficult for continental legal systems simply have not arisen in the same way in the United Kingdom.[96] However, it is still remarkable that so few Article 6 findings have been made against the United Kingdom.

Though the right to fair trial might be thought of as a procedural guarantee, the Court has on occasion found that the rights contained in Article 6 may give rise to substantive obligations on the part of the Contracting states. In the landmark decision of *Golder v. United Kingdom*[97] the Court found that the refusal by the Home Secretary to allow a prisoner to consult a solicitor, with a view to bringing a civil action for libel against a prison officer, was a violation to the right of access to a court which was implicit within Article 6(1). This right of access to a court constituted an aspect of the "right to a court", to which the Article also added various further procedural guarantees as regards the organisation and composition of the court and the conduct of the proceedings. The thrust of the Government's submission had been that Article 6(1) contained purely procedural guarantees, to ensure the fairness of the trial of proceedings already pending, and did not create a new right of access to a court. In countering this argument the Court invoked the principle of the rule of law as one of the founding principles of the Convention, finding that "in civil matters one can scarcely conceive of the rule of law without there being a possibility of having access to the Courts ... [and that] the principle whereby a civil claim must be capable of being submitted to a judge ranks as one of the universally 'recognised' fundamental principles of law".[98]

Following the decision in *Golder*, in a number of other cases concerning prisoners'

---

[94] Article 6(1): In the determination of his civil rights and obligations or of any criminal charge against him, everyone is entitled to a fair and public hearing within a reasonable time by an independent and impartial tribunal established by law. Judgment shall be pronounced publicly but the press and public may be excluded from all or part of the trial in the interest of morals, public order or national security in a democratic society, where the interests of juveniles or the protection of the private life of the parties so require, or to the extent strictly necessary in the opinion of the court in special circumstances where publicity would prejudice the interests of justice.

[95] See, for example, *Sutter v. Switzerland*, Series A, No. 74, at para. 26; (1984) 6 EHRR 272.

[96] In relation to the latter of these points the controversies within the Court in determining what constitutes a "civil right" for these purposes have not been an issue in most of the Article 6 cases concerning the United Kingdom. However, as will be shown below, given that this is a primary issue which determines how deeply Art. 6 bites, English lawyers ignore it at their peril.

[97] Series A, No. 18; (1979–80) 1 EHRR 524. This was the first ever Court decision involving an individual's application against the United Kingdom.

[98] *ibid.* para. 34–35.

71

access to legal advice violations of Article 6(1) were found.[99] The independent nature of the rights protected by Article 6(1) was established again in *Campbell and Fell*,[1] where prison disciplinary procedures before the Board of Visitors were held to involve the determination of what were considered criminal charges to which the full guarantees of Article 6 should attach. It is clear that *Golder* and the subsequent judgments on prisoners contributed to a change in attitudes towards prisoners' rights observable in the United Kingdom since approximately 1980.[2]

The nature of the court, which must be and must be seen to be independent and impartial, was raised in relation to the system of courts-martial operating prior to the coming into force of the Armed Forces Act 1996, in the case of *Findlay v. United Kingdom*.[3] The issue in this case was the impartiality of a court-martial, in which the Convening Officer was both central to the prosecution, convened the tribunal, which was made up of officers of subordinate rank to himself, had power to appoint prosecuting and defending advocates, and also acted as confirming officer (with certain powers of review of the sentence of the court). In these circumstances a clear violation of Article 6 was found, though the Court did not seek to comment upon the amendments to the courts-martial procedure under the 1996 Act.

Once *Golder* had established the "right to a court", the next issue for the Court was what questions such a court should be able to decide. How far should a court to which Article 6 applied be able to decide both fact and law? In a series of disparate cases,[4] the European Court held that such a court must be of "full jurisdiction"[5] to make a "determination of the individual's rights in issue".[6] In relation to the "full jurisdiction" requirement, the adequacy of judicial review to provide this review has been raised before the Commission and the Court in Strasbourg on several occasions, notwithstanding that it is not a review of the merits, but rather a narrower review based on the administrative law notions of legality, procedural propriety and reasonableness.

In the notable group of cases concerning parental access to children in local authority care[7] where judicial review was found to be insufficient, much depended upon the Court's appreciation of what was the precise nature of the "civil rights" of the applicants in issue. The Court found that parental rights of access were civil rights; they

---

[99] See *Silver v. United Kingdom*, Series A, No. 61; (1983) 5 EHRR 347; also the cases of *Kiss, Hilton, Brady, Marritt, Jenkinson, Farrant* and *Byrne* which went before the Committee of Ministers.

[1] Series A, No. 80; (1985) 7 EHRR 165.

[2] For examples of the change in the approach of the English courts, see *Raymond v. Honey* [1982] 1 All E.R. 756, H.L. and *R. v. Secretary of State for the Home Department, ex parte Anderson* [1984] 1 All E.R. 920, D.C., both of which drew inspiration directly from the requirements of the Convention.

[3] Judgment of February 25, 1997.

[4] *Le Compte, Van Leuven and de Meyer*, Series A, No. 54; (1983) 5 EHRR 183; *Albert and Le Compte*, Series A, No. 58; (1983) 5 EHRR 533; *Benthem*, Series A, No. 97; (1986) 8 EHRR 1; *Deumeland*, Series A, No. 100; (1986) 8 EHRR 448.

[5] *Van der Mussele*, Series A, No. 70; (1984) 6 EHRR 163. The French (original) text may imply a distinction between such a jurisdiction and the more limited scope of administrative court proceedings in certain European countries. The scope of such proceedings varies widely, however, and is a poor guide to the "true" scope of Art. 8(1).

[6] This combined test is usually interpreted as requiring that the court is "empowered to make a review of matters of both fact and law".

[7] The cases of *O. v. United Kingdom, H. v. United Kingdom* (Series A, No. 120; (1988) 10 EHRR 95), *W. v. United Kingdom, B. v. United Kingdom*, and *R. v. United Kingdom* (Series A, No. 121; (1988) 10 EHRR 74); for discussion of the Court's findings in these cases in relation to Art. 8 see text below.

constituted part of the bundle of parental rights which remained with the parents after a "parental rights resolution"[8] had been made by a local authority vesting in itself most of the other rights and duties which by law the mother and father have in relation to a legitimate child and his or her property. The Court's decision was that, in view of their nature, a proper "determination" of these civil rights, for the purposes of Article 6(1), required that the parent should be able to apply to a tribunal with power to review the local authority decision on the merits.[9] Unfortunately, the Court does not identify the criteria upon which this finding was made.

It is worth noting briefly some of the cases in which violations of Article 6 have been alleged but not upheld by the Court,[10] for whilst the importance of *Golder* is indisputable, there are also numerous cases establishing limitations to the substantive rights found there. In *Powell and Rayner v. United Kingdom*[11] the applicants, who lived close to Heathrow Airport, claimed that a statutory provision limiting their rights to bring actions in trespass or nuisance against aircraft operators had the effect *inter alia* of removing their right of access to a court for the purposes of Article 6(1). The Court rejected the complaint on the basis that as the limitation of liability was statutory and therefore part of English law, the applicants could not be said to have any "civil right" in English law to which Article 6(1) could apply.

The case of *Fayed v. United Kingdom*[12] is also relevant in this respect. The case arose out of the report into certain business dealings of the applicants in the course of a hotly contested takeover, prepared by independent inspectors appointed by the Secretary of State for Trade and Industry, the findings of which were published by the Secretary of State. The Court held that the inspectors' investigations role was investigative rather than adjudicative, and so they made no determinations of a civil right.[13] However, the applicants' second complaint was that they were denied access to a court to challenge the findings of the report, which had been published to the world at large and contained statements damaging to their reputations. Had they sued in defamation, the inspectors would have had the defence of privilege, and judicial review, not being an investigation of the merits of the impugned decisions, would have been inadequate. The Court found that the right of access to a court was subject to some regulation by the state and that in so regulating this right the state enjoyed a certain margin of appreciation. On the other hand, it found that the right should not

---

[8] See s. 2(1) Children Act 1948, and now s. 3(1) Children Act 1989.

[9] See, for example, the cae of *O. v. United Kingdom*, Series A, No. 120, at para. 63; (1988) 10 EHRR 82. By way of contrast see the Commission's findings in the case of *Kaplan v. United Kingdom*, 21 DR 5.

[10] A further case where a violation of Art. 6(1) was the main finding against the United Kingdom in relation to England and Wales was *Darnell v. United Kingdom*, Series A, No. 272; (1994) 18 EHRR 205. The issue here concerned the reasonableness of the length of time taken in reaching determination of the applicant's complaints regarding the termination of his employment as a consultant microbiologist and director of a public health laboratory. The length of time involved from initial complaint to the industrial tribunal to final judgment by the Employment Appeal Tribunal was nine years, and the Government did not contest the complaint before the Court in Strasbourg.

[11] Series A, No. 172; (1990) 12 EHRR 355; for comment and criticism see F. Hampson, "Restrictions on Rights of Action and the European Convention on Human Rights: the case of *Powell and Rayner*" (1990) 61 BYBIL 279.

[12] Series A, No. 294-B; (1994) 18 EHRR 393.

[13] This conclusion depended upon the precise terms of the inspectors' remit on the facts of this case and may not represent a general rule.

be so limited that its very essence is impaired, that any restrictions must pursue a legitimate aim and that there should be a reasonable relationship of proportionality between the means employed and the aim pursued. In relation to the requirements of proportionality, the Court was favourably impressed by the safeguards in favour of the applicants contained in the inspectors' procedures, and the long-stop of judicial review to ensure procedural fairness.[14]

However, it has been established subsequently that whilst DTI inspectors in performance of their investigative function may not be subject to the procedural requirements of Article 6, the evidence they obtain may not necessarily be used in subsequent criminal proceedings. Among the guarantees contained in Article 6 are the right against self-incrimination and, closely related to it, the right to silence. Though neither is expressly recognised in Article 6, the Court has found them to be generally recognised international standards, lying at the heart of a fair procedure as guaranteed by Article 6, and related to the presumption of innocence contained in Article 6(2).[15] In the case of *Saunders v. United Kingdom*[16] the DTI investigators exercised their compulsory powers of investigation, questioning the applicant about alleged wrongdoing in the battle between Guinness PLC and the Argyll Group for the takeover of the Distillers' Company. If the applicant failed to cooperate with the inspectors' investigation, he risked imprisonment or a fine. The transcripts of his interviews with the inspectors were passed to the prosecuting authorities, and used in evidence against him in subsequent criminal proceedings, in which he was convicted and received a custodial sentence. The European Court of Human Rights found that whilst the compulsory powers of investigation exercised by the inspectors did not in themselves offend the right against self-incrimination, the subsequent use of material so obtained in criminal proceedings against the person who had been forced to provide that evidence was a violation of Article 6. However, the Court's judgment leaves open the question as to how evidence existing independently of that given by the interviewee, but discovered as a result of his cooperation with the inspectors, should be considered.

Interpretation of Article 13 in Cases Concerning England and Wales[17]

The Commission and the Court have wrestled[18] to establish a satisfactory interpretation of the difficult text of this Article, which deals too briefly with the interrelationship between the Convention and domestic law. This has been an issue of special relevance in cases concerning England and Wales because of the particular place of the Conven-

---

[14] See also the case of *Bryan v. United Kingdom*, Series A, No. 335-A; (1996) 21 EHRR 342, for similar reasoning.
[15] See *Funke v. France*, Series A, No. 256-A; (1993) 16 EHRR 297.
[16] (1997) 23 EHRR 313.
[17] Article 13 provides: "Everyone whose rights and freedoms are set forth in this Convention are violated shall have an effective remedy before a national authority notwithstanding that the violation has been committed by persons acting in an official capacity."
[18] Some authors would suggest they have done so in vain.

tion in English Law[19] and the importance traditionally attached to the protection of the rights of individuals in the history of the common law.

The Court held at an early stage in its work that Article 13 does not impose a requirement of incorporation of the Convention into domestic law.[20] As a result it has been left with the difficulty of determining how this provision should apply to create a remedy in cases in which "rights and freedoms as set forth in this Convention are violated",[21] where the finding of such a violation can only be made by the Court. When this provision is considered with the basis of the Commission's jurisdiction to receive applications from "any person . . . claiming to be the victim of a violation",[22] there is a practical question as to whether there are any circumstances in which a person who claims to be such a victim would not inevitably seek to allege that they had not enjoyed a remedy in respect of the violation in question.[23]

In *Silver*[24] the Court had to consider this problem in respect of complaints of unjustified interference with prisoners' correspondence. The main complaint was under Article 8[25] but the Court also found that the absence of a remedy breached Article 13.[26] However, in order to limit the scope of Article 13 the Court has developed the doctrine of arguability—*i.e.* a complaint under Article 13 need be considered only where the complaint based upon the substantive Article is "arguable".

This approach is illustrated in the Court's approach to remedies in the *Soering* case.[27] The applicant complained that his extradition would expose him to the "death row phenomenon", contrary to Article 3. He also complained that he had no remedy in England whereby the risk to which he was exposed if extradited could be considered by reference to the Convention or an equivalent standard. The Court found that extradition would violate Article 3; the applicant's complaint therefore satisfied the arguability threshold. On examination, however, the Court found that the scope of judicial review of the decision of the Secretary of State to extradite the applicant was sufficient to provide the necessary remedy.[28] On the facts, this conclusion could not be tested because the applicant had not sought judicial review of the Secretary of State's decision. The respondent Government relied on the "anxious scrutiny" which the House of Lords had established as the appropriate review in cases of life and limb. It may be doubted whether judicial review would in fact have resulted in the questioning of the Secretary of State's decision had the remedy been tried. This must have been the appropriate consequence under Article 13 in a case in which that decision did

---

[19] See the section headed The Convention in English Law below.

[20] See the *Swedish Engine Drivers' Union* case, Series A, No. 20; (1979–80) 1 EHRR 617.

[21] See the text of Art. 13; this text is to be interpreted together with the (equally authentic) French text: ". . . *dont les droits et libertés reconnus dans la présente Convention ont été violés* . . ."

[22] Art. 25(1); see genrally the introductory section to this chapter.

[23] If they had had a remedy in their domestic legal system, they would not have been able to claim to be a "victim" any longer.

[24] Series A, No. 61; (1983) 5 EHRR 347.

[25] As to which see the section on Qualified Rights below.

[26] See Series A, No. 61, at p. 44, para. 119. Contrast *Boyle and Rice*, Series A, No. 131; (1988) 10 EHRR 425, covering Scotland.

[27] Series A, No. 161; (1989) 11 EHRR 439; see the section on Non-derogable Rights above.

[28] The case raised difficulties as to the true extent of judicial review which are considered briefly in the section The Convention in English Law below.

violate Article 3. However, the question also arises why this remedy, if sufficient for Article 3, was not a necessary prerequisite for the application to be lodged by virtue of Article 26.[29]

By way of contrast to the Court's findings in both *Soering* and *Vilvarajah*,[30] where judicial review proceedings were found to be an effective remedy in cases of threatened or actual removal where the applicant maintained that such removal put him at risk of ill-treatment contrary to Article 3, in the case of *Chahal*[31] the Court found that it was an insufficient remedy. The Court was able to distinguish those earlier cases on the basis that Chahal was threatened with deportation on grounds of national security, and in those circumstances judicial review before the English court was of much more limited scope. As the complaint was made under Article 3, limitations on the effectiveness of remedies necessitated by national security, which might have been acceptable in relation to complaints under Articles 8 or 10, were not appropriate because of the importance which the Court attaches to Article 3. Whilst the Court accepted that scrutiny of the deportee's claim that there was a real risk of ill-treatment contrary to Article 3 did not have to be performed by a judicial authority, the procedural shortcomings of the Advisory Panel procedure[32] were such that it could not have provided the applicant with sufficient procedural safeguards for the purposes of Article 13.

Interpretation of Article 14 in Cases Concerning England and Wales[33]

The prohibition on discrimination contained in Article 14 is an ancillary protection to those provided by each of the other individual Articles in Section 1 of the Convention. Hence the Article protects against discrimination in the enjoyment of those rights and not against discrimination *per se*. As a result, discrimination may be an aggravating feature of an allegation of a violation of the Convention but it cannot normally be the whole basis for a complaint.

Two cases referred to elsewhere in this Chapter will illustrate the limits of this general rule. First, in the *East African Asians* case[34] the allegation of discrimination based on race was considered under Article 3 as degrading treatment. In fact, it is difficult to see how an arguable allegation of a violation of Article 3 is enhanced by adding the terms of Article 14, at least where the basis of the main complaint is an allegation of an implicit racial motivation for the matters complained about.

The extent to which Article 14 may extend the basis of a complaint is nevertheless illustrated in the case of *Abdulaziz and Others*.[35] The applicants' complaints concerned

---

[29] The Commission may only deal with a matter after all domestic remedies have been exhausted, according to the generally recognised rules of international law, and within a period of six months from the date on which the final decision was taken.

[30] Series A, No. 215; (1992) 14 EHRR 248.

[31] (1997) 23 EHRR 413.

[32] See note 83 above.

[33] Art. 14 provides: "The enjoyment of the rights and freedoms set forth in this Convention shall be secured without discrimination on any ground such as sex, race, colour, language, religion, political or other opinion, national or social origin, association with a national minority, property, birth or other status."

[34] See above, p. 58.

[35] Series A, No. 94; (1985) 7 EHRR 471.

denial of rights of entry into the United Kingdom to their husbands, where it was not contested that the applicants could lawfully and safely join their husbands in a third country. According to the established case law, Article 8 does not guarantee the right to enter a country and the husbands' exclusion was therefore a justifiable interference with the right to respect for family life. The force of the complaint derived from the difference in treatment between husbands of those lawfully settled and the wives of lawfully settled men; the former were excluded, the latter permitted to enter. In these circumstances, the fact that the applicants could allege a difference in treatment without a legitimate justification allowed them to succeed under the Convention.

This last mentioned case also illustrates the limitations of ancillary protection against discrimination. The United Kingdom Government was able to comply for the future with the requirements of the Convention by refusing wives entry to the United Kingdom in the same way that the applicants' husbands had been refused.[36] It follows that the weakness of the discrimination protection under the Convention compares unfavourably with the more general protection of this principle in the economic sphere under European Community law.[37]

Qualified Rights: Articles 8 to 11

The characteristic of this group of rights is that they are not merely derogable in times of emergency, they are also not expressed in absolute terms. Their interpretation raises special problems, both in the provision of justice in individual cases and in the provision of readily appreciable standards prospectively.

The structure of each Article is broadly similar. The right protected is set out in the first paragraph. The second paragraph identifies the criteria upon which an interference with that right may be justified. To be justified the interference must be lawful, pursue a legitimate aim, and be necessary in a democratic society, which entails the requirement that it be proportionate to the aim sought to be achieved. The Court considers first whether there is an infringement of the right described in the first paragraph of these Articles. If so, it will consider whether the infringement was "prescribed by law", pursued a "legitimate aim" and was "necessary in a democratic society". These requirements are cumulative. The first two are largely formal, although compliance with domestic law will not necessarily suffice for the lawfulness standard.

The requirement that the infringement be "necessary in a democratic society" suggests that a judgment as to the substance of the infringement must be made; essentially, was the decision right? The Court has developed a number of principles to delimit its review of an infringement of one of these qualified rights: (i) the infringement must answer to a pressing social need; (ii) the respondent state has some margin of appreciation (of a varying width depending upon the right and infringement in

---

[36] Though this is not always the outcome of discrimination complaints. Compare the *Belgian Linguistics* case, Series A, No. 6; (1979–80) 1 EHRR 252.

[37] The basis of protection against discrimination is more specifically linked to the "four freedoms" and to the general terms of Art. 7 EEC and, in relation to sex discrimination, Art. 119 EEC.

question) in its perception of the social need and the measures taken to meet it; and (iii) the infringement must be proportionate to the legitimate aim pursued.

However, at times, in reaching its conclusions the Court has considered its task as a balancing exercise, in which the individual right is simply an *interest*, to be weighed against the competing public justification offered by the respondent state. The Court has stressed the supervisory nature of its jurisdiction, emphasising that it is not in a position to take the place of the national authorities. Therefore, on occasion, the Court has found procedural protections and guarantees of these rights to be sufficient; *i.e.* provided that there is some domestic procedure by which a similar balancing exercise may be undertaken in the domestic legal system and in which the applicant has had the chance properly to participate, compliance may be found to be sufficient. The fact that the United Kingdom has not incorporated the Convention, nor has any equivalent domestic Bill of Rights, puts it in a particularly interesting position. The lack of a legal remedy, or the limited scope or availability of such a remedy, has been at the heart of several of the major cases before the Court covering England and Wales.

Interpretation of Article 8 in Cases Concerning England and Wales[38]

Article 8 is a complex right made up of a number of different elements. It requires respect for private life, family life, the home and correspondence. Its application by the Court has been wide, covering matters as diverse as telephone-tapping and trans-sexuality. The "right to respect requires not only protection by the State in respect of infringements by its own agents, but also the prevention of infringements by third Parties."[39] Given the breadth of the right(s) in question, and also the fact that the law of England and Wales recognises no equivalent right(s) in express terms, a degree of pessimism would not appear to be necessary in approaching the United Kingdom's ability to comply with these obligations. Indeed there are a relatively large number of cases on Article 8, but what is perhaps more interesting is that they raise a comparatively small range of issues on which the United Kingdom has been found to be in violation.

Prisoner Correspondence

The case of *Golder*,[40] in which a prisoner was prevented from seeking legal advice with a view to pursuing an action in defamation against a prison officer, was found to violate both Articles 6(1) and 8. The landmark finding on Article 6(1) has been

---

[38] Article 8:

"1. Everyone has the right to respect for his private and family life, his home and his correspondence.
2. There shall be no interference by a public authority with the exercise of this right except such as is in accordance with the law and is necessary in a democratic society in the interests of national security, public safety or the economic well-being of the country for the prevention of disorder or crime, for the protection of health or morals, or for the protection of the rights and freedoms of others."

[39] See, *e.g. Marckx v. Belgium*, Series A, No. 31; (1979–80) 2 EHRR 330; for another aspect of the positive duty it places upon the contracting States see *Airey v. Ireland*, Series A, No. 32; (1979–80) 2 EHRR 305.

[40] Series A, No. 18; (1979–80) 1 EHRR 524.

considered above, and it is noticeable how closely the finding on Article 8 is linked to the finding on Article 6(1). The Government argued that the right to correspond was implicitly qualified *ab initio* for prisoners because they were deprived of their liberty. This approach is difficult to reconcile with the very general words of Article 1 of the Convention[41] and it was rejected.

The Court found that there were no implied limitations on the rights contained in Article 8 simply because the applicant was a prisoner, but then went on to consider whether the limitations on the applicant's right to respect for correspondence fell within the relevant categories under Article 8(2). The Court unanimously found that the limitation could not be said to be "necessary" for the purpose of the prevention of disorder or crime, the protection of health or morals, or the protection of the rights and freedoms of others. It reached this conclusion on the basis that none of these reasons could justify the restriction on the applicant's ability to obtain legal advice. Effectively the Court was concerned that this restriction on correspondence by the Home Secretary essentially prejudged the prospects of the action which the applicant was considering; the applicant should have been allowed to obtain legal advice and a ruling by a court as to merits of any action he brought as a result.[42] In *Silver*[43] the issue of prisoners seeking legal advice also arose, with the same result as *Golder*. However, a number of the claimants also sought to challenge broader restrictions on correspondence. In English law such restrictions could be imposed by virtue of the Prison Act 1952, which gave the Home Secretary the power to make Rules (these cases related to the Prison Rules 1964). The Rules were supplemented by the Home Secretary through more detailed Standing Orders and Circular Instructions, whose aim was to ensure uniformity of practice (they did not purport to have the force of law but were rather statements of policy); however, prison governors were required to comply with them, unless authorised to do otherwise. These Orders and Instructions were unpublished.

The Court in *Silver* reviewed the restrictions on correspondence, first by considering whether they were "in accordance with law". The Court recalled the procedural safe-guards that it had laid down in the *Sunday Times* case[44] in this respect, *i.e.* that the law must be (i) accessible and (ii) formulated with sufficient precision to enable the citizen to adjust his or her behaviour accordingly. The Court considered that notwith-standing that the Orders and Instructions were not accessible, some of the restrictions they contained were foreseeable from the wording of the Rules or in some cases from an explanatory memorandum which was issued to prisoners concerning the "prior ventilation rule".[45] Certain other restrictions did not meet this requirement, thus resulting in an automatic violation of Article 8.[46]

---

[41] "The High Contracting Parties shall secure to everyone within their jurisdiction the rights and freedoms defined in Section 1 of the Convention."

[42] The narrowness of the Court's view is clear: the interference was not justifiable because it affected the exercise of another Convention right, access to court. The actual need for a restriction of this kind—*i.e.* the policy—was scarcely considered.

[43] Series A, No. 61; (1983) 5 EHRR 347.

[44] See the subsection on Art. 10 below.

[45] *i.e.* the rule that a prisoner not be allowed access to legal advice concerning complaints relating to treatment/conditions in prison until he or she had first raised these complaints through the internal prison procedures.

[46] The requirement of lawfulness is axiomatic. No interference with the rights protected by Arts. 8, 9, 10 or 11 can be justified unless it is lawful.

In those cases where it had found that the restrictions were "in accordance with law" the Court went on to consider whether the interferences were necessary in a democratic society. The Government did not contest that a large number of the restrictions were not necessary in a democratic society (such as the prohibition on the inclusion in letters to legal advisers and MPs of unventilated complaints about prison treatment); however, in relation to the items it did contest, the Court found that a degree of censorship of prisoner correspondence was not inconsistent with the Convention and the Government succeeded on all of the items it contested at this stage.

In *Campbell and Fell*[47] the Strasbourg proceedings were again largely concerned with procedural matters in relation to disciplinary proceedings before the Board of Prison Visitors (as regards Article 6, see above). The Government did not seek to contest the Commission's findings of violations of Article 8 in respect of the prior ventilation rule, and also the prohibition of the personal correspondence of one of the applicants with persons other than relatives or pre-existing friends.

The United Kingdom Government's response to these cases has been criticised as "piecemeal, often half-hearted and inadequate".[48] First, in response to *Golder* the Prison Rules were amended to enable prisoners to correspond with a solicitor for the purpose of obtaining legal advice in relation to "any action to which the prisoner may become a party in civil proceedings or for the purpose of instructing the solicitor to issue such proceedings". However, first in a Circular Instruction and then in a Standing Order, proceedings arising out of the imprisonment were subject to the prior ventilation rule.[49] This rule essentially provided that a prisoner could not have access to legal advice unless he had first exhausted the internal prison complaints procedures. In *Reed v. United Kingdom*[50] the prior ventilation rule was challenged, and the United Kingdom as part of a friendly settlement undertook its abolition. The Court's findings in both *Silver* and *Campbell and Fell* concerned events prior to the abolition, but were reached after the rule had been abolished. This explains the Government's failure to contest these claims.

The prior ventilation rule was replaced by the "simultaneous ventilation rule",[51] allowing access to legal advice in respect of matters arising from imprisonment provided that a complaint had first been lodged with the Secretary of State. This again was found to be a violation of Article 6 by the Committee of Ministers.[52] However the rule had already been found to be *ultra vires* by the Divisional Court insofar as it applied to correspondence with legal advisers.[53] The rule was finally abolished in its entirety in England and Wales by a revised Standing Order 5.

The Government had also sought to amend some of the other restrictions on correspondence criticised in *Silver* in advance of the hearing, both in respect of the identity of the correspondents and its subject matter. Churchill and Young express some con-

---

[47] Series A, No. 80; (1985) 7 EHRR 165.
[48] See R. R. Churchill and J. R. Young, "Compliance with Judgments of the European Court of Human Rights and Decisions of the Committee of Ministers: The Experience of the United Kingdom, 1975–87" (1991) 62 BYBIL 283 at 331.
[49] See note 45 above.
[50] 25 DR 5.
[51] See Order 5B34j, discussed in *Silver*, Series A, No. 61 at p. 21 para. 49; (1983) 5 EHRR 347.
[52] See *Byrne v. United Kingdom*, Res DH (87)7 of March 20, 1987.
[53] See *R. v. Secretary of State for Home Department, ex p. Anderson* [1984] 1 All E.R. 920.

cern at some of the current restrictions on the subject matter of correspondence,[54] and also the complexity of Order 5. Even so, greater openness in respect of the prison regime in England and Wales means that many of the Standing Orders including Order 5 are at least now published.

Clearly the Government response has been piecemeal and at times insufficient. The cases also show that the Court has sometimes confined its findings so narrowly that they take on more of a procedural than a substantive character. The United Kingdom Government could thus claim to have complied with what was required of it by the Court and Committee of Ministers, if not with the spirit of the Convention itself. It is submitted that the procedural preoccupation of the Court's approach, particularly in its case law concerning prisoners, is not an inevitable consequence of the distillation and clarification of the rights contained in the Convention. The Court in these cases was considering a very specific context of persons in the direct care of the State for most aspects of their lives. The prisoners could have expected the Court to require a more substantive answer to be given to their complaints.[55]

Local Authority Care of Children

Procedural rather than substantive aspects of Article 8 are also strongly in evidence in a series of cases brought against the United Kingdom by parents whose children had been taken into local authority care. In the cases of *W, B* and *R*[56] the claims arose out of the decision-making process of local authorities in reaching decisions terminating parental access to children taken into care. In all of these cases the Court found violations of Article 6(1)[57] but also found Article 8 applicable, making the following statement:

"It is true that Article 8 contains no explicit procedural requirements, but this is not conclusive of the matter. The local authority's decision-making process clearly cannot be devoid of influence on the substance of the decision, notably by ensuring that it is based on the relevant considerations and is not one-sided and, hence, neither is nor appears to be arbitrary. Accordingly the Court is entitled to have regard to that process to determine whether it has been conducted in a manner that, in all the circumstances, is fair and affords due respect to the interests protected by Article 8. Moreover the Court observes that the English courts can examine, on an application for judicial review of a decision of a local authority, the question whether it has acted fairly in the exercise of a legal power.

The relevant considerations to be weighed by a local authority in reaching decisions on children in its care must perforce include the views and interests of the natural parents. The decision-making process must therefore in the Court's view be such as to secure that their views and interests are made known to and

---

[54] Churchill and Young, *op. cit.* p. 307.
[55] But see the Court's change of heart, at least in respect of ill-treatment of persons in detention in *Tomasi*, Series A, No. 241-A; (1993) 15 EHRR 1.
[56] Series A, No. 121; (1988) 10 EHRR 29.
[57] See above. p. 73.

duly taken into account by the local authority and that they are able to exercise in due time any remedies available to them."[58]

In each of these cases the decision-making procedures of the local authority on access were found to be in violation of Article 8. In contrast, in the case of O,[59] despite making a similar finding under Article 6(1) in relation to the possibilities of challenging parental access restrictions imposed by the local authority, the Court held that, as there was some uncertainty as to the extent to which the applicant was informed of the measures taken, the material before it was insufficient to make a finding in respect of Article 8.

A further violation of Article 8 was found in H,[60] where it was held that the delays in proceedings challenging restrictions on access might have the effect of a *de facto* determination of the matter at issue, since delays in the proceedings would lengthen the period in which a young child had no contact with the parent, and thus prejudice the question of the parent's future relations with the child.

Given the procedural nature of the findings, compliance with the judgment was comparatively straightforward, and was included within the much wider reform of the law relating to children in the Children Act 1989. Section 34 provides for parental contact with children in care, and section 22 includes a duty upon the local authority so far as is reasonably practicable to ascertain the wishes and feelings of *inter alia* parents in making decisions with respect to children whom they are looking after. Neither provision appears to have been controversial in the passage of the Act through Parliament, and no cases challenging the adequacy of these measures has been brought before the Court or the Committee of Ministers in Strasbourg.

The minor's rights, rather than those of the parents, were at issue in *Gaskin*,[61] where the applicant sought access to the records held by the local authority in whose care he was as a child. The right he sought was procedural in nature: the Court emphasised that the applicant neither challenged the fact that information was stored about him nor alleged that any use was made of it to his detriment. Thus the Court's finding was again confined to a procedural criticism:

"... a system like the British one, which makes access to records dependent on the consent of the contributor, can in principle be considered to be compatible with the obligations under Article 8, taking into account the margin of appreciation. The Court considers however that under such a system the interests of the individual seeking access to records relating to his private or family life must be secured when a contributor to the records either is not available or improperly refuses consent. Such a system is only in conformity with the principle of proportionality if it provides that an independent authority finally decides whether access has to be granted in cases where a contributor fails to answer or withholds consent."[62]

[58] Series A, No. 121 at p. 28, para. 62–63.
[59] Series A, No. 120; (1988) 10 EHRR 82.
[60] Series A, No. 120, at p. 63, para. 89–90.
[61] Series A, No. 160; (1990) 12 EHRR 36.
[62] *ibid.* at p. 20 para. 49.

The Government has stated that it intends to bring forward legislation in order to comply with this need for scrutiny, but has not yet done so.[63]

Immigration

In *Abdulaziz, Cabales and Balkandali*,[64] the Court was faced with a challenge to immigration legislation which allowed entry to, and leave to remain in, the United Kingdom for the wives and fiancées of United Kingdom-settled men, but did not allow entry/leave to remain for the husbands and fiancés of United Kingdom-settled women. Women in this position complained that disallowing entry/leave to remain to their husbands was a breach of their right to respect for family life under Article 8, and was a discriminatory interference with this right under Article 14 taken together with Article 8. The Court held that Article 8 was applicable. The Court found that ''although the essential object of Article 8 is to protect the individual against arbitrary interference by the public authorities, there may in addition be positive obligations inherent in an effective 'respect' for family life.''[65] However, as the notion of respect was not clear cut, States should be given ''a wide margin of appreciation in determining the steps to be taken to ensure compliance with the Convention with due regard to the needs and resources of the community and of individuals''. Given that the case concerned immigration, the Court held as a matter of well-established international law, and subject to supervening treaty obligations, that a state has the right to control the entry of non-nationals into its territory. Thus it found that the duty imposed by Article 8 cannot be considered as extending to respect the choice by married couples of the country of their matrimonial residence and to the acceptance of non-national spouses for settlement in that country.

However, the Court noted two additional facts: (i) that the applicants had not shown that there would be any difficulties for them to stay in their husbands' home countries, and (ii) that the women, in advance of their marriages, knew or could or should have known that their husbands-to-be would require entry clearance/leave to remain and that it was likely to be refused. These seem to be factors which weighed with the Court notwithstanding that they are of a formal character rather than relating to the substance of the right to respect for family life.

The applicants were, however, successful in their claim that the refusal of entry/ leave to remain to their husbands or fiancés was discriminatory on the grounds of sex, since, had they been settled men, entry clearance/leave to remain would have been granted to their wives or fiancées. As noted above, the Government response was to remove the discrimination by removing the right of the wives and fiancées of settled men to enter or remain.[66] Gearty suggests that the United Kingdom was able to do this because equality, as protected by Article 14, is a procedural rather than a substantive goal.[67] Had the Court found that the treatment was a violation of Article 8 or of

---

[63] See *Hansard*, H.C. December 17, 1993, col. 960w.
[64] Series A, No. 94; (1985) 7 EHRR 471.
[65] *ibid*. at para. 67.
[66] See Immigration Act 1988, s. 1.
[67] C. A. Gearty, ''The European Convention on Human Rights and the Protection of Civil Liberties: an overview'' [1993] CLJ 89, at 114–115.

Article 3 (on the basis that the applicants' treatment was also degrading) the Government would have had to take measures to allow in the spouses and fiancés of both settled men and women.[68]

Interference with Communications

One of the most important civil liberties cases to be brought against the United Kingdom in Strasbourg was the *Malone* case.[69] Malone had discovered during criminal proceedings against him for handling stolen goods (in which he was eventually acquitted) that the police had tapped his telephone. He also suspected that his mail had been intercepted by the police and that his telephone had been "metered".[70] In civil proceedings Megarry V.-C. had concluded that the tapping of his telephone had been legal; Parliament had recognised the Home Secretary's prerogative power to authorise tapping and there was no general right to privacy.[71] Malone complained under the Convention. The Court started its judgment by saying it was solely concerned with interceptions by the police in the context of a criminal investigation, together with the legal and administrative framework relevant to such interceptions.

The Court, after finding that these interceptions were an infringement of the right in Article 8(1), considered the justification offered by the Government under Article 8(2). Its judgment centres on the lawfulness requirement. The Court held that these words required the existence of domestic law governing the situation, and that the law in question should reflect the rule of law:

> "... the phrase thus implies—and this follows from the object and purpose of Article 8—that there must be a measure of legal protection in domestic law against arbitrary interferences by public authorities with the rights safeguarded by paragraph 1. Especially where a power of the executive is exercised in secret, the risks of the arbitrariness are evident ... the law must be sufficiently clear in its terms to give citizens an adequate indication as to the circumstances in which and the conditions on which public authorities are empowered to resort to this secret and potentially dangerous interference with the right to respect for private life and correspondence ..."[72]

It followed that, as the implementation in practice of measures of secret surveillance of communication is not open to scrutiny by the individuals concerned or the public at large, the law which confers a discretion to undertake these activities must indicate the scope of that discretion and manner of its exercise, with sufficient clarity to give the individual adequate protection against arbitrary interference. The Court found the law of England and Wales was lacking in this respect, and so did not need to go

[68] See the discussion of the *East African Asians* case above.
[69] Series A, No. 82; (1985) 7 EHRR 14.
[70] *i.e.* all numbers dialled from his telephone had been recorded.
[71] *Malone v. Commissioner of Police of the Metropolis (No. 2)* [1979] 2 All E.R. 620, Ch. D.
[72] Series A, No. 82 at p. 32, para. 67.

further to consider the more substantive question of whether the tapping of Mr. Malone's telephone was "necessary in a democratic society".

The Government response was to introduce the Interception of Communications Act 1985, which makes clear that the interception of communications without a warrant is illegal. Warrants may be issued (i) in the interests of national security; (ii) for the purposes of preventing or detecting serious crime; and (iii) to safeguard the economic well-being of the United Kingdom (but only to obtain information in relation to acts or persons outside the United Kingdom).[73] A number of safeguards on the issue of warrants, aimed at limiting the possibility of abuse by the Secretary of State, are provided. A tribunal is established to investigate complaints, as well as a Commissioner to keep the system under review and to assist the tribunal in its functions. It should be noted here that Churchill and Young[74] have serious reservations as to whether the system provided in the Act meets the requirements of the Convention as interpreted in the *Malone* and *Klass*[75] judgments. However criticism might also be levelled at the Court for its failure to provide guidance on the substantive right that Article 8 protects in this respect.

Interpretation of Article 10 in Cases Concerning England and Wales

Cases concerning England and Wales based on Article 10 show significant examples of the Court deciding whether "the right decision was made". In the *Sunday Times (No. 1)* case,[76] the newspaper challenged an injunction which prevented the publication of an article concerning the cases of children born disabled as a result of their mothers having taken the drug Thalidomide during pregnancy. The proposed article was part of a campaign to pressurise the manufacturer of the drug to come to a more generous settlement. The injunction had been imposed on the grounds that publication would be a contempt of court. The injunction was upheld by the House of Lords, but there were five separate speeches, which revealed a split in the basic approach to the common law of contempt of court between the "prejudgment principle" and the "pressure principle".

The Court in Strasbourg, finding that there was an interference with the right in Article 10(1), considered whether it could be justified under Article 10(2). The first question the majority considered was whether the rules were "prescribed by law". The Court concentrated upon English domestic law, finding that it had to be accessible to the citizen and formulated with sufficient precision to enable the citizen to regulate his or her conduct: "he must be able, if need be on legal advice, to foresee, to a degree that is reasonable in the circumstances, the consequences which a given course of action may entail."[77] Despite the differences between the speeches of the House of Lords, the Court found that these criteria were met.

---

[73] *cf.* the restrictions allowable under Art. 8(2).
[74] Churchill and Young, "Compliance with Judgments of the European Court of Human Rights and Decisions of the Committee of Ministers: The Experience of the United Kingdom, 1975–87" (1991) BYBIL 283 at 323–326.
[75] Series A, No. 28; (1979–80) 2 EHRR 214.
[76] Series A, No. 30; (1979–80) 2 EHRR 245.
[77] *ibid.* p. 31, para. 49.

The Court then turned to the question of whether the restriction was "necessary in a democratic society" for maintaining the authority of the judiciary. The Court found that the margin of appreciation of the state in this case was more limited than it had been in the earlier case of *Handyside*,[78] where the restrictions had been imposed for the protection of morals, a less objective concept than the maintenance of the authority of the judiciary. To be justifiable, the interference complained of had to correspond to a "pressing social need" and to be proportionate to the legitimate aim pursued. The Court held that on the facts here it was not. The Court reviewed the need for an injunction, as the domestic courts had, and found it unjustified. This is therefore one of the rare cases where the Court and the English courts were faced with the same issue and disagreed.

The response of the Government to the *Sunday Times (No. 1)* case was the introduction of the Contempt of Court Act 1981, which deals with wider aspects of the law on contempt than those raised in the Strasbourg proceedings.[79] Under section 10 of the 1981 Act, the court may exceptionally require a journalist to disclose the source of his information where "that disclosure is necessary in the interests of justice or national security or for the prevention of disorder or crime". In the case of *Goodwin v. United Kingdom*[80] the applicant, was a journalist who had obtained highly sensitive and confidential information about the finances of a company, from a source on an unattributable basis. The applicant, intending to write an article based on this information, telephoned the company to check the facts and elicit its comments. The company immediately sought and was granted an injunction restraining publication. The company also sought and was granted an order under section 10 that the applicant disclose his source, on the basis that disclosure was in the interests of justice as the company wished to recover its document and damages for the expense to which it had been put, but could not do so until it knew the identity of the source. The applicant refused to comply with the disclosure order, and was fined £5,000 for contempt of court.

The European Court of Human Rights, there being no dispute that there had been an interference with the applicant's freedom of expression under Article 10(1), turned to Article 10(2). Having found the interference to be "prescribed by law" and in pursuit of a "legitimate aim", decided that it could not be said to be "necessary in a democratic society". Stressing the vital role of freedom of the press in a democratic society, and noting the potentially chilling effect of a disclosure order on that freedom, the Court considered that the granting of the injunction against publication of the information had largely neutralised the threat of damage to the company. Thus the disclosure order merely served to reinforce the injunction and was found to be disproportionate to the legitimate aim pursued. Thus, rather in the same way as in the *Sunday Times (No. 1)* case, the European Court had been faced by the same issue as the English court,[81] but had reached an opposite conclusion.

The *Spycatcher* cases[82] concerned the imposition of interlocutory injunctions against the newspapers preventing disclosure of the contents of *Spycatcher* (the memoirs of a

---

[78] Series A, No. 24; (1979–80) 1 EHRR 737.
[79] For doubts as to adequacy see Churchill and Young, *op. cit.*
[80] (1996) 22 EHRR 123.
[81] See *X Ltd v. Morgan Grampian (Publishers) Ltd* [1990] 2 All E.R. 1, H.L.
[82] Series A, Nos. 216 and 217; (1992) 14 EHRR 153 and 229.

former MI5 officer), pending the determination of the application for permanent injunctions based on breach of confidence. These interlocutory injunctions had been upheld by a majority in the House of Lords. One of the criticisms of that decision was that the memoirs were circulating without restriction in published form in several other countries where individuals in England and Wales could place orders without restriction. The Court in Strasbourg found that the principles on which interlocutory injunctions were made[83] were sufficiently accessible and foreseeable to be "prescribed by law". The Court also found that the joint aims of the maintenance of the authority of the judiciary and the requirement of national security were legitimately in issue and recognised by Article 10(2). However, when it came to the question whether the interferences with freedom of expression were "necessary in a democratic society", the Court divided the period of the duration of the injunctions between the period until the book's publication in the USA and the subsequent period until their discharge on the final determination of the substantive English proceedings.

As regards the first period the Court found that the injunctions were necessary in a democratic society, finding that at this stage the reasons for their imposition were "relevant", "sufficient" and "proportionate to the aim pursued". The Court was impressed favourably by the fact that the English courts "had recognised that the present case had involved a conflict between the public interest in preventing and the public interest in allowing disclosure of the material in question, which conflict they resolved by a careful weighing of the relevant considerations on either side.[84] The Court was strengthened in this view by the potential prejudice which publication would bring to the breach of confidence actions against the author, and in this respect underlined the central position of Article 6 of the Convention. The Court's main reasons for finding the injunctions to be proportionate were that they were limited in scope and duration. Thus the Court found that the national authorities were entitled to consider the injunctions necessary in a democratic society.

The second period was that following publication in the USA. The Court found that the reason for continuing injunctions at that stage was asserted by the Government to be the maintenance of the authority of the judiciary. The Court held that reason to be insufficient. The interest in maintaining the confidentiality of the material for the judicial proceedings had ceased to exist with publication. Further, in respect of national security, any damage the publication might cause would by then have been caused. The only grounds for continuing the injunctions by that time were the promotion of the efficiency and reputation of the Security Service and this was an insufficient reason for interfering with freedom of expression.[85]

Finally, in the recent case of *Tolstoy v. United Kingdom*[86] the Court considered the compatibility of a £1.5 million libel award with Article 10. The Court ostensibly managed to find that the award could be said to be "prescribed by law". It found

---

[83] As set forth in *American Cyanamid v. Ethicon Ltd* [1975] 1 All E.R. 504.
[84] Series A, No. 216, at p. 32, para. 63.
[85] Gearty finds the importance of the case in the Court's upholding of the injunctions in the first period, noting that "without the United States Constitution's first amendment, which protected the book from injunction in the American courts, the Convention would have been of little assistance to the press", *op. cit.*
[86] Series A, No. 323; (1995) 20 EHRR 442.

flexibility was required to enable juries to assess damages appropriately, and it could not be a requirement of the "prescribed by law" notion that a person, even with legal advice, could anticipate with any degree of certainty the quantum of damages that would be awarded in a particular case. The Court also noted that there were a number of limitations and safeguards limiting the discretion enjoyed by juries, including the power of the Court of Appeal to set aside awards on grounds of irrationality.[87] However, when considering whether or not the award could be said to be "necessary in a democratic society" the Court found that the magnitude of the award violated the Convention. The question remains whether this violation is due to the size of the award, or the absence of review. If the latter, it seems that if the Court of Appeal decided not to exercise its new powers under the Courts and Legal Services Act to interfere with a jury award of £1.5 million,[88] there would be no violation of the Convention.

Interpretation of Article 11 in Cases Concerning England and Wales

A contrasting approach has been taken by the Court in relation to Article 11, in particular in the case of *Young, James and Webster v. United Kingdom*.[89] Here the Court was concerned with the position of employees who were dismissed for refusing to join a union following the introduction of a post-entry closed shop. The Court found that the negative aspect of freedom of association, *i.e.* the right not to be forced to join an association, did not fall completely outside Article 11. However the Court explicitly refrained from seeking "to review the closed shop system as such in relation to the Convention or to express an opinion on every consequence or form of compulsion which it may engender". It limited itself to examining the effect of this system on the applicants.

The Court assumed that the negative aspect of freedom of association was not guaranteed by Article 11 on the same footing as the positive aspect: compulsion to join a particular trade union may not always be contrary to the Convention. The factors which the Court found to be crucial were (i) that the compulsion was serious because the applicants were threatened with the loss of their livelihoods, (ii) that the applicants had little or no choice as to which union they had to join, and (iii) that the applicants had deeply held objections to union membership, so that there was an interference with aspects of Article 11, which were also protected by Articles 9 and 10, relating to freedom of thought, conscience and religion and freedom of expression.

Having confined itself to facts rather than principle, the Court took a rather broader approach in deciding whether the interference was justifiable under Article 11(2). The Court assumed that the interferences were "prescribed by law" and "pursued a legitimate aim", and considered only whether the interferences were "necessary in a

---

[87] The libel action against Tolstoy took place before the entry into force of s. 8(2) of the Courts and Legal Services Act 1990, which gives the Court of Appeal the power to set aside jury awards on the grounds that they are excessive or inadequate (see *Rantzen v. Mirror Group Newspapers* cited below).

[88] Though at present it would appear unlikely, given the judgment of the Court of Appeal in *John v. MGN Ltd* [1996] 2 All E.R. 35, where the Convention was cited in support of the court's conclusions on excessive libel damages (though these had been reached independently of the Convention).

[89] Series A, No. 44; (1982) 4 EHRR 38.

democratic society". In deciding this question in the negative the Court noted that the need for safeguards for existing non-union employees on the introduction of a closed shop had been recognised elsewhere, and that there was no reason justifying the failure to make such safeguards for the applicants in this case. The Court found that the union would in no way have been prevented from striving to protect its members' interests through the operation of the closed shop agreement even if it had not been lawful to compel non-union employees with objections to join a specified union. As a result, the Court did protect the applicants' substantive right to be free from compulsion to join a union, in this case (though in places the language is suggestive of a procedural right—*e.g.* a right to safeguards from dismissal).[90]

Restrictions on the closed shop in the Employment Acts of 1980 and 1982 go much further than is strictly required by the judgment in *Young James and Webster*. However, this must be seen in the political context of the early 1980s, when the relatively new Conservative government aimed to reduce the power of trade unions as a major plank of economic and social policy; this considerably narrowed the areas of dispute before the Court in Strasbourg.

Interpretation of Article 1 of Protocol No. 1 in Cases Concerning England and Wales[91]

Of all the rights protected under the Convention and its Protocols, the right to the peaceful enjoyment of possessions has proved to be one of the most difficult both to draft and agree in the first instance, and to interpret and apply in the particular circumstances of any given case.

At the time when the Convention was drafted, it was disputed whether the right to property was a fundamental right and whether it should be protected at all. It was originally omitted from the Convention as a result of the difficulties which had arisen in achieving an agreed text but was finally incorporated as one of the principal rights added to the Convention in the First Protocol in 1952.

This background provides one explanation for the unusual drafting of this provision. The Convention itself is not exemplary for the consistency of its drafting.[92] Thus the Article first refers to both natural and legal persons as being entitled to the protection of the right in question whereas the extent to which the other rights in the Convention might or might not be enjoyed by legal as opposed to natural persons is unspecified

---

[90] The narrowness of the factual base in which the right would be protected is underlined also in the *Sibson* case, Series A, No. 258-A; (1994) 17 EHRR 193.

[91] Article 1 of Protocol No. 1 provides:

"Every natural or legal person is entitled to the peaceful enjoyment of his possessions. No one shall be deprived of his possessions except in the public interest and subject to the conditions provided for by law and by the general principles of international law.

The preceding provisions shall not, however, in any way impair the right of a State to enforce such laws as it deems necessary to control the use of property in accordance with the general interest or to secure the payment of taxes or other contributions or penalties."

[92] *e.g.* the various references to conformity with law in Arts. 8(2), 9(2), 10(2) and 11(2) and generally the different ways in which the exceptions to those rights are drafted.

except by implication in Article 12.[93] The content therefore of the right which is protected and the circumstances in which there may be an interference with it are not easy to glean from the choice of words adopted for the text which bears little relationship to the second paragraphs of Articles 8, 9, 10 and 11 with which Article 1 of Protocol No. 1 might otherwise be compared.[94] Nevertheless, the important interests at stake in the protection of property have given rise to very substantial cases concerning interferences with property rights in England and Wales.

As with other provisions of the Convention, the Commission has established the most extensive repertoire of case law in determining the boundaries of whether a claim is arguable by reference to this provision or manifestly ill-founded under the terms of Article 27(2) of the Convention. For many years the Commission's case law was effectively blighted by the rather superficial decision of the Court in the *Handyside* case.[95] That case concerned criminal prosecutions against the proprietor of a publishing firm for offences of obscenity in publishing and distributing *The Little Red School Book*. As a result of the prosecution, the applicant's stock of books was ordered to be destroyed and he complained to the Commission and then the Court first in respect of the interference with his right to freedom of expression and secondly in relation to the seizure and destruction of the book stock.

Curiously, the Court regarded the seizure and subsequent destruction of the books as a control over their use rather than a deprivation of the applicant's possessions and accordingly held that the wide permissive exceptions in the final sentence of the Article precluded closer examination of the property issues. The separate opinion of Judge Zeeker is persuasive that a fuller examination was merited which the Court would itself adopt in later cases. In the light of this decision, for some years the Commission was able to find that a large variety of complaints fell within the scope of protection of Article 1 of Protocol No. 1 but that the measures taken were nevertheless justified under the derogations implicit in the second sentence of the second paragraph of that provision.

Three major cases from England and Wales contributed to the review of this analysis and greatly improved the clarity of the interpretation of the protection afforded by Article 1 of Protocol No. 1, with regard to both the control of use and also the deprivation of possessions.[96] The first of these cases concerned nationalisation and the vexed question of whether compensation was available where the assets of nationals are taken by the state. As the *travaux préparatoires* of Article 1 of the First Protocol

---

[93] Art. 12 grants men and women of marriageable age the right to marry and found a family. The right is obviously not exercisable by legal persons but the general terms of the other provisions of the Convention referring to everyone or no-one (and more specifically in the French text to *nul* or *toute personne*) are thereby implicitly of application to all persons whether natural or legal.

[94] But see in particular the Commission's interpretation of the provisions of the second paragraph of Art. 1 of Protocol No. 1 in Application No. 9261/78, 28 DR 177, where the Commission concluded that the interpretation of this provision should reflect the equivalent terms of Art. 8(2) at least where the complaint concerned interferences with the right to respect for property which was the applicant's home.

[95] See judgment of December 7, 1976, Series A, No. 24; (1979–80) 1 EHRR 737, especially paras 60–63.

[96] *Lithgow and Others*, Series A, No. 102; (1986) 8 EHRR 329; *James and Others*, Series A, No. 98; (1991) 13 EHRR 431; and *AGOSI*, Series A, No. 108; (1987) 9 EHRR 1.

show,[97] the difficulties of agreeing a text for the Article included the question whether nationalisation should be regulated under the terms of the Convention and any protection by way of compensation afforded to those whose assets were taken by the state in such circumstances.

This was the issue which arose by virtue of the provisions of the Aircraft and Shipbuilding Industries Act 1977, which nationalised certain parts of the aircraft and shipbuilding industries, notably those providing materials and ships for naval purposes. These proposals were extremely controversial on a domestic political level and the companies whose assets were threatened with nationalisation mounted a major lobbying exercise to restrict or avoid the scope of nationalisation. Partly as a result and partly because of the political uncertainties of the relevant period, the legislative process was very protracted. It began on July 31, 1974, when the Secretary of State for Industry announced that the shipbuilding and ship-repair industries would be taken into public ownership and that legislative provisions for safeguarding their assets would take effect from the date of his announcement. A further statement was made to the House of Commons on November 4, 1974 after the intervening general election which had given the new Government a working majority in the House of Commons. Thereafter, in March 1975, the Secretary of State for Industry announced the introduction of the Aircraft and Shipbuilding Industries Bill to give effect to the nationalisation proposals. At this stage the basis for compensation by reference to the value of the shares of the companies to be acquired, during a reference period which preceded the election of the then Government, was disclosed.

The first Bill lapsed as a result of lack of Parliamentary time at the close of the Parliamentary session and a second Bill, essentially similar, was introduced in November 1975. There were protracted procedural discussions and disputes within the House of Commons as to the appropriate approach to this legislation and to the provisions for compensation. The discussion and debate in the House of Commons was concluded on July 29, 1976 when the Bill was transferred to the House of Lords, but major amendments were made there which were unacceptable to the Government. The issues in dispute could not be resolved before the close of the Parliamentary session and the second Bill also lapsed. A third Bill was introduced to the House of Commons on November 26, 1976 and completed its procedural stages there by December 7. It was introduced to the House of Lords under the Parliament Acts and received the Royal Assent on March 17, 1977.

This extended legislative history, together with the very rapid rate of inflation in the period between the reference period for valuation (in 1974) and the date of actual payment of compensation (available from the date of operation of the Bill) gave rise to some largely unforeseeable but very large variations in the asset values of the companies which were taken into public ownership. This provided the basis for the complaints to the Commission and to the Court in what has been the largest single group of cases with which the institutions have had to deal.

In an exhaustive examination of the scope and interpretation of Article 1 of Protocol No. 1, the Court implied into it a right to compensation for an individual deprived of

---

[97] To which the Court has had frequent recourse in interpreting the text.

91

his or her possessions in the particular circumstances of the cases, but limited its review of the compensation terms essentially to the reasonableness of the system adopted rather than its operation in practice.[98]

The case is overwhelmingly important as an illustration of the way in which legislation may be challenged for non-conformity with the Convention. Whether this eventuality was envisaged by the drafters of the Convention may well be doubted, as it is a type of review provided by only some of the constitutional systems in Western Europe and frequently subject to elaborate safeguards in relation to standing as well as the consequences of a judgment.

A similar challenge to the operation of legislation *per se* was mounted in the *James and Others*[99] case, relating to the operation of the leasehold reform provisions whereby tenants of properties let on long leases could compel the freeholder to convey the freehold on advantageous terms. The applicants were the trustees of the Duke of Westminster's Estate and thereby the owners of large parts of Central London where leasehold provisions had retained the value and consistency of the relevant areas in a form of early private planning control.

The legislation in question had been introduced initially in order to enfranchise tenants whose long leases of modest properties, especially in South Wales, were shortly to expire and who would then be left without any security of tenure. The application of the provisions to Central London properties operated in a completely different and perhaps unexpected way. By virtue of the operation of the Act, it was possible for the holders of the remnant of a long lease to enfranchise the property on terms which resulted in an enormous gain in value to themselves for no very clear social purpose.

The trustees of the Duke of Westminster's Estate complained both about the legislation as such and about individual transactions which illustrated its operation in practice. For reasons which can only be ascribed to procedural economy, it appears that the latter complaints were effectively subsumed into the general challenge to the legislation and were treated as merely illustrative of the applicants' legitimate status as purported victims for the purposes of Article 25 of the Convention (for the decision on admissibility).

The Court considered that the operation of the leasehold reform provisions resulted in the applicants being deprived of their possessions within the meaning of the second sentence of Article 1 of Protocol No. 1. While this approach appears to be correct, it is difficult to reconcile with the analysis adopted by the Court in the earlier *Handyside* decision.[1] In assessing whether the deprivation was justified under the terms of that

---

[98] *Lithgow and Others*, Series A, No. 102; (1986) 8 EHRR 329. And even here the review is a narrow one in a nationalisation case: "Accordingly the Court's power of review in the present case is limited to ascertaining whether the decisions regarding compensation fell outside the United Kingdom's wide margin of appreciation; it will respect the legislature's judgment in this connection unless that judgment was manifestly without reasonable justification", *ibid.* para. 122, p. 51. This may be contrasted with the Commission's less narrow approach, *ibid.* Rep. Comm. para. 374, p. 95.

[99] Series A, No. 98; (1986) 8 EHRR 123.

[1] Series A, No. 24; (1979–80) 1 EHRR 737. The case concerned *inter alia* the destruction by the authorities of publications which were seized. The Court, mainly concerned with questions of freedom of expression, held the seizure and destruction were a "control of the use of property" rather than a deprivation of property, with the result that scrutiny under the Convention was attenuated.

n the Convention are violated shall have an effective remedy before a
thority''. Despite this, the European Court of Human Rights has consist-
d that the non-incorporation of the Convention into domestic law does not
a violation of either of these obligations.[7] However, the non-incorporation
vention, together with the lack of a Bill of Rights equivalent to the constitu-
uments of many other European countries, might suggest that the position
ted Kingdom is likely to be particularly vulnerable in proceedings in Stras-

er, the fact that the Convention does not have a clear place in English
ld not lead to the conclusion that Convention can safely be ignored in
sh courts. Internationally, as the United Kingdom as a state is bound by
other human rights conventions, its international responsibility is engaged
s of all and any of its organs, including the acts and decisions of its
[8] Thus, so far as possible within the constitutional framework and limita-
its powers, the judiciary should seek not to act in such a way as to
nternational obligations which the state has undertaken. This appears to be
n what Bennion describes as "a principle of legal policy that the municipal
ld conform to public international law".[9]

wing awareness of the Convention in recent years has prompted the courts
greater account of arguments based on the Convention than the narrow
ld justify, and the result is that the Convention has had some influence
me important developments in the law. At times the courts have taken into
the jurisprudence of both the European Court of Human Rights and, less
tly, the European Commission of Human Rights. On occasion the English
have shown themselves willing to take on some of the important concepts
jurisprudence, including the balancing of other public interests with an
ual right,[10] as required in respect of many of the Convention rights, and
move towards the adoption of the concept of proportionality.[11] The case law

gards Art. 1, see *Ireland v. United Kingdom*, "the absence of a law expressly prohibiting this or
iolation does not suffice to establish a breach since such a prohibition does not represent the sole
od of securing the enjoyment of the rights and freedoms guaranteed''; as regards Art. 13 see *inter*
Swedish Engine Drivers' Union case, Series A, No. 20 at p. 18; (1979–80) 1 EHRR 617, and *Silver*
ited Kingdom, Series A, No. 61 at p. 42; (1983) 5 EHRR 347. See also J. A. Frowein, "Incorpora-
of the Convention into Domestic Law'' in J. P. Gardner (ed.), *Aspects of Incorporation of the*
pean Convention on Human Rights into Domestic Law (1993), pp. 3–11.
R. Higgins, "The Relationship between International and Regional Human Rights Norms and
estic Law'' (1992) 18 *Commonwealth Law Bulletin* 1268.
Bennion, *Statutory Interpretation*, section 270, and see section on statutory interpretation below.
ever, the case law suggests that the principle is wider than simply one of statutory interpretation but
ld inform other areas of judicial functioning as well: see sections below on development of the
mon law and exercise of judicial discretion. This may suggest that the Convention is an exception
e strict application of the narrow rule.
, for example, the *Spycatcher* litigation above.
Jowell and Lester, "Proportionality: Neither Novel Nor Dangerous,'' in Jowell and Oliver (eds.)
Directions in Judicial Review, pp. 51–72; see also Lord Diplock in *Council for the Civil Service*
ons v. Minister of the Civil Service [1984] 3 All E.R. 935 at 950; Lord Templeman in *R. v. Independ-*
Television Commission, ex parte TSW Broadcasting Ltd, The Times, March 30, 1992; and also Neill
in *R. v. Secretary of State for the Environment, ex p. NALGO, The Times*, December 2, 1992.

provision, the Court recalled that it had jurisdiction to enquire into the factual basis for the justification pleaded by the respondent Government.[2] It held, however, that that review was limited to examining whether the legislature's assessment of the relevant social and economic conditions came within the state's margin of appreciation. The Court therefore agreed with the Commission's original conclusion that the belief of the United Kingdom Parliament in the existence of a social injustice in the operation of an unreformed leasehold system "was not such as could be characterised as manifestly unreasonable".

The Court held that the deprivation rule in Article 1 of Protocol No. 1 included one further protection for the applicant, namely that there should be a reasonable relationship of proportionality between the means employed and the aims sought to be realised or, in other words, that there should be a fair balance struck between the demands of the general interests of the community and the requirements of the protection of the individual's fundamental rights. The principal basis of the applicants' complaints in this respect was that the compulsory sale of the freehold interest to the leasehold tenant of a house in Belgravia resulted in what was referred to as "the merger value", *i.e.* a windfall profit to the purchaser in the event of a subsequent resale of the freehold with vacant possession. However, as the Court pointed out, this windfall benefit was under the structure of the legislation not so much a deprivation of the rights of the freeholder as a disproportionate advantage to the leaseholder who exercised the right of enfranchisement when compared with previous leaseholders who had either not had the opportunity to do so or not exercised the right which they had been granted under the relevant legislation.

The third, *AGOSI* case,[3] arose from even more bizarre facts than those at issue in the first two applications. The applicant company, registered in the Federal Republic of Germany, sought to recover gold coins which had been purchased from it by two fraudsters who had been apprehended by customs officers on attempting to smuggle the coins into England at Dover. The customs authorities took proceedings to order the coins forfeit and the applicant company sought to recover them on the basis that they had not been party to the illegal attempts to import the coins and that their title to the coins was preserved under the terms of their contract with the fraudsters, in view of the latters' failure to pay the contract price.

Although in these circumstances the applicant company had clearly been deprived of its possessions by the seizure of the coins by the customs authorities and the forfeiture proceedings, the Commission and the Court analysed the case by reference to the second paragraph of Article 1 of Protocol No. 1 as being an example of the operation of "such laws as [the respondent government] deems necessary to control the use of property in accordance with the general interest". In its opinion, the Commission recognised that customs law frequently envisages the forfeiture of smuggled goods. However, it considered that the principle of proportionality protected by the Convention and expressed as the principle of balance between the rights of an owner and the general interest in respect of Article 1 of Protocol No. 1 could only be respected where there was a genuine link between the owner and the smuggling of the goods. The

[2] Series A, No. 98, at p. 33, para. 49.
[3] Series A, No. 108; (1987) 9 EHRR 1.

Court rejected this approach, whilst accepting that a balance must nevertheless be struck between the rights of the owner and the general interest. It emphasised that these rights might be secured in a procedural way, *i.e.* by providing a remedy for the owner to claim innocence or to put at issue a refusal by the customs authorities to restore the goods to him or her.

The Court's view was doubtless influenced by the decision[4] of the Divisional Court to allow judicial review of the decision of the Commissioners of Customs and Excise to order forfeit a yacht which had been chartered by its owners to individuals who had subsequently used it in connection with drug smuggling. The owner of the yacht had successfully obtained judicial review to challenge the decision of the authorities in relation to the yacht, claiming he had no connection with the charterers beyond the contract for the use of his yacht which they had entered into. In reliance upon *Hawarth* the Court concluded that a remedy had been available to *AGOSI* whereby it could have sought to challenge the decision of the Commissioners of Customs and Excise and thereby obtain the necessary measure of balance required by Article 1 of the First Protocol.[5]

It is interesting to note what the effect of the incorporation of the rights protected by Article 1 of Protocol No. 1 into the domestic law of England and Wales would have been in this particular case. It appears that had those rights been incorporated, it would have been open to *AGOSI* to argue that the original forfeiture proceedings initiated by the customs authorities were contrary to the Convention. It is hard to imagine that a domestic court would reach the same conclusion as that of the European Court that the availability of yet other proceedings to review the decision of the customs authorities would satisfy the substantive protection of the peaceful enjoyment of possessions contained in Article 1 of Protocol No. 1.[6]

Some concluding remarks in relation to the operation of Article 1 of Protocol No. 1 are appropriate. The cases from England and Wales which have given rise to the analysis of this provision by the Court have been complex and have involved substantial financial interests. The *Handyside* case illustrates the extent to which the Commission and the Court were, at least in the early years, ill-equipped to cope adequately with the interaction of difficult issues of private law and the operation of state powers of forfeiture following the seizure of goods which gave rise to criminal proceedings. The Commission has not yet had to consider, in relation to a case concerning England and Wales, the extent to which an order of forfeiture of an equivalent kind, interfering with the right to the peaceful enjoyment of possessions, could lawfully be made where the entity making that order did not comply with the requirements of Article 6 of the Convention. Such a complaint may easily be anticipated.

---

[4] *R. v. Commissioners of Customs & Excise, ex p. L. Hawarth*, Divisional Court, July 17, 1985. The Commission's Report had been adopted on October 11, 1984 and the case referred to the Court on December 19, 1984; the hearing was held on January 20, 1986 and judgment given on October 26, 1986, more than eleven years after the coins were smuggled into England.

[5] The proceedings in this case had already involved a reference from the criminal proceedings against the two rogues to the European Court of Justice as well as proceedings for forfeiture at first instance and before the Court of Appeal.

[6] Such a possibility is even more difficult to imagine when it is recalled that the order of forfeiture made under the Customs and Excise Act 1952 was made on March 10, 1978, more than seven years before the judgment was given in the *Hawarth* case. To their credit, the applicants' representatives in the domestic proceedings specifically relied in their statement of claim upon Art. 1 of Protocol No. 1.

A second point relates to the special and anomalous Convention in the domestic law of England and Wales. the nationalisation legislation under the Aircraft and Ship is a stark example of the extent to which the Convention not otherwise available in English law. This is not only b part of domestic law, but also because, even if it were, it it would then allow the courts to consider the legitimacy of application of legislation to particular circumstances.

An associated point also follows, both from the interes tions and the involvement of a group of specialist practition had extensive experience of the Convention machinery. Th vention might have relevance to major commercial disput the total number of applications which are ultimately lodg proceedings. This view, if correct, supports the analysis th are "so many" cases brought against the United Kingdom cases taken to Strasbourg concerning England and Wales is tion. More relevant is the question why so few cases are tak cases which could provide applications to Strasbourg with a cess are nevertheless not pursued.

The Convention in English Law

As in many other countries, foreign affairs powers of the U general exercised by the executive rather than the legislature. T provides that foreign affairs powers, including those of negotia treaties or Conventions, are exercisable by the Crown by virtue ive. Of course, these powers are in fact usually exercised by m of a Minister of the Crown. However, in accordance with the doc supremacy, such an executive act cannot alter the substance of E if a treaty is to change English law, or give rise to new rights enforce directly in national courts, it must be incorporated by leg

It is important to note, however, that at the level of internation has been ratified by the United Kingdom the state's internationa be engaged, whether or not it has incorporated the terms of the tre its ratification of the European Convention on Human Rights, the bound by its terms (including the obligation it has undertaken by n under Article 25, allowing individuals to petition Strasbourg) at the However, the non-incorporation of the treaty into national law by le suggests that formally the Convention does not give rise to rights enforceable in the English courts at the instance of individuals. referred to as the narrow rule, and it is not entirely easy to reco recent decisions of the higher courts.

The Convention spells out in Article 1 that the government is u to "secure" the rights and freedoms set out in the Convention to ev jurisdiction, and in Article 13 requires that "Everyone whose rights

suggests that there are four main areas in which the courts have taken account of the Convention,[12] to extend the narrow rule.

Statutory Interpretation

Bennion finds that the principle of conformity of municipal law with international law requires that "[t]he court when considering in relation to the facts of the instant case, which of the opposing constructions of the enactment would give effect to the legislative intention, should presume that the legislator intended to observe this principle". There is authority that, even in the case of a treaty which has not been incorporated by legislation, this presumption will operate in the interpretation of legislation, in favour of the interpretation most consistent with the international obligations of the United Kingdom. In *Garland v. B.R. Engineering Ltd*[13] Lord Diplock found that there was "a principle of construction of United Kingdom statutes, now too well established to call for the citation of authority, that the words of a statute after the treaty has been signed and dealing with the subject matter of the international obligation of the United Kingdom are to be construed, if they are reasonably capable of bearing such a meaning as intended to carry out the obligation and not to be inconsistent with it". It appears Lord Diplock was in fact the first to formulate this as a "prima facie presumption" in the case of ambiguous statutory provisions, some years earlier.[14] The House of Lords affirmed this principle in relation to the Convention in *Brind v. Sec. of State for Home Department*,[15] albeit that it was not actually applicable in that case because the legislation was not ambiguous. Lord Bridge found, "it is already well settled that in construing any provision in domestic legislation which is ambiguous in the sense that it is capable of a meaning which either conforms to or conflicts with the Convention, the courts will presume that Parliament intended to legislate in conformity with the Convention and not in conflict with it".[16] Whereas Lord Ackner preferred the negative formulation, "If Parliament has legislated and the words of the statute are clear, the statute must be applied even if its application is in breach of international law".[17]

It might be thought that in the hands of ingenious lawyers, well-practised at finding ambiguities and alternative interpretations, this rule would enable frequent reference

---

[12] For an enumeration of the occasions on which the ECHR may be referred to before the Courts, see *R. v. Secretary of State for Environment, ex p. NALGO* CA, 26.11.92, *The Times*, December 2, 1992; see also the judgment of Balcombe L.J. in *Derbyshire CC v. Times Newspapers* [1992] 1 Q.B. 770, C.A.

[13] [1982] 2 All E.R. 402 at 415C.

[14] See *Saloman v. Commissioners of Customs* [1966] 3 All E.R. 871 at 875, and *Post Office v. Estuary Radio* [1967] 3 All E.R. 663 at 682 and *per* Lord Scarman in *A-G v. BBC* [1980] 3 All E.R. 161 at 177; see also *per* Lord Denning in *R. v. Secretary of State for Home Affairs, ex p. Bhajan Singh* [1975] 2 All E.R. 1081 at 1083.

[15] [1991] 1 All E.R. 720.

[16] *ibid.* p. 722.

[17] *ibid.* p. 733. The difference between these two approaches is significant. On it depends whether the international obligation in the treaty can be relied upon to illustrate that there is an ambiguity in the legislation—see Dicey and Morris, *The Conflict of Laws* (12th ed.) pp. 10–11 as to the question of ambiguity in relation to interpretation of statutes implementing treaties.

to be made to the Convention and other human rights treaties which the United Kingdom has ratified. In fact, there are very few cases in which the Convention has made an impact in this way. In most cases, like *Brind* itself, the courts appear to have been unable to find an ambiguity in the words of the legislation.[18] In *Morris v. Beardmore*[19] Lord Scarman found support for his strict construction of the statutory requirements in respect of police powers to request a breath test in both a fundamental right of privacy at common law and in Article 8 of the Convention.[20] In *A-G v. British Broadcasting Corporation*, Lord Scarman, with whom Lord Fraser agreed, approached a question which others had treated as a question of interpretation (of the Rules of the Supreme Court) as one of legal policy, finding that it was necessary to consider this "country's international obligation to observe the European Convention as interpreted by the European Court of Human Rights".[21]

Where a statutory provision has been enacted following the finding of violation of the Convention by the Court in Strasbourg, the courts appear to be more willing to presume that Parliament intended that the new legislation should conform with the Convention and the decisions of the Court.[22] Bratza also makes the point that there are a number of cases in which the Convention has been used by the courts in the interpretation of the prohibition on "cruel and unusual punishments" contained in the Bill of Rights 1688.[23] Overall, however, the extent to which the narrow rule may be widened by reference to statutory ambiguity depends in turn on what criteria are used for statutory interpretation. The traditional view has been to give a statutory text its clear and natural meaning. That approach is already a commitment against finding ambiguity. The question is therefore whether knowledge of the Convention is relevant to identifying an ambiguity, or merely to resolving it.

---

[18] See, for example, *A-G v. Associated Newspapers* [1994] 1 All E.R. 556, where the Convention arguments were considered, but only after the statute was found to be unambiguous; also *Champion v. Chief Constable of the Gwent Constabulary* [1990] 1 All E.R. 116, *per* Lord Ackner at 125 (on the substantive issue in this case it was argued that statutory restrictions on the spare time activities of policemen were an infringement of the right to private life contained in Art. 8 of the ECHR, whereas an interesting comparison may be made with the case of *R. v. Secretary of State for the Environment, ex p. NALGO, The Times*, December 2, 1992, where the restrictions on the political activities of local government officers were challenged on the basis of Article 10).

[19] [1980] 2 All E.R. 753 at p. 762.

[20] It is noticeable, though, in his speech in the same case that Lord Diplock specifically excluded the European Convention on Human Rights from his reasoning.

[21] In this respect see also Lord Wilberforce's judgment in *Raymond v. Honey* [1982] 1 All E.R. 756, in which he considered the decision of the European Court of Human Rights in *Golder* as one of two basic principles underlying his interpretation of s. 47 of the Prison Act 1952, and the Prison Rules made thereunder. See also *R. v. Broadcasting Complaints Commission, ex p. BBC, The Times*, February 24, 1995. Brooke J. found that very clear language was required to interpret legislation in a way which might have the effect limiting the right of free expression as contained in Art. 10.

[22] *R. v. Cannons Park Mental Health Authority, ex p. A* [1994] 1 All E.R. 481, reversed C.A. [1994] 2 All E.R. 659, but see *per* Kennedy L.J., esp. at p. 684; *R. v. Secretary of State for Home Dept, ex p. T* [1994] 1 All E.R. 794; *Re Lonrho* [1989] 2 All E.R. 1100 at 1116; *R. v. Secretary of State, ex p. Leech* [1993] 4 All E.R. 539.

[23] See Bratza, "The Treatment and Interpretation of the European Convention on Human Rights by the English Courts" in J. P. Gardner (ed.), *Aspects of Incorporation of the European Convention on Human Rights into Domestic Law* (1993), p. 70, where he cites the cases of *Williams v. Home Office (No. 2)* [1981] 1 All E.R. 1211); *R. v. Secretary of State for Home Dept., ex p. Herbage* [1986] 3 All E.R. 209) and *Weldon v. Home Office* (especially C.A. [1990] 3 All E.R. 673,H.L. [1991] 3 All E.R. 733).

Development of the Common Law

The courts have more frequently used the Convention to inform the development of the common law. Formally speaking the judicial function is to declare what the common law already, in its wisdom, provides, rather than to make the law. In fact, what the role of the judge is now more generally accepted as being is to decide how the law should develop, according to principle, but in the light of prevailing social and moral values.[24] In so doing the role of the court is a complex one; it must involve the consideration of numerous factors, including the rule of *stare decisis*, the need for certainty and predictability in the law, and the need to do justice in the instant case. If these matters are not in conflict, it is unlikely that the case will be reported or even litigated.

In reaching such decisions there are numerous occasions on which assistance has been gained from comparative material. Needless to say, reference to such material is not regarded as having any binding quality within the English legal system. Sir John Laws develops this approach, arguing that in exactly the same way the English courts may consider the Convention and its case law.[25] Indeed, such arguments may be strengthened by observing that at the level of international law the courts, as the judicial arm of a state which is party to the Convention and other human rights treaties, are bound to consider the requirements of these treaties in developing the law in an area which Parliament has left to regulation by the common law. As a matter of international law the responsibility of a state which is party to the Convention may be engaged by the decisions of the courts, particularly so where the constitutional arrangements of that state provide for the courts to develop the law in a certain area.[26]

In recent years the courts have displayed an increasing willingness to have regard to the provisions of the Convention in this context. Reference to the Convention has been made in respect of numerous rights it protects but many of the most notable decisions have concerned the right to freedom of expression. Since the decision of the European Court of Human Rights in the *Sunday Times (No. 1)* case in 1979, where the common law was clearly found to be lacking in its protection for freedom of expression, there has been a great deal more attention paid to the requirements of Article 10 of the Convention. Dicta can be found in a number of cases from the early 1980s in which Article 10 was considered as a factor relevant to the decision, but the most emphatic endorsement of the Convention standards as reflected in the common law can be found in the *Spycatcher* litigation. In *Spycatcher (No. 1)*[27] the balancing of the interests required under Article 10 was conducted explicitly in Lord Templeman's speech. In the second case[28] Lord Goff made the following comments:

---

[24] See Cross and Harris, *Precedent in English Law* (4th ed.) especially at pp. 24–36; see also Lord Reid, "The Judge as Law Maker" (1972) 12 JSPTL 22, and A. Lester, "English Judges as Law Makers" [1993] P.L. 269.

[25] See "Is the High Court the Guardian of Fundamental Constitutional Rights?" [1993] P.L. 59 at 63. See also his comments at first instance in *R. v. Cambridge District Health Authority, ex p. B, The Times,* March 15, 1995.

[26] See *Sunday Times No. 1*; see also Beddard, "Retrospective Crime" [1995] N.L.J. 663.

[27] [1987] 3 All E.R. 316.

[28] *Spycatcher (No. 2)* [1988] 3 All E.R. 545.

"I can see no inconsistency between English law on this subject and Article 10 of the European Convention on Human Rights and Fundamental Freedoms. This is scarcely surprising since we may pride ourselves that freedom of speech has existed in this country perhaps as long, if not longer than, it has existed in any other country in the world. The only difference is that whereas Article 10 of the Convention, in accordance with its avowed purpose, proceeds to state a fundamental right and then to qualify it, we in this country (where everybody is free to do anything, subject only to the provisions of the law) proceed rather on the assumption of free speech, and turn to our law to discover the established exceptions to it. In any event I conceive it to be my duty when I am free to do so, to interpret the law in accordance with the obligations of the Crown under this treaty. The exercise of the right to freedom of expression under Article 10 may be subject to restrictions (as are prescribed by law and are necessary in a democratic society) in relation to certain prescribed matters, which include 'the interests of national security' and 'preventing the disclosure of information received in confidence'. It is established in the jurisprudence of the European Court of Human Rights that the word necessary in this context implies the existence of a pressing social need, and that interference with freedom of expression should be no more than is proportionate to the legitimate aim pursued. I have no reason to believe that English law, as applied in the courts, leads to any different conclusion."[29]

This statement has been relied on as an accurate exposition of the law in numerous subsequent cases. The courts have considered Article 10 in dealing with a number of common law restrictions on free speech. In respect of libel, and in particular the question whether suits in defamation lay at the instance of local authorities, the Court of Appeal relied primarily on the Convention in deciding this question in the negative.[30] The decision was affirmed by the House of Lords, largely on grounds other than application of the Convention provisions, but Lord Keith, after considering the requirements of Article 10 in the light of its interpretation by the European Court of Human Rights, approved the Court of Appeal's reasoning and added:

". . . I have reached my conclusion upon the common law of England without finding any need to rely upon the European Convention. Lord Goff of Chieveley in *A-G v. Guardian Newspapers Ltd (No. 2)* expressed the opinion that in the field of freedom of speech there was no difference in principle between English law on the subject and Article 10 of the Convention. I agree, and can only add that I find it satisfactory to be able to conclude that the common law of England is consistent with the obligations assumed by the Crown under treaty in this particular field."[31]

This somewhat Delphic utterance is not easy to analyse. What is its authority? Its

---

[29] *ibid.* p. 660.
[30] *Derbyshire County Council v. Times Newspapers* [1993] 3 All E.R. 65, C.A.
[31] [1993] 1 All E.R. 1011 at 1021.

principal function appears to be to reinforce the appropriateness of referring to the Convention in order to ensure that there is no inadequacy in the common law, equivalent to an ambiguity in legislation. This seems to have been the approach of the Divisional Court in respect of the law of blasphemy, in reaching its decision on an application for judicial review of a magistrate's refusal to issue summonses for blasphemous libel against Salman Rushdie and the publishers of *The Satanic Verses*.[32] The court had to decide whether the common law of blasphemy should be extended to protect religions other than Christianity and, in reaching its decision against such an extension, found it "necessary . . . in the context of this case, to attempt to satisfy [itself] that the United Kingdom is not in any event in breach of the Convention",[33] even though the common law was apparently certain on the point. A fairly detailed examination was given, in particular, to the extent of Convention obligations in respect of the right of free expression and the right to freedom of religion, and to affording these rights on a non-discriminatory basis, with reference made both to judgments of the European Court of Human Rights and to decisions of the European Commission of Human Rights. As a result the court concluded that "the Convention does not demand . . . the creation of a law of blasphemy for the protection of Islam so that as signatory to the Convention the United Kingdom be in conformity",[34] suggesting a consciousness by the court of its own responsibility for the United Kingdom international obligations. This is certainly a step further than the House of Lords felt required to go in *Derbyshire*.

In contrast to their attitude towards the Convention's requirements in relation to freedom of expression, the English courts have shown greater reticence in dealing with the Convention's requirements under Article 8. Article 8, broadly described, contains a "right to respect for privacy", but this is in fact made up of a number of elements, aimed at ensuring that the individual can live his or her life with the minimum of governmental interference as to, *inter alia*, their person, home or family. In particular it is worth noting that the right is to "respect for" privacy, which implies a positive obligation upon a state to provide protection from infringements by third parties, rather than a merely negative obligation on a state and its organs to abstain from particular actions or practices.[35]

In *Morris v. Beardmore*,[36] the House of Lords appeared to recognise that breathalyser legislation to combat drunken driving curtailed common law rights of the individual to personal privacy, and as such should be construed so as to ensure that interference with individual rights was restricted to the minimum extent consistent with the aim of the legislation. Thus, where the police officer was trespassing on the land of the accused at the time the breath test was requested, the request would be an unlawful exercise of the powers contained in the legislation and the evidence of it

---

[32] See *R. v. Chief Magistrate, ex p. Choudhury* [1991] 1 All E.R. 306: the law of blasphemy was reviewed by the House of Lords in *R. v. Lemon* [1979] 1 All E.R. 898, where, interestingly, only Lord Scarman considered the requirements of the ECHR (see p. 927), but he found that the offence of blasphemy fell within the permissible restrictions on free speech contained in Article 10(2).

[33] *R. v. Chief Magistrate, ex parte Choudhury* [1991] 1 All E.R. 306 at 320.

[34] *ibid.* at 322.

[35] See *Marcx v. Belgium*, Series A, No. 30; (1979–80) 2 EHRR 330.

[36] [1990] 2 All E.R. 753; *cf. R. v. Khan (Sultan)* [1994] 4 All E.R. 426, C.A., affirmed [1996] 3 All E.R. 289, H.L.

would be inadmissible. Lord Scarman based his judgment on a "fundamental right to privacy of the home" long recognised by the common law, and also protected by the European Convention on Human Rights. However, it should also be noted that whilst others of their Lordships analysed the case in terms of rights to liberty and personal privacy, Lord Diplock took a more restrictive approach, characterising the police action as simply tortious (in the absence of specific legislative authority for entering on to private land in this respect) and thus he held that his findings owed nothing to the Convention. Other writing has suggested that a right to personal privacy may be established by extension of the law of confidentiality,[37] but there are some obvious limitations as to the extent to which judicial activism in this respect is possible or desirable.[38]

The English courts have also been cautious in using the Convention as a basis for the development of common law rights in respect of family life, though Article 8 has been invoked in particular by parents in relation to their children.[39] In *Re KD (a minor) (Ward: termination of access)*,[40] Lord Templeman compared the approach of English law, which was concerned with the best interests of the child, and Article 8 in the following terms:

"The English rule was evolved against an historical background of conflict between parents over the upbringing of their children. The Convention rule was evolved against an historical background of claims by the State to control the private lives of individuals. Since the 1939–45 war interference by public author-ities with families for the protection of children has greatly increased in this country. In my opinion there is no inconsistency of principle or application between the English rule and the Convention rule. The best person to bring up a child is the natural parent. It matters not whether the parent is wise or foolish, rich or poor, educated or illiterate, provided that the child's moral and physical health are not endangered. Public authorities cannot improve on nature. Public authorities exercise a supervisory role and interfere to rescue a child when the parental tie is broken by abuse or separation. In terms of the English rule the court decides whether and to what extent the welfare of the child requires that the child shall be protected against harm caused by the parent, including harm which could be caused by the resumption of parental care after separation has broken the parental tie. In terms of the Convention rule the court decides whether and to what extent the child's health or morals require protection from the parent and whether and to what extent the family life of parent and child has been supplanted by some other relationship which has become the essential family life for the child."[41]

[37] See Sir John Laws, "Is the High Court the Guardian of Fundamental Constitutional Rights?" [1993] P.L. 59.
[38] See the judgment of Megarry V.-C. in *Malone v. Commissioner of Police (No. 2)* [1979] 2 All E.R. 620, especially at 647–649.
[39] In this respect see Hampson, "Children in Care and the ECHR" in J. P. Gardner (ed.), *Aspects of Incorporation of the European Convention on Human Rights into Domestic Law* (1993), especially 84–86.
[40] [1988] 1 All E.R. 577.
[41] *ibid.* at p. 578.

On the facts of the case, access to the ward of court was denied to his mother. Lord Oliver however, with whom Lord Templeman agreed and who gave the leading judgment, considered the nature of the "right" of parental access to his or her child. After examination of the Convention case of *R v. United Kingdom*,[42] he found that the right of parental access (which he described also as a "claim" and as a "privilege") was always to be qualified by consideration of what is best for the welfare of the child. The same approach has been taken in respect of a parent's application for a Residence Order which is opposed by a local authority, under the Children Act 1989.[43] Parental rights at common law which accord with Article 8 of the Convention have also been considered in relation to a woman prisoner whose Category A security status meant that she was separated from her very young baby. However, the Court of Appeal found that the second paragraph of Article 8 was also relevant and that therefore such rights could be restricted *inter alia* on the grounds of national security, public safety or the economic well-being of the country, for the prevention of disorder or crime, for the protection of health or morals, or for the protection of rights and freedoms of others.[44]

Exercise of Judicial Discretion

In accordance with the responsibility of the courts to ensure the conformity of their decisions with the international obligations of the United Kingdom, insofar as they are permitted to do so under the Constitution, a third area where the courts have taken the requirements of the Convention into account has been when exercising a discretion. In the *Spycatcher* litigation[45] the question arose as to whether the interlocutory injunctions against the *Guardian* and *Observer* newspapers should be maintained, notwithstanding that the book was available elsewhere in the world and was being imported into the United Kingdom, and that other newspapers had printed extracts from it.[46] At the same time an application to commit *The Sunday Times* for contempt was made for its subsequent publication of extracts of the book. The House of Lords, by a majority of three to two, decided in favour of maintaining the injunctions. Lord Templeman, as part of the majority (and on this point Lord Ackner specifically agreed with him), found that in this case it was appropriate to examine the requirements of Article 10 of the Convention and he considered in some detail the balance to be struck between the right of freedom of expression and the permissible restrictions in the public interest.[47]

The Court of Appeal has also found it necessary to consider the implications for free expression of the granting of an injunction against the members of a trade union issuing leaflets urging the public not to purchase certain goods, in their pursuit of an

---

[42] Series A, No. 121; (1988) 10 EHRR 74.
[43] See *Re K (a minor)*, Court of Appeal, December 15, 1994 (unreported).
[44] See *R. v. Secretary of State for the Home Department, ex p. Togher*, Court of Appeal, February 1, 1995 (unreported).
[45] See p. 87 and pp. 100–101 above.
[46] See [1987] 3 All E.R. 316.
[47] *ibid.* pp. 355–357. Note also the dissenting opinion of Lord Bridge, especially in relation to the ECHR at pp. 346–347.

industrial dispute. It is particularly noticeable that the Court raised the relevance of Article 10 of the Convention apparently of its own motion.[48] Again in the context of freedom of expression, the Court of Appeal found that it was entitled to consider the requirements of Article 10 of the Convention in deciding whether to exercise its powers under the Courts and Legal Services Act 1990 to set aside a jury's award of damages in a libel case on the basis that it was excessive. Neill L.J. found that an almost limitless discretion of the jury in respect of libel damages "fails to provide a satisfactory measurement for deciding what is 'necessary in a democratic society' or 'justified by a pressing social need' ".[49]

Again in this category of cases it is clear that the Convention has been referred to most often in respect of rights of free expression. [50] However the potential breadth of this category suggests that it may be possible to use it in other contexts.[51]

Judicial Review

Given that the negotiation and ratification of treaties are matters for the executive, it might seem consistent to expect that actions of the executive should comply with the requirements of such treaties. The argument has been put that, given that Parliament is presumed by the courts to have legislated in conformity with the United Kingdom's international obligations for the purposes of resolving legislative ambiguities, then where legislation has granted a discretion to the executive which may be exercised so as either to conform or to conflict with the United Kingdom's international obligations, such discretion should be exercised so as to conform with those obligations. However this argument was rejected in respect of the exercise of executive discretion in conformity with the Convention by the House of Lords in *R v. Secretary of State for the Home Dept, ex parte Brind*[52] on the basis that it would effectively incorporate into domestic law a treaty which Parliament had chosen not to incorporate by legislation.[53] The case involved an exercise by the Home Secretary of his discretion to issue directives under the Broadcasting Act 1981, prohibiting the broadcasting of direct statements of members of certain organisations in Northern Ireland, including Sinn Féin, Republican Sinn Féin and the Ulster Defence Association. Although the House of

---

[48] *Middlebrook Mushrooms Ltd v. TGWU* [1993] I.C.R. 612 at 620.

[49] *Rantzen v. Mirror Group Newspapers* [1993] 4 All E.R. 975 at 994. See also *John v. MGN Ltd* [1996] 2 All E.R. 35.

[50] Though in *Re H-S (minors: protection of identity)* [1994] 3 All E.R. 391 the Court of Appeal balanced the right of free expression (Art. 10) with the right to respect for private and family life (Art. 8) in deciding the extent of an injunction in respect of publicity in relation to custody proceedings. See also *Re W (a minor) (wardship: freedom of publication)* [1992] 1 All E.R. 794.

[51] See *R. v. Khan (Sultan)* [1994] 4 All E.R. 426, from which it would appear that rights to privacy as protected by Article 8 of the ECHR may be a relevant factor in exercising the discretion of whether to exclude evidence under s. 78 of the Police and Criminal Evidence Act 1984, though what weight it should be given is not clear from the judgment. An interesting case from the point of view of procedural law is the decision of *Sparks v. Harland, The Times*, September 9, 1996, where proceedings which were statute-barred under the Limitation Act 1980, were stayed rather than struck out pending the decision in the European Court of Human Rights in a similar case, which might have resulted in the introduction of retroactive legislation amending the Limitation Act.

[52] [1991] 1 All E.R. 721.

[53] See Lord Bridge, *ibid.* p. 723.

Lords was unanimous in refusing the application for judicial review, the various judgments of their Lordships are not entirely consistent in their approach to the Convention in such proceedings. Lord Ackner (with whom Lord Lowry agreed) appeared to take the most restrictive approach in considering that the sole standard which the court was called to apply in this case was that of *Wednesbury* unreasonableness; the question of whether a human right was in issue apparently made no difference, and the test was no higher than "was the decision of the Home Secretary so unreasonable that no reasonable Home Secretary could ever have reached it?" Further, the *Wednesbury* test did not require the court to examine whether the Secretary of State had had proper regard to the Convention in exercising his discretion, since to require that would be incorporating the Convention into English law "by the back door".

On the other hand Lord Bridge, with whom Lord Roskill agreed, having accepted that there was no presumption that the Secretary of State should have exercised this statutory discretion so as to conform with the Convention, went on to say:

> "But I do not accept that this conclusion means that the courts are powerless to prevent the exercise by the executive of administrative discretions, even when conferred, as in the instant case, in terms which are on their face unlimited, in a way which infringes fundamental human rights. Most of the rights spelled out in terms of the Convention, including the right to freedom of expression, are less than absolute and must in some cases yield to the claims of competing public interests. Thus Article 10(2) of the Convention spells out and categorises the competing public interests by reference to which the right to freedom of expression may have to be curtailed. In exercising the power of judicial review we have neither the advantages nor the disadvantages of any comparable code to which we may refer or by which we are bound. But again, this surely does not mean that in deciding whether the Secretary of State, in the exercise of his discretion, could reasonably impose the restriction he has imposed on the broadcasting organisations, we are not perfectly entitled to start from the premise that any restriction of the right to freedom of expression requires to be justified and that nothing less than an important competing public interest will be sufficient to justify it. The primary judgment as to whether the particular competing public interest justifies the particular restriction imposed falls to be made by the Secretary of State to whom Parliament has entrusted the discretion. But we are entitled to exercise a secondary judgment by asking whether a reasonable Secretary of State, on the material before him, could reasonably make that primary judgment."[54]

Lord Templeman also appeared to consider that something more that the *Wednesbury* test pure and simple could be applied in terms when considering a question raising human rights questions:

> "The English courts must, in conformity with the *Wednesbury* principles, consider whether the Home Secretary has taken into account all relevant matters and

[54] *ibid.* p. 723.

has ignored irrelevant matters. These conditions are satisfied by the evidence in the case, including evidence by the Home Secretary that he took the Convention into account. If these conditions are satisfied, then it is said on *Wednesbury* principles that the court can only interfere by way of judicial review if the decision of the Home Secretary is 'irrational' or 'perverse'.

The subject matter and date of the *Wednesbury* principles cannot in my opinion make it either necessary or appropriate for the courts to judge the validity of an interference with human rights by asking themselves whether the Home Secretary has acted irrationally or perversely. It seems to me that the courts cannot escape from asking themselves only whether a reasonable Secretary of State, on the material before him, could reasonably conclude that the interference with freedom of expression which he determined to impose was justifiable. In terms of the Convention, as construed by the European Court of Human Rights, the interference with freedom of expression must be necessary and proportionate to the damage which the restriction is designed to prevent.''[55]

Thus it appears that the Convention may well have some place in judicial review of the exercise of administrative discretion, although exactly what this place is may be questioned. Lord Ackner's insistence on *Wednesbury* principles in their traditional form stemmed from his concern that the "supervisory" (as opposed to "appellate") nature of the court's jurisdiction in judicial review be maintained. Lord Bridge's description of the court's judgment as being "secondary" suggests a similar limitation, but the way in which it is expressed may be interpreted as giving the court a somewhat broader scope to this jurisdiction. According to this view, instead of the simple *Wednesbury* test, the court in assessing the reasonableness of the exercise of a discretion which has the effect of restricting a fundamental human right will have to ask "could a reasonable Home Secretary reasonably conclude that there is an important competing public interest which justifies the restriction?" Though it is not said explicitly, the implication of Lord Bridge's judgment is that the "important competing public interests" which might justify a restriction on freedom of expression would be those contained in Article 10(2) of the Convention. There are similar public interest qualifications to a number of the other rights, and so a similar exercise might be imagined in relation to those. It is less clear how the courts would deal with Convention rights which are absolute on their face.[56]

There have been a few decisions since *Brind* which appear to bear out this reading, at least in part, though there remain a number of uncertainties. In *R v. Secretary of State for the Environment, ex p. NALGO*,[57] which concerned a challenge to Regulations made by the Secretary of State preventing certain local government officers from

---

[55] *ibid.* pp. 725–726. He found that the interference with freedom of expression was minimal and the Home Secretary's reasons were compelling.

[56] In this respect see *per* Lord Bridge in *R. v. Secretary of State, ex p. Bugdaycay* [1987] 1 All E.R. 940, at 952.

[57] *The Times*, December 2, 1992. This case has recently been suggested as authority for the proposition that "the *Wednesbury* threshold of unreasonableness is not lowered in fundamental rights cases" (Lord Irvine, "Judges and Decision-Makers: the Theory and Practice of Wednesbury Review" [1996] P.L. 59 at 64).

political activities, on the grounds *inter alia* that they infringed freedom of expression as guaranteed by Article 10 Convention, Neill L.J. considered the judgment in *Brind*. He found that *Brind* was authority for the proposition that "... where fundamental human rights including freedom of expression are being restricted the Minister will need to show that there is an important competing [factor] sufficient to justify the restriction". This suggests a means of weighing the two, akin to proportionality. However, Neill L.J. also found that, with the exception of what he described as a dictum by Lord Templeman, he was unable to extract from the other speeches any real support for the view that the latitude to be given to a Minister is to be confined with tighter limits when his decision impinges on fundamental human rights. It is submitted that these two findings may not easily be reconciled.

In *R. v. Secretary of State for the Home Department, ex p. Ozminnos*[58] Auld J. in reviewing *Brind* found it authority for the following proposition:

> "even though there is no presumption that the Secretary of State's discretion has to be exercised in accordance with the Convention, restrictions of the rights upheld by it need to be justified. As Lord Bridge indicated ... the judiciary are entitled to exercise a secondary judgment where Convention matters are raised by asking themselves whether a reasonable Secretary of State, aware that the United Kingdom was a signatory to the Convention, could reasonably disregard its provisions."

His conclusion was in fact that the Secretary of State had not exercised his discretion in a way which was "*Wednesbury* unreasonable, tested by the approach indicated by the House of Lords in *Brind* where articles of the European Convention on Human Rights have at least some role as relevant factors in the taking of a decision."[59]

The *Ozminnos* case is also interesting because it is one of a number of immigration cases in which the Convention has been relied upon because the Home Office policy has been publicly revealed to seek conformity with the Convention.[60] First of all, in *Hlomodor v. Secretary of State for the Home Department*,[60a] the applicant sought review of the Home Secretary's decision to deport him, claiming *inter alia* that his deportation would involve his separation from his wife and children and that the Home Secretary had not given sufficient weight to these relationships in reaching his decision. In correspondence prior to the hearing the Home Secretary had acknowledged the relevance of Article 8 of the Convention in reaching his decision. Thus the Court of Appeal found, only for the purposes of this case, that Article 8 was a relevant factor to take into account in reviewing that decision, but its judgment gives little indication of the weight it attached to it. Similar reasoning, though in relation to a

---

[58] [1994] Imm. A.R. 287.

[59] *cf.* the decision in *Kwapong v. Secretary of State for the Home Department* [1994] Imm. A.R. 207, C.A., where the Court of Appeal did not consider the ECHR relevant in reviewing the exercise of discretion. However, it might be distinguishable in that in this case the Court of Appeal was dealing with the argument that was quite categorically rejected in *Brind* that there was a presumption that a statutory discretion must be exercised in accordance with the ECHR.

[60] It should be noted that the findings quoted above could be applied to judicial review of discretion generally and not simply merely to cases where these Home Office Guidelines are at issue.

[60a] [1993] Imm. A.R. 534.

broader range of cases, underlies the reference to the Convention in some subsequent decisions again concerning the exercise of discretion to deport in cases where the applicant's family life would be disrupted. In *Iye v. Secretary of State for the Home Department*[61] the applicant obtained a copy of an internal Home Office document offering guidance from the Home Secretary to immigration officers exercising the discretion to deport. In particular the guidance addressed in terms the requirements of Article 8, as interpreted by the European Court of Human Rights, in relation to persons whose deportation would separate them from a spouse or children in this country. Though the document had not become a public document, Glidewell L.J. found that its significance was as follows:

"... having embarked upon the exercise of deciding whether to exercise his discretion because of compassionate grounds, the Home Secretary's officers are required by him to act within the general terms of the guidance he gives. If it became clear a particular officer had disregarded the guidance, that would be a valid reason for saying the decision was wrongly made. But if it appears that the guidance has been followed, the question then arises whether it can be said that following the guidance no sensible Home Secretary or officer on his behalf could properly ever arrive at the decision which has been made."[62]

In *R. v. Secretary of State, ex p. Amankwah*[63] the Divisional Court was also referred to the same internal document. In this case Popplewell J. quashed the decision of the Secretary of State to deport, on the basis that "the decision of the Secretary of State is not in conformity with the policy document, or at any rate it does not appear from the reasons he has given to be in conformity with the policy document. To that extent I consider that the decision is not fair and is therefore perverse."

Brind has imposed an obstacle on the development of this area of the law. On its facts, the case was weak and the subsequent application to the Commission was rejected as inadmissible. Part of the difficulty of interpreting the scope of the decision derives from this factual background. Another important aspect was emphasised in *R. v. Ministry of Defence, ex p. Smith*,[64] a case concerning the review of the rule precluding homosexuals from serving in the armed forces. As with *Brind*, the rule was a general one, akin to legislation, rather than a specific decision based upon the facts of a particular case. The court emphasised the limited scope of review where policy considerations were prominent and where the courts would find themselves considering issues with which they were unfamiliar and perhaps which they are unsuited to determine.[65] The Court recognised a role for the Convention in attuning the scrutiny

[61] [1994] Imm. A.R. 63.
[62] *ibid.* at 66. See also the judgment of Evans L.J., where he states that it is unsatisfactory that in this type of case the respondents were unable to make clear the Secretary of State's position on the following three issues: (i) whether the Secretary of State considered that he was bound to comply with the guidance; (ii) whether the guidance was intended to give effect to Article 8 ECHR, as interpreted by the European Court of Human Rights; and (iii) if the answer to those questions was yes, why the decision letter did not make it abundantly clear that this was the way by which the decision had been reached.
[63] [1994] Imm. A.R. 240.
[64] [1996] 1 All E.R. 257.
[65] *ibid.* p. 264g–j and p. 272e–g.

on *Wednesbury* criteria in cases where life and liberty are at stake and, it is submitted, where the executive decision under review relates to the particular circumstances of the individual concerned. Such an approach may provide a good basis for distinguishing *Brind*[66] (and *Smith* itself) from cases concerning individual circumstances.

Parliament and the Convention

Though the Convention has not yet been incorporated into English law, there have been a number of attempts by Parliamentarians from both Houses and from each of the three largest parties, to introduce Private Members' Bills.[67] Though some of these have passed through all of their stages in the House of Lords, none has received the support of the Government in the Commons. However, it is beyond the scope of the present chapter to discuss the techniques by which incorporation might be achieved,[68] and instead a more modest task of examining how Parliament has used the Convention in legislative debate will be considered.

Perhaps unsurprisingly under a Constitution whose central tenet is the supremacy of Parliament, the use which Parliament has made of the Convention in the course of legislative debate has been rather limited. It has not been possible to research the use of the Convention in Parliamentary scrutiny of legislation or of Executive actions in a general way. Instead, the comments which follow are based on a review of the Parliamentary passage of the pieces of primary legislation introduced in response to findings by the Strasbourg organs that English law was in violation of the Convention, during the period since 1980.[69] Though generalisations are of limited value in this context, it must be observed that close analysis of the provisions of the Convention and the specific findings by the European Court of Human Rights is rarely undertaken in legislative debate. Within the scope of the research which the writers have carried out, where the legislation was introduced to remedy violations of the Convention, usually the Government Minister has recorded this fact when opening the debate on Second Reading. As is to be expected, in most cases it was not until the Committee Stage that close attention was given to the requirements of the Convention.[70] It is

---

[66] See *per* Sir Thomas Bingham M.R. at 264j. It may be recalled that *Brind* has been criticised in Australia and New Zealand. See *Tavita v. Minister of Immigration* [1994] 2 N.Z.L.R. 257 and *Minister for Immigration and Ethnic Affairs v. Teoh*, 128 A.L.R. 353.

[67] The two most recent of these have been introduced in the House of Lords by Lord Lester of Herne Hill. In May 1997 the Labour Government included in the Queen's Speech a commitment to incorporate the European Convention into British law during the 1997–98 parliamentary session.

[68] For discussion of earlier attempts at incorporation, see R. Blackburn, "Draft Legislation to Incorporate the European Convention on Human Rights into U.K. Domestic Law", in *Aspects of Incorporation of the European Convention on Human Rights into Domestic Law*, J. P. Gardner (ed.), 1993. See also the Report *Human Rights Legislation* published by the Constitution Unit in November 1996.

[69] The aCts whose legislative history has been traced for these purposes are Contempt of Court Act 1981; Employment Act 1982; Marriage Act 1983; Mental Health (Amendment) Act 1982; Interception of Communications Act 1985; Immigration Act 1988; Children Act 1989; Criminal Justice Act 1991.

[70] In relation to the Contempt of Court Act 1981, see especially *Hansard*, H.L. Vol. 416, col. 179 (though fairly frequent reference was made to the ECHR and the *Sunday Times* judgment at almost all stages of the passage of this Act); Employment Act 1982, see esp. *Hansard*, H.L. Vol. 431, col. 831–845; Mental Health (Amendment) Act 1982, see esp. *Hansard*, H.L. Vol. 426, col. 759–766, Vol. 427, col. 863–870 & 874–882; Interception of Communications Act 1985, see esp. *Hansard*, H.L. Vol. 464, col. 855–

perhaps more noteworthy that the most detailed analysis of the Convention's require-ments took place generally at the House of Lords' Committee Stage, usually led by practising and academic lawyers and some leading judges and former judges.

It is suggested that the Convention should have a greater role in the legislative process, as providing an additional framework of principles against which legislative proposals might be considered, but one on which there is likely to be a degree of consensus amongst the main political parties. There is of course an obvious difference in the style of drafting between the Convention, in its concise but general terms, and most English legislation, which seeks to establish certainty in the law through preci-sion and inevitably detail. Where the proposal is introduced to remedy a violation of the Convention, the task may be made easier as there is usually a judgment of the European Court of Human Rights translating the broad principle into the particular area of English law and (it is hoped) spelling out, at least by implication, the Conven-tion's requirements in that context.

However, where the judgment is not so specific and the legislator simply has the words of the Convention, the generality of the Convention's words may cause prob-lems. For example, in the course of passage of the Interception of Communications Act 1985, which followed as a result of the *Malone* case, Article 8 of the Convention was discussed at some length in the debates. The qualifications to the right contained in Article 8(2) in particular were considered in relation to reasons for which the Secret-ary of State may issue a warrant for interception. The wording of the Bill drew to a large extent on Article 8(2): the warrant was to be *necessary* (a) in the interests of national security; (b) for the purpose of preventing or detecting serious crime; or (c) for safeguarding the economic well-being of the United Kingdom (though this was limited to obtaining information which is considered necessary to acquire, being information relating to the acts or intentions of persons outside the British Islands). The legislative debates show that the last ground caused considerable concern to the Opposition in its apparent breadth, but the Government was able to point out that it was a more restrictive basis, given its territorial limitations, than the words of Article 8(2) would allow.[71] Further, the point was raised that Article 8(2) would also allow a potentially broad category of warrants on the basis of the protection of health or morals, though the Government had felt that this would be unduly restrictive of civil liberties.[72] No mention was made of the interpretation of these limitations or of the principle of proportionality as adopted by the European Court of Human Rights.

The level at which the Convention's requirements are discussed in the legislature could clearly be improved. Whilst the discussion of the Convention is at present larg-ely conducted by lawyers in both Houses, it is submitted that its interest certainly goes much wider than the legal community, and correspondingly that wider participa-tion would be beneficial. Numerous suggestions could be made as to how this could best be achieved, but at the very least a major problem which could be remedied

---

880; Immigration Act 1988, Standing Committee D, 24.11.87–26.1.88, at col. 3940, 92, 105–106, 124, 147–154, 165–174, 234, 363, 370, & 435–438; Criminal Justice Act 1991, see esp. *Hansard*, H.C. Vol. 193, col. 897–911 and Vol. 195, col. 309–322, Standing Committee A, 15.1.91 col. 328–339; see also *Hansard*, H.L. Vol. 529, col. 59–72 and Vol. 530, col. 1006–1035.

[71] See *Hansard*, H.L. Vol. 464, col. 877–878 and Vol. 465, col. 962.
[72] *Hansard*, H.L. Vol. 464, col. 878.

without undue difficulty is simply the informational one. It is believed that draft legislation is already scrutinised by government lawyers with expertise on the Convention,[73] and indeed as a state party to the Convention which takes seriously its international obligations, it would be surprising if the United Kingdom did not do this. Such advice is, of course, given confidentially. However when it comes to the stage of presenting a Bill to Parliament, the Government has presumably taken an informed view that its proposals will not violate the Convention. There seems, therefore, to be little reason why a short summary of the human rights implications of the Bill could not be included in the explanatory memorandum that accompanies the Bill in the same way as is done for financial implications. It would appear that the explanatory memorandum has no legal status, even following *Pepper v. Hart*,[74] and so it would make no inroad into the principle of Parliamentary supremacy. It would serve simply to improve the quality of debate and understanding of the international obligations which the United Kingdom has undertaken, if anything enhancing the role of Parliament.[75]

Conclusions

Some conclusions may be drawn from the foregoing review of cases concerning England and Wales which have been brought before the European Commission and Court of Human Rights.

First, the variety of cases must be recognised. Cases have been brought before the Court relating to most of the Articles of the Convention and relating to an extraordinary variety of different factual circumstances. As a result, the pattern of cases brought to Strasbourg concerning England and Wales has been different from that concerning most other jurisdictions, from which cases have largely concentrated on a relatively small section of the Convention.

Secondly, the position of the applicant in these cases should be considered. To what extent has the Convention machinery provided a solution for the complaints of individuals, whose cases have been taken to the Commission and the Court and have resulted in the finding of a violation of the Convention? Even discarding the acute problems of delay which beset the duplicative system established under the Convention as it currently operates, it may be doubted whether the majority of these complaints are more suitably dealt with by an international petition system than by the domestic legal system. It is certainly remarkable that a case such as *Reed v. United Kingdom*,[76] in which the facts were largely not in dispute, should nevertheless require resolution on the international rather than on the domestic plane.

---

[73] See A. W. Bradley, "Protecting Government from Legal Challenge" [1988] P.L. 1, at 3.
[74] [1993] A.C. 591.
[75] *cf.* the position in Canada where legislative proposals are scrutinised by the Department of Justice for their compliance with the *Canadian Charter of Rights and Freedoms* and the Minister is required to report any inconsistency to the House of Commons at the first convenient opportunity, s.4.1 (1) of the Department of Justice Act, RSC 1985 c.J-2. For explanation see the comments of M. Dawson in "Symposium: the Impact of the Charter on the Public Policy Process" (1992) 30 *Osgoode Hall Law Journal* 501–660.
[76] Application No. 7360/76, 19 DR 113.

Such considerations lead inevitably to the uneasy place of the Convention in domestic law. Notwithstanding the formal position that the Convention is not part of domestic law, the courts have increasingly shown a preparedness to entertain argument relating to it and to refer to it in reaching judgments. This has been especially true in cases that relate to the availability of discretionary remedies, such as the granting or refusal of an injunction, or in cases relating to the judicial review of decisions made in the many regulatory areas into which that jurisdiction has extended its control, in the thirty years since individual applications have concurrently been possible under the Convention.

One clear consequence of the uneasy place of the Convention in English law is the rarity with which the European Court of Human Rights has had to consider precisely the same issue which the domestic courts have previously analysed. The significance of the *Sunday Times*[77] case may be that it was one of the rare cases where an appeal was made successfully from a decision of the House of Lords, which had actually considered the same question that the Court ultimately had to determine in Strasbourg. The place of the Convention in judicial review proceedings, and in particular as an element in the test of irrationality under the *Wednesbury* criteria, has not yet been finally settled, although the case of *R. v. Ministry of Defence, ex p. Smith*[78] affirms the relevance of the Convention.

Each of these factors taken together, however, tend to reinforce the question with which this Chapter opened, which is why there is a perception that there are a large number of cases concerning England and Wales brought before the European Court of Human Rights. On the evidence, not only are there few cases in absolute terms, the per capita application rate is far lower than in the majority of European countries and major comparable jurisdictions such as France and Italy have had far more cases in a much shorter period. Given the variety of issues which may be and have been taken to the Court from England and Wales, the overall number of cases on any given topic is shown to be even lower.

The question why this should be and how far it would be altered by the introduction of an accelerated and simplified system in Strasbourg, or by the incorporation of the Convention into domestic law and hence by the availability of such arguments in ordinary proceedings, would be a legitimate topic for empirical study.

---

[77] Series A, No. 30; (1979–80) 2 EHRR 245.
[78] [1996] 1 All E.R. 257.

CHAPTER 4

SCOTLAND AND THE EUROPEAN CONVENTION

For a legal system which prides itself on its continental roots, Scots law has displayed a curious reluctance to acknowledge the European Convention on Human Rights. There is little evidence that the treaty has had any real impact upon the consciousness of practitioners or judges, and it may be no exaggeration to suggest that, in any "league table" of legal influence of the Convention, its standing is the weakest in Scotland in comparison with the position in other West European countries.[1] Executive suspicion of incorporation explains legislative inaction, but it does not justify judicial hostility, which only in 1996 has begun to show some signs of moderation. In turn, this lack of accommodation for the Convention in domestic law has encouraged a corresponding lack of awareness amongst members of the legal profession of the treaty's contents and scope for providing remedies for litigants. In short, the links between the Scottish legal system and the Strasbourg organs are still tenuous. While this chapter may have less to say about domestic cases which have given rise to issues under the treaty and about the use made of the Convention in domestic law, it does seek to examine the wider issue as to why Scots law has failed to embrace the challenge and opportunities accorded.[2]

The ECHR in Domestic Case Law

The Convention has had little use in the domestic courts of Scotland, either as a tool for developing the common law or as an aid in the interpretation of statute, in marked contrast to the position adopted by courts in England and Wales.[3] The deliberate rejection of the English approach may well have been encouraged by a determination to uphold the separateness and distinctiveness of the Scottish legal system through the

---

[1] The distinction between Scots law and English law is often overlooked partly as a result of the tendency of commentators to use the term "British" as a synonym for "English": *e.g.* A. Drzemczewski, "Authority of the Findings of the Organs of the European Human Rights Conventions in Domestic Courts" (1979) 1 LIEI 1 at 43. For a recent discussion of the status of the European Convention on Human Rights in those West European domestic legal systems where the Convention has direct effect, see I. Polaciewicz and V. Jacob-Foltzer, "The European Human Rights Convention in Domestic Law" (1994) 12 HRLJ 65 and 125.

[2] Some of the discussion in this chapter draws upon an earlier article published in [1991] P.L. 40.

[3] See Chapter 3.

over-strict application of constitutional doctrine, but the practical result has been to minimise the availability of argument based upon human rights principles. If through-out West Europe—and since 1989, in most Central and East European countries also—the Convention has gradually asserted itself as the new *ordre public* of the continent,[4] such developments have passed Scotland by. It would be an overstatement that its citizens were badly served by its judiciary in this respect, for reforms to Scots law and to administrative practices to meet Strasbourg obligations have regularly occurred through legislative and executive action, albeit that most reforms have been prompted by successful English applications.[5] The primary question has always been whether this difference between Scots and English law could be maintained since the tide was clearly not going to turn back south of the border. Only in 1996, through certain dicta of the Lord President in the Inner House of the Court of Session, came the first real indication of a possible future change of judicial policy with an observation that this distinction could no longer be justified,[6] but it is too early to confirm whether this will result in a realignment with English law. This chapter, then, has a Janus-feel to it: it dwells upon the recent past, but with an eye to future possibilities, much in keeping with the Scottish tradition as the old year ends of reflecting on what has recently been achieved and on opportunities missed, but with the optimism with which the New Year is welcomed.

Initial Jurisprudence: Kaur and Moore

Kaur v. Lord Advocate[7] and *Moore v. Secretary of State for Scotland*[8] have stood for long as the twin watchdogs at the doors of the Scottish legal system, effectively preventing entry of the European Human Rights Convention without legislative authority in the shape of a statute transforming the treaty into domestic law. There is some irony in that the first of these two cases was brought in part to help support a planned application to Strasbourg,[9] and there is some regret in that in disposing of the extravagant arguments in the pleadings based upon the treaty the Scottish courts

---

[4] cf. J. A. Frowein, "The ECHR as the Public Order of Europe" in European University Institute, *Collected Courses of the Academy of European Law* (1992), pp. 293–295.

[5] See A. W. Bradley, "The United Kingdom before the Strasbourg Court 1975–1990" in W. Finnie, C. M. G. Himsworth, and N. Walker, eds, *Edinburgh Essays in Public Law* (1991), pp. 185–214.

[6] *T, Petitioner*, 1997 S.L.T. 724, 1996 GWD 28-1653.

[7] 1981 S.L.T. 322 (Outer House).

[8] 1985 S.L.T. 38 (Inner House).

[9] One month before being deported, Mrs Kaur had lodged an application before the European Commission on Human Rights. In its observations on admissibility made after Kaur's deportation, the British Government argued that Kaur had failed to exhaust her domestic remedies. An earlier attempt to prevent deportation by means of interim interdict was unsuccessful, although any grant of a declarator of breach of rights under the Convention would have had the practical result of her readmission to the United Kingdom (*Kaur v. Lord Advocate*, above, at 326). But this would have been a concession admitted by the Crown and not one prompted by any legal rule. While Lord Ross was undoubtedly right in remarking that "once a decision has been given in the present action . . . it will be clear that any domestic remedy will have been exhausted . . ." (at 331), it is also clear from the decisions of the Commission that exhaustion of the statutory remedies provided for in the legislation would have sufficed: only remedies which are considered effective and adequate need be employed. See further, P. van Dijk & G. D. van Hoof, *Theory and Practice of the European Convention on Human Rights* (2nd ed., 1990), 81–98; *Uppal Singh v. United Kingdom*, No. 8244/78; 17 DR 149 (1979).

discouraged any more moderate use of the Convention. Scots law—as in the other legal systems in the United Kingdom and in the Republic of Ireland—proceeds upon the fundamental principle that, while the executive has power to enter into a binding treaty in international law with other sovereign states, the provisions of the treaty will not become part of domestic law unless "transformed" by means of a statute passed by the legislature.[10] International law and national law are two distinct spheres.[11] *Kaur* was an attempt to persuade the Outer House of the Court of Session to rewrite this fundamental principle of constitutional law and, as such, was doomed to fail.

In *Kaur* the pursuer sought a declarator that certain of her rights and those of her three children under the Convention (in particular, respect for family life in terms of Article 8, and prohibition of expulsion of nationals provided for by Article 3 of Protocol No. 4) had been violated when she had been deported as an illegal immigrant. This had taken place some eighteen months after the earlier deportation of her husband from Scotland. Although the three young children of the marriage had been born in the United Kingdom and qualified as "patrials" with a right of abode, Kaur decided to take them with her when she herself was deported. Her conclusion for declarator was based on the assertion that the Convention gave her and her children rights "which are recognised by the law of Scotland and which are enforceable in the Scottish courts".[12] She argued, first, that the Convention and Protocol were already part of Scots law; second, that she and her children had acquired rights under the Convention by virtue of application of analogous legal doctrines; and third, that in any case the Convention had been brought into Scots law by the law of the European Union.

What Kaur in effect was asking the Outer House to do was to incorporate the Convention into Scots law and hold it hierarchically superior to an Act of Parliament. This was to propose a fundamental revision of the doctrine of sovereignty of parliament. Further, since the United Kingdom had not ratified Protocol No. 4, the court was also being asked to modify the clear principle of international law that a treaty or international obligation which provides for ratification will only bind a state once it has specifically ratified it.[13] Ratification of the Convention by the Government required Scots judges, it was argued, to reject this "dualist" approach in favour of a "monist" one in which rules of international law may be directly applicable and thus able to be relied upon by individuals in domestic courts.[14] The argument was partly based upon the principle of *quoad fieri debet infectum valet* to the effect that Parliament's failure to incorporate the treaty should be ignored by the court so as to ensure that the applicants could still rely upon the legal obligations of the United Kingdom.

---

[10] The leading case in British constitutional law is that of *The Parlement Belge* (1879) 4 P.D. 129, (1880) 5 P.D. 157. See, further, O. H. Phillips & P. Jackson, *O. Hood Phillips' Constitutional and Administrative Law* (7th ed., 1987), pp. 285–287. An example of the "transformation" of international legal norm into domestic law is to be found in the Criminal Justice Act 1988, ss. 134–138, where the provisions of the UN Convention Against Torture are given effect by statute.

[11] *cf. Mortensen v. Peters* (1906) 8F (J) 93, where the High Court of Justiciary reaffirmed that the courts would give effect to an Act of Parliament, even where it violated international law. This is similar to the constitutional position in the Nordic countries (although most of these states have now incorporated the ECHR into domestic law) and in Ireland. For discussion of transformation of treaty into statute, see F. A. Mann, "The Interpretation of Uniform Statutes" (1946) 62 L.Q.R. 278.

[12] *Kaur v. Lord Advocate*, 1981 S.L.T. 322 (Outer House) at 327.

[13] *cf. Vienna Convention on the Law of Treaties*, 1969, Art. 14.

[14] See further A. Drzemczewski, *European Human Rights Convention in Domestic Law* (1983), p. 177.

Further, the Scots law principle in private law of *ius quaesitum tertio*, it was submitted, would allow the court to conclude the Government had intended in ratifying the Convention to confer the "benefits" of human rights protection in a directly-effective manner upon individuals. This was also to misunderstand what the Convention required of contracting states, since it is left up to each state to determine how the substantive rights are to be protected within its own legal systems.[15]

The judge, Lord Ross, had little difficulty in dismissing the three arguments. First, "the Convention cannot be regarded in any way as part of the municipal law. ... A treaty or convention is not part of the law of Scotland unless and until Parliament has passed legislation giving effect to the treaty provisions".[16] The pursuer could not succeed on account of her arguments based upon *quoad fieri debet infectum valet* or by arguing that in ratifying the Convention and by at least signing Protocol No. 4 an *ius quaesitum tertio* had been created in favour of Kaur by the Government. While Lord Ross certainly accepted that "in certain circumstances what ought to be done avails although not done", here there was no issue of personal bar but instead the hurdle of a fundamental constitutional point: "even if the government had failed in an [international] obligation ... I do not see how that could create in favour of the pursuers a right which only Parliament and not the British government could give them".[17] Nor could he accept any private law argument that the Government had constituted the public at large a *tertius* and thus conferred rights upon individuals in domestic law by "contracting" with other States.[18] Only the pursuer's final argument that the Convention could become enforceable in domestic law as part of the European Union legal order had any attraction for Lord Ross, who accepted the European Court of Justice's recognition that respect for fundamental human rights formed part of the general principles of law it has recourse to in judgments.[19] But the lack of any "economic feature" and any particular issue raising a specific question of European Union law was crucial, and Kaur was not even a national of any E.U. state.

Kaur is thus hardly more than a reaffirmation that it is Parliament rather than the executive which can change domestic law. The harm to the subsequent development of Scots law came with Lord Ross's further discussion of existing English case law on the place of the European Convention in domestic law. While in England the Convention was also not part of municipal law, "if there is any ambiguity in a United Kingdom statute, the court in England may look at it and have regard to the Convention as an aid to construction".[20] It was this that caused Lord Ross most difficulty

---

[15] *Belgian Linguistic Case*, July 23, 1968, Series A, No. 6, at 35; (1979–80) 1 EHRR 252; *Swedish Engine Drivers' Union Case*, February 6, 1976, Series A, No. 20, at 18; (1979–80) 1 EHRR 617.

[16] *Kaur v. Lord Advocate*, above, at 327.

[17] *ibid.* p. 330.

[18] Lord Ross had serious doubts as to whether any such intention had been present, and whether the public at large could be considered a *tertius*. Superficially, however, these arguments are attractive: by Article 1 of the Convention states undertake to "secure to everyone within their jurisdiction" the rights specified, and by Article 13 to provide "an effective remedy before a national authority" to resolve violations of the Convention.

[19] See Chapter 2.

[20] *Kaur v. Lord Advocate*, above, at 328; *cf.* the cases considered by Lord Ross, especially *Salomon v. Commissioners of Customs and Excise* [1976] 2 Q.B. 116; *R. v. Secretary of State for Home Affairs, ex p. Bhajan Singh* [1976] Q.B. 198; and *Pan-American World Airways v. Dept of Trade* [1976] 1 Lloyd's Rep. 257.

since "if the Convention does not form part of the municipal law, I do not see why the court should have regard to it at all". Although Parliament will at least have had sight of the Convention when it was laid before both Houses prior to ratification by virtue of the Ponsonby rule, to interpret ambiguities in subsequent legislation by making use of the Convention he considered would be indeed constitutionally improper "because the court is then challenging the well-settled principle that the executive cannot by itself make law".[21] He continued:

> "So far as Scotland is concerned, I am of opinion that the court is not entitled to have regard to the Convention either as an aid to construction or otherwise. I respectfully share the view . . . to the effect that a convention is irrelevant to legal proceedings unless and until its provisions have been incorporated or given effect to in legislation. To suggest otherwise is to confer upon a convention concluded by the executive an effect which only an Act of the legislature can achieve".[22]

This is strictly *obiter*,[23] but is what turned *Kaur* from a simple and straightforward reaffirmation of constitutional principle into a major hurdle to be overcome before the Convention could be introduced into legal argument in Scotland. Academic reaction to *Kaur* was muted but broadly sympathetic.[24] This unfortunate case with its unnecessary *obiter* gained approval from the Inner House of the Court of Session in an equally unlikely legal action four years later.

In *Moore v. Secretary of State for Scotland*,[25] Moore was a party litigant who at the time of the action was incarcerated in Peterhead prison. He sought damages and a "declarator of erroneous conviction" in the civil courts. This was an attempt to persuade a civil court to overturn a criminal conviction using averments which were speculative and irrelevant. The pleadings also contained references to Article 6 of the Convention's guarantees of a fair trial, which Moore claimed had been violated. To the Inner House, the pursuer's submissions were no more than "an illegitimate stratagem". The requirements of Article 6, the court declared, were already met by domestic law, and the legal system already provided a remedy to review criminal convictions. Instead of merely dismissing the action, the court took the opportunity of confirming the rejection of the Convention's use in domestic law in *Kaur*: "Lord Ross was per-

---

[21] *Kaur v. Lord Advocate*, above, at 329, quoting with approval O. Hood Phillips, *Constitutional and Administrative Law* (6th ed., 1978), p. 446: "Indeed, one might argue that the fact that parliament has hitherto refrained from incorporating the European Convention into our law indicates an intention that its provisions should not be taken into account by the courts, so that the Convention ought not to be cited by counsel or looked at by the judges".

[22] *Kaur v. Lord Advocate*, at 330, quoting with approval Diplock L.J. in *Salomon v. Commissioners of Customs & Excise* [1967] 2 Q.B. 116.

[23] Lord Ross himself noted that Kaur's counsel had accepted that the issues did not raise any issue of the interpretation of statute: *Kaur v. Lord Advocate* at 330.

[24] *cf.* W. Finnie, "The European Convention on Human Rights" (1980) 25 J.L.S.S. 434 at 439: "however much the practical effect of the decision may be deplored, it is correct and desirable, given the more important constitutional principle underlying it"; J. M. T. "*Kaur v. Lord Advocate*" (1982) 98 L.Q.R. 183 at 186: "[the decision] brought back the virtues of simplicity and certainty into an important area of constitutional law".

[25] 1985 S.L.T. 38.

fectly correct in holding that the Convention plays no part in our municipal law so long as it has not been introduced into it by legislation''.[26]

Subsequent Use of the ECHR in Domestic Proceedings

Despite this seemingly firm denunciation from the Inner House, litigants in Scotland have made sporadic use of the Convention in submissions, no doubt on account of the continued reliance of the treaty as an aid to statutory interpretation or in developing the common law in England.[27] Not all of these references to the treaty in written pleadings have made it through to the stage of oral debate,[28] but on occasion the courts have appeared willing to consider the treaty as having some moral persuasive force without admitting it as a formal source of law.

This distinction is important. Abuse of the Convention by seeking to use it as a *formal* source (as in *Kaur*) will end in failure. Lord Templeman's remark in the House of Lords in *Lord Advocate v. The Scotsman Publications*[29] that, while the courts should follow any guidance contained in a statute as to the extent of restraints on free speech, ''if that guidance is inconsistent with the requirements of the Convention that will be a matter for the Convention authorities and for the United Kingdom government'' rather than for the courts, is clearly a restatement of the dualist approach and one not at odds with the English courts' decision to permit the treaty to be used in interpreting ambiguities in legislation since this is a ''mere canon of construction which involves no importation of international law into the domestic field''.[30] For example, in *Ferns v. Management Committee & Managers, Ravenscraig Hospital*,[31] a sheriff court considered it was unable to obtain assistance from a decision of the European Court of Human Rights in deciding a question as to the extent of new statutory appeals in mental health cases. The issue was to be decided solely by reference to the terms of the legislation introduced in response to an adverse ruling from Strasbourg, and not by recourse to the ruling itself.

Where counsel has tried to rely upon European notions of ''fairness'' under Article 6 to advance an appellant's case, the courts have proved singularly unimpressed, just

---

[26] *ibid.* p. 41.
[27] *cf.* P. J. Duffy, ''English Law and the ECHR'' (1980) 29 I.C.L.Q. 585; G. McCouch, ''Implementing the ECHR in the United Kingdom'' (1982) 18 Stan. J. Int'l L. 147; O. H. Phillips & P. Jackson, *Constitutional and Administrative Law* (7th ed., 1987) 429–433; A. Lester, ''The Impact of Europe on the British Constitution'' (1992) 3 Pub. Law Rev. 228; C. Warbrick, ''Rights, the European Convention on Human Rights and English Law'' (1994) 19 M.L.R. 34.
[28] References to the Convention may be withdrawn by the pursuer (*e.g. McDonald v. Rifkind*, unreported, October 4, 1990 (Inner House)) or summarily dismissed by the court as not competent or helpful (*cf. Murray v. Rogers*, 1992 S.L.T. 221 at 224A (Inner House); *L v. H*, 1996 S.L.T. 612 at 617D).
[29] 1989 S.C. (H.L.) 122 at 167–168. Reaction in Scotland to this House of Lords case itself is of some interest. While there was extensive discussion of the requirements of Article 10 in relation to free speech guarantees, the case does not appear to have been taken as establishing any precedent for directing any change of attitude towards the Convention. The case seems not even to have been considered by Lord President Hope in *T, Petitioner*, above; indeed, Lord Hope accepts that Lord Ross's decision in *Kaur* was ''widely quoted in the text books as still representing the law of Scotland on this matter'' (above, at 733K).
[30] *R. v. Secretary of State for the Home Department, ex p. Brind* [1991] 1 A.C. 696, *per* Lord Bridge at 748.
[31] 1987 S.L.T. (Sh.Ct.) 76 (*per* Sheriff Principal Caplan).

as in *Moore*. Thus, in *Ralston v. H.M. Advocate*,[32] the High Court of Justiciary was asked to consider whether prejudice had been caused to the accused at his trial when his solicitor withdrew from the case with his consent leaving the accused conducting his case himself for half a day before obtaining the assistance of an advocate who had not had the opportunity of hearing all the Crown evidence. The appeal in part was based upon Article 6's guarantees of a fair hearing, but this was summarily dismissed: "[E]ven if Article 6 is regarded as showing the sort of rights which every citizen enjoys, there was no question in the present case of the appellant being denied a fair and public hearing".[33] In *Montes v. H.M. Advocate*, when a question arose as to the fairness of interrogations involving foreigners whose command of English was limited, Lord Weir felt that Scots law itself provided an ample test of fairness to an accused in such circumstances and decided it was unnecessary "even if it is competent to do so" to refer to Strasbourg jurisprudence for assistance.[34] And in *Anderson v. H.M. Advocate* the High Court of Justiciary considered that reference to Strasbourg decisions on the availability of legal aid in Scotland were not relevant in a criminal appeal concerning fair trial issues since these were to be answered in accordance with domestic law alone.[35]

The first breakthrough for the Convention in Scots law—though it has always been a tentative one—was found in administrative law, where certain judges have accepted that the Convention and its jurisprudence can help in deciding the reasonableness or otherwise of executive decisions. If Lord Ross's reticence was largely founded upon the impropriety of letting the Convention in by the back door, as it were, without Parliamentary approval, there should be less reluctance on the part of the judiciary in using the Convention in the area of judicial review of executive action since it is the executive branch of government itself which has ratified the treaty. Thus the Convention could be seen as providing a convenient test of the reasonableness or otherwise of executive action.[36] The first indication of a thaw in attitude is probably to be found in *Martin v. City of Edinburgh District Council*, where a question arose as to the fiduciary responsibilities of council members as trustees. In protest at apartheid, the ruling Labour group had decided to withdraw from all investments involving South Africa. Lord Murray in the Outer House remarked at the outset that the case was "not about the legality or morality of apartheid. Prima facie, South African apartheid would not be legally enforceable in Scotland if only because of its apparent incompatibility with [race relations legislation] and with Article 14 of the European Convention on Human Rights".[37]

The first real inkling that such arguments could actually succeed in persuading a court to consider the Convention, *Kaur* and *Moore* notwithstanding, came in the 1988

---

[32] 1989 S.L.T. 474.
[33] *ibid.* p. 478.
[34] 1990 SCCR 645 at 673.
[35] 1996 S.L.T. 155.
[36] Application of the test of reasonableness in domestic law in any case mirrors the recognition by the Strasbourg organs of a "margin of appreciation" on the part of the state; *cf.* R. St. J. Macdonald, "The Margin of Appreciation" in Macdonald, Matscher and Petzold, eds., *The European System for the Protection of Human Rights* (1993) 83–124.
[37] 1988 S.L.T. 329 at 330.

Outer House decision of *Budh Singh*.[38] Lord Morison was asked to consider whether the decision of an immigration official to deport Mr Singh and his wife as illegal immigrants was unreasonable, *inter alia* on the ground that general immigration policy as applied by the Home Office amounted to a breach of Article 8 of the Convention by failing to respect the pursuer's family life. While Lord Morison decided that in this particular case it was unnecessary to determine whether he was bound by the Convention guarantee, "if the policy of the Home Office is one which ignores the obvious humanitarian principle of respect for family life, it would in my view be unreasonable and subject to the Court's review".[39] Thus, while avoiding the issue of the status of the Convention within Scots law, Lord Morison seemed to accept that the legality of executive action could be measured against the provisions of the Convention at least for some purposes of judicial review. And to give substance to such an open-ended concept as "respect for family life", Lord Morison was prepared to examine the jurisprudence of the European Court of Human Rights. Executive practice required, as Lord Morison summarised it, "something out of the ordinary in regard to family circumstances to justify departure from the general practice of removing illegal entrants", and in order to assess whether such a position existed, he turned to the European Court's decision in *Abdulaziz, Cabales and Balkandali v. United Kingdom*[40] for guidance. Since this decision confirmed that Article 8's guarantee of respect for family life did not require state respect for choice of matrimonial residence, Lord Morison thus concluded that the Home Office policy "could not be described as one which involves a lack of respect for family life, unless there existed a general obligation such as the European Court rejected". The action accordingly was unsuccessful.

A similar approach is found in another Outer House decision, *Irfan Ahmed*.[41] Ahmed had been given entry clearance to take part in an arranged marriage with a named individual, and shortly after a civil ceremony of marriage the couple divorced. Ahmed thereupon entered into a hastily arranged civil marriage with another U.K. national after notice of intention to deport had been served upon him. Lord Coulsfield considered the petitioner's arguments based upon Article 8 as merely a "side issue", intended to give emphasis to his point that in domestic law the Secretary of State was required to give serious consideration in exercising his discretion to deport to any effect upon the family life of the petitioner, but he did cite *Budh Singh* with approval and did accept that, were the Secretary of State to have ignored any "obvious humanitarian principle" involved, this would have been one factor in helping establish that executive policy was unreasonable. *Abdulaziz, Cabales and Balkandali v. United Kingdom* was again considered in some detail but with the similar conclusion reached that reliance upon this case could not assist the petitioner.

These two cases, then, suggest that recourse to Convention requirements may help a court decide whether executive action is so unreasonable as to fail the *Wednesbury* test of reasonableness[42] or the *GCHQ* test of whether the decision "is so outrageous

---

[38] 1988 S.C. 349.
[39] *ibid.* p. 352.
[40] May 28, 1985, Series A, No. 94; (1985) 7 EHRR 471.
[41] October 26, 1994 (unreported).
[42] *Associated Provincial Picture Houses v. Wednesbury Corporation* [1948] 1 K.B. 223.

in its defiance ... of accepted moral standards".[43] However, they constitute only a tentative advance for the Convention into Scots law. Other judges have been much less sympathetic. In *Leech v. Secretary of State for Scotland*[44] a prisoner sought judicial review of prison rules and standing orders which permitted interference with correspondence between a prisoner and his legal adviser. Much of Leech's arguments were based upon Convention case law, which contains several successful challenges to British law and practice on this matter. Lord Caplan, however, accepted the Secretary of State's contentions that the treaty was not part of domestic law and accordingly dismissed submissions based upon Court decisions.[45] The extent of sympathy for Convention arguments seems thus in part dependent upon the attitude of the particular judge involved.

There are also, however, sound reasons of principle against the further advance of the Convention in judicial review. Arguments based upon the notion of personal bar are restrained by the extent to which the executive may fetter in advance the exercise of its discretion, as much as by constitutional concerns about any usurpation of the proper powers and responsibilities of the legislature by the courts. Nor is the notion of legitimate expectation—defined by Lord Fraser as arising from "an express promise given on behalf of a public authority or from the existence of a regular practice which the claimant can reasonably expect to continue"[46]—likely to act as an alternative conduit for the Convention. In England, the Court of Appeal has already rebuffed an attempted advance on this front.[47] In Scotland, arguments that a legitimate expectation existed that domestic law and practice would be altered in the light of a decision from Strasbourg were similarly rejected in the unreported case of *Hamilton v. Secretary of State for Scotland*.[48] Hamilton sought to argue that the Secretary of State had been wrong not to alter administrative arrangements to meet the requirements of Convention requirements despite the existence of a general "practice" of bringing domestic law and administrative systems into line with European Court of Human Rights jurisprudence. Hamilton had been convicted of murder and detained during Her Majesty's pleasure as a minor. He was subsequently released on licence, but after various incidents was recalled to prison by the Secretary of State. Hamilton was not accorded the possibility of challenging any adverse report, since the decision to recall him was taken without reference to the Parole Board, and was not given the opportunity of having sight of the documents available to the Secretary of State. His application for judicial review of the recall decision was based upon the European Court's decision in *Weeks v. United Kingdom*,[49] which considered the recall of an individual initially sentenced by the trial court to a discretionary sentence of life imprisonment partly on

---

[43] *Council of Civil Service Unions v. Minister for the Civil Service* [1985] 1 A.C. 374, *per* Lord Diplock at 669.

[44] 1991 S.L.T. 910 (Outer House).

[45] *ibid.* p. 917K.

[46] In *Council of Civil Service Unions v. Minister for the Civil Service* [1985] 1 A.C. 374 at 401.

[47] *cf. Chundawadra v. IAT* [1988] Imm. A.R. 161, *per* Glidewell L.J. at 174: "[Since the Convention has not been incorporated] it may not be looked at or prayed in aid in relation to matters in these courts save where a question of ambiguity in a statute or other legal text arises. That not being the case here, it may not be looked at at all and no expectation that it should be followed can arise."

[48] December 18, 1990 (unreported).

[49] *Weeks v. United Kingdom*, March 2, 1987, Series A, No. 114; (1988) 10 EHRR 293.

account of public safety and partly to facilitate treatment of the prisoner's mental condition. Since any subsequent decision to recall Weeks to prison had to be based upon a ground which was consistent with the trial court's objectives to satisfy Article 5(1)(a), the European Court ruled that Weeks was entitled under Article 5(4) to a determination of the lawfulness of his recall. In the *Hamilton* case, the court was prepared to enter into submissions based upon the Convention's guarantees to dispose of the arguments that in the present instance there had also been a breach of Article 5(4). Counsel argued that Hamilton had a legitimate expectation that the Government would have taken steps to give effect to the decision in *Weeks* by altering domestic law based upon "the declared policy and practice of the Government", and alternatively that the "practice in the Courts of the United Kingdom" was to give effect to Strasbourg decisions "so far as consistent with U.K. law". The submissions were ultimately unsuccessful. Lord Milligan distinguished the present case from *Weeks*, where there had been a discretionary sentence of life imprisonment involving treatment considerations and where personal circumstances were likely to have fluctuated over time, as opposed to a mandatory sentence of life imprisonment which is imposed to mark the gravity of the crime of murder. Further, the argument based upon the "legitimate expectation" that the Government would take steps to implement the *Weeks* decision had this been considered to be in point was also rejected since this would have extended application of the doctrine beyond its established limits:

> "In the present case, the petitioner's case is not that the respondent departed from an established practice or system with regard to the provision of adverse information: on the contrary, it is that he failed to change such practice in the light of a decision of the European Court of Human Rights. . . . It is right to say that [Government statements of policy] from time to time over the years might encourage the hopes of persons anticipating promotion of legislation to bring domestic law into conformity with decisions of the European Court of Human Rights, at least where derogation under Article 15 is not in contemplation. But [the petitioner's counsel] also regarded what he described as the 'practice of the courts' as being important to his submission and it seems to me that on this matter a further formidable difficulty arises in his submission. The problem is that the Convention and decisions of the European Court of Human Rights have achieved recognised significance in English law but not, as yet at least, in Scottish courts."

Perhaps the most noteworthy feature of the judgment is that Convention arguments were examined at such length.[50] Indeed, Lord Milligan noted that counsel for the

---

[50] For further discussion of the case, see W. C. Gilmore and S. C. Neff, "On Scotland, Europe and Human Rights", in H. L. MacQueen, ed., *Scots Law into the 21st Century* (1996) pp. 269–270, where the authors question whether the U.K. Government can indeed now be taken to have given an express promise to adhere to the Convention by virtue of a written answer to a Parliamentary Question in 1994. But the answer (that Ministers and civil servants have a general obligation to adhere to the treaty) was no more than a simple reaffirmation of obligations under international law, and the contention that this could perhaps found a legitimate expectation within domestic law still fails to consider the issue of the fettering of executive discretion which worried Lord Bridge in the *GCHQ* case, above.

Secretary of State had not attempted to argue that precedent prevented the court from considering any decision of the European Court of Human Rights "for any purpose in determining the duties of the respondent". While these arguments based upon the Convention ultimately failed, the case gives further weight to the thin line of authority which suggests that admission of the Convention and examination of Strasbourg jurisprudence in actions for judicial review is not constitutionally improper. But this development is still tentative and should not be overestimated. While *Budh Singh* may go further than English decisions[51] and suggests a potentially fruitful line for development, there have been but a handful of judicial review cases in which such arguments have been advanced by counsel and considered by courts. Lord Milligan's willingness in *Hamilton* to consider Convention guarantees is still atypical.

By the end of 1995, then, the only limited advances the Convention had made were in administrative law. *Kaur* and *Moore* remained in Scotland as bulwarks against assimilation with English law,[52] but also against any major adoption of Strasbourg guarantees into the domestic legal system. Such a position isolated the Scottish legal system, for even elsewhere in West Europe where there was no formal incorporation of the Convention—as with Norway—the courts were prepared to use the Convention for certain purposes.[53] Scots law stood apart and alone.

Individual Applications

This lack of accommodation of the Convention in domestic law is reflected in a lack of interest amongst practitioners as to the potential use of the treaty in challenging domestic practices in Strasbourg. While the United Kingdom has been involved in a substantial number of applications disposed of by the Strasbourg organs,[54] the number

---

[51] cf. *R. v. Secretary of State for the Home Department, ex p. Brind* [1991] 1 A.C. 696, *per* Lord Bridge at 697: "[W]here Parliament has conferred on the executive an administrative discretion without indicating the precise limits within which it must be exercised, to presume that it must be exercised within Convention limits would be to go far beyond the resolution of an ambiguity. It would be to impute to Parliament an intention not only that the executive should exercise the discretion in conformity with the Convention, but also that the domestic courts should enforce that conformity by the importation into domestic administrative law of the text [and case law]". This dictum has been criticised by C. Warbrick in "Rights, the European Convention on Human Rights and English Law" [1994] E.L.R. 34. P. J. Duffy, in "English Law and the European Convention on Human Rights" (1980) 29 I.C.L.Q. 585 at 597, has argued that interpretation of statutes which confer administrative powers on ministers involves similar considerations as to the use of the Convention as apply to interpretation of statutes generally. Cf. *Bennett v. Horseferry Road Magistrates Court* [1993] 3 All E.R. 138, where the courts considered the issue of improper extradition to England by reference *inter alia* to USA decisions but were not referred to the European Court's ruling in *Bozano v. France*, December 18, 1986, Series A, No. 111; (1987) 9 EHRR 297, a case which was arguably in point.

[52] cf. *Anderson v. H.M. Advocate*, 1996 S.L.T. 155, where the High Court of Justiciary decided it was unnecessary in the present case to consider whether the Scottish courts should follow the English practice of using the Convention in cases of statutory ambiguity.

[53] cf. K. Eggan, "Incorporation and Implementation of Human Rights in Norway" in M. Scheinin, *International Human Rights Norms in the Nordic and Baltic Countries* (1996), pp. 207–208.

[54] In 1996, 471 of the 4758 applications registered by the Commission concerned the United Kingdom: *Survey of Activities and Statistics 1996*. By the start of 1997, 69 cases had been referred to the Court which involved the United Kingdom, and in over half of these cases at least one violation was established.

of cases emanating from Scotland[55] is comparatively low. It has often been suggested that the high number of British cases is attributable to Britain's non-incorporation of the Convention, but this is open to doubt: first, it is "apparently impossible to establish a clear causal connection between a country's incorporation of the [treaty] and the number of (successful) applications brought before the Strasbourg organs";[56] and second, it does not explain why Scottish cases are proportionally rare in comparison with those involving England and Wales or Northern Ireland respectively. It may be more likely that the number of applications from any jurisdiction reflects the level of awareness of the Convention amongst legal practitioners as well as the standing of the Convention in the domestic legal system. Of course, any survey of *Scottish* cases raises in any case problems of labelling. The specific "nationality" of any British application may often be of little relevance where Scots law or administrative practice is replicated elsewhere in the United Kingdom. Thus cases such as *Reid v. United Kingdom*,[57] in which a Scottish employee challenged his dismissal for failure to join a trade union following the Court's decision in *Young, James and Webster*,[58] have no distinctive Scottish dimension. Further, a Scots applicant may well be challenging action which in fact took place in England as in *Christie v. United Kingdom*.[59] Similarly, a decision from Strasbourg in the case of an application arising from England may often result in the consequential amendment of law or practice in Scotland (either through the introduction of measures applying throughout Britain[60] or through Scottish measures which follow those elsewhere in the United Kingdom[61]). Yet any survey of Scottish applications may be of value more for the paucity of its content than for the development of Convention jurisprudence or for the prompting of change in domestic legal systems. Certainly, the issues challenged by applicants from Scotland have tended to be of mainly domestic interest. Only *Campbell and Cosans*[62] has had any

---

Only Italy exceeded this figure (although some two-thirds of these cases concerned recent referrals almost exclusively concerned with length of proceedings in domestic courts).

[55] Decisions and Reports of the Commission and Court decisions do not distinguish between cases arising in Scotland, England and Wales and Northern Ireland. I am indebted to Dr Stanley Naismith of the Secretariat of the Commission for assistance in tracing reported Scottish applications. This survey attempts to discuss applications in which decisions have been made public as at the end of 1994, but inevitably some have been missed.

[56] J. G. Polakiewicz, "Implementation of the ECHR and of the Decisions of the European Court of Human Rights" (1992) 2 AEHRYB 147, at 157.

[57] Application No. 9520/81, October 12, 1983, (1983) 34 DR 107 (friendly settlement secured).

[58] August 13, 1981, Series A, No. 44; (1983) 5 EHRR 201.

[59] Application No. 21482/93, June 27, 1994, 78-A DR 119 (complaint relating to interception of communications sent to applicant in Scotland by GCHQ based in England).

[60] As with the Contempt of Court Act 1981 passed as a result of the decision in the *Sunday Times* case, judgment of April 26, 1979, Series A, No. 30; the Employment Act 1982 following the decision in *Young, James and Webster*, above; the Interception of Communications Act 1985 following the case of *Malone v. United Kingdom*, judgment of August 2, 1984, Series A, No. 82; and changes to the Immigration Rules following *Abdulaziz, Cabales and Balkandali v. United Kingdom*, judgment of May 28, 1985, Series A, No. 94; (1985) 7 EHRR 471. *Cf. Hansard*, H.C. Vol. 234, cols 959–962, for a list of Court judgments involving the UK and any consequential domestic action taken; and European Court of Human Rights, *Survey of Activities 1959–1990* and subsequent years.

[61] As with changes to standing orders affecting prisoners' correspondence after the *Golder* case, judgment of February 21, 1975, Series A, No. 18; (1979–80) 1 EHRR 524, and the *Silver and Others* case, judgment of March 25, 1983, Series A, No. 61; (1983) 5 EHRR 347.

[62] *Campbell and Cosans* case, judgment of February 25, 1982, Series A, No. 48; (1982) 4 EHRR 293. This resulted in the enactment of the Education (No. 2) Act 1986 (which abolished corporal punishment in

major impact on the law and practices in other parts of the United Kingdom; and only *Lithgow and Others*—a case involving both Scottish and English applicants and even a French citizen—has advanced understanding of the Convention interpretation of issues of interest arising outwith Britain. As suggested, one conclusion that immediately presents itself is that the Convention's lack of standing in the domestic legal system has encouraged lack of awareness of its utility in challenging domestic laws and practices in international law. Nevertheless, this survey—however brief—of attempts to use the Convention to challenge Scots law illustrates the type of issue which has found its way from Scotland to Strasbourg.

"Fair Trial" Guarantees under Article 6

Article 6 gives rise to a substantial case load on account of the nature of the fundamental rights protected,[63] and it is thus not surprising that the bulk of Scottish applications concerns interpretation of these provisions guaranteeing a fair hearing in civil and criminal cases. The particular features of Scots law challenged at Strasbourg have included such issues as the right of access to courts, security measures during trials, criminal appeals, bias on the part of jurors, the non-availability of legal aid in criminal cases, and certain features of the children's hearing system.

The general issue of the applicability of Article 6(1) is not without controversy. The text refers to the "determination of . . . civil rights and obligations", but the extent to which disciplinary hearings within the public sector are included still causes difficulty. An illustration of the type of issue which can arise is *C. v. United Kingdom*,[64] where a janitor at a Scottish school was dismissed for petty theft after a hearing before a local authority educational officer and the school's headmaster. The dismissal was subsequently upheld by an industrial tribunal. The collection of evidence had involved some ineptitude on the part of the police, and a charge of theft was dismissed in the criminal courts. The Commission considered that Article 6(1) need not apply to internal disciplinary proceedings in the public service, but where a contract of employment permits access to civil courts and tribunals, then any such proceedings may be said to have "determined" an individual's civil rights within the meaning of the Convention's guarantee. Since the applicant had not challenged the fairness of the tribunal proceedings, this part of the application had to be considered manifestly ill-founded. Cases which do meet the "civil rights and obligations" threshold test give rise to further issues. Access to a court under Article 6 is not unlimited and may be subject to restrictions in the public interest. In *H. v. United Kingdom*[65] the applicant

---

state schools). Other decisions have led to administrative changes. The *McCallum* case, judgment of August 30, 1990, Series A, No. 183; (1991) 13 EHRR 596, and the *Campbell* case, judgment of March 25, 1992, Series A, No. 233-A; (1993) 15 EHRR 137, each led to reforms in prison standing orders. The decision in *Granger*, judgment of March 28, 1990, Series A, No. 174, led to the issue of a practice rule. No action was considered necessary in respect of the *Boyle and Rice* case, judgment of April 27, 1988, Series A, No. 131; (1988) 10 EHRR 425.

[63] For a recent survey, see A. Grotrian, *Article 6 of the European Convention on Human Rights: The Right to a Fair Trial* (1994).
[64] Application No. 11882/85, (1987) 54 DR 162.
[65] Application No. 11559/85, December 2, 1985, 45 DR 281.

complained that his right of access to the judicial system was impeded since he was subject to the status of vexatious litigant and accordingly required the authority of a Court of Session judge before being permitted to initiate court proceedings.[66] He had not been granted such permission when he sought to raise an action against a police officer since he was unable to establish to the satisfaction of the court that he had a prima facie case. There was no right of appeal against this decision. The Commission considered that access to a court is but one aspect of the general right to a fair hearing provided by Article 6, and since Scots law did not limit the applicant's right of access completely, and the restrictions on a vexatious litigant were not disproportionate to the acceptable state aim of ensuring the proper administration of justice, his application had consequently to be declared manifestly ill-founded.

In the sphere of criminal procedure, several applications have allowed the Commission the opportunity to consider the extent to which Scots law meets Article 6 requirements. In the *C. v. United Kingdom* application discussed above, C further alleged that his dismissal and the determination of his case by an industrial tribunal involved assessments of his dishonesty and thus violated paragraph 2 of the Article, which provides that "everyone charged with a criminal offence shall be presumed innocent until proved guilty". Here, the Commission drew a distinction between civil and criminal proceedings: only in the latter instance did the need for "scrupulous observation of the principle of innocence" arise. Consequently, this part of the application was declared incompetent *ratione materiae*. In *Campbell v. United Kingdom*,[67] the question was whether the applicant's handcuffing to a prison officer throughout appeal proceedings in court breached Article 6(1). The Commission considered it was not called upon in the present case to consider the extent to which the security measure was justified but merely whether this had interfered with the right to a fair hearing, and in the present case this had not arisen: while handcuffing of an individual in public was undesirable, security considerations could justify interference with certain rights of prisoners, including that of privileged communication with legal representatives. More recently, the administration of the jury system has been challenged in *Pullar v. United Kingdom*,[68] where the Commission had considered that the applicant's rights had been breached when it transpired that one of the members of the jury which eventually returned a guilty verdict was employed by the principal prosecution witness and knew another of the witnesses, but the Court (by five votes to four) held that there was no violation of Article 6(1) since the particular juror had no personal knowledge of the issues and the system of jury trial in Scotland offered important safeguards such as the random way in which jurors were selected and the nature of the sheriff's charge to the jury to consider in a dispassionate manner the evidence presented.

Several applications have called for scrutiny of the disposal of criminal appeals. For example, in *Grant v. United Kingdom*[69] the power of the High Court in Scotland to increase a sentence of a trial court on appeal was considered. During appeal proceedings, the applicant's counsel had sensed that the court was coming round to the

[66] In terms of the Vexatious Actions (Scotland) Act 1898.
[67] Application No. 12323/86, July 13, 1988, 57 DR 148.
[68] Judgment of June 10, 1996.
[69] Application No. 12002/86, March 8, 1988, 55 DR 218.

opinion that the trial court's sentence of six years' imprisonment was too light, and accordingly during the proceedings had attempted to abandon the appeal. This had been refused, and the sentence was increased to one of ten years. The Commission considered that the proceedings had to be looked at as a whole, and it was inevitable that an appeal court must form an "initial inclination or view" from the appeal papers and other materials from the trial court before the opening of the appeal hearing. Furthermore, the court had benefitted from hearing submissions on the sentence. Scots law did permit an individual to abandon his appeal, but in this case the motion to seek authority to do so had been made after the start of the hearing. This application again was considered manifestly ill-founded.

Restrictions on the availability of legal aid in Scottish criminal proceedings at trial and at appeal have been challenged in a series of applications under Article 6(3)(c), which provides that an individual has the right to "defend himself in person or through legal assistance of his own choosing" (with the state providing free legal assistance if an individual lacks sufficient means) when the interests of justice so require.[70] A key issue in Scottish applications has been the refusal of free representation to accused persons or at appeal hearings. In *McDermitt v. United Kingdom*[71] a stipendiary magistrate rejected an application for legal aid in a criminal case involving a breach of the peace and assault of a police officer, since as a matter of policy he considered "interests of justice" did not apply to breaches of the peace or to resisting arrest by a police officer. In this case, the matter was disposed of by way of a friendly settlement in the form of an *ex gratia* payment by the Government which accepted that the application for legal aid had not been appropriately dealt with by the magistrate.

More difficult questions have arisen on account of the ready right of access to an appeal court traditionally recognised by Scots law and the restricted availability of free legal representation. This tension between openness and ensuring "equality of arms" has resulted in violations in three cases, and paradoxically in the cutting back of appeal rights in order to ensure Scots law meets European human rights standards. Where an appellant's grounds of challenge were considered to have no likelihood of success, no legal aid would be made available, nor would an advocate be prepared to act on the appellant's behalf in accordance with the code of professional ethics of the Faculty of Advocates. However, an appellant would still be able to gain access to the appeal court, at which any oral submissions would be answered by counsel for the Crown. The situation could thus have arisen during a hearing involving an unrepresented appellant where the court became convinced that some legal issue of difficulty did indeed exist, but where the appellant was unable to represent himself properly. In other words, the ready access to a court accorded by Scots law had the potential drawback of appearing more illusory than real. On three occasions the Strasbourg Court has examined the matter, and on each occasion has established that there has been a violation of Article 6. In *Granger*,[72] the applicant had given statements to the

---

[70] This does not mean an individual has unlimited choice in selecting legal representation: Application No. 7572/76, *Ensslin v. FR Germany*, July 8, 1978, 14 DR 64. An individual receiving legal representation through a legal aid scheme has no right to choose his or her representative: Application No. 9285/78, *X v. United Kingdom*, October 9, 1978, 15 DR 242.

[71] Application No. 11711/85, May 15, 1987, 52 DR 244.

[72] Judgment of March 28, 1990, Series A, No. 174; (1990) 12 EHRR 469.

police in connection with serious charges of wilful fire-raising and murder in which he named the persons he believed responsible. At the trial he denied having made any such statements, but was subsequently convicted of perjury. Legal aid had covered the preparation, trial, and initial appeal stages, but further legal aid for representation at the appeal hearing was refused by a legal aid committee, which had received counsel's opinion that there were no reasonable prospects that any appeal would succeed.[73] Granger presented his own appeal by reading a statement presented by his solicitor who had continued to give him advice but could not appear since he had no rights of audience in the appeal court. The court decided it could not dispose of the appeal without obtaining a transcript of parts of the evidence, and adjourned the hearing. The appeal subsequently failed. The European Court considered that there had been a violation of paragraph 3(c) taken together with paragraph 1 of Article 6.[74] A matter of some complexity calling for an adjournment had arisen during the appeal, and legal aid at least for the adjourned hearing should have been made available; further, the applicant was not in a position to oppose the arguments advanced by the Crown or even fully to comprehend the prepared address he read out. In short, the appeal court had not had the benefit of "expert legal argument from both sides on a complex issue".[75]

The *Granger* decision led to the making of a practice direction by the Lord Justice-General to the effect that where legal aid had been refused for an appeal but where during the hearing the court considered that an appellant might have a substantive case and it was in the interests of justice that he be represented, the court would adjourn and recommend that the refusal of legal aid be reviewed. In such circumstances, legal aid would in practice be awarded.[76] This allowed the ready disposal by the Commission of several other pending Scottish applications.[77] But two subsequent Court decisions ruled against this solution, which had attempted to resolve the tension between open access and the availability of legal aid. In the *Boner*[78] and *Maxwell*[79] cases, the factual situation in *Granger* was in each instance distinguished in that the legal issues were "not particularly complex", but the inability of each applicant denied legal aid at the appeal stage to make an effective contribution was deemed crucial. By the time of these appeals, legislation had provided that legal aid should be granted if an individual had "substantial grounds" for any appeal in the High Court and if it was "reasonable in the particular circumstances" that such should be awarded.[80] The practice direction introduced after *Granger* also provided an additional safeguard. During Boner's trial, a prospective prosecution witness entered the

---

[73] In terms of the Legal Aid (Scotland) Act 1967, s. 1(7).
[74] The Commission was of the opinion that paragraph 3(c) alone had been violated, and that no separate issue arose under paragraph 1.
[75] *Granger*, above, at para. 47.
[76] *cf. Boner* case, below, paras 30–31; *Maxwell* case, below, paras 27–28.
[77] Application Nos. 14778/89, *Higgins v. United Kingdom*, report of February 13, 1992, 73 DR 95; 16212/90, *R. v. United Kingdom*, report of February 1992; 15861/89, *M v. United Kingdom*, report of August/September 1992; and 18123/91, *WW v. United Kingdom*, report of March/April 1993, Commission Information Notes Nos. 103, 107 and 111 (three *ex gratia* payments of £1200 and one of £900).
[78] Judgment of October 28, 1994, Series A, No. 300-B; (1995) 19 EHRR 246.
[79] Judgment of October 28, 1994, Series A, No. 300-C; (1995) 19 EHRR 97.
[80] Legal Aid (Scotland) Act 1986, s. 25(2).

courtroom and spoke to a co-accused. The trial judge exercised his discretion to permit the witness to give evidence,[81] and after his conviction Boner sought to have this discretion reviewed on appeal. In the second case, Maxwell's appeal concerned instructions to his representatives and the reliability and sufficiency of evidence. In neither instance had counsel concluded that there was any reasonable prospect of success and thus neither appellant had been legally represented. The Strasbourg Court found a breach of Article 6(3)(c) in both applications. Of significant importance was the severity of the penalty imposed (eight years' and five years' imprisonment respectively) and "the limited capacity of an unrepresented appellant to present a legal argument": these factors led the Court to consider that the interests of justice did indeed require the provision of legal aid.[82]

The choice facing the British Government in deciding how to deal with the *Boner* and *Maxwell* judgments was straightforward: either it could take steps to ensure that legal aid would be awarded to any person sentenced to a substantial period of imprisonment who sought to challenge the conviction by producing some argument, however spurious, or it could seek to limit the traditionally wide right of access to the criminal appeal court. Reflection would have suggested that any adverse decision in Strasbourg could have led only to the latter response as a matter of practical politics. In any case, the open door policy of the High Court of Justiciary in appeal matters relied to a large extent—as the Court at least noted—upon the rule which provides that "counsel cannot properly occupy the time of the court in advancing arguments which he knows to be without foundation".[83] The judgments did not address this central issue. Nor did they recognise the Crown's more neutral (as opposed to adversarial) role as representative of the public interest at appeal stage. Article 6 jurisprudence places greater emphasis upon "equality of arms" than upon the (logically prior) issue of access to a court, which was the emphasis found in Scots law.[84] The *Granger* solution provided a compromise which maintained ready court access supported by measures to ensure this was effective whenever a genuine concern was identified. The "open door" right of appeal in criminal cases has now been closed: leave to appeal in such instances is required[85] which, if granted, will bring with it free representation.

Prisoners' Rights

Not surprisingly, substantial numbers of applications to Strasbourg are made by persons deprived of their liberty and who seek to have the justification for detention or its continuation scrutinised. Article 5 in particular provides tests of the lawfulness of deprivation of liberty and associated procedural safeguards, and two applications have permitted the Commission to consider Scottish procedures. In *Gordon v. United*

[81] In terms of the Criminal Procedure (Scotland) Act 1975, s. 140.
[82] *Boner* case, above, paras 40–44; *Maxwell* case, above, paras 37–41.
[83] *Boner* case, above, para. 23; *Maxwell* case, above, para. 20.
[84] The concurring opinion of the British judge, Sir John Freeland, further confuses the issues by seeming to read the text's reference to "interests of justice" as if this were to be interpreted as "appearance of injustice".
[85] By virtue of the Criminal Procedure (Scotland) Act 1995, s. 42.

Kingdom[86] an individual confined to a mental hospital by a criminal court[87] challenged his return to a secure hospital after having spent a period in an ordinary mental hospital with leave privileges. Scots law did not make provision for periodic review of the need for continuing detention at the time when the application was made, a deficiency which had been condemned by the Court when it considered similar English legislation as failing to meet the requirements of Article 5(4).[88] Accordingly, the Commission applied the Court's decision, but since Scots law had been subsequently amended[89] to meet the problem, the Committee of Ministers resolved that no further action was required.[90] *Nelson v. United Kingdom*[91] sought to challenge differences between Scots and English law in the release of prisoners who had been sentenced as minors. Scots law did not provide remission of sentence (as distinct from parole or release on licence) for juvenile offenders, and Nelson claimed this was a form of discrimination prohibited by Article 14 since there was no objective or reasonable justification for such distinctions in the domestic laws of the United Kingdom. The Commission considered the application manifestly ill-founded since the Convention did not confer a general right to question the length of any sentence, although, if any aspect of sentencing policy did appear to affect individuals in a discriminatory way, there could well be an issue under Article 5 taken with Article 14. Distinctions in sentencing policy based upon age reflected the state's need to ensure flexibility in treatment, while differences between the "penal legislation of two regional jurisdictions" were not related to personal status.

Persons deprived of their liberty have also attempted to rely upon other guarantees contained in the Convention.[92] In particular, Article 8's protection of privacy and family life has been interpreted as implying that authorities must assist prisoners in maintaining effective contact with their close relatives and friends, but always having regard to the "ordinary and reasonable requirements of imprisonment and to the resultant degree of discretion" which must be accorded the national authorities in regulating contact.[93] This is illustrated by an application such as *Ballantyne v. United Kingdom*.[94] The applicant complained that the decision to house him in penal establishments several hundred miles away from where his family lived rather than in local prisons breached state obligations to respect family life, but the Commission in holding the application inadmissible noted that the Convention could not be interpreted as conferring a general right on prisoners to choose the place of their detention, and in

---

[86] Application No. 10213/82, report of October 9, 1985, 47 DR 36.
[87] In terms of the Mental Health (Scotland) Act 1960, ss 55 and 60.
[88] In the case of *X v. United Kingdom*, judgment of November 5, 1981, Series A, No. 46; (1982) 4 EHRR 188.
[89] By the Mental Health (Amendment) (Scotland) Act 1983, s. 21.
[90] Resolution DH (86) 9.
[91] Application No. 11077/84, Ocotber 13, 1986, 49 DR 170.
[92] See, further, J. Murdoch, "The Work of the Council of Europe's Torture Committee" (1994) 5 E.J.I.L. 220 at 231. In Application No. 10239/83, *Wardlaw v. United Kingdom*, report of April 11, 1989, 60 DR 71, the Commission struck off its list for want of interest on the part of the applicant under rules 44 and 49 of its Rules of Procedure an application made by a prisoner who had been detained in the segregation unit at Inverness Prison and who had claimed the detention conditions were in violation of Article 3's prohibition of inhuman or degrading treatment.
[93] *Boyle and Rice* case, Series A, No. 131, para. 74; (1988) 10 EHRR 425.
[94] Application No. 14462/88, April 12, 1991 (unreported).

any case the applicant's move to prisons offering more secure regimes was as a consequence of his own behaviour.

Violations of Article 8 have been established in a series of cases concerning the censorship of mail and have led to the progressive narrowing of the ability of authorities to interfere with prisoners' correspondence to the extent necessary to meet state interests.[95] Several of these applications have come from Scotland. *McComb v. United Kingdom*[96] led to a friendly settlement with the Government's introduction of new standing orders narrowing the power of the authorities to censor correspondence with a legal adviser.[97] In *Boyle and Rice*,[98] complaints concerned restrictions on communications by letter and on visiting and special leave entitlement. The Court ruled that the censorship of a letter as "objectionable matter" since it was intended for publication or for use in a broadcast[99] was a violation of Article 8[1] but found no other violation of the Convention to have taken place.[2] In the *McCallum* case,[3] again restrictions on a prisoners' correspondence[4] were challenged. The letters which were stopped were variously intended for the applicant's solicitor, his Member of Parliament, a journalist, an academic, and a public prosecutor. As in the *Boyle and Rice* case, the Government once more conceded that these interferences constituted breaches of Article 8. In the most recent of these cases, *Campbell v. United Kingdom*,[5] correspondence between the applicant and his solicitor relating to various civil and criminal matters, an application under the Convention and correspondence directly with the Commission had been subjected to interference by the prison authorities under standing instructions issued by the Secretary of State.[6] In this instance, however, the Government contested the application claiming that the only way to establish whether correspondence con-

---

[95] In particular, in the *Golder* case (1975), Series A, No. 18; (1979–80) 1 EHRR 524; *Silver and Others* case, Series A, No. 61; (1983) 5 EHRR 347; *Campbell & Fell* case, Series A, No. 80; (1985) 7 EHRR 165; *Boyle and Rice* case, Series A, No. 131; (1988) 10 EHRR 425; *Schönenberger and Durmaz* case, Series A, No. 137; (1989) 11 EHRR 202; *McCallum* case, Series A, No. 183; (1991) 13 EHRR 596; *Campbell* case, Series A, No. 233; (1993) 15 EHRR 137. *Cf. T v. United Kingdom* (1986) 49 DR 5 (blanket prohibition on communication of artistic or scientific material not justified).

[96] Application No. 10621/83, report of May 15, 1986, 50 DR 81.

[97] Standing Order Ma8, discussed in *Campbell* case, above, at para. 23.

[98] Judgment of April 27, 1988, Series A, No. 131.

[99] Under Rule 74(4) of the Prison (Scotland) Rules 1952 (S.I. 1952 No. 565) and Standing Order Ic.2(3), made by the Secretary of State.

[1] The British Government also accepted this, and asked the Court to rule accordingly: *Boyle and Rice* case, above, para. 48.

[2] *cf. X v. United Kingdom* (1982) 30 DR 113 (restrictions on visits with persons campaigning about prison medical treatment did not violate Art. 8); Application No. 14452/88 v. *United Kingdom*, April 12, 1991 (refusal to transfer disruptive prisoner to institution closer to home of elderly mother was not a violation of Art. 8; separation from family is an inevitable consequence of imprisonment).

[3] Judgment of August 30, 1990, Series A, No. 183; (1991) 13 EHRR 596.

[4] In terms of Standing Order Ic. 3 and 4, made by the Secretary of State.

[5] Judgment of March 25, 1992, Series A, No. 233-A; (1993) 15 EHRR 137.

[6] During the course of the application proceedings, changes in Standing Orders introduced after the *McComb* friendly settlement noted above had been introduced by which correspondence relating to Commission proceedings was only to be read if the Governor had reason to believe that the correspondence contained prohibited or other material in addition, but it was established that some of the letters to the Commission had been opened: para. 16. By the time of the Court's judgment, rule 74 of the Prison (Scotland) Rules 1952, which provides for the reading of letters to and from a prisoner, had been upheld in the case of *Leech v. Secretary of State for Scotland*, discussed above.

tained prohibited material was to read the letters, and that in any case state authorities enjoyed a wide margin of appreciation in this sphere. The Court by eight votes to one (with the British judge dissenting) considered that while the interference was for the legitimate state aim of preventing disorder or crime, the necessity of doing so "in a democratic society" had not been established. Although some measure of control over correspondence was compatible with the Convention, "the fact that the opportunity to write and to receive letters is sometimes the prisoner's only link to the outside world" should not be overlooked, especially since the general interest required consultations with a lawyer to be under circumstances "which favour full and uninhibited discussion". Only when state authorities had reasonable cause to believe a letter "contains an illicit enclosure which the normal means of detection have failed to disclose" should a letter be opened—but not read—and with the provision of "suitable guarantees" such as opening the letter in the presence of the prisoner.[7] The *Campbell* case goes much further than other cases and may well mark the maximum advance of the Court in this area, at least as far as communication with legal advisers is concerned. The decision has resulted in further changes to prison standing orders.[8]

Parental Rights, Juvenile Justice and Educational Provision

Determination of human rights issues involves balancing individual rights with the collective good, but education and juvenile care cases can involve more complex triangular conflicts in resolving the proper weight to be given to the interests of the child, parents and the state respectively. In turn, domestic resolutions of such issues as detention of a child for educational purposes or for the protection of his or her physical or moral health are subject to Convention supervision. In Scotland, the particular questions which have resulted in challenges in Strasbourg have concerned juvenile justice and parental interests in educational practices, matters which have both resulted in international criticism.

For over a quarter of a century, the Scottish system of children's hearings has attempted to place primary emphasis upon ascertaining the best interests of the child in juvenile justice and care proceedings cases. The premise is that specially-trained lay persons are better placed than a court to determine these interests, but in the *McMichael* case[9] the extent to which this welfare-oriented approach was compatible with a human rights one—in essence, whether it met the requirements of fair procedures and gave due respect to family life—called for examination. An infant was made subject to compulsory measures of care since it was considered that lack of parental care was "likely to cause him unnecessary suffering or seriously to impair his health or development".[10] The children's hearing in taking the decision, and the sheriff court in subsequently reviewing the disposal, had sight of documents which were withheld from the parents although the substance of their contents had been disclosed. The child was ultimately adopted by foster parents, but only after a court had decided to

---

[7] *Campbell* case, above, paras 42–48.
[8] *Hansard*, H.C. Vol. 234, cols 959–962.
[9] Judgment of February 24, 1995, Series A, No. 307-B.
[10] In terms of the Social Work (Scotland) Act 1968, s. 32(c).

dispense with the necessity of obtaining the consent of the natural parents.[11] The first issue under the Convention concerned the inability of the parents to consider the reports. The Court considered that there had been a violation of Article 6(1)'s guarantee of a fair hearing by an independent tribunal in the determination of the mother's civil rights and obligations, but not as regards the father's rights since he had not taken the required steps in Scots law to acquire parental rights. The Court also found there had been a violation of the rights of both parents (since father and mother were living together as a family unit) under Article 8's guarantees of respect for private and family rights because the decision-making process leading to interference with the "mutual enjoyment by parent and child of each other's company" had not been fair.[12] The decision has led to a review of the procedures of children's hearings,[13] but early indications suggest that the practical effect has been to reduce the amount of relevant information made available to members of the hearing, rather than to increase parental access to documentation. Sensitive or confidential reports are now more likely to be withheld by the Reporter, with the almost certain result that hearings will now find it more difficult to discharge their duty to determine what is in the best interests of the individual child. The pursuit of procedural justice—as perhaps with the *Boner* and *Maxwell* decisions discussed above—has resulted in an outcome which is only superficially attractive in favouring means rather than ends.

Other Scottish applications have concerned the extent of the guarantees provided by Article 1 of Protocol No. 2, which contains two separate provisions: first, protection against deprivation of "the right to education" and, second, recognition of the religious and philosophical convictions of parents in state provision of educational functions. This second duty applies to matters such as the organisation and financing of education as well as actual instruction,[14] but in Britain's case is subject to a reservation.[15] In *X and Y v. United Kingdom*,[16] the applicants sent their three children to a Rudolf Steiner school which provided education in accordance with their own views and outlooks based upon the so-called "anthroposophical movement". The complaint of the parents concerned the lack of state funding for the school. This was rejected by the Commission as manifestly ill-founded (even without need to consider the reservation) since the Article could not be interpreted as obliging the state to establish or support any educational establishment serving any particular set of religious beliefs or convictions, and in any case the state had indeed shown "respect" by granting the

---

[11] In terms of the Adoption (Scotland) Act 1978, s. 16(2).

[12] *McMichael v. United Kingdom*, above, at paras 76–93.

[13] *cf. Implementation of the Children (Scotland) Act 1995: Draft Children's Hearings Rules* Docs ICSA(4) and (19), The Scottish Office, 1996. In particular, Draft Rules 6(3)–(5) propose that the Reporter must make available a copy "to each relevant person in relation to the child whose case is being considered" of any document supplied to the members of the children's hearing. This will include the father of the child if living together with the mother of the child "as if they were husband and wife". The Scottish Office is apparently still considering whether such documents should also be made available to the child itself.

[14] *Kjeldsen, Busk Madsen and Pedersen* case, judgment of December 7, 1976, Series A, No. 23, para. 50; (1979–80) 1 EHRR 711.

[15] At the time of ratification of this Protocol, the United Kingdom accepted the principle "only so far as it is compatible with the provision of efficient instruction and training, and the avoidance of unreasonable public expenditure".

[16] Application No. 9461/81, December 7, 1982, 31 DR 210.

school charitable status and extending the assisted places scheme to it. This decision, though, does not perhaps dispose of all issues of state funding of education. The Scottish system of publicly-funded denominational education could well be seen as discriminatory when Article 14 is read alongside Article 2 of Protocol No. 1: while the issue has not been raised, the continuing refusal to accord Moslem parents public-sector denominational schooling in communities in which there is a real demand for this and where similar demands from other faiths are accommodated does arguably give rise to a violation of Convention guarantees.[17]

One particular Scottish case decided by the European Court above all others has made an impact upon the popular consciousness and upon educational provision throughout the United Kingdom. *Campbell and Cosans*[18] successfully challenged the long-established practice of inflicting corporal punishment upon school pupils, a practice sanctioned by the common law, which conferred immunity upon teachers from prosecution or civil action for assault providing the chastisement was moderate and inflicted for a proper purpose.[19] Despite agreement in principle being reached with the teaching profession to eliminate the punishment over a period of time, it was a standard and frequently-used (and abused) disciplinary device in the vast majority of schools, and apparently generally supported by teachers, by parents and even by pupils.[20] Mrs Campbell had sought unsuccessfully an assurance from the educational authority that her son would not be subject to beatings; Mrs Cosans' son was told that he was to be given corporal punishment for taking a short-cut home, had refused the punishment on his father's advice and had subsequently been suspended from school until he had indicated he was prepared to be punished. Both parents alleged violations of Article 3, which prohibits inhuman or degrading treatment or punishment and also of Article 2 of Protocol No. 1. Since in neither instance had the pupils in fact been subjected to corporal punishment the Court considered Article 3 was irrelevant. The Court did accept that the "mere threat" of a beating could constitute a violation "provided it is sufficiently real and immediate", but here the apprehension felt by the son of the second applicant had not reached the minimum level of severity required to trigger a violation of the Article.[21] However, both applicants were found to have been victims of a violation of the second sentence of Article 2 of Protocol No. 1.[22] The Court considered that since corporal punishment was apparently used in the "development and moulding of the character and mental powers" of pupils, there was a duty upon the state to take into account any expressed wishes of parents on such matters. A state could not hide behind the common law, which conferred disciplinary powers directly upon teachers, since the state had assumed a general responsibil-

---

[17] *cf.* J. L. Murdoch, "Religion, Education and the Law" (1989) 34 J.L.S.S. 258 at 261.

[18] Judgment of February 25, 1982, Series A, No. 48; (1982) 4 EHRR 293.

[19] *cf.* A. F. Phillips, "Teachers, Corporal Punishment and the Criminal Law" [1992] J.R. 3.

[20] *Campbell and Cosans v. United Kingdom*, above, para. 18.

[21] *ibid.* paras 25–26 and 30.

[22] In addition, the Court found that the son of the second applicant was also a victim of a violation of the first sentence of the Article in that his right to education had been denied when he was forbidden to attend school by reason of his parents' refusal to accept the infliction of corporal punishment in any future instance: *ibid.* paras 39–41. The British judge dissented in this opinion.

ity for shaping educational policy.[23] Subsequent applications led to a spate of friendly settlements in which the British Government made payments for the actual infliction of corporal punishment or for suspensions for refusal to accept the punishment,[24] but only in those instances where parental opposition to corporal punishment had been drawn to the attention of educational authorities. Where this had not occurred—as in *X, Y and Z v. United Kingdom*[25]—there was no corresponding breach of the Article. Despite uncertainties as to whether actual infliction of corporal punishment could also violate Article 3 and, if so, whether national authorities were also liable for infliction of corporal punishment in private schools,[26] this form of discipline rapidly began disappearing from both state and independent schools largely on account of practical difficulties in implementing a "two-tier" disciplinary system in classrooms.[27]

Property Rights

Article 1 of Protocol No. 1 guarantees a general right to peaceful enjoyment of property and prohibits state deprivation of possessions except where justified in the public interest, while at the same time recognising state interests in regulating the use of property in the general interest.[28] The Article is often invoked in conjunction with Article 6, which guarantees a fair hearing in the determination of civil rights, since interference with property rights invariably also raises issues under this heading.[29] In the *Lithgow and Others* case[30] state nationalisation of shipbuilding and aircraft concerns on the Clyde and elsewhere in Britain[31] was challenged by eight individuals and companies principally upon the issue of calculation of the compensation which fell to be paid. The Court held that a right to compensation was implied by the Article, but did not accept that any scheme adopted must meet the full market cost of any property affected since state interests in achieving social justice or economic reform had also to be taken into account. Further, the type of consideration behind a decision to nationalise an undertaking was such that a wide "margin of appreciation" had to be accorded state authorities, which could be challenged only if "manifestly without

---

[23] *ibid.* paras 33–34.

[24] *e.g.* Application No. 9114/80, *Durairaj v. United Kingdom*, report of July 16, 1987, 52 DR 13; and Application No. 10592/83, *A v. United Kingdom*, report of July 16, 1987, 52 DR 150.

[25] Application No. 8566/79, October 13, 1982, 31 DR 50 (parents had advised 15-year-old pupil in Tayside not to accept corporal punishment only if "unjustified", and views not brought to the attention of the authorities).

[26] *cf. Costello-Roberts* case, judgment of March 23, 1993, Series A, No. 247-C; (1995) 19 EHRR 112 (corporal punishment of seven-year-old boy in English private boarding school did not meet the minimum threshold of severity under Article 3, but state functions assumed in relation to supervision, etc. of private schools brought them within ambit of Convention guarantees).

[27] The infliction of corporal punishment was prohibited in state schools and in relation to "assisted places" pupils in independent establishments by the Education (Scotland) Act 1980, s. 48A, inserted by the Education Act 1986.

[28] *Sporrong and Lönnroth v. Sweden*, judgment of September 23, 1982, Series A, No. 52, para. 61; (1983) 5 EHRR 35.

[29] *ibid.* para 79; *cf.* L. Sermet, *The European Convention on Human Rights and Property Rights*, Human Rights Files No. 11, Council of Europe (1992).

[30] Judgment of July 8, 1986, Series A, No. 102; (1986) 8 EHRR 329.

[31] In terms of the Aircraft and Shipbuilding Industries Act 1977.

reasonable foundation".[32] In this respect this case[33] has raised issues beyond Scots domestic law in ruling that the Article confers a general right to reasonable compensation.

The Scottish Legal System and the Strasbourg Machinery

In Scotland, then, the Convention has proved to be at most a device which may assist in ascertaining the reasonableness or otherwise of executive action in judicial review cases, but only where submissions to this effect are advanced by counsel and where the particular judge is prepared to accept such arguments. Other uses—in interpreting statutory ambiguities or in helping develop the common law—were ruled out by *Kaur* and *Moore*. While the failure to incorporate the treaty into Scots law means that individuals who claim that rights under the Convention have been infringed must turn to Strasbourg for assistance, the number of applications from Scotland still remains comparatively low; but since legal rules and administrative practices often replicate those found south of the border, it is unlikely that this can be explained by a greater compatibility of Scots law with treaty guarantees. The temptation is to suggest that Scots lawyers do not use the Convention since they have little understanding of it. Only a handful of Scottish solicitors[34] and even fewer advocates[35] have had any direct experience of Convention matters. Other aspects of law and practice peculiar to Scotland await identification as potential violations of European norms. This reluctance to use the Convention in applications to the Commission is attributable to the failure of domestic courts to remove the barriers provided by *Kaur* and *Moore*. If awareness is to be raised, the Convention has to be seen as of relevance both in Scots law as well as in international law.

Reversing domestic case law and thereby generating domestic interest in the Convention appears to have been an ambition of Lord Hope while Lord President of the Court of Session. His efforts to reverse *Kaur* appear to have started in 1991. In the context of a review article, he criticised the "too-ready assumption" that the English approach of allowing the Convention's use as an aid to interpretation of statute had been rejected by Lord Ross since "the proper view would seem to be that the views [of Lord Ross in Scotland, and Lord Denning in the English courts] are consistent with each other and that there is in fact no difference in approach between the Scottish and English courts".[36] But this was precisely what Lord Ross had indeed ruled out in

---

[32] *Lithgow and Others* case, above, paras 120–122. Nor was any breach of Article 6 established in any of the various applications.

[33] The case is hardly a distinctly Scottish case: two of the applicants were Scots, one was French, and the remainder were companies registered either in Scotland or in England.

[34] Solicitors appear to have been involved in over 60 per cent of the applications from Scotland, a percentage which is in line with applications from other jurisdictions. However, closer examination of these applications indicates that a large proportion has involved the same handful of firms.

[35] Applicants in two of the earliest Court hearings instructed English counsel: *i.e.* in *Lithgow and Others* (although one of the applicants was represented by Scottish counsel) and *Boyle and Rice*. Senior counsel addressed the Court on behalf of the applicants in *Campbell and Cosans* and in *Boner*, and junior counsel appeared in *McCallum*. Solicitors addressed the Court in *Granger*, *Campbell* and *McMichael*.

[36] [1991] J.R. 122 at 126–127 (review of Stair Memorial Encyclopaedia chapter on public international law).

unambiguous language: that on constitutional grounds it would be inappropriate to make use of the treaty "at all".[37] The following year in an address, Lord Hope warned of the "danger of isolation by unfamiliarity" with European law. In discussing the problems Scots lawyers have in gaining an understanding of both Community and Convention law (difficulties "accentuated by the fact that we in the United Kingdom appoint our judges relatively late in the course of their working lives"), he concluded that the remedy lay in self-education: Scots lawyers must become familiar with Community and Convention concepts "by reading, by attending legal education courses and conferences or by any other appropriate methods". Certainly, "access to the relevant case law and other working materials on these subjects is extremely difficult for the judges, as it is indeed for most practitioners". But more crucial is a practical (and self-imposed) obstacle:

> "On [matters of European law] the judges are especially dependent upon the researches of counsel. This is true both north and south of the border—it is not, I must emphasise, a peculiarly Scottish problem. I have heard it said that English judges are reluctant to explore the significance of the developing jurisdiction under the Convention and that, this being known, it has its effect on counsel who do not wish to spend days researching into a topic on which the judge is likely to cut them short. As a result the judges have not had the jurisprudence cited to them, and it has not found its way into their judgments."[38]

Here lay the essence of the matter. What Lord Hope identified was that Scots lawyers would be unlikely to seek to gain awareness of the Convention until it was perceived as relevant: that is, until the two watchdogs of *Kaur* and *Moore* were somehow pensioned-off. This "catch-22" arose through the accepted wisdom that attempts at persuading the courts to use the Convention were likely to be futile (*Budh Singh* notwithstanding). Without judicial reversal of existing case law, the Convention would continue to be ignored; but without the opportunities arising during court pleadings to urge reversal, the Court of Session would be unable to review its earlier decisions.

T, Petitioner

The 1996 case of *T, Petitioner*[39] was likely to be a rare opportunity to urge reversal of *Kaur* and one which most certainly would have been Lord Hope's last as Lord President. From a human rights standpoint, *Kaur* is a principled judgment which results in an unfavourable outcome; *T, Petitioner* on the other hand is (on this point) a poorly reasoned opinion but which may open the door to the Convention's entry into Scots law. The case raised the question whether there was any objection in Scots

---

[37] See above, pp. 116–117.
[38] *From Maastricht to the Saltmarket*, Society of Solicitors in the Supreme Courts of Scotland, Biennial Lecture 1992, pp. 16–17.
[39] 1997 S.L.T. 724, GWD 28-1653. Discussed by A. Brown in "The European Convention on Human Rights in Scottish Courts", 1996 S.L.T. (News) 267–270, and A. Grotian in "The European Convention—A Scottish Perspective" [1996] 1 E.H.R.L.R. 511 at 521–522.

law to the adoption of a young boy by a homosexual man who lived with his male partner. While the decision ultimately turned on issues of Scots private law, the Lord President (who by the time of the decision was known to be likely to be leaving the Court of Session to move to the House of Lords) reaffirmed his stance that Scots law could not continue to hold its isolated position in refusing to allow the use of the Convention as an aid to statutory interpretation. The petitioner himself had not sought to raise any issue of international law: it was indeed the *amicus curiae* in the case who in written submissions had noted that no conflict with the Convention would arise were the Scottish courts in interpreting domestic legislation to hold that the application to adopt the child fell outwith the true meaning of the statute.[40] This intervention provided Lord Hope with his opportunity. As in *Kaur*, so too is discussion in the judgment of the Convention's place in domestic law strictly *obiter*. But instead of examining the foundations of *Kaur*, the Lord President's approach relies more upon the winds of change than the even keel of constitutional principle. For Lord Hope, *Kaur* "has been looking increasingly outdated in the light of subsequent developments". In his opinion, "with respect, it is time that it was expressly departed from":

"It is now clearly established as part of the law of England and Wales, as a result of decisions in the House of Lords, that in construing any provision in domestic legislation which is ambiguous . . . the courts will presume that Parliament intended to legislate in conformity with the Convention, not in conflict with it. . . . [It is also] now an integral part of the general principles of European Community law that fundamental human rights must be protected, and that one of the sources to which regard may be made for an expression of these rights is international treaties for the protection of human rights on which Member States have collaborated or of which they are signatories. . . . I consider that the drawing of a distinction between the law of Scotland and that of the rest of the United Kingdom on this matter can no longer be justified. In my opinion the courts in Scotland should apply the same presumption as that described by Lord Bridge [in *R v. Home Secretary, ex p. Brind*[41]], namely that, when legislation is found to be ambiguous in the sense that it is capable of a meaning which either conforms to or conflicts with the Convention, Parliament is presumed to have legislated in conformity with the Convention, not in conflict with it."[42]

Public policy and the dictates of European Union law are thus the motives for a change of direction. Scots law must realign itself with the approach adopted elsewhere in the United Kingdom; and membership of the E.U. has brought with it respect for Convention guarantees. Neither justification is perhaps entirely satisfactory. Certainly, if both the English and the Northern Irish judiciary have embarked upon a policy of using the Convention as an aid to the construction of statutes,[43] there may be good reason for the Scottish courts to follow this line in order to minimise differences in

---

[40] In terms of decisions of the Commission such as Application No. 15666/89, *Kerkhoven, Hinke & Hinke v. the Netherlands*, May 19, 1992.
[41] [1991] A.C. 696 at 747–748.
[42] *T, Petitioner*, above, at 733L–734C.
[43] See Chapter 5.

the interpretation of public rights,[44] but this reflects merely the interest of convenience rather than the constitutional propriety that Lord Ross so strongly emphasised. Even if assimilation were an acceptable ground for reversal of *Kaur*, reference to dicta of the House of Lords in *Lord Advocate v. Scotsman Publications*[45] could have strengthened the argument.[46] And the assertion that the European Communities Act 1972 has resulted in the effective incorporation of the Convention into domestic law on account of the European Court of Justice's acceptance of respect for human rights as part of the general principles of Community law raises additional issues which were not addressed concerning the extent of the mutual recognition by the two European Courts of each's jurisdiction and sphere of interests.[47] Neither justification is entirely satisfactory; and the constitutional doubts voiced by Lord Ross are left unanswered.

Tackling these constitutional questions directly could have assisted in understanding why the approach adopted by English law was worthy of emulation and why Scots law reflected the very lack of awareness or understanding of the nature of the Convention highlighted by Lord Hope in his 1992 address. *Kaur* proceeds upon the assumption that any use of the treaty not authorised by statute would contradict legislative supremacy and implicitly confer law-making powers on the executive, and thus this absence of standing as a formal legal source of rights in domestic law means the Convention cannot be used by the judiciary as a source or restatement of public policy in helping interpret ambiguous statutes or in developing the common law. Until Parliament enacts the Convention it is clearly not part of domestic law; but this by no means further implies its very existence is irrelevant. There is a crucial distinction between treating the Convention as a source of *law* and one of *public policy*. This seems to have been missed by Lord Ross. *Kaur* denies that judges take into account propositions of social, commercial and public morality and experience in the process of judicial reasoning as "law-makers" by suggesting the judge's role is confined to that of "law-finder" through the consideration of legal sources alone.[48] Judicial activism is restrained in any case by generally accepted principles. In matters of statutory interpretation, Parliament is supreme, and its statutes must be followed even if in clear conflict with international law;[49] likewise, "where the meaning of the statutory words is plain and unambiguous, it is not for the judges to invent fancied ambiguities as an excuse for failing to give effect to its plain meaning because they themselves consider that the consequences of doing so would be inexpedient, or even unjust or immoral".[50] However, in cases of clear and genuine ambiguity courts may properly proceed upon the basis that Parliament did not intend to have acted contrary to international law, an

---

[44] *cf. Lord Advocate v. Dumbarton District Council*, 1990 S.L.T. 158, *per* Lord Keith at 163: "There would appear to be no rational grounds on which a different approach to the construction of a statute [which applies to the whole of the United Kingdom] might be adopted for the purpose of ascertaining whether or not the Crown is bound by it according to the jurisdiction where the matter is being considered."

[45] 1989 S.C. 122, H.L. This case is briefly discussed above at p. 118.

[46] A. Brown, "The European Convention on Human Rights in Scottish Courts", 1996 S.L.T. (News) 267 at 268.

[47] *cf.* Brown, *ibid.*, at 269.

[48] See, further, M. Eisenberg, *Theory of Adjudication* (1990); R. Dworkin, *Taking Rights Seriously* (1977), Chap. 4, and *Law's Empire* (1986).

[49] *Mortensen v. Peters* (1906) 8 F. 93; *Salomon v. Commissioners of Customs & Excise* [1967] 2 Q.B. 116.

[50] *Duport Steels v. Sirs* [1980] 1 All E.R. 529, *per* Lord Diplock at 541.

approach which is based upon a more realistic view of the legislative process in which constitutional theory presupposing a strict separation of powers between executive and legislature as adopted by Lord Ross is displaced by recognition of the key role of the executive in drafting and ensuring legislative passage of Government proposals. Thus on one occasion when the question arose whether a statute could be applied retrospectively, Lord Reid remarked that "[i]t is hardly credible that any Governmental department would promote or that Parliament would pass retroactive criminal legislation" in view of Article 7 of the European Convention on Human Rights.[51] While there is continuing academic debate on statutory interpretation,[52] there seems no compelling constitutional reason for rejecting this approach.

The widened use of the Convention urged by Lord Hope in *T, Petitioner* appears limited to statutory interpretation.[53] The effect of *Kaur* on the treaty's possible use in the development of the common law was left untouched, but here too Lord Ross's approach requires discussion. The common law is generally accepted to be shaped by perceived notions of constitutional morality and propriety, theories of democracy, and presumptions against retroactive lawmaking.[54] Recourse to an external body of principle such as the Convention could indeed be seen to restrict judicial discretion and to strengthen the appearance of judicial impartiality by stressing the minimalist's view of the judicial function as that of "the disinterested application of known law",[55] since the treaty is essentially a collection of values which infuse the common law. The drafters were concerned to ensure that the Convention was to contain only those particular substantive and procedural rights recognised by long usage in developed Western legal systems, and hence the lengthy initial consideration given to whether there should be included such matters as the rights to marry and found a family (which eventually were included in the Convention) and such rights as the peaceful enjoyment of property and of parents to have their wishes taken into account in the education of their children (two matters which were not contained in the original Convention, but which later were to form the basis of Protocol No. 1).[56] The substance of Convention guarantees thus contains values which are commonplace: equality before the law, fair hearings, impartiality of judges, no retroactive lawmaking, protection against discrimination and against wrongful deprival of liberty, recognition of the concept of marriage, freedom of conscience and respect for privacy and belief, and protection of property rights. Such ideas have been articulated and developed by the judiciary long before the Convention's ratification. Use of the Convention to help shape the common law is indeed supported by a fundamental principle of the legal system that "[e]quity

---

[51] *R v. Miah* [1974] 2 All E.R. 377 at 379.

[52] *cf.* D. R. Miers and A. C. Page, *Legislation* (2nd ed., 1990), pp. 163–191.

[53] A. Brown, above, at 269.

[54] *cf.* G. H. Gordon, *Criminal Law* (2nd ed., 1978), pp. 23–43, where the author discusses the declaratory power of the High Court; K. Greenawalt, "Discretion and Judicial Decision: The Elusive Quest for the Fetters that Bind Judges" (1975) 75 Colum.L.Rev. 359; and "The Enduring Significance of Neutral Principles" (1978) 78 Colum.L.Rev. 982.

[55] *cf.* L. Jaffe, *English and American Judges as Law Makers* (1969), quoted with approval by Lord Devlin, *The Judge* (1980), pp. 2–3. J. A. Griffith in *The Politics of the Judiciary* (3rd ed., 1985) at 225–226 denies that the judiciary can be a "neutral arbitral force" since it is part of the "machinery of authority" of the state which determines questions presented as "public interest" issues in an illiberal and conservative way.

[56] See, further, A. H. Robertson and J. G. Merrills, *Human Rights in Europe* (3rd ed., 1993), pp. 10–12.

remains a valid and unexhausted source of Scots law in that it is still open to a court to delimit a rule or principle in the light of what seems consistent with reason and natural justice".[57] The Scottish Law Commission itself has accepted the Convention as a source of public policy which it takes into account in drafting recommendations for law reform, a point noted by Lord Hope in his 1992 address.[58] Further, while any criticism that the text of the Convention was in places so open and uncertain as to be almost devoid of worth[59] was earlier just, by now the jurisprudence of the Commission and Court is sufficiently developed to give real substance to the minimum require-ments of textual guarantees. If such arguments are persuasive, then they should have been employed in *T, Petitioner* to encourage revision of *Kaur* and *Moore* so as to permit use of the Convention also in the development of the common law.

The impact of Lord Hope's *obiter dicta* in *T, Petitioner* will only become clear with the passage of time. Assuming it is not seen so much as a Pandora's box as a lifeline to pull Scots law back into the mainstream current of European human rights protection, the challenge for the Scottish legal system will be a real one. To switch metaphors, the building of a solid bridge between Scotland and Strasbourg to recog-nise this "increasing interdependence" of legal systems requires the triggering of that process of self-education amongst practising lawyers and judges which Lord Hope advocated. Failure to seize the initiative offered will result in a continuing lack of awareness.

The building of this bridge can be assisted in an additional way. The appointment of respected Scots lawyers to the European Court of Justice as Advocates-General or as Judges has allowed the Scottish legal system to have a personal link with Luxem-bourg. Symbolically and functionally this has been important. The practice—perhaps now a convention—of ensuring that at least one of the three British appointments to the courts of the European Union is a Scottish jurist ensures Luxembourg has ready access to expertise in Scots law; and through addresses, articles and papers directed at fellow Scottish lawyers, appointees to Luxembourg can help spread understanding of European Union law. Yet there is no similar practice of ensuring that at least one of the two Strasbourg appointments[60] is a Scottish jurist, and indeed, successive British Governments have failed to nominate even one Scots lawyer for appointment to the European Court of Human Rights.[61] Only one Scot has served (albeit briefly) as a member of the Commission.[62] There is no sense in which Scots law is represented at

---

[57] D. M. Walker, *The Scottish Legal System* (6th ed., 1990), p. 459; *cf.* D. M. Walker, "Equity in Scots Law" (1954) 66 J.R. 103.

[58] *From Maastricht to the Saltmarket*, above, at 15, citing Scottish Law Commission, *Report on Evidence: Report on Documentary Evidence and Proof of Undisputed Facts in Criminal Proceedings* (1992), para. 4.17.

[59] *e.g. Ahmad v. ILEA* [1978] Q.B. 36, *per* Lord Denning at 41: "[Art. 9's guarantees of thought, conscience and religion] are drawn in such vague terms that it can be used for all sorts of unreasonable claims."

[60] While the process of appointing members of the Commission and Judges of the Court appears complex, in practice the first-placed nominee is invariably selected by the Parliamentary Assembly. For appoint-ments to the Commission and the Court, see Articles 21 and 22 and Articles 39 and 40 (as amended by Protocols No. 5 and No. 8).

[61] See Parliamentary Assembly Docs 918 (December 18, 1958); 2063 (April 30, 1966); 3388 (January 16, 1974); 4604 (September 23, 1980); 4996 (December 3, 1982); 5925 (July 8, 1988); and 6542 (January 10, 1992).

[62] Professor A. E. Anton served for a short period in 1984 before resigning. For declarations of elections of British members, see Committee of Ministers Resolutions (54) 9; (60) 15; (62) 1; (66) 27; (72) 15;

Strasbourg, an issue which is likely to become even more difficult when Protocol No. 11 comes into force and the Commission and Court are combined. The lack of a distinguished Scottish presence has an obverse: on occasion it can result in errors in Strasbourg in disposing of applications raising issues of Scots law. For example, in *Harkin v. United Kingdom*[63] a Northern Irish citizen who had landed at a Scottish port and who was detained under British anti-terrorist legislation claimed that British law did not provide an effective remedy to challenge the legality of detention as called for by Article 5(4). The Commission disposed of this issue by reaffirming an earlier decision[64] that the remedy of habeas corpus was sufficient to meet Convention requirements without realising that this English law remedy is not available in Scots law. More crucially as far as the current discussion is concerned, the lack of a Scottish presence on the Commission or Court hinders propagation of understanding of the Convention within the Scottish legal system. The Scottish legal system has thus failed to be accorded due recognition by the United Kingdom Government in its influencing of judicial appointments.

Conclusion

In the absence of incorporation of the Convention into domestic law, its use by the Scottish courts has been minimal in contrast to the greater willingness in other parts of the United Kingdom and in Ireland to permit its restricted use as a source of public policy in developing the common law and in the interpretation of statutory ambiguity, but always with caution and with an awareness of the proper limit of judicial creativity. A more realistic analysis of the legislative process or a more sophisticated appreciation of the judicial function would overcome constitutional scruples voiced in Scotland as to the danger of introduction of the Convention into legal argument. A fruitful area for the Convention appears to lie in administrative law where more recently a willingness to consider arguments based on the treaty and on its interpretation given by the European Court of Human Rights has been expressed. The opportunity for revision which has arisen in *T, Petitioner* may have been weakened by too hasty dicta which failed to address the fallacies in the *Kaur* judgment. At the root of the issue is a general lack of awareness of Convention matters, perhaps accentuated in Scotland by lack of representation of its legal system in appointments to the Commission and Court, and evidenced by a low level of usage of the Convention by Scots lawyers both in domestic courts and in applications to Strasbourg. Cause and effect are intermingled: the overall result is that the promotion of the effective safeguard of personal liberty and freedom through European norms remains restricted.

(78) 36; (84) 2; (85) 5; and (90) 9. The lists of candidates for appointment to the Commission are held in Committee of Ministers documents which remain confidential for 30 years.
[63] Application No. 11539/85, July 12, 1986, 48 DR 237.
[64] Application Nos 8022/77, 8125/77 and 8027/77, *McVeigh, O'Neill and Evans v. United Kingdom*, report of March 18, 1981, 25 DR 15.

CHAPTER 5

NORTHERN IRELAND AND THE EUROPEAN CONVENTION

Introduction

Although Northern Ireland is a separate part of the United Kingdom, with its own legal system, on many matters its statute law is identical to that of England and Wales and its judges are usually content to follow the decisions of appellate courts there. Northern Ireland has therefore been indirectly affected by the large number of cases successfully taken to Strasbourg against the United Kingdom government by individuals resident in England and Wales, for whenever English law has been changed as a result of such cases the change has invariably filtered through to Northern Ireland too. However, numerous applications have placed the specific laws of Northern Ireland under the European microscope. It is not possible to give the precise number of these applications, since the Secretariat in Strasbourg does not keep statistics on the place of residence of applicants within each member state, but most are connected with the civil unrest prevailing in Northern Ireland since 1968. Various "emergency" laws have been enacted to deal with this unrest, some of them confined to Northern Ireland, others extending throughout the United Kingdom.[1] A few applications to Strasbourg have, on the other hand, challenged the "ordinary" law.

In this chapter a survey is conducted, first, of all the significant cases respecting Northern Ireland that have been heard in Strasbourg whether by the Court or just by the Commission and, second, of all the cases where the Convention has been referred to in Northern Ireland's own courts. Northern Ireland has certainly been a severe testing ground for the Convention, for on many occasions it has raised in a stark form the age-old question of how far human rights can justifiably be limited for the sake of a greater good, in this case the struggle of democracy against terrorism. No other legal jurisdiction within the Council of Europe's domain has caused the commissioners and judges in Strasbourg so much anguish. The efforts of these decision-makers to strike the appropriate balance would need to be carefully examined before any step is taken by the United Kingdom or Ireland to incorporate the European Convention directly into domestic law, for if the Strasbourg jurisprudence is out of line with prevailing judicial and political attitudes in those jurisdictions incorporation could be

---

[1] See C. Warbrick, "The European Convention on Human Rights and the Prevention of Terrorism" (1983) 32 I.C.L.Q. 82.

a recipe for unseemly attempts by Parliament and the judiciary to evade or distort the Convention's requirements. This could occur whether the more liberal stance is that adopted internally or by the Strasbourg organs.

European Court Judgments Concerning Northern Ireland[2]

Seven cases directly concerning Northern Irish law have reached the European Court of Human Rights. Two further cases are indirectly relevant in that they concern incidents occurring elsewhere but arising out of the conflict in Northern Ireland. The present survey, which here is chronological, begins with one of these indirectly relevant cases.

Lawless v. Ireland was in fact the first decision ever rendered by the European Court, on July 1, 1961.[3] Quite apart from the substantive issues at stake it is therefore a significant decision from the procedural point of view, since it deals with matters such as the nature of the Commission's role in proceedings before the Court and the right of lawyers representing an individual applicant to be heard. The connection with Northern Ireland lies in the fact that, from July to December 1957, Mr Lawless had been interned without trial in the Republic of Ireland for allegedly acting on behalf of the Irish Republican Army. He unsuccessfully attempted to seek habeas corpus in the Irish High Court and Supreme Court.[4] The European Court held unanimously (7 votes to 0) that the detention was lawful: although it was in contravention of Articles 5(1)(c) and 5(3) of the Convention,[5] the Republic's derogation notice issued pursuant to Article 15 was a valid excuse for the breach. The Court measured the derogation notice against the requirements of Article 15 and decided (a) that there *was* a "public emergency threatening the life of the nation", (b) that the measures taken *were* "strictly required by the exigencies of the situation", and (c) that there was nothing to show that the measures were "inconsistent with [Ireland's] other obligations under international law". The Court stated that the meaning of the words "public emergency threatening the life of the nation" was clear, namely "an exceptional situation of

---

[2] Some of the material in this section has already appeared under the title "The European Convention on Human Rights and Northern Ireland" in *Présence du Droit Public et des Droits de l'Homme: Mélanges offerts à Jacques Vélu* (1992), pp. 1407–1429. See also C. Gearty, "The Cost of Human Rights: English Judges and the Northern Irish Troubles" (1994) 47 *Current Legal Problems* 19.

[3] Judgments of November 14, 1960, April 7, 1961 and July 1, 1961, Series A, Nos. 1–3, (1979–80) 1 EHRR 1, 4 Ybk of the ECHR 438. The first and second judgments concerned procedural points which need not detain us here. For the Commission's decision on admissibility, see 2 Ybk of the ECHR 308. See M.-A. Eissen [1960] *Annuaire français de droit international* 444; D. J. Harris (1961) 10 I.C.L.Q. 616; D. G. Valentine (1961) 10 I.C.L.Q. 899; P. O'Higgins [1962] C.L.J. 234; A. Robertson [1960] BYBIL 343 and [1961] BYBIL 536. See also Chapter 6 of this book.

[4] *In re O'Laighleis* [1960] I.R. 93.

[5] Art. 5(1)(c) reads: "Everyone has the right to liberty and security of the person. No one shall be deprived of his liberty save in the following cases and in accordance with a procedure prescribed by law ... (c) the lawful arrest or detention of a person effected for the purpose of bringing him before the competent legal authority on reasonable suspicion of having committed an offence." Art. 5(3) reads: "Everyone arrested or detained in accordance with the provisions of paragraph (1)(c) of this Article shall be brought promptly before a judge or other officer authorized by law to exercise judicial power and shall be entitled to trial within a reasonable time or to release pending trial. Release may be conditioned by guarantees to appear for trial."

crisis or emergency which affects the whole population and constitutes a threat to the organised life of the community of which the State is composed."[6] The Irish government had reasonably deduced the presence of such an emergency from a combination of factors:

"in the first place, the existence in the territory of the Republic of Ireland of a secret army engaged in unconstitutional activities and using violence to attain its purposes; secondly, the fact that this army was also operating outside the territory of the State, thus seriously jeopardising the relations of the Republic of Ireland with its neighbour; thirdly, the steady and alarming increase in terrorist activities from the autumn of 1956 and throughout the first half of 1957."[7]

The European Court rejected rather summarily the suggestions that there were other means available to the Irish Government in 1957 for controlling the IRA and its splinter groups, means such as the use of the ordinary criminal law, or of special criminal or military courts, or the sealing of the border between the Republic of Ireland and Northern Ireland.

Whether or not one agrees with the Court's conclusions, it can hardly be denied that the judgment in *Lawless* displays considerable reserve in its analysis of a country's reaction to civil disturbance. As a recent American commentary has put it, in its first foray into adjudicating upon alleged state violations "the Court seemed anxious to reassure its member states that it would be sensitive to their concerns and traditions".[8] The reticence and very format of the judgment are reminiscent of judgments handed down by French domestic courts and perhaps reflect the heavy influence which civil law systems were exercising on the Strasbourg organs during this early period in their history. By the time of the next case concerning Northern Ireland both the Commission and the Court had developed a more independent identity.

This case is *Ireland v. United Kingdom*, still the only interstate application to have reached the European Court.[9] Applications were lodged by the Irish Government in 1971 and 1972, alleging violations of Articles 3, 5, 6, 14 and 15 of the European Convention. The claims were that persons arrested in Northern Ireland under emergency powers had been mistreated, that these powers were themselves inconsistent with the Convention, and that they had been applied in a politically discriminatory fashion. The European Commission examined a range of "representative" cases and declared on January 25, 1976 that the United Kingdom had violated Article 3[10] in

---

[6] (1979–80) 1 EHRR 15 at 31, para. 28.

[7] *ibid.*

[8] M. W. Janis and R. S. Kay, *European Human Rights Law* (1990), p. 95; this statement appears to have been dropped from the second edition of this book: M. W. Janis, R. S. Kay and A. Bradley, *European Human Rights Law: Text and Materials* (1995). For another analysis of the development of the Court's approaches, see P. Mahoney, "Judicial Activism and Judicial Self-Restraint in the European Court of Human Rights: Two Sides of the Same Coin" (1990) 11 HRLJ 57.

[9] Series A, Nos 25, (1979–80) 2 EHRR 25, 15 Ybk of the ECHR 76 (decision on admissibility), 19 Ybk of the ECHR 512 (Commission's Report).

[10] "No one shall be subjected to torture or to inhuman or degrading treatment or punishment."

that it had tortured and inhumanly treated detainees by employing five interrogation techniques (hooding, exposure to noise, deprivation of food and drink, deprivation of sleep and enforced standing against a wall). Surprisingly the United Kingdom did not contest this conclusion, but the European Court insisted on examining the situation for itself and decided on January 18, 1978, by 13 votes to four, that the five techniques did not amount to torture but, by 16 votes to one,[11] that they did amount to a practice of inhuman and degrading treatment. When considering the meaning of such treatment the Court said:

> "As was emphasised by the Commission ill-treatment must attain a minimum level of severity if it is to fall within the scope of Article 3. The assessment of this minimum is, in the nature of things, relative; it depends on all the circumstances of the case, such as the duration of the treatment, its physical or mental effects and, in some cases, the sex, age and state of health of the victim."[12]

The Court unanimously recognised that it could not command the United Kingdom government to take criminal or disciplinary action against the officials who, directly or indirectly, were responsible for the mistreatment. And although it was irrelevant to Article 3—because the rights it enshrines are non-derogable rights[13]—the Court again held that the state's notice of derogation with respect to Article 5 was valid, though one judge did say that the measures taken went beyond what was within the government's margin of appreciation as to what was strictly required and two considered that the emergency arrest powers had been used discriminatorily against Republicans in Northern Ireland.

Ireland v. United Kingdom illustrates how far the European Court had come by the late 1970s in its fact-finding[14] and norm-setting functions, but the Convention's weaknesses on the remedial side are also demonstrated. The British government gave an undertaking that use of the five techniques in question had been discontinued, but no further steps were taken to punish those who had resorted to them in the first place or to indemnify the victims. The Irish government did not ask for any compensation for the individuals who had been subjected to the inhuman treatment, so the Court did not make an award under Article 50 of the Convention.

Something of the same criticism can be levelled against the Convention when we look at the next Northern Irish case to reach the Court, *Dudgeon v. United Kingdom*.[15] This was not a case connected with Northern Ireland's civil unrest, but rather a com-

---

[11] The dissenting voice was that of the United Kingdom judge, Sir Gerald Fitzmaurice, though he did agree, more generally, that in the autumn of 1971 there existed at Palace Barracks in Holywood, County Down, a practice of inhuman treatment: (1979–80) 2 EHRR 25 at 131–137, paras 22–30.

[12] (1979–80) 2 EHRR 25 at 79, para. 162.

[13] Art. 15(2).

[14] For security reasons certain evidence was collected at hearings in Norway. See generally K. Boyle and H. Hannum, "Ireland in Strasbourg: An Analysis of the Northern Irish Proceedings before the European Commission of Human Rights" (1972) 7 Ir. Jur. 330; K. Boyle and H. Hannum, "Ireland in Strasbourg: Final Decisions in the Northern Irish Proceedings before the European Commission of Human Rights" (1976) 11 Ir. Jur. 243.

[15] Judgment of October 22, 1981, Series A, No. 45, (1982) 4 EHRR 149. For the decision of the Commission, see (1981) 3 EHRR 40. *Cf. Norris v. Ireland*, judgment of October 26, 1988, Series A, No. 142, (1991) 13 EHRR 186, where the same Victorian legislation was in question.

plaint that the law on male homosexuality in Northern Ireland (which had not been liberalised at the same time as the law in England and Wales in 1967 and therefore still prohibited homosexual intercourse even between consenting males over 21[16]) was in contravention of Article 8 of the Convention (guaranteeing the right to a private life). In January 1976 Mr Dudgeon had been extensively questioned about his sexual activities while in police custody on a drugs charge. Although he was eventually informed, in February 1977, that he was not to be prosecuted for breaking the laws on homosexuality, he proceeded with an application lodged with the European Commission in May 1976. Besides relying on Article 8, he argued that Article 14 had been violated in that he was being treated differently from homosexuals in other parts of the United Kingdom and from both female homosexuals and all heterosexuals in Northern Ireland.

The European Court, agreeing with the Commission, held by 15 votes to four that Article 8 had been violated by the very existence of the repressive legislation in Northern Ireland, quite apart from whether or not it was applied in practice. For once, in a sense, the Court dealt with an issue *in abstracto*. It did not matter that Mr Dudgeon had not himself been victimised through being prosecuted. The majority of the judges also held, unfortunately, that it was unnecessary to decide the claim under Article 14, thereby leaving it uncertain whether differential treatment under the law within one member state of the Council of Europe can ever be a legitimate ground for complaint under any of the Convention's provisions. Perhaps the judgment's main significance lies in its refusal to allow the United Kingdom government to shelter behind the fact that majority public opinion in Northern Ireland was apparently against a liberalisation of the homosexuality laws: a draft reforming measure had been published in July 1978 but was withdrawn a year later because of widespread public disapproval. It seems, therefore, that in a matter of private morality the Court is prepared to grant less scope to the margin of appreciation of the respondent state than it is in a matter to do with emergency criminal law.[17] In a later judgment dealing with Mr Dudgeon's claims for compensation under Article 50, the Court awarded him £3,315 for his costs and expenses but nothing for the financial losses he had allegedly suffered.[18] As a consequence of the judgment the Homosexual Offences (NI) Order 1982 was passed, bringing the law on male homosexuality in Northern Ireland into line with that in the rest of the United Kingdom at the time.

In some ways the most significant of the Northern Irish cases dealt with in Strasbourg to date has been *Brogan and Others v. United Kingdom*, decided by the European Court on November 29, 1988.[19] At issue here was the validity of the seven-day detention power conferred on the police by section 12 of the Prevention of Terrorism (Temporary Provisions) Act 1984 (the PTA),[20] an anti-terrorist law which applies

---

[16] Offences against the Person Act 1861, ss. 61 and 62.

[17] For discussions of the doctrine of margin of appreciation, see P. van Dijk and G. J. H. van Hoof, *Theory and Practice of the European Convention on Human Rights* (1990), pp. 583–606; T. A. O'Donnell, ''The Margin of Appreciation Doctrine: Standards in the European Court of Human Rights'' [1982] HR Qtly 474.

[18] Judgment of February 24, 1983, Series A, No. 59; (1983) 5 EHRR 573.

[19] Series A, No. 145B, (1989) 11 EHRR 117; W. Finnie (1989) 523 M.L.R. 703; S. Livingstone (1989) 40 N.I.L.Q. 288.

[20] Now s. 14 of the 1989 Act of the same name.

throughout the United Kingdom but which has always been invoked most frequently in Northern Ireland. The four applicants made six specific allegations, five based on Article 5 and one based on Article 13. First, they argued that there had been a breach of Article 5(1)(c) in that the deprivation of liberty they had suffered was not because they were suspected of having committed an "offence" but because they were suspected of involvement in unspecified acts of terrorism, something which of itself does not constitute a breach of the criminal law in Northern Ireland.[21] By 16 votes to three the Court rejected this argument, but instead of giving specific reasons for doing so the majority simply followed the Court's own finding in the earlier case of *Ireland v. United Kingdom*, where it had said that terrorism, as defined in Northern Ireland's emergency legislation,[22] was "well in keeping with the idea of an offence". The majority seemed to think that Article 5(1)(c) was satisfied by the applicants being questioned within a few hours of their arrest about their suspected involvement in specific offences.

The applicants' second argument in *Brogan* was that there had been a breach of the same provision in that the purpose of their arrest was not to bring them before a competent legal authority but to gather information or harass them. They relied upon the fact that, along with the vast majority of other persons arrested in Northern Ireland under this emergency power, they had been released without being charged.[23] The Court was able to reject this contention by pointing out that just because no charges were laid this was

> "no reason to believe that the police investigation in this case was not in good faith or that the detention of the applicants was not intended to further that investigation by way of confirming or dispelling the concrete suspicions which ... grounded their arrest."[24]

Third, the applicants alleged a breach of Article 5(3), which requires detainees to be brought promptly before a judge or other officer authorised by law to exercise judicial power. The Commission, citing earlier cases involving the Netherlands and Belgium,[25] had held that, in the context of terrorism, detention for up to four days and 11 hours was justified but detention for five days and 11 hours was not. The Court, perhaps surprisingly, went further and held by 12 votes to seven[26] that all of the

---

[21] Though Lord Lloyd, in his *Inquiry into Legislation against Terrorism*, recommended that there should be an individual offence of being concerned in the preparation of an act of terrorism: 1966, Cm 3420, para. 6.13.

[22] "Terrorism" is defined by s. 20 of the Prevention of Terrorism (Temporary Provisions) Act 1989 and s. 58 of the Northern Ireland (Emergency Provisions) Act 1996 as meaning "the use of violence for political ends [including] any use of violence for the purpose of putting the public or any section of the public in fear".

[23] The Government's own figures on this point reveal that of the 19,872 persons arrested in Northern Ireland under the Prevention of Terrorism legislation between 1974 and the end of September 1995, 318 (1.6 per cent) were charged with offences created by that legislation and 5,602 (28.2 per cent) with other offences. This leaves 14,492 (70.2 per cent) who were released without being charged.

[24] (1989) 11 EHRR 117 at 131, para. 53.

[25] *X v. the Netherlands*, Application No. 2894/66, (1966) 9 Ybk of the ECHR 564, 568 and *X v. Belgium*, Application No. 4960/71, (1973) 42 CD 49 at 54–55.

[26] The dissenters included Sir Vincent Evans, the United Kingdom judge. Judge Walsh, from Ireland, held that there was also a breach of Art. 5(1)(c).

detentions in the cases before it were unjustified. It said that "promptness" in Article 5(3) was to be assessed in each case according to its special features, but that the significance attached to those features could never be taken to the point of impairing the very essence of the right guaranteed. What is more, "the undoubted fact that the arrest and detention of the applicants were inspired by the legitimate aim of protecting the community as a whole from terrorism is not on its own sufficient to ensure compliance with the specific requirements of Article 5(3)."[27]

It followed, moreover, that there had also been a breach of Article 5(5), which guarantees everyone who has been the victim of an arrest or detention in contravention of Article 5(3) an enforceable right to compensation. The United Kingdom Government unsuccessfully argued that this simply meant that compensation should be available if domestic Northern Irish law had been violated.

The applicants' fifth allegation, that an effective review of the lawfulness of their detention as required by Article 5(4) was precluded, was unanimously rejected by the European Court on the ground that the remedy of habeas corpus was available in Northern Irish law (even though, of course, this can never prevail against a specific legislative provision such as the PTA). Similarly, the applicants failed with respect to Article 13, which contains less strict requirements concerning an "effective remedy before a national authority". No decision was reached at this time on whether compensation was payable under Article 50, but in later proceedings the claim was lost, providing yet further evidence of the Convention's limitations in this regard,[28] or at any rate of the Court's reluctance to develop such provisions as do exist.

Understandably, the Court's decision in *Brogan* that there had been a violation of Article 5(3) caused quite a stir within official legal circles in Britain and the Government had to decide how to react in order to meet the Convention's standards. Within a month, on December 23, 1988, it announced that, rather than introduce new judicial procedures for checking on the lawfulness of detentions, it would enter a further derogation notice under Article 15.[29] An earlier notice (itself the latest of a series) had been withdrawn on August 22, 1984, though it had not covered the area of law in issue in the *Brogan* case. The new notice exempted the Government from complying with Article 5(3) but it was itself quickly challenged for failing to comply with all the requirements of Article 15. In the first such challenge, *McConnell v. United Kingdom*,[30] the applicant had been detained by the police on two occasions, each of them for three and a half days, once before the notice of derogation was issued and once thereafter. The Commission of Human Rights decided that, quite apart from the derogation, neither period of detention disclosed any breach of Article 5(3); it considered the maximum permissible period of detention in a situation such as exists in Northern Ireland to be four days. The derogation notice was also considered by the Commission, and then by the Court of Human Rights, in *Brannigan and McBride v. United Kingdom*.[31] The application was initially declared admissible by the Commis-

---

[27] (1989) 11 EHRR 117 at 136, para. 62.
[28] (1991) 13 EHRR 439.
[29] For a critique of the Government's *Note Verbale*, see P. van Dijk and G. J. H. van Hoof, *Theory and Practice of the European Convention on Human Rights* (1990), pp. 557–558.
[30] Application No. 14671/89.
[31] Application Nos. 14553/89 and 14554/89, December 3, 1991.

sion but was then rejected, by eight votes to five, on the merits.[32] The Commission examined the statistics on terrorist activity in Northern Ireland and concluded, contrary to the applicants' argument, that the measures taken under the derogation notice *were* "strictly required by the exigencies of the situation" and were *not* "inconsistent with [the United Kingdom's] other obligations under international law". The European Court, by 22 votes to four, decided likewise.[33] The Court held that the United Kingdom had not stepped beyond the margin of appreciation which Strasbourg was prepared to allow to each state when deciding what steps to take to combat terrorism:

> "By reason of their direct and continuous contact with the pressing needs of the moment, the national authorities are in principle in a better position than the international judge to decide both on the presence of such an emergency and on the nature and scope of derogations necessary to avert it. Accordingly, in this matter a wide margin of appreciation should be left to the national authorities."[34]

Prior to the Court's decision in *Brannigan and McBride v. United Kingdom*, it had occasion to render judgment in another Northern Irish case, *Fox, Campbell and Hartley v. United Kingdom*,[35] decided on August 30, 1990. Again this involved the legality of arrest powers, those conferred by section 11 of the Northern Ireland (Emergency Provisions) Act 1978.[36] The main contention was that the lack of any requirement that there be "reasonable suspicion" before an arrest could occur under this section was a contravention of Article 5(1)(c). The contention succeeded, by four votes to three,[37] although by this time the law had already been changed in Northern Ireland. A subsidiary contention was that Article 5(2) had been violated through the detainees not being told promptly of the reasons for their arrest. This succeeded before the Commission but was rejected unanimously by the Court (seven votes to 0) on the ground that it was sufficient for the detainees to be made aware of the reasons for their arrest through the nature of the questions put to them by their interrogators. The decision is regrettable as it appears to contravene a principle enunciated by the Court in the *Brogan* case—that the special circumstances of a situation should not be allowed to undermine completely the purpose of a Convention provision.

Emergency arrest powers were again in question in *Margaret Murray and Others v. United Kingdom*, the first of two *Murray* cases decided by the European Court.[38] Mrs Margaret Murray complained that her arrest by a soldier in 1982, under section 14 of the Northern Ireland (Emergency Provisions) Act 1978, was unlawful. Her counsel observed that the UK had withdrawn its notices of derogations from the Convention on August 22, 1984 because the Convention's provisions were now "being fully

---

[32] Extracts from the Commission's Report are included at (1994) 17 EHRR 539 at 553–564.

[33] Series A, No. 258B, (1994) 17 EHRR 539. The dissenters included Judge Walsh from Ireland.

[34] (1994) 17 EHRR 539 at 569, para. 43.

[35] Series A, No. 182, (1991) 13 EHRR 157.

[36] Now s. 17 of the Northern Ireland (Emergency Provisions) Act 1996. The 1978 Act was amended in 1987 to take account of the judgment in *Fox, Campbell and Hartley*—the word "reasonable" was inserted before "suspicion".

[37] Again the U.K. judge, Sir Vincent Evans, was one of the dissenters.

[38] On the domestic decisions in this case see C. Walker, "Army Special Powers on Parade" (1989) 40 N.I.L.Q. 1.

executed". But the first instance judge in the case (also called Murray!) refused to hold that section 14 was affected by the Convention (in particular by Article 5(1)(c)) because in a recent case on section 11 of the 1978 Act (which allowed arrests by the police) the House of Lords had not treated Article 5 as affecting the construction of that section.[39] He thought that sections 14 and 11 were "very similar".[40] The Court of Appeal largely endorsed Murray J.'s conclusions,[41] as did the House of Lords, where no reference was made to the Convention.[42]

By the time the case reached Strasbourg, however, the European Court of Human Rights in *Fox, Campbell and Hartley v. United Kingdom*[43] had already proved Murray J. wrong by finding that section 11 of the 1978 Act was *not* in compliance with Article 5(1)(c) and the Government had changed the wording of sections 11 and 14 so that they now included the adjective "reasonable".[44] The European Court had reached this conclusion despite emphasising that the "reasonableness" of arrests for terrorist-type offences could not always be judged according to the same standards as are applied when dealing with conventional crime. Nevertheless, in *Margaret Murray v. United Kingdom* the European Court, contrary to the Commission in the same case, held that on the facts before it there had *not* been a breach of Articles 5(1), 5(2) or 5(5).[45] In particular, the Court decided that there had been enough suspicion of Mrs Murray's illegal fund-raising activities to make that suspicion "reasonable" as required under Article 5(1)(c) for a lawful arrest. A similar conclusion was reached in *Oscar v. Chief Constable of the RUC*,[46] where the Court of Appeal of Northern Ireland looked at both *Brogan v. United Kingdom*[47] and *Fox, Campbell and Hartley v. United Kingdom*[48] before rejecting counsel's argument that his client's arrest in connection with two armed robberies had been unlawful because of a lack of reasonable suspicion. Likewise, the House of Lords has recently held, in *O'Hara v. Chief Constable of the RUC*,[49] though without reference to the *Murray* case, that an arresting officer can formulate a reasonable suspicion against someone purely on the basis of what was in his or her own mind at the time: the officer's suspicion does not have to be based on his or her personal observations. The Lords did make it clear, though, that an arresting officer could not formulate a reasonable suspicion simply on the basis of an order issued by a superior officer: the latter has to supply the arresting officer with some

---

[39] *McKee v. Chief Constable of the RUC* [1985] 1 All E.R. 1. See C. Walker, "Emergency Arrest Powers" (1985) 36 N.I.L.Q. 145 and "A Barrister", "Reasonable Suspicion and Planned Arrests" (1992) 43 N.I.L.Q. 66.

[40] [1985] 12 NIJB 1 (H.C.). Murray J. also noted that the events in the case before him had occurred in 1982, prior to the United Kingdom's withdrawal of its derogation, but he did not base his decision on this point because it was not argued before him.

[41] [1987] 3 NIJB 84 (C.A.: Gibson and Kelly L.J.J.; this was two months before Gibson L.J.'s assassination). Mrs Murray was awarded £250 because the Ministry of Defence had not discharged the onus of proving a justifiable reason for conducting a body search, but this was a relatively minor part of the case.

[42] [1988] 2 All E.R. 521.

[43] Series A, No. 182, (1991) 13 EHRR 157.

[44] s. 25 and Sched. 1 of the Northern Ireland (Emergency Provisions) Act 1987.

[45] (1995) 19 EHRR 193; (1994) 15 HRLJ 8.

[46] [1991] NI 290.

[47] Series A, No. 145B, (1989) 11 EHRR 117.

[48] Series A, No. 182, (1991) 13 EHRR 157.

[49] [1997] 1 All E.R. 129.

information grounding the order. In view of the European Court's attitude to arrest powers in the Margaret Murray case, it is unlikely that an application to Strasbourg by Mr O'Hara would get very far.

In *John Murray v. United Kingdom*[50] the issue at stake was whether the applicant had received a fair trial within the terms of Article 6 of the Convention. He submitted that in three respects he had not: first, he had been denied access to a solicitor for the first 48 hours of his detention;[51] second, his solicitor had not been permitted to be present during interviews which took place after that period;[52] third, the court had been permitted to draw inferences of guilt from the fact that he had remained silent in the face of police questioning.[53] The European Commission of Human Rights held by 13 votes to four that the lack of access to a solicitor did violate the applicant's rights of defence under Articles 6(1) and 6(3)(c) but by 15 votes to two that Northern Ireland's legal provisions on a defendant's right to silence did not violate Articles 6(1) or 6(2).[54] The Court mirrored these conclusions—by 12 votes to seven on the first point and by 14 votes to five on the second—but the majority made it clear that the denial of access was a violation only because at the same time the defendant's silence could lead to inferences of guilt being drawn.[55] The logical conclusion of this is that, because the provisions on the right to silence affect *all* detainees, whether arrested under the emergency laws or not, in any case where access to a solicitor is denied in Northern Ireland the detainee in question will stand a very good chance of showing that Article 6 has been breached. The Government has not yet announced, a year and a half after the European Court's ruling in *John Murray*, how it intends to avoid this consequence and in the meantime further applications to Strasbourg are pending by detainees who have since been dealt with in the same way as Mr Murray was. However, the Government has no doubt breathed a sigh of relief that its provisions on the right to silence in Northern Ireland have not *per se* been held to violate the Convention, not least because Northern Ireland's provisions on this matter have recently been adopted in England and Wales too.[56]

The last of the Northern Irish cases to be decided by the Court of Human Rights, *McCann and Others v. United Kingdom*, is, like *Lawless v. Ireland*, one that originated in a different jurisdiction, this time Gibraltar. In 1988 two men and a woman were shot dead there by undercover British soldiers who apparently believed that they were IRA terrorists planting a bomb in the colony. It later transpired that there was no bomb, although the three people in question had collected explosives across the border in Spain. Their relatives issued writs suing the Ministry of Defence on the basis that unlawful force had been used, but the Foreign Secretary issued certificates excluding proceedings against the Crown. This effectively prevented any court case from proceeding either in Gibraltar or in any part of the United Kingdom: the applicants sought

---

[50] (1996) 22 EHRR 29, (1996) 17 HRLJ 39 (February 8, 1996); B. Dickson (1996) 21 E.L.R. 424; S. Nash and M. Furse (1996) New L.J. 261.
[51] Northern Ireland (Emergency Provisions) Act 1987, s. 15 (now s. 47 of the 1996 Act).
[52] No law expressly permitted or disallowed this.
[53] As permitted by the Criminal Evidence (NI) Order 1988.
[54] (1994) 18 EHRR CD 1.
[55] The Court awarded Mr Murray £15,000 in costs, but no compensation.
[56] Criminal Justice and Public Order Act 1994, ss 34–37.

leave to apply for judicial review to challenge the legality of the certificates, but this was denied and the actions were then struck off the court list. The applicants therefore went directly to Strasbourg. In March 1994 the Commission held by 11 votes to six that there had been no violation of the right to life guaranteed by Article 2 of the Convention but it nevertheless referred the case to the Court. In September 1995 the Court held by the narrowest of majorities, 10 votes to nine,[57] that Article 2 *had* been violated. As in the second *Murray* case (decided some five months later) the Court ordered the Government to pay some of the applicants' legal costs (to the tune of £38,700) but did not award any compensation; many commentators on the case, Deputy Prime Minister Michael Heseltine amongst them, blurred this distinction and condemned the European Court for its "ludicrous" decision which would give "succour to terrorists". The decision renewed calls from some quarters, again neglecting to distinguish between organs of the European Union and those of the Council of Europe, that the United Kingdom should "pull out of Europe altogether".

McCann was the first case on Article 2 to reach the European Court from any jurisdiction.[58] What was said about the interpretation of that Article is therefore extremely important, especially for the many other applications from Northern Ireland which have already been lodged relying on the same provision.[59] The Court stressed that Article 2 was one of the most fundamental provisions in the Convention and that it had to be strictly construed. It added that in assessing the actions in question it had to consider not only the actions themselves but also the manner in which they were planned and controlled. On the facts before it the Court found that the soldiers who fired the shots honestly believed that it was necessary to do so in order to prevent the three people detonating a bomb and causing loss of life; that was enough to exonerate the soldiers from a breach of Article 2. On the other hand, the Court said, the Government had not convinced it that there was no other way of preventing the detonation of the supposed bomb (*e.g.* why were the suspects, who were being kept under surveillance, not arrested at the border if they were believed to be on a bombing mission?); this suggested a lack of appropriate care in the control and organisation of the arrest operation. In a sense the Ministry of Defence was hoisted with its own petard, for, having refused to make public the details of the training received by the undercover soldiers, it was then unable to show to the Court's satisfaction that it had taken proper

---

[57] Series A, No. 324, (1996) 21 EHRR 97. The states in the majority were Estonia, Greece, Italy, Lithuania, Luxembourg, Malta, Poland, Portugal, Slovakia and Spain. Those in the minority were Finland, Germany, Hungary, Iceland, Norway, Slovenia, Sweden, Turkey and the United Kingdom.

[58] Art. 2 reads: "(1) Everyone's right to life shall be protected by law. No one shall be deprived of his life intentionally save in the execution of a sentence of a court following his conviction of a crime for which this penalty is provided by law. (2) Deprivation of life shall not be regarded as inflicted in contravention of this article when it results from the use of force which is no more than absolutely necessary: (a) in defence of any person from unlawful violence; (b) in order to effect a lawful arrest or to prevent the escape of a person lawfully detained; (c) in action lawfully taken for the purpose of quelling a riot or insurrection."

[59] These include applications by relatives of eight IRA men shot by the army at Loughgall, County Armagh, in 1987; by Hugh Jordan, the brother of Pearse Jordan killed by the army in a police ambush of an IRA gang in 1992; by the widow of Patrick Finucane, killed allegedly with the connivance of the British armed forces in 1989; and by Eleanor Creaney, a relative of Gervaise McKerr killed by the RUC in 1982. I am grateful to British Irish Rights Watch, a London-based campaigning group, for this information.

care to ensure that soldiers knew when less than lethal force might be an adequate response in a particular situation.[60]

What the European Court refused to do was to condemn the United Kingdom merely because its domestic law on the use of force was formulated differently from that in Article 2. The domestic law in question here was Gibraltarian law and according to Article 2 of the Gibraltar Constitution such force ''as is reasonably justifiable'' can be used to effect a lawful arrest or prevent the commission of a crime. This is similar to the test in English and Northern Irish law[61] and appears less strict than the requirement in the Convention that the force be ''absolutely necessary''. True to its tradition of not dealing with comparisons of laws *in abstracto*[62] the Court then said that in its view ''the difference between the two standards is not sufficiently great that a violation of Article 2(1) could be found on this ground alone''.[63] The Court also affirmed that the right to life in Article 2 presupposed that there was a system in place in each state for effectively reviewing the lawfulness of the use of force by state authorities, but it found that the inquest which had been held in Gibraltar, even if flawed in the ways alleged by groups such as Amnesty International, was still a thorough, impartial and careful examination of the circumstances surrounding the killings.

The *McCann* decision is a startling one, although because it is confined to its particular facts it is unlikely to have any significant legal effect beyond requiring a rethink of the (still officially unpublished) firing instructions issued by the Ministry of Defence to its soldiers. Of greater import is the manner in which the European Court reasoned when deciding the case. In this respect the Court has evolved appreciably since that first decision in *Lawless* some 35 years earlier. Then it was rather supine and conservative; today it is more interventionist and liberal. The Court is now prepared to second-guess member states' legislative choices on matters such as arrest powers, detention periods and use of force instructions. The Northern Irish cases have in this sense helped the Court to earn its jurisprudential spurs and to assert itself more firmly on the European stage.

European Commission Decisions Concerning Northern Ireland

Many cases from Northern Ireland have got as far as the Commission but have not proceeded to the Court because the application has been declared inadmissible, because having been lost on the merits it has not been referred to the Court by any body with a power to do so, or because the Commission has succeeded in effecting a ''friendly settlement'' of the application under Article 28 of the Convention. The easiest way of reviewing these cases is according to the Convention Articles con-

---

[60] Para. 212.
[61] Police and Criminal Evidence Act 1984, s. 117; Criminal Law Act (NI) 1967, s. 3; Police and Criminal Evidence (NI) Order 1989, Art. 88.
[62] Notwithstanding *Dudgeon v. United Kingdom*. The Court's refusal to consider in the abstract the compatibility of legislation with the provisions of the Convention goes back to its decision in *Klass v. Germany* (1978) 2 EHRR 214 at 227, para. 33.
[63] Para. 155.

cerned. One or two applications concerning Article 8 (right to a family life) have also been brought: for example, Irish Republican prisoners in English jails have unsuccessfully sought to challenge the government's refusal to transfer them to prisons in Northern Ireland.[64] In the early days of the troubles in Northern Ireland various general and specific complaints were made to the Commission by the Campaign for Social Justice and the Northern Ireland Civil Rights Association; they related to the Civil Authorities (Special Powers) Act 1922, to gerrymandering of electoral constituencies, to discrimination by the Northern Ireland government in public housing, employment and education and to controls on civil rights marches. Unfortunately, all of these complaints were struck out by the Commission in December 1970, largely it seems because the Commission could not obtain from the applicants or their lawyers all the information it required, despite a visit to Northern Ireland by the secretary to the Commission.[65]

The Right to Life

The cases on the right to life fall into two categories, the first comprising killings, or threats to kill, by members of the security forces in Northern Ireland and the second embracing deaths caused by paramilitary organisations.[66] It should be noted that even though the Commission recognises the right to life as the most important in the Convention it nevertheless applies just as rigidly the procedural rules concerning the lodging of applications. Thus, when the 14 Bloody Sunday deaths were included in Ireland's application against the United Kingdom in 1972 this part was declared inadmissible because there had been no exhaustion of domestic remedies;[67] likewise, in *McDaid and Others v. United Kingdom* applications in relation to the same incident were rejected for being out of time.[68] Nor did the Commission think that time had started to run again when the Prime Minister stated that no new inquiry would be held.

A significant case in the first category is *Farrell v. United Kingdom*,[69] where the applicant's husband had been killed by British soldiers in 1971 because they suspected that he was in the act of planting a bomb at a bank in Newry, County Down, over which they had been keeping watch. On December 11, 1982 the Commission of Human Rights declared the widow's complaint under Article 2 to be admissible and, in accordance with Article 28, proceeded to "place itself at the disposal of the parties concerned with a view to securing a friendly settlement of the matter on the basis of

---

[64] *McCotter v. United Kingdom*, Application No. 18632/91, (1993) 15 EHRR CD 98; *S v. United Kingdom*, Application No. 19085/91, (1993) 15 EHRR CD 106.

[65] Application No. 3625, (1970) 13 Ybk of the ECHR 340.

[66] See, generally, "The Use of Lethal Force under Article 2 of the European Convention of Human Rights", a paper delivered by M. O'Boyle at a meeting of Directors and representatives from Police Academies and Police Training Institutions, Strasbourg, November 26–28, 1990. Since November 1982, 75 persons have been killed by the security forces in Northern Ireland.

[67] Application No. 5310/71, (1972) 41 *Collections of Decisions* 3.

[68] Application No. 25681/94, (1996) 22 EHRR CD 197, 85A DR 134.

[69] Application No. 9013/80, (1983) 5 EHRR 465. Mrs Farrell was unsuccessful in her claims brought within the domestic legal system, which went as far as the House of Lords: see [1980] 1 W.L.R. 172 and D. S Greer, (1980) 31 N.I.L.Q. 151.

respect for human rights as defined in this Convention".[70] In October 1984, after two meetings with the parties in London in June and July 1984, the Commission announced that a friendly settlement had been reached, under the terms of which the Government agreed to pay Mrs Farrell £37,500, and to make a contribution towards her legal costs, but did not admit any legal liability for her husband's death. A spokesman for the Government declared that the death had been "an unfortunate mistake".[71] One of the consequences of this settlement, of course, was that it prevented the case from creating any kind of judicial precedent. Also, because the instructions issued to soldiers on when to open fire were not, and are still not, public documents, it is not possible to say whether the settlement led to any changes being made to those instructions. It is interesting that the applicant had tried to argue in the domestic courts that she should be entitled to compensation on account of the negligent planning and organisation of the surveillance operation. The House of Lords refused her permission to do so because this was not part of her original statement of claim. Had she been granted permission it is still likely, given the state of the law of negligence at the time, that she would have lost. We have seen that in *McCann v. United Kingdom* the European Commission and Court *have* shown themselves prepared to consider condemning a state's authorities for just such negligence.

In *Stewart v. United Kingdom*[72] the death in question was that of the 13-year-old son of the applicant. He had been killed by a plastic baton round (also referred to as a plastic bullet) fired by a British soldier in Belfast in 1976.[73] In 1979 Mrs Stewart failed in her attempt to obtain £1,000 compensation through the Belfast courts and a few months after losing an appeal in 1982 she lodged an application in Strasbourg complaining of breaches of Articles 2, 3 and 14. In July 1984 she lost on all three counts. With respect to Article 2, the Commission considered the arguments on the basis of facts established by the courts in Northern Ireland, no new evidence having been brought before the Commission nor any indications having been made that the trial judge in Belfast had incorrectly evaluated the evidence before him. The Commission accordingly held that there had been a riot in progress at the time of the incident, that the lives of the army patrol were in peril and that the death of Brian Stewart resulted from the use of force which was no more than "absolutely necessary . . . in action lawfully taken for the purpose of quelling a riot", the relevant test laid down in Article 2(2)(c). It followed from this that there was no inhuman treatment or punishment under Article 3. Nor was there any evidence to support the allegation that plastic bullets had been used only against Roman Catholics or the Republican community in Northern Ireland. To this day it remains the case that none of the victims of plastic bullets have succeeded in winning a case in Strasbourg, though one or two have obtained damages through the domestic courts.

Probably the most important aspects of the Commission's decision in the *Stewart* case are the rejection of the Government's argument that Article 2 concerned only

---

[70] 30 DR 96 (1982).
[71] 38 DR 44 (1984).
[72] Application No. 10044/82, (1985) 7 EHRR 453, 39 DR 162.
[73] Altogether 17 people have been killed by rubber or plastic bullets in Northern Ireland during the present unrest; eight of these were under 18 when they died.

intentional killing and had no application to accidental or negligent killing and the statement that the lawful use of lethal force envisaged by Article 2(2) must be:

"strictly proportionate to the achievement of the permitted purpose ... [and in] assessing whether the use of force is strictly proportionate, regard must be had to the nature of the aim pursued, the dangers to life and limb inherent in the situation and the degree of risk that the force employed might result in loss of life."[74]

This is a stiffer standard than that laid down in Northern Ireland's domestic law by section 3 of the Criminal Law Act (NI) 1967, which simply says:

"[a] person may use such force as is reasonable in the circumstances in the prevention of crime, or in effecting or assisting in the lawful arrest of offenders or suspected offenders or of persons unlawfully at large."

The House of Lords, unfortunately, has interpreted this standard in a manner which allows considerable discretion to the security forces.[75] Given the European Court's pronouncements in *McCann v. United Kingdom*, discussed above, it is possible that in a future case the courts in Northern Ireland will give preference to the *Stewart* and *McCann* standards over those laid down by the House of Lords, although as we shall see in the next section the Northern Irish courts have to date been very reluctant to allow the Convention to take precedence over established domestic principles. They seem less willing even than the House of Lords to adopt Strasbourg's interpretation of the Convention.

Mrs Stewart lost in Strasbourg because of the exception concerning riots enshrined in Article 2(2)(c). A different exception was under the microscope in *John Kelly v. United Kingdom*, namely that in Article 2(2)(b) concerning the effecting of a lawful arrest. The applicant's 17-year-old son had been shot by the army in 1985 while driving a stolen car which tried to evade a checkpoint at a roundabout. Mr Kelly sued the Ministry of Defence in the High Court of Northern Ireland but lost; his appeal to the Court of Appeal also failed.[76] The judges held that the soldiers, believing on reasonable grounds that the car contained terrorists and not just joyriders, had used reasonable force to prevent crime or to effect a lawful arrest, as permitted by section 3(1) of the Criminal Law Act (NI) 1967. An application to the European Commission was also declared inadmissible,[77] the Commission holding that the force used was justified as an attempt to effect an arrest and that the arrest in turn would have been lawful (if the victim had survived) because the harm to be averted by preventing the escape of terrorists outweighed the harm likely to be caused by the shooting. This reasoning is most unfortunate because it assumes that in Northern Irish law such an

---

[74] (1985) 7 EHRR 453 at 458, para. 19.
[75] See *The Attorney-General for Northern Ireland's Reference (No. 1 of 1975)* [1977] A.C. 105 and *Farrell v. Secretary of State for Defence* [1980] 1 W.L.R. 172; S. Doran, "The Use of Force by the Security Forces in Northern Ireland: A Legal Perspective" (1987) 7 *Legal Studies* 291.
[76] [1989] N.I. 341.
[77] (1993) 16 EHRR CD 20; see J. C. Smith [1994] New L.J. 354.

arrest would also have been lawful, and that is by no means clear. If the killing was at all justified it was surely on the basis that it was to prevent a serious crime that was about to be committed, but that is an exception to the right to life which Article 2 does not recognise. What the European Commission appears to have endorsed, as Smith has observed, is the doctrine "that would allow a fleeing person to be shot down because, if he gets away, *sooner or later*, he is likely to participate in acts of violence."[77a] It is regrettable that the Commission did not decide this case on its merits and then refer it to the Court. The Court's approach in *McCann* suggests that it might not have decided *Kelly* in the same way as the Commission.

In *McQuiston v. United Kingdom* the issue was not a killing but a threat to life.[78] Loyalist prisoners at Magilligan Prison, who had taken part in an abortive hunger strike in 1984 to try to persuade the authorities to segregate Loyalist and Republic inmates, claimed that they were obliged to remain in their cells for 23 hours each day since they feared for their own safety if they left their cells to go for meals, wash or associate with other prisoners. On March 4, 1986 the Commission rejected the claim on the ground that the applicants' isolation was voluntary: "[t]he facts do not support their contention that the situation was so dangerous that they were compelled to protest in this way".[79] With reference to a complaint under Article 3 of the Convention, the Commission decided that, as integration of prisoners had been introduced following the withdrawal of special category status pursuant to one of Lord Gardiner's recommendations in 1975,[80] the policy of integration was not inherently inhuman or degrading. Nor was the Commission sympathetic to a point raised under Article 14 (the non-discrimination provision): even though segregation of prisoners was *de facto* permitted at another Northern Irish prison, the Commission did not think that Article 14 obliged state authorities to follow the same policy in every prison when dealing with prison disputes.

The cases falling into the second category concerning the right to life have all been taken by the relatives of persons killed in Northern Ireland by Republican terrorist groups. Strangely, no applications seem to have been made in relation to deaths caused by Loyalist terrorists, nor have there been any applications in relation to the punishment beatings or "kneecappings" which both sets of paramilitary organisations frequently carry out. The allegation made has been that the U.K. Government has not done enough to guarantee the right to life of Protestants living in terrorised areas or of persons employed in the security forces. The applications have also been lodged against the Government of the Republic of Ireland, but the Commission has dealt summarily with these if the death actually occurred in the North.[81] While all of the cases have been lost, the Commission has nevertheless recognised that the obligation

---

[77a] J. C. Smith [1994] New L.J. 354.
[78] Application No. 11208/84, 46 DR 182 (1986).
[79] 46 DR 182, 189.
[80] Report of a Committee to consider, in the context of civil liberties and human rights, measures to deal with terrorism in Northern Ireland (1975), Cmnd 5847.
[81] *X v. United Kingdom and Ireland*, Application No. 9348/81, 32 DR 190, (1983) 5 EHRR 504; *H v. United Kingdom and Ireland*, Application No. 9833/82, 42 DR 53 (1985), lost on the six months rule; *M v. United Kingdom and Ireland*, Application No. 9837/82, 47 DR 27 (1986); *X v. United Kingdom and Ireland*, Application No. 9825/82, (1986) 8 EHRR 49, also lost on the six months rule.

imposed by Article 2 is not merely of a negative character—it also embraces positive duties to protect citizens.

In *X v. United Kingdom and Ireland*[82] the applicant complained of violations on behalf of herself and her two dependent children in respect of the murders of her brother in Northern Ireland in 1981 and of her husband in the Republic in 1990; the latter was a quarry owner, a farmer, a declared Unionist and an ex-member of the Ulster Defence Regiment (a regiment of the British Army). She argued that the Governments were not adopting adequate or effective measures to protect her in the face of a terrorist campaign which was being waged with the calculated genocidal intent of driving members of the Protestant community from their lands, homes and businesses in certain border areas. In finding no breach in the circumstances of this case, the Commission cited an earlier case taken against the Republic alone,[83] where the Commission had declared inadmissible an application by a person who, after an attack on his life by the IRA, had received police protection for several years and then lost it; the Commission said there that the applicant was not entitled to a personal bodyguard for an indefinite period of time. One wonders if the same conclusion would be reached if, say, an unguarded prominent politician were to be killed.

In *M v. United Kingdom and Ireland*[84] the applicant's murdered husband was a member of the Territorial Army and Volunteer Reserve. His request to be issued with a firearm for personal protection had been refused and the Commission accepted the Government's contention that this was justifiable because possession of firearms would make members of the TAVR even more likely to be targeted by terrorists. The same argument is likely to defeat any application by, say, a Sinn Féin activist based on the refusal to him or her of a licence to carry a firearm for personal protection.

The Right Not to Be Ill-Treated

The earliest of all the cases taken to Strasbourg from Northern Ireland was *Donnelly and Others v. United Kingdom*, decided by the Commission on December 15, 1975.[85] Seven applicants alleged that, following their arrest in April 1972, they had been subjected to treatment by the security forces in violation of Article 3 of the Convention. They also alleged, relying on a principle elaborated by the Commission in the interstate cases involving Cyprus and Greece,[86] that the treatment formed part of a continuing administrative practice encouraging or permitting torture or inhuman or degrading treatment. The Commission declared three of the applications inadmissible on the merits, since the applicants had not exhausted the local remedies available to them within the Northern Irish legal system; the other four applications were also declared inadmissible but on the ground that adequate remedies had already been

---

[82] See the first case in the previous note.
[83] Application No. 6040/73, 44 CD 121.
[84] See note 81 above.
[85] Application Nos. 5577–5583/72, (1973) 43 CD 122 and (1975) 4 DR 4.
[86] *Greece v. United Kingdom*, Application No. 176/56, (1956–57) 2 Ybk of the ECHR 182, and *Denmark, Norway, Sweden, the Netherlands v. Greece*, Application Nos 3321–3323/67 and 3344/67, (1968) 11 Ybk of the ECHR 730.

obtained within Northern Ireland, compensation amounting to more than £16,000 having been paid out in settlements. The complaint about a continuing administrative practice was rejected because, although situations could be envisaged where a practice was of such a nature as to render the available domestic remedies ineffective or inadequate, this was not so in this case. The Commission did not, however, refuse to deal with the claim about the administrative practice just because the issue was also involved in the *Ireland v. United Kingdom* application, which at that time was still under consideration by the Commission: to be excluded from consideration under Article 27(1)(b) of the Convention a petition has to be "substantially the same as a matter which has *already been examined*[87] by the Commission or has already been submitted to another procedure of international investigation or settlement and if it contains no relevant new information".

Another early case concerning Article 3 of the Convention was *X v. United Kingdom*, decided in 1980.[88] This involved an application by an Irishman imprisoned in England for Provisional IRA activities. He was given a life sentence in 1976 for attempted murder and possession of firearms and explosives. The gist of his complaint was that he had been forced to spend 760 days in solitary confinement, which he alleged amounted to torture or to inhuman or degrading treatment or punishment. In the Commission's view, while the solitary confinement was unusual and undesirable, it was not arbitrary or of such severity as to fall within the scope of Article 3.

A second case involving procedures in prisons, but one arising directly from Northern Ireland, is *McFeeley, Nugent, Hunter and Campbell v. United Kingdom*.[89] In May 1980 the Commission declared inadmissible the bulk of the applicants' complaints, which had to do with the conditions under which Republican prisoners were being held in the Maze Prison in Northern Ireland. The applicants had refused, on grounds of conscience and in order to claim a special status as political prisoners,[90] to wear prison clothing or footwear or to engage in prison work. As their own clothing had been removed, they remained naked throughout their imprisonment. They relied upon Articles 3, 6, 8, 9, 10, 11, 13, 14 and 18. The Commission decided that the right to a preferential status in prison was not among those protected by Article 9 (on freedom of conscience) and that the loss of remission for a breach of prison discipline did not constitute inhuman or degrading treatment. But it stressed that prison authorities do remain under Convention obligations even in the face of unlawful challenges by prisoners:

"[T]he Convention requires that the prison authorities, with due regard to the ordinary and reasonable requirements of imprisonment, exercise their custodial authority to safeguard the health and well-being of all prisoners including those engaged in protest in so far as that may be possible in the circumstances. Such a requirement makes it necessary for the prison authorities to keep under constant

---

[87] Emphasis added.
[88] Application No. 8158/78, (1980) 21 DR 95. *Cf. X v. Ireland*, Application No. 9554/81, (1984) 6 EHRR 336, where an unsuccessful claim of inhuman treatment was made by an IRA prisoner in an Irish jail.
[89] Application No. 8317/78; (1980) 20 DR 44, (1981) 3 EHRR 161.
[90] The government had previously granted this status to some prisoners but abolished it for persons convicted of offences committed on or after March 1, 1976.

review their reaction to recalcitrant prisoners engaged in a developing and protracted protest."[91]

The Commission adjourned its consideration of complaints under Articles 8 and 13. These concerned the limitations on the number of letters which the prisoners could send and receive, the reading by the prison authorities of letters and the stoppage of some of them, and an inadequate supply of writing materials. The adjournment was to allow time for the European Court to decide *Silver and Others v. United Kingdom*, which it did in March 1983.[92] The Secretary to the Commission then wrote to the applicants' solicitor, also referring to a reform in the prison censorship rules which the government had already implemented in Northern Ireland. No reply was received to the inquiry whether the applicants wished to maintain their applications, so, after consulting the U.K. Government, the Commission decided in October 1984 to strike the applications off its list.

In *X v. United Kingdom*[93] the applicant alleged a breach of Article 8 in that she could not visit her husband, an IRA prisoner, without their conversations being listened to by prison officers. The Commission rejected the complaint on the ground that the exceptional security risks involved in imprisoning terrorists justified the eavesdropping as "necessary . . . in the interests of . . . public safety . . . [or] for the prevention of disorder or crime . . . or for the protection of the rights and freedoms of others".[94]

The Right to Liberty

The right to liberty, guaranteed by Article 5 of the Convention, has been the focus of attention in several Northern Irish cases. The first applications related to internment without trial, a policy which was in operation in Northern Ireland from 1971 to 1975. These were all struck out by the Commission because of the U.K. Government's notice of derogation in place at the time.[95] Apart from *Brogan and Others v. United Kingdom*, *Fox, Campbell and Hartley v. United Kingdom* and *Brannigan and McBride v. United Kingdom*, already mentioned in the previous section, the most significant decision is that rendered by the Commission in 1979 in *McVeigh, O'Neill and Evans v. United Kingdom*.[96] This concerned the examination and detention of travellers at

---

[91] (1981) 3 EHRR 161 at 196, para. 46.
[92] Judgment of March 25, 1983, Series A, No. 61, (1983) 5 EHRR 347. For an examination of this and related cases, see A. Jones, "Prisoners' Rights to Privacy and Article 8 of the European Convention on Human Rights", in the 16th Annual Report of the Standing Advisory Commission on Human Rights in Northern Ireland, (1990–91) H.C. 488, pp. 251–265. See also Chapter 3 above.
[93] 14 DR 246.
[94] Art. 8(2).
[95] *McMillen and Heaney v. United Kingdom*, Application No. 5459, (1972) 40 *Collections & Decisions* 75; *McMillen v. United Kingdom*, Application No. 5470, (1972) 42 *Collections & Decisions* 110; see generally Niall Osborough, "Northern Ireland and the European Convention on Human Rights" (1970) 5 Ir. Jur. 303.
[96] Application Nos. 8022/77, 8025/77 and 8027/77, (1979) 18 DR 66 and (1981) 25 DR 15, (1983) 5 EHRR 71; C. Warbrick (1983) 32 I.C.L.Q. 757.

ports under the Prevention of Terrorism legislation.[97] Articles 5 and 8 of the Convention were invoked, but the only breach which the Commission identified was of Article 8 in respect of the authorities' failure to contact the wives of two of the detained persons during the 45 hours of their detention. The detaining, questioning, searching, photographing and fingerprinting were all held to be justifiable in the circumstances. The law on communication with relatives and friends has now been altered so as to permit a detainee to make one such contact "as soon as practicable", though delays of up to 48 hours are possible if certain (not very restrictive) conditions are fulfilled.[98] What remains unchanged is the power to examine persons at ports even though the examiner has no suspicion that the person is involved in terrorism: the Commission did not think that this contravened Article 5 of the Convention, especially as Article 5(1)(b) permits the detention of a person "in order to secure the fulfillment of any obligation prescribed by law". Since 1984, however, the examination can continue beyond 12 hours only if the examining officer reasonably suspects that the person is involved in terrorism, a reform which was relied upon by the Commission in two subsequent applications concerning the port examination powers, *Harkin v. United Kingdom* and *Lyttle v. United Kingdom*.[99] The former applicant tried to distinguish the *McVeigh* case on the ground that there the applicants were resident in Britain and were returning from a place outside the United Kingdom (the Republic of Ireland) while in his own case he was travelling internally within the United Kingdom (and had crossed to Scotland a few days earlier with no problems). The Commission did not accept this distinction, saying "a security check on leaving the mainland following a visit is clearly provided for in the legislation and fulfils an equally evident security requirement".[1] The Commission also followed *McVeigh* as far as Article 5(2) was concerned: "the information provided to the applicant was sufficient to make him aware of the purpose and reasons for his detention".[2]

In *Brennan v. United Kingdom* an application concerning an allegedly unlawful arrest was declared inadmissible because of the six months rule.[3] In another application brought by Terence Brogan the Commission refused to decide whether, in the light of the government's notice of derogation of 1988, future detentions under the Prevention of Terrorism Act would comply with Article 5(1);[4] this underlines Strasbourg's reluctance to answer hypothetical questions. Finally, in *O'Neill v. United Kingdom* and *Gerard Kelly v. United Kingdom*[5] the Commission declared inadmissible applications concerning restrictions on the applicants' freedom of movement. Mrs O'Neill had had to stay in her house with her two baby children for more than three

---

[97] Now s. 16 and Sched. 5 of the Prevention of Terrorism (Temporary Provisions) Act 1989, and Orders made thereunder. See generally D. Bonner, "Combatting Terrorism in the 1990s: the Role of the Prevention of Terrorism (Temporary Provisions) Act 1989" [1990] P.L. 440 at 446–451; also D. Jackson, "Prevention of Terrorism: The U.K. Confronts the European Convention on Human Rights" (1994) 6 *Terrorism and Political Violence* 507.

[98] Now s. 46 of the Northern Ireland (Emergency Provisions) Act 1996.

[99] Application No. 11539/85, (1986) 48 DR 237, and Application No. 11650/85, (1987) 9 EHRR 350.

[1] 48 DR 237 at 242, para. 7.

[2] 48 DR 237 at 243, para. 13.

[3] Application No. 19805/92, (1994) 18 EHRR CD 114.

[4] *Brogan v. United Kingdom*, Application No. 14672/89, (1993) 75 DR 21.

[5] Application Nos. 17441/90 and 17711/91 (August 1992).

hours during a police and army search of the house, while Mr Kelly had had to accompany the police to the Maze Prison and wait for about two and a half hours whilst his car was searched. Both searches were conducted under the anti-terrorist legislation. The main ground for the Commission declaring the applications inadmissible was that each applicant was still in the process of suing the Ministry of Defence for compensation and so had not yet exhausted their domestic remedies. It is probable that had the Commission considered the merits of the applications it would have held against them on the basis that Article 5(1)(b) permits detention "in order to secure the fulfilment of any obligation prescribed by law".

The Right to a Fair Trial

The chief alteration made to criminal procedure in Northern Ireland as a response to the troubles has been the abolition of jury trial for persons charged with "scheduled" offences, which are the offences commonly committed by terrorists.[6] But jury trial is not a right guaranteed by the European Convention, so the validity of this change cannot be tested in Strasbourg. Nor does the Convention contain any such provision as that in Article 26 of the United Nations' International Covenant on Civil and Political Rights, which begins: "All persons are equal before the law and are entitled without any discrimination to the equal protection of the law",[7] so a person tried by a judge alone in a Diplock court cannot complain under the European Convention that he or she has not been treated equally with a person tried by a judge and jury. Other aspects of the trial process for persons charged with scheduled offences *have* been challenged in Strasbourg.

In *Orchin v. United Kingdom*[8] the issue was the legality of the applicant's four-year period on bail in respect of charges of possession of firearms and ammunition. He had been released on bail in February 1974 but the Director of Public Prosecutions (the DPP) did not enter a *nolle prosequi* (a declaration that the prosecution would not be pursued) until March 1978. The Government argued that Mr Orchin could have applied to the court to fix a date for the hearing of the outstanding charges but that he had chosen not to do so. Unsurprisingly, the Commission gave short shrift to such a contention:

"Although in many States there are procedures whereby the accused can accelerate the proceedings, it is generally for him to decide, in complete freedom and in accordance with his own view of his best interests, whether to make use of them. If such procedures were held to be 'effective and sufficient remedies' which the accused had to exhaust before he could complain of the duration of the pro-

---

[6] Now listed in Sched. 1 of the Northern Ireland (Emergency Provisions) Act 1996. The Crown Court sitting without a jury is known as a Diplock court, after the Law Lord who chaired the Commission that recommended the establishment of the juryless courts.

[7] *cf.* the beginning of Art. 14(1), on the right to a fair trial: "All persons shall be equal before the courts and tribunals".

[8] Application No. 8435/78, (1982) 26 DR 18 (admissibility) and (1983) 34 DR 5 (merits), (1984) 6 EHRR 391.

eeedings, he would effectively be required to step into the role of the prosecution and advance the proceedings against himself whenever the prosecution failed to do so sufficiently speedily themselves."[9]

The application was therefore declared admissible and by 13 votes to one[10] the Commission decided that there had been a breach of Article 6(1) in that the duration of the proceedings exceeded "a reasonable time". However, in October 1983 the Committee of Ministers of the Council of Europe resolved, under Article 32 of the Convention, not to take any further action in this case. It noted that the DPP for Northern Ireland had issued further instructions to his staff with the object of expediting trials and obtaining the prompt disposal of all pending proceedings and that, following the enactment of the Judicature (NI) Act 1978, a practice was now in operation whereby the listing of cases for trial on indictment was the responsibility of an officer of the Northern Ireland Court Service. These administrative changes persuaded the Committee of Ministers that the case should be closed. It remains a little-known, but worth-remembering, example of the reforming effect which an application to Strasbourg—albeit belatedly—can produce.[11]

In *X v. United Kingdom* a challenge was made to the practice of screening witnesses at trials. This too was rejected,[12] as it mostly has been within Northern Ireland's own courts.[13] The Commission also declared inadmissible an application lodged by Bernadette Devlin MP after she had been convicted by a magistrates' court in Northern Ireland of indulging in and inciting riotous behaviour.[14] She alleged, first, that the magistrate's refusal to allow her to call up to 50 witnesses to show that past conduct of the police justified her actions was a breach of Article 6(3)(d) of the Convention;[15] second, that the Court of Appeal in Northern Ireland was biased against her in breach of Article 6(1); and third, that contrary to Article 13 she had no effective remedy in Northern Ireland for these two breaches. The Commission decided that there was no breach of the Convention: national authorities have a wide latitude to decide what evidence is relevant or not, the consistency of an appeal court's ruling on a point of law with pre-existing domestic law is of no concern to the Commission, and the refusal to grant a certificate that a point of law of general public importance was

---

[9] 26 DR 18 at 20, para. 3.

[10] The published documents do not reveal which state's Commissioner this was.

[11] Further illustrations are provided by two cases brought to Strasbourg by Irish prisoners in England. In *McComb v. United Kingdom*, Application No. 10621/83, (1986) 50 DR 81, the applicant objected to the opening of letters to and from his solicitors. There was a friendly settlement after the Government agreed to issue an instruction that such correspondence should not be opened save in the prisoner's presence. In *Byrne, McFadden, McCluskey and McLarnon v. United Kingdom*, Application Nos. 7879/77, 7931/77, 7935/77 and 7936/77, (1985) 51 DR 5, (1986) 8 EHRR 272, the Commission held that preventing the applicants from having confidential consultations with their solicitors was a breach of Art. 6(1) but that no breach arose from refusing to allow a prisoner facilities for an independent medical examination. The Committee of Ministers resolved that no further action was called for in view of the Government's revised Standing Order on consultations with legal advisers: DH (87), March 20, 1987.

[12] (1993) 15 EHRR CD 113.

[13] See the next section of this chapter.

[14] *Devlin v. Armstrong* [1971] N.I. 13: the decision was upheld by the Court of Appeal.

[15] "Everyone charged with a criminal offence has [the right] . . . to obtain the attendance and examination of witnesses on his behalf. . . ."

involved (for an appeal to the House of Lords) is not part of a court's "determination of a criminal charge" within Article 6(1).[16]

The Right to Freedom of Expression and Conscience

The Northern Irish troubles have, of course, had an impact in Great Britain as well as in Ireland and there is a significant strand of British opinion which believes that the British army should not be employed in controlling the disturbances in the province. In *Arrowsmith v. United Kingdom*[17] the applicant had distributed leaflets to troops stationed at an army camp in Great Britain urging them to desert or to refuse to obey orders if they were posted to Northern Ireland. She was charged with two offences under the Incitement to Disaffection Act 1934—endeavouring to seduce members of Her Majesty's forces from their duty to Her Majesty, and possessing a document the distribution of which among Her Majesty's forces would constitute an offence. She was convicted, in London, and sentenced to 18 months' imprisonment (of which she actually served seven before being released). Her application to Strasbourg claimed violations of Articles 9 (freedom of thought, conscience and religion), 10 (freedom of expression), and 14 (non-discrimination). Although the Commission declared the application admissible in May 1977, its final report, issued in October 1978, rejected the complaints. While recognising that pacifism is a belief protected by Article 9, it held that the distribution of the leaflets in question was not a *manifestation* of that belief because they were not addressed to the public in general. It also held by 11 votes to one[18] that interference with, and punishment of, such distribution was a necessary curb in a democratic society on the right to free speech: "in view of the applicant's manifest intention to continue her action unless stopped by prohibitive measures, the decision to prosecute her was necessary for the protection of national security and the prevention of disorder in the army."[19] Citing *Handyside v. United Kingdom*,[20] the Commission added: "the notion 'necessary' implies a 'pressing social need' which may include the clear and present danger test [as developed by the United States Supreme Court] and must be assessed in the light of the circumstances of a given case."[21] The decision in *Arrowsmith* was a tough one and the reasoning of the Commission seems strained and even circular. It may well be that if a case with similar facts were to occur today the by now more enlightened Strasbourg organs would decide it differently.

In the autumn of 1988 the British government introduced what became known as "the broadcasting ban", which prohibited all radio and television stations in the United Kingdom from broadcasting interviews with or speeches by any member of

---

[16] *Devlin v. United Kingdom*, Application No. 4607, (1970) 37 *Collections & Decisions* 146, (1971) 14 Ybk of the ECHR 634.

[17] Application No. 7450/75, (1977) 8 DR 123 and (1978) 19 DR 5, (1981) 3 EHRR 218.

[18] The dissenter was the Norwegian Commissioner Torkel Opsahl, who in 1992 was to chair a commission looking at ways forward in Northern Ireland.

[19] (1981) 3 EHRR 2318 at 233, para. 97.

[20] Judgment of December 7, 1976, Series A, No.24, (1979–80) 1 EHRR 737.

[21] (1981) 3 EHRR 218 at 233, para. 85.

certain paramilitary organisations, not all of which were unlawful. A challenge to this ban failed at the highest level in the British courts,[22] and so did the application presented to the Commission at Strasbourg.[23] This was almost inevitable given that, in June 1991, in *Purcell v. Ireland*,[24] the Commission had already rejected a challenge to the more extensive broadcasting ban which had operated in the Republic of Ireland since 1971. Both bans have since been lifted, the United Kingdom's in the autumn of 1994 in the wake of the IRA and Loyalist ceasefires.

In *Rai, Allmond and "Negotiate Now" v. United Kingdom* a non-governmental organisation seeking to promote peace in Northern Ireland, even in the absence of any ceasefire by the paramilitary groupings there, was refused permission by the Department of National Heritage to hold a rally in Trafalgar Square, London. Somewhat surprisingly perhaps, the application to Strasbourg was declared inadmissible because the ban on "not uncontroversial" demonstrations relating to Northern Ireland in Trafalgar Square was deemed to be necessary in a democratic society for the prevention of disorder and protection of the rights and freedoms of others, as permitted by Article 10(2) of the Convention.[25]

In *Magee v. United Kingdom* a challenge was raised by a barrister against the nature of the oath which is required to be sworn when a person is appointed Queen's Counsel. He argued that his freedom of conscience was violated by the requirement that he swear allegiance to the Queen. The Commission declared the application inadmissible because it did not raise an issue of conscience in the sense intended by Article 9.[26]

Rights under Protocol No. 1

Protocol No. 1 was at issue in *S v. United Kingdom*,[27] where the applicant argued that the decision of the Lands Tribunal in Northern Ireland to extinguish the restrictive covenants of which she had the benefit was a deprivation of the peaceful enjoyment of her possessions as guaranteed by Article 1 of Protocol No. 1.[28] However, the Commission did not consider that Mrs S. had been deprived of her possessions (as she still received £100 per annum rentcharge), nor that the "dispossession" was unnecessary or disproportionate (she had received £350 compensation from the Lands Tribunal); the control exercised by the Tribunal was "in accordance with the general interest". Similarly, in *X v. United Kingdom* the Commission rejected an application under

---

[22] *Brind v. Secretary of State for the Home Dept* [1991] 1 A.C. 696, H.L.
[23] *Brind v. United Kingdom*, Application No. 18714/91, (1994) 18 EHRR CD 76, 77 DR 42; also *McLaughlin v. United Kingdom*, Application No. 18759/91, (1994) 18 EHRR CD 84. Both applications were declared inadmissible.
[24] Decision of the Commission, April 17, 1991.
[25] Application No. 25522/94, 81 DR 46.
[26] (1995) 19 EHRR CD 91.
[27] Application No. 10741/84, (1984) 41 DR 226.
[28] "Every natural or legal person is entitled to the peaceful enjoyment of his possessions. No one shall be deprived of his possessions except in the public interest and subject to the conditions provided for by law and by the general principles of international law. The preceding provisions shall not, however, in any way impair the right of a State to enforce such laws as it deems necessary to control the use of property in accordance with the general interest or to secure the payment of taxes or other contributions or penalties."

Article 2 of Protocol No. 1[29] by parents who wanted their children to be educated in an "integrated" school in Northern Ireland, that is, not in a Catholic or in a state (in practice overwhelmingly Protestant) establishment.[30] Perhaps predictably, the Commission was of the opinion that Article 2 did not impose an obligation on a state "to establish, or to subsidize, education of a particular type".

A further topic on which applications have been made from Northern Ireland is the election process. In *Lindsay and Others v. United Kingdom*[31] the applicants were leaders of the British Union Dominion Party. They complained that the European Assembly Elections Act 1978 provided for a simple majority system of voting in Great Britain but for a proportional representation system in Northern Ireland. They argued that in a free and democratic society—which the Council of Europe requires all its members to be—a vote must have the same consequence irrespective of the area of the state in which it is cast and that to deprive a section of the inhabitants of representation which they would otherwise achieve deprives them of rights, status and dignity as citizens of the United Kingdom and is degrading treatment within Article 3. They also alleged that the 1978 Act discriminated under Article 14 because the grounds there listed (especially "political or other opinion" and "national or social origin") included the characteristics which differentiate the British electors in Northern Ireland from those in "the Irish Republican irredentist community". The elections, moreover, were supposedly not "free" as required by Article 3 of Protocol No. 1.[32] Taking the last point first, the Commission had no difficulty in declaring the complaint to be manifestly ill-founded within Article 27(2): assuming, without deciding, that Protocol No. 1 applied to European elections and not just to national elections, the election in Northern Ireland was still free because "a system taking into account the specific situation as to majority and minority existing in Northern Ireland must be seen as making it easier for the people to express its opinion freely".[33] With regard to Article 14 (and, impliedly, Article 3), the Commission announced that:

> "the United Kingdom has specific reasons for applying a different electoral system in one part of the country, namely the protection of the rights of a minority.
>
> The electoral system complained of is, therefore, based on reasonable and objective criteria which justify the differentiation applied. Moreover, it does not appear that there is no reasonable relationship of proportionality between the means employed and the aim sought to be realised."[34]

---

[29] "No one shall be denied the right to education. In the exercise of any functions which it assumes in relation to education and to teaching, the State shall respect the right of parents to ensure such education and teaching in conformity with their own religious and philosophical convictions."

[30] Application No. 7782/77, (1978) 14 DR 179.

[31] Application No. 8364/78, (1979) 15 DR 247.

[32] "The High Contracting Parties undertake to hold free elections at reasonable intervals by secret ballot, under conditions which will ensure the free expression of the opinion of the people in the choice of the legislature".

[33] 15 DR 247 at 251, para. 1.

[34] *ibid.* para. 2.

This is one instance, then, of a Strasbourg organ directly addressing a disparity between the laws of different parts of the same member state, something which the European Court in *Dudgeon* refused to do two years later. The fact that on the facts the applicant's argument based on disparity was rejected ought not to dissuade future applicants from raising the same point in an appropriate situation.

A comparable case is *M v. United Kingdom*.[35] Seamus Mallon had been nominated as a member of Ireland's Senate by the Prime Minister of Ireland in May 1982. Five months later he was elected to the Northern Ireland Assembly, a regional Parliament without real powers which existed from 1982 to 1986. An electoral court in Armagh held shortly thereafter that, under the Northern Ireland Assembly Disqualification Act 1975, Mr Mallon was disqualified from membership of the Assembly because he was already a member of the legislature of a country outside the British Commonwealth. The Commission held that there were doubts over whether the Assembly was a ''legislature'' within the meaning of Protocol No. 1 but that in any event ''a condition that one must not be a member of another legislature is a requirement which is reconcilable with the rights enshrined in Article 3'' of that Protocol. In response to Mr Mallon's claim that he was being discriminated against because of his ''association with a national minority'' (within the terms of Article 14) the Commission said:

> ''The distinction which arises between the members of a legislature inside the Commonwealth and members of other legislatures finds a reasonable and object-ive justification in the special historical tradition and special ties that are shared by members of the British Commonwealth of which Ireland does not form part.''[36]

Such a comment is perhaps disingenuous given the special links which have also long existed between the United Kingdom and Ireland. Today those links would certainly be stronger than those between the United Kingdom and some of the newer members of the Commonwealth such as Cameroon and Mozambique!

This last case illustrates well the diversity of matters which the European Commission has been asked to consider from Northern Ireland over the past 30 years or so (the United Kingdom has allowed individual petitions only since 1966). Taken together the cases demonstrate that the European Convention is very much alive and well in Northern Ireland. There is now a critical mass of local solicitors and barristers who are knowledgeable about the workings of the Commission and who are not slow to test those workings to the full. The academic and NGO communities in Northern Ireland have also done much to foster a high level of awareness. A number of applications to the Commission are in the pipeline and we can expect no let up in the flow. The fact that the great majority of the applications made to date have come to naught is not likely to diminish the enthusiasm of litigants and lawyers for challenging and at the very least embarrass-ing public authorities.

---

[35] Application No. 10316/83, (1984) 37 DR 129.
[36] 37 DR 129 at 135, para. 3.

The Convention in Northern Irish Courts[37]

It is an interesting fact that only two of the seven Northern Irish cases that have reached the European Court of Human Rights have been preceded by proceedings within the Northern Irish courts, and only one of those went as far as the House of Lords.[38] This section looks not just at those cases but also at the many other cases where Northern Irish judges have referred to the Convention, two of which have also reached the House of Lords.[39] Not all of the cases, unfortunately, are yet fully reported.[40]

The European Convention has been referred to in at least 34 cases so far,[41] the first dating from May 1977. The flow has been fairly steady, except for two lean spells in the early 1980s and early 1990s. All but one of the cases[42] are connected in some way with the "troubles" in Northern Ireland; 16 are applications for judicial review (six involving prisoners' rights), 13 are criminal cases, and five are civil suits. In this section they will be surveyed on a topic-by-topic basis.

Retrospectivity

In view of the eventual outcome it had, the very first in the long series of cases is in some ways the most startling. In *R. v. Deery*[43] the defendant had been convicted in January 1977 of two firearms offences committed in April 1976. In August 1976 the maximum penalty for these offences had been increased from five to 10 years'

---

[37] Some of the material in this section has already appeared in print at (1996) 1 EHRLR 496–510.

[38] *John Murray v. United Kingdom* arose out of the proceedings in *R v. Martin and Others* [1992] 5 N.I.J.B. 1 (C.A.). It is *not* the same case as *Kevin Sean Murray v. DPP* [1994] 1 W.L.R. 1 (H.L.), though the law on the right of silence is central to both. *Margaret Murray and Others v. United Kingdom* was preceded by *Murray v. Ministry of Defence* [1985] 12 N.I.J.B. 1 (H.C.), [1987] 3 N.I.J.B. 84 (C.A.), [1988] 2 All E.R. 521 (H.L.). *Fox, Campbell and Hartley v. United Kingdom* arose in part out of the arrest of Bernard Fox in February 1986, but he was released before his application for habeas corpus came on for hearing in the Northern Irish courts; Fox was again arrested in January 1987, when once more he applied for habeas corpus only to be released prior to the hearing: *R. v. Chief Constable of the RUC, ex p. Fox*, Lexis transcript, January 16, 1987. *McCann and Others v. United Kingdom* was taken to Strasbourg only after the Ministry of Defence had issued a public interest immunity certificate which in effect made it pointless to pursue a remedy in a Gibraltarian or Northern Irish court.

[39] *McCann v. Mullan* [1984] N.I. 186, [1985] A.C. 528 (*sub nom. Re McC (A minor)*) and *Re Hone and McCartan's Application* [1988] A.C. 379, [1988] 1 All E.R. 321 (*sub nom. R v. Board of Visitors of H.M. Prison The Maze, ex p. Hone and McCartan*). *Murray v. Ministry of Defence* (see previous note) and *Re Hone and McCartan's Application* are discussed in S. Livingstone, "The House of Lords and the Northern Ireland Conflict" (1994) 57 M.L.R. 333.

[40] Only in mid-1997 were the *Northern Ireland Law Reports* for 1993 published. Publication of the *Northern Ireland Judgments Bulletin* was terminated in 1993.

[41] The NILAW library of the Lexis database contains all cases reported in the *Northern Ireland Law Reports* or in the *Northern Ireland Judgments Bulletin* from January 1945, as well as the transcripts of most unreported cases from March 1984. The Bar Library in Belfast also has copies of as yet unreported judgments.

[42] *Re Applications to Adopt A-MDW and GICW*, Lexis transcript, May 1, 1992 (H.C.). *McKay v. Northern Ireland Public Service Alliance*, Lexis transcript, October 28, 1994 (C.A.), can, on one reading, also be categorised as a non-troubles case.

[43] [1977] N.I. 164 (C.C.A.).

imprisonment[44] and the judge therefore sentenced the defendant to six years' imprisonment for each of his two offences. When the defendant appealed to the Court of Criminal Appeal,[45] Lowry L.C.J.[46] held that the increased penalty was not applicable: given that the legislation providing for the increase was ambiguous as to when it was to take effect, he decided it should be construed so as not to have retrospective effect. This had the consequence, he said, of avoiding any breach by the Government of its obligations under Article 7(1) of the European Convention on Human Rights.[47] Lowry L.C.J. cited with implicit approval the words of Lord Diplock in *Salomon v. Commissioners of Customs and Excise*:

> ". . . there is a prima facie assumption that Parliament does not intend to act in breach of international law, including therein specific treaty obligations; and if one of the meanings which can reasonably be ascribed to the legislation is consonant with the treaty obligations and another or others are not, the meaning which is consonant is to be preferred."[48]

While the application of this principle in *R. v. Deery* is to be welcomed (and it has since been vindicated by the European Court itself[49]), we must note that Lowry L.C.J. stopped short of saying that he was deciding the case as he did *because* of the European Convention. He was not according the Convention any status other than as a tie-breaking mechanism in the event of domestic legislation being ambiguous; even then he was not suggesting that the Convention was necessarily determinative of the result in the case.

It is possible that in giving such prominence to Article 7 of the Convention Lowry L.C.J. remembered that a few years earlier the United Kingdom Government had given an undertaking to the Council of Europe that, although it had introduced the Northern Ireland Act 1972 in order to confer legitimacy on what had been held by Lowry L.C.J. and two other judges to be *ultra vires* orders by British soldiers to demonstrators,[50] it would not be applying this Act retrospectively so as to charge demonstrators for failing to comply with those orders.[51] However, in *R. v. Gorman*,[52] where the question was whether the accused had escaped from "lawful" custody after having been arrested by a soldier under an *ultra vires* regulation, Lowry L.C.J. held

---

[44] By the Firearms (Amendment) (NI) Order 1976.

[45] This court was merged with the Court of Appeal by the Judicature (NI) Act 1978.

[46] Lord Lowry later served as a Law Lord from 1988 to 1994.

[47] Art. 7(1) reads: "No one shall be held guilty of any criminal offence on account of any act or omission which did not constitute a criminal offence under national or international law at the time when it was committed. Nor shall a heavier penalty be imposed than the one that was applicable at the time the criminal offence was committed."

[48] [1966] 3 All E.R. 871, 875.

[49] *Welch v. United Kingdom* (1995) 20 EHRR 247.

[50] The illegitimacy of these orders was established by the Divisional Court in *R. (Hume) v. Londonderry Justices* [1972] N.I. 91 (Lowry L.C.J., Gibson and O'Donnell J.J.). The Northern Ireland Act 1972 was rushed through Parliament in one day in order to counter the effects of this decision.

[51] See Application No. 5451/72, decided by the Commission on October 1, 1972: 15 Ybk of the ECHR 228–240 and 254–256. Ireland withdrew the application after learning of the U.K. Attorney-General's undertaking.

[52] [1974] N.I. 152.

that the custody *had* been retrospectively validated by the 1972 Act. A year earlier a contrary conclusion had been reached in the similar case of *R. v. Meehan*.[53] The European Convention was not cited in either of these cases.

Extraction of Confessions

Article 3 of the Convention (torture, inhuman and degrading treatment or punishment) has been scrutinised on several occasions by Northern Irish courts. As mentioned in the first section of this chapter, in 1971 the Republic of Ireland lodged an interstate application against the United Kingdom complaining that army and police interrogation practices in Northern Ireland were in breach of Article 3. This issue could not be directly tested in Northern Irish courts because Article 3 had not been incorporated into domestic law, and there was no identifiable administrative decision which could be challenged by an application for judicial review, but when "emergency" measures were introduced to deal with the terrorist problem in Northern Ireland in 1973 the law on the admissibility of confession evidence was altered in a way which *borrowed* from Article 3: a confession was to be admissible in evidence only if the prosecution could prove beyond a reasonable doubt that it had not been obtained as a result of torture or inhuman or degrading treatment.[54]

In *R. v McCormick*,[55] decided by a judge sitting without a jury, McGonigal L.J. made express reference to the report of the European Commission of Human Rights in the interstate case taken by Ireland, where the Commission had held that the interrogation practices amounted to torture,[56] but McGonigal L.J. used the report to support a related point, namely that when considering whether to exercise his common law discretion to exclude confession evidence he was entitled to ask not only whether the treatment in question was unacceptable but also whether its *effect* was "such as to drive the individual to act against his will or conscience." In the judge's view, unacceptable treatment was not *per se* a ground for excluding evidence, only if it induced a confession. Just over a year later, in *R. v. Milne*,[57] the same judge reiterated this opinion, though *obiter* because on the facts of the case there had been no physical ill-treatment at all. Strangely, McGonigal L.J. did not at this stage refer to the judgment of the European Court of Human Rights in the interstate case, even though it had been issued eight months previously.[58]

Six months later, in March 1979, Lowry L.C.J. in *R. v. O'Halloran*[59] was more

---

[53] Unreported, January 26, 1973. See generally B. Hadfield, "A Constitutional Vignette—From SR & O 1970/214 to SI 1989/509" (1990) 41 N.I.L.Q. 54.

[54] s. 6 of the Northern Ireland (Emergency Provisions) Act 1973, encapsulating a recommendation of the Diplock Commission (1972; Cmnd 5185). In 1978 this section was amended so as to exclude in addition evidence obtained by "any violence or threat of violence" (as per the recommendation in the Baker Report 1984; Cmnd 9222). The relevant section today is s. 12 of the Northern Ireland (Emergency Provisions) Act 1996.

[55] [1977] N.I. 105 (May 23, 1977).

[56] *Ireland v. United Kingdom*, 15 Ybk of the ECHR 76 and 19 Ybk of the ECHR 512; see K. Boyle and H. Hannum [1976] Ir. Jur. Rep. 243.

[57] [1978] N.I. 110 (September 15, 1978).

[58] (1979–80) 2 EHRR 25.

[59] [1979] N.I. 45 (C.A.) (March 13, 1979).

demanding than McGonigal L.J. He held that, when deciding whether a confession should be excluded from evidence, a judge would find it difficult to envisage any form of physical violence which did not trigger the exclusion. On the other hand, in *R. v. McGrath*,[60] where the defendant argued that he had been the victim of inhuman or degrading treatment in that he had twice been arrested and interrogated in relation to the same offence (murder), Lowry L.C.J. was not so lenient: he held that, even if someone had been the victim of a negligent arrest, this did not amount to torture or inhuman or degrading treatment. Counsel for the defendant did rely upon several passages in the judgment of the European Court of Human Rights in *Ireland v. United Kingdom*, but to no avail. Some years later, in *R. v. Cowan and Others*,[61] the Court of Appeal approved Lowry L.C.J.'s words in *R. v. O'Halloran* and *R. v. McGrath* and held that evidence obtained from a detainee as a result of an inducement (the police had allegedly offered to make deals with each of the appellants) does not have to be excluded—the trial judge retains a discretion in this regard.

In all of these five cases dealing with the admissibility of confessions the court did not treat the European Convention as central to the point at issue, perhaps because counsel relied only on Strasbourg jurisprudence relating to Article 3. If counsel had also cited case law concerning Article 6, the fair trial provision, the Northern Irish courts would have had to confront head on the issue whether common law rules of evidence are in harmony with the Convention's standards. Given the generally laxer approach to evidential requirements adopted in civil law countries, it is likely that the Northern Irish judges would have discovered no disharmony. The Convention, after all, is worded in very general terms, not with specific rules of evidence in mind, and its framers did not intend it to be used as a means whereby all decisions on the facts in domestic courts could be re-opened in Strasbourg.

Prisoners' Rights

Article 3 of the Convention was more directly at issue in the first of the six cases involving prisoners' rights. In *McKernan v. Governor of H.M. Prison Belfast*,[62] a remand prisoner sought judicial review of the governor's decision to keep him in solitary confinement, arguing that it constituted inhuman or degrading treatment. The case is important because it is the first in which the judge who later became the Lord Chief Justice of Northern Ireland, Sir Brian Hutton,[63] was able to express his views on the status of the European Convention in Northern Irish law. Hutton J. considered counsel's argument, based on a publication from the Council of Europe,[64] that solitary confinement could in certain circumstances breach Article 3 even though the European Commission had not yet so held in any case. Conveniently, having found that on the facts before him there was no breach of Article 3, his Lordship felt it unnecessary to

---

[60] [1980] N.I. 91 (C.A.).
[61] [1987] N.I. 338 (C.A.: MacDermott, Murray and Carswell J.J.).
[62] [1983] N.I. 83 (C.A.).
[63] Sir Brian Hutton was appointed Lord Chief Justice of Northern Ireland in 1988 and in January 1997 became a Lord of Appeal.
[64] Human Rights Files No. 5 (1981).

give an opinion on how a domestic remedy could have been made available if the solitary confinement had constituted inhuman treatment.

In four further cases involving applications for judicial review by prisoners the Convention again failed to supplement existing protection for rights under domestic law. In *Re Lillis' Application*[65] a prisoner at the Maze Prison sought judicial review of the decision by a Board of Visitors, the body responsible for dealing with breaches of prison discipline, not to allow him legal representation, or even an adjournment to prepare his defence, when he was answering two charges of assaulting a prison officer. Gibson L.J.[66] considered at some length the decision of the European Court of Human Rights in *Campbell and Fell v. United Kingdom*[67] but distinguished it:

> "My conclusion therefore, is that the considerations which primarily weighed with the court in *Campbell*'s case in deciding that the charges were criminal point to an opposite result in this case. In my view the charges are of a non-criminal nature reading the word 'criminal' in the sense in which it ought to be construed—and indeed, has been construed in Article 6 of the Convention."[68]

In approaching his judicial task in this manner Gibson L.J. seemed to be conceding that a decision of the European Court of Human Rights had indeed altered the domestic law of the United Kingdom. The implication is that, had he not been able to distinguish the facts of the case before him, he would have "followed" *Campbell and Fell*, even without reference to the new English legislation and changes in practice which had implemented the European Court's decision. The learned judge added, incidentally, that in construing the effect of the European Convention upon domestic law he would accept the stance of Lowry L.C.J. in *R. v. Deery*[69] and the statement in *Halsbury's Laws of England* that "where possible, statutes must be interpreted so as not to conflict with any relevant rule of international law."[70] The fact remains that in the case before him Gibson L.J. was prepared to consider the relevance of the European Convention in a context where the common law, not a statute, was the contested ground.

The very issue discussed in *Re Lillis' Application* arose once more in *Re Hone and McCartan's Application*,[71] a case from Northern Ireland that went all the way to the House of Lords.[72] Two prisoners again argued that they had a right to representation when appearing before a Board of Visitors. All eight judges who considered the case held against the applicants, but they took the argument based on *Campbell and Fell*

---

[65] [1984] 15 N.I.J.B. (October 18, 1984).

[66] Gibson L.J. and his wife were murdered by the IRA in April 1987.

[67] (1984) 7 EHRR 165. This case was decided by the European Court less than five months earlier than *Re Lillis's Application*, on June 28, 1984.

[68] *ibid.* pp. 15–16. Gibson L.J. was assisted in his deliberations by the attention given to the legal representation point in the then recent decision of the English Divisional Court in *Ex p. Tarrant* [1984] 1 All E.R. 799.

[69] [1977] N.I. 164.

[70] *Halsbury's Laws of England* (4th ed.), Vol. 18, para. 1404.

[71] [1987] N.I. 160 (C.A.: Lowry L.C.J. and Kelly J.). The first instance judge was again Gibson L.J.

[72] *Sub nom. R. v. Board of Visitors of H.M. Prison The Maze, ex parte Hone and McCartan* [1988] A.C. 379.

v. United Kingdom very seriously. In holding the offences in question not to be criminal offences, the judges expressly applied the criteria laid down by the European Court in that case.

In *Re Hardy's and Whelan's Applications*[73] two prisoners sought judicial review of the Life Sentence Review Board's decision not to recommend that they be given a provisional release date.[74] Carswell J., as he then was,[75] was referred to *Weeks v. United Kingdom*,[76] where the European Court of Human Rights, two years earlier, had held against the United Kingdom on whether, under Article 5(4) of the Convention, judicial review was an adequate form of proceedings for deciding the lawfulness of a discretionary lifer's detention when he was recalled to prison after having been released on licence. It would have been possible for Carswell J. simply to distinguish *Weeks* from the case before him, where no release on licence had yet occurred,[77] but instead he chose to go further in discouraging reliance on the Convention: "It is not for a domestic court, however, to concern itself with the Convention, except where it may be relevant to the interpretation of statute law."[78] This dictum, with great respect, is unfortunate, for it purports to rule out reliance on the Convention in all cases where the common law, as opposed to legislation, is at issue. Not only is such a position out of step with the use made of the Convention in other Northern Irish cases, including the two earlier decisions on prisoners' applications, it also runs counter to judicial practice in England and Wales.

In *Re Baker and Others' Applications*[79] Carswell J. faced judicial review applications from 15 female prisoners who had been charged with failing to obey an order to submit to a body search.[80] The judge held against the applicants on all the grounds argued, as did the Court of Appeal. It is not entirely clear from the Lexis transcript in what way the European Convention was called in aid, but counsel for the applicants seems to have accepted that even if Article 8 were deemed relevant (protection of the right to a private life) it would not have been breached if a prisoner being searched

---

[73] [1989] 2 N.I.J.B. 81.

[74] One was an ordinary lifer, the other a person detained "at the Secretary of State's Pleasure" because he was under 18 when he committed the murder for which he was convicted.

[75] Sir Robert Carswell became Lord Chief Justice of Northern Ireland in January 1997.

[76] (1987) 10 EHRR 293.

[77] Such a situation did arise in *R. v. Secretary of State for Northern Ireland, ex p. Crawford* (Lexis transcript, November 17, 1994), where the applicant, a juvenile when first sentenced, was complaining about the revocation of his release from prison on licence. In answer to counsel's argument that this was a suitable case for the application of the principle of proportionality, in that the decision to revoke the applicant's licence was wholly disproportionate to the risk involved to the public, Kerr J. referred in passing to the Convention when quoting a sentence from the speech of Lord Ackner in the *Brind* case, [1991] 1 A.C. 696 at 763, to the effect that unless and until Parliament incorporates the European Convention into domestic law "there appears to be at present no basis upon which the proportionality doctrine applied by the European Court can be followed by this country." Perhaps surprisingly, counsel in *Ex p. Crawford* does not otherwise seem to have relied upon the Convention.

[78] [1989] 2 N.I.J.B. 81, 95.

[79] [1992] 8 N.I.J.B. 86 (H.C.) and Lexis transcript, April 18, 1994 (C.A.).

[80] Contrary to r. 31(18) of the Prison Rules (NI) 1982. Six were also charged with offending against security or good order and discipline (r. 31(19)) in that they had erected barricades to obstruct entry to their cells.

had been told, as was the case here, that the purpose of the search was to look for an unauthorised article.[81]

Liberty and Freedom of Movement

In *McCann v. Mullan*[82] a 14-year-old boy had been ordered by a juvenile court to attend a training school because he had failed to attend an attendance centre in compliance with a previous court order. Before being ordered to attend the training school, however, the boy had not been told of his statutory right to apply for legal aid[83] and in an application for judicial review the Divisional Court quashed the order for that reason. The boy then sought damages against the members of the juvenile court for false imprisonment, trespass to the person, negligence and breach of statutory duty. At first instance, Hutton J. held that there had been no breach of any right for which compensation could be claimed, but the Court of Appeal, and the House of Lords as well, held to the contrary. In both the High Court and the Court of Appeal, but not, it seems, the House of Lords, the boy's counsel, Richard Ferguson, Q.C., cited Article 5 of the European Convention (which protects the right to liberty but says nothing about the right to legal aid). He accepted, however, that the boy did not have a separate and distinct cause of action under that Article. The Court of Appeal[84] simply noted Article 5, but Hutton J., in the High Court, was not as dismissive of the point. Rather than say that a plaintiff could never rely on Article 5 in a Northern Irish court, he held that Article 5 was not applicable on the facts before him for three reasons: those facts did not involve any ambiguity in a statutory provision,[85] there was no lack of certain authority in the existing corpus of law and nothing from Strasbourg suggested that Article 5 was intended to give an enforceable right to compensation where a superior court had ordered the release of a sentenced person due to some defect or irregularity in the procedure before a lower court.[86]

Freedom of movement arose in a different context in *Re Atkinson*.[87] The applicant, a member of a Loyalist flute band, was seeking judicial review of a police decision to stop the bus on which he was travelling from proceeding to a town 30 miles away, where a rerouted parade was to be held. Hutton J. held that the police action was lawful, because the police officer concerned had reasonable grounds for believing that his action was necessary to preserve the peace.[88] This meant, according to the judge,

---

[81] Art. 8 was also mentioned in *Re Applications to Adopt A-MDW and GICW* (Lexis transcript, May 1, 1992), where Higgins J. reviewed two earlier U.K. cases which had reached Strasbourg when he had to decide whether dispensing with a parent's consent to an adoption order was a breach of the protection of family life; on the facts before him he held that it was not.

[82] [1984] N.I. 186 (H.C., C.A., H.L.), [1984] 3 All E.R. 908 (H.L.).

[83] Under Art. 15(1) of the Treatment of Offenders (NI) Order 1976.

[84] Lowry L.C.J., Jones and O'Donnell L.JJ.

[85] Such as arose, *e.g.* in *R. v. Deery*, [1977] N.I. 164 (C.C.A.).

[86] This seems to be correct: none of the victims of recent miscarriages of justice in England and Wales appear to have succeeded in obtaining compensation through the Strasbourg system. For a case brought by the Birmingham Six, see *Callaghan and Others v. United Kingdom* (1989) 60 DR 296.

[87] [1987] 8 N.I.J.B. 6 (H.C.).

[88] Applying the test laid down by the Irish Court of Appeal in *O'Kelly v. Harvey* (1883) 14 L.R.Ir. 105.

that the restrictions on freedom of movement, assembly and association were "prescribed by law and necessary in a democratic society", as required by Article 11(2) of the Convention and Article 2 of Protocol No. 4. It is interesting that his Lordship was willing to consider Protocol No. 4 even though the United Kingdom has never ratified it, and he expressly chose not to endorse, even *obiter*, the view of Megarry V.-C. in *Malone v. Metropolitan Police Commissioner*[89] that the European Convention does not confer any direct rights on applicants which can be enforced in domestic courts. As he had done in *McKernan v. Governor of H.M. Prison Belfast*[90] and *McCann v. Mullan*,[91] Hutton J. left the door open for a more adventurous application of the Convention should the occasion arise in future. Unfortunately, the opportunities which have arisen since have not been grasped.

District Council Cases

A most unusual use was made of the European Convention in two 1985 cases concerning the right of a local authority to exclude certain councillors from its proceedings, Craigavon Borough Council having set up a special committee which excluded Sinn Féin councillors. In *Re Curran and McCann's Application*[92] Sinn Féin successfully sought judicial review of this decision, on the basis that the council resolution was *ultra vires*. In a bold *obiter dictum* Hutton J. said that if the resolution had not been *ultra vires* it would not have been unreasonable in a *Wednesbury* sense; this was because the exclusion of Sinn Féin would have been in conformity with Article 17 of the European Convention, a provision which is not well known even among human rights experts:

"Nothing in this Convention may be interpreted as implying for any state, group or person any right to engage in any activity or perform any act aimed at the destruction of any of the rights and freedoms set forth herein or at their limitation to a greater extent than is provided for in this Convention."

Although it is distinctly arguable that Article 17 was inapplicable to the facts of the case, because the activity in which Sinn Féin councillors wanted to engage—serving on a council committee—was not itself aimed at the destruction of rights and freedoms set down in the Convention, the basis upon which Hutton J. resorted to the Convention at all is worthy of note for it is probably the most progressive pronouncement to date on the Convention by a Northern Irish judge: "In determining a point on which there is no direct authority under the common law I consider that it is permissible to look at the European Convention on Human Rights and Fundamental Freedoms."[93] This appears to conflict with the view of Carswell J. in *In re Hardy's and Whelan's*

[89] [1979] Ch. 344 at 378.
[90] [1983] N.I. 83 (C.A.).
[91] [1984[N.I. 186 (H.C., C.A., H.L.), [1984] 3 All E.R. 908 (H.L.).
[92] [1985] N.I. 261 (Q.B.).
[93] At pp. 270–272 Hutton J. went on to cite the European Court in *Lawless v. Ireland* (1979–80) 1 EHRR 1.

Applications[94] that the Convention can be used only as an aid in the construction of ambiguous statutory material.

As if in reliance on his dictum on Article 17, a month or so after Hutton J.'s judgment Craigavon Borough Council passed another resolution requiring councillors to sign a declaration against violence and making express reference to the Convention.[95] This was in turn challenged by two other political parties, the Workers' Party and the Social Democratic and Labour Party, again successfully. In *Re French and Others' Applications*[96] Carswell J. held that a council's common law power to protect itself did not extend to the power to exclude councillors or to require a declaration on security grounds.[97] His Lordship did not seek to rely on Article 17 of the European Convention.

Article 17 was later called in aid by an applicant for judicial review of a district council's decision to limit access to the council's public gallery to persons who held passes.[98] The first instance judge (Campbell J.) and the appeal court (through Murray L.J.) had no difficulty in holding that the pass system was operated in a reasonable and permissible manner and they did not deem it necessary to explore the implications of Article 17 in any way.

Freedom of Expression and Discrimination

Two cases impinge upon the Convention's provisions protecting freedom of expression and conscience. In *re McLaughlin*[99] Carswell J. rejected a Sinn Féin activist's challenge to the Government's ban on broadcasts by supporters of violence. In doing so he relied upon the reasoning of the English Court of Appeal in *R. v. Secretary of State for the Home Department, ex parte Brind*, where it was held, *inter alia*, that the European Convention (here Article 10, protecting freedom of expression) could not be used as an aid to the construction of delegated legislation.[1] Likewise, in *R. v. Secretary of State for Northern Ireland, ex parte Stewart*,[2] where the applicant for judicial review was a police officer who had been disciplined for taking part in activities of the Orange Order and the Apprentice Boys, Carswell L.J. refused to permit reliance upon Article 9 of the Convention (the right to freedom of conscience). In line with his attitude to the Convention in *Re Hardy's and Whelan's Applications*,[3] he held

---

[94] [1989[2 N.I.J.B. 81.
[95] The declaration began: "That the Members of this Council condemn all persons and organisations who engage in any activity or perform any act aimed at the destruction or limitation of any of the rights set forth in the European Convention on Human Rights and Fundamental Freedoms."
[96] [1985] N.I. 310 (Q.B.).
[97] It is worth noting that the Elected Authorities (NI) Act 1989 now requires all election candidates in Northern Ireland to sign a declaration indicating their lack of support of violence for political ends.
[98] *R. v. Strabane District Council, ex p. Kelly*, Lexis transcript, September 15, 1993.
[99] [1990] 6 N.I.J.B. 41. An application by Mr McLaughlin to the European Commission was declared inadmissible in May 1994: (1994) 18 EHRR CD 84.
[1] [1990] 1 All E.R. 469. The decision was affirmed by the House of Lords: [1991] 1 A.C. 696 (Lord Lowry, as he had by then become, was one of the Law Lords in this case). The European Commission also declared an application by Mr Brind inadmissible: (1994) 18 EHRR CD 76, (1994) 77-A DR 42.
[2] Lexis transcript, January 12, 1996.
[3] [1989] 2 N.I.J.B. 81.

that the disciplinary regulation in question was adequately clear and that to insist that the domestic court's conclusion should coincide with that of the European Commission and Court would be to incorporate the Convention into domestic common law by the back door, contrary to the views expressed by Lords Ackner and Bridge when the *Brind* case reached the House of Lords.[4]

Two further cases relate to discrimination on religious or political grounds. The right not to be discriminated against on these grounds in the employment sphere is established by the Fair Employment (NI) Acts 1976 and 1989, but the European Convention, on the other hand, does not protect employment rights *per se*. It merely says, in Article 14, that the rights set forth in the Convention shall be secured without discrimination on any ground, including "political or other opinion". Nevertheless, in *McKay v. Northern Ireland Public Service Alliance*[5] Hutton L.C.J. recited Article 14 in order to show that the term "political opinion" in the Fair Employment Acts was not ambiguous or obscure but had a meaning which was recognised and used both in legal documents and in everyday speech. He went on to hold, though not expressly because of Article 14, that the prohibition of discrimination on the basis of political opinion in those Acts was not to be interpreted as confined to political opinions about the constitutional status of Northern Ireland.

As with other anti-discrimination legislation in the United Kingdom, the fair employment legislation in Northern Ireland permits the Secretary of State, under section 42 of the 1976 Act, to issue a certificate to the effect that an act has been done for the purpose of safeguarding national security, public safety or public order. The section even says that the certificate must be taken as conclusive evidence that the act has been done for that purpose. A challenge was raised against one of these certificates in *R. v. Secretary of State for Northern Ireland, ex parte Devlin*.[6] Counsel for the applicant argued that section 42 could be interpreted in two different ways, one of which justified a certificate only where the act done would otherwise have been discriminatory (which was not the Secretary of State's position here). Counsel then contended that the court should resolve this ambiguity by referring to relevant European law and he submitted that it was a cardinal principle of European jurisprudence, as reflected in Articles 6 and 13 of the Convention on Human Rights, that there should be effective judicial control over disputes between parties where, for instance, an allegation of unlawful discrimination had been made. Kerr J., adopting the strict approach to the Convention favoured by Carswell L.J. in other cases, held that there was nothing ambiguous about section 42 and that the Fair Employment Tribunal was as a result totally precluded from hearing the applicant's complaint.[7] He noted, however, that a case was already pending before the European Commission of Human Rights on whether judicial review provides a sufficient remedy in these cases to satisfy

---

[4] [1991] 1 A.C. 696.
[5] Lexis transcript, October 28, 1994 (C.A.).
[6] Lexis transcript, September 6, 1995.
[7] Unfortunately, the judge does not seem to have been referred to *R. v. Secretary of State for Northern Ireland, ex p. Gilmore*, April 10, 1987 (unreported except on Lexis), where Carswell J. said in relation to s. 42 that it "cannot apply to issues which are not referable to complaints of unlawful discrimination contrary to the terms of the Act." See, further, B. Dickson, "Judicial Review and National Security" in B. Hadfield (ed.), *Judicial Review: A Thematic Approach* (1995), Chap. 7.

Articles 6 and 13 of the Convention. This application has since been declared admissible and a decision on the merits is awaited.[8]

Access to Solicitors and Witness Evidence

In recent years most of the Northern Irish cases referring to the European Convention have involved challenges to the pre-trial or trial stages of prosecutions for terrorist offences. The most important decisions are probably *R. v. O'Kane* and *R. v. Dougan*,[9] which each deal with the right of access to a solicitor. It has always been the practice of the police in Northern Ireland not to permit solicitors to be present during the interrogations of terrorist suspects, contrary to the practice with other suspects in Northern Ireland and with all suspects in England and Wales. In *R. v. O'Kane* and *R. v. Dougan* the legitimacy of this practice came before the Court of Appeal of Northern Ireland after the decision of the European Commission, but before that of the European Court, in *John Murray v. United Kingdom*.[10] The Commission and the Court both decided that Northern Ireland's law permitting detainees to be denied access to solicitors for certain periods, when coupled with the restrictions on the right to silence, violated Article 6 of the Convention (the fair trial provision), but neither body examined the issue of whether a denial of access to a solicitor at interview was also a breach of the Convention. In *R. v. O'Kane* Hutton L.C.J. and his colleagues had to consider whether, in the light of the European Commission's view, he should overturn the decision of the trial judge, MacDermott L.J., that a confession was admissible in evidence even though the detainee had been denied access to a solicitor prior to being interrogated and during the interrogation. The Lord Chief Justice decided that he should not. Not only did he re-affirm that the Convention—and the decisions of the Commission and Court—were not part of domestic law, he also held that it was not irrational (in a *Wednesbury* sense) for a judge to fail to refer to the Convention's standards when exercising his or her discretion on whether to admit a confession in evidence. His Lordship saw no need for such a reference because "the principles upon which the discretion given by section 11(3) [of the Northern Ireland (Emergency Provisions) Act 1991] should be exercised have been clearly established by the statutory provisions and by the previous decisions in this jurisdiction." MacDermott L.J. expressed the same views in *R. v. Dougan*, where he quoted the words of Lord Bridge in *R. v. Secretary of State for the Home Dept, ex parte Brind*[11] dismissing the suggestion that the executive must exercise an administrative discretion within the limits of the requirements of the Convention.

The same issue came up for consideration the following year in a Divisional Court

---

[8] *Tinnelly & Sons and McElduff v. United Kingdom*, Application Nos. 20390/92 and 21322/92, (1996) 22 EHRR CD 62.

[9] Both unreported, June 1995. See too *R. v. McMullan* (1994, Kerr J.), *Re Begley* (March 25, 1996, Q.B.) and *R. v. McWilliams* (September 20, 1996, C.A.), all unreported but available through Lexis.

[10] (1994) 18 EHRR CD 1 (Commission), (1996) 22 EHRR 29 (Court). This application to Europe was made by one of the accused in *R. v. Martin and Others* [1992] 5 N.I.J.B. 1, 56 (C.A.), Lexis transcript, May 8, 1991 (H.C.); the European Convention does not seem to have been relied upon either at the trial or on appeal.

[11] [1991] 1 A.C. 696, 748.

appeal of a judicial review application, *Re Russell and Others*.[12] Again the leading judgment was that of Hutton L.C.J. In it he went out of his way to cite parts of European Court jurisprudence[13] to the effect that a democracy had the right to defend itself and its citizens against terrorism and he quoted extensively from various official reports on the emergency laws in Northern Ireland to show that at no time did Parliament opt in favour of altering the law to provide that a confession should be excluded where it had been obtained in the absence of a solicitor at interview. Having endorsed what MacDermott L.J. said in *R. v. Dougan* and he himself in *R. v. O'Kane*, Hutton L.C.J. concluded that "the decision of the European Court [in *John Murray*] . . . falls short of holding that in every case where a terrorist suspect is interviewed without the presence of his solicitor, there will be a breach of Article 6 of the Convention".[14] He added:

"If this court were considering whether it was open to it to develop the rules of the common law to hold that criminal suspects should have a right to have a solicitor present at interview, and if a very grave terrorist threat did not exist in Northern Ireland, and if Parliament had not enacted Section 6 of the 1973 [Emergency Provisions] Act and the similar sections in the subsequent Acts to give effect to the recommendations of the Diplock Report, this court might have accepted and given effect to the arguments advanced."[15]

It should be noted that these same arguments could have been cited by the Northern Irish courts when faced with the proposition that the original section 6 of the 1973 Act had abolished the judicial discretion to exclude a confession even where it was otherwise admissible under the Act. On that occasion the judges did not accede to the "intention of Parliament" argument, which is always a suspect one when based on what Parliament did not say rather than on what it did say. Instead the judges contrived to affirm that their discretion had survived Parliament's intervention.[16] Of course, that was a situation where the pre-existing common law clearly conferred a discretion; there is no such clarity in the common law *vis-à-vis* the right of access to a solicitor at interviews.

In two cases the practice of screening witnesses from the courtroom has come under judicial scrutiny. In *R. v. Murphy and Maguire*[17] one ground of appeal advanced against the conviction of two men for the murder of two British army corporals was that at their trial the names, addresses and faces of Crown witnesses had been concealed from the defendants (though not from their lawyers). Counsel argued that this was a breach of Article 6(1) of the Convention, but the Court of Appeal held that the practice fell within the exceptions allowed by that provision. Kelly L.J. stressed that,

---

[12] Unreported, October 1996.
[13] In particular the European Court's decisions in *Ireland v. United Kingdom* (1979–80) 2 EHRR 25; *Brannigan and McBride v. United Kingdom* (1994) 17 EHRR 539; and *Margaret Murray v. United Kingdom* (1995) 19 EHRR 193, (1994) 15 HRLJ 8.
[14] Page 49 of the unreported judgment.
[15] Pages 52–53 of the unreported judgment.
[16] *R. v. Corey* (1973) N.I.J.B. (December).
[17] [1990] N.I. 306 (C.A: Kelly and MacDermott L.JJ. and Higgins J.).

although there seemed to be no other reported case where the witness's face had been kept concealed, the witnesses here were not giving evidence which directly implicated the accused but were merely proving that they had taken films of the incident leading to the prosecutions. He took judicial notice of the fact that in Northern Ireland even prosecution witnesses whose evidence was merely formal could suffer considerable anxiety for their safety. He noted, moreover, that the trial judge, Hutton L.C.J., had indicated that defence counsel was still able to ask witnesses whether they had seen the accused (shown in photographs) in places different from where the Crown alleged. This local interpretation of the Convention's relevance in such a context has since been approved by the European Commission itself, which has declared inadmissible an application from Mr Murphy.[18]

In *Doherty v. Ministry of Defence*,[19] however, where in a preliminary action during a civil suit against them the Ministry of Defence sought to have their soldier witnesses screened from the court at the main hearing, a judge refused the application. On appeal the judges thought the application should be dealt with only once the main hearing had begun, but they hinted strongly that even then it should not be granted. They suggested it would be enough to allow the names and addresses of the soldiers to be concealed (referring to them as Soldiers A, B, C, etc.). Not surprisingly perhaps, the Ministry's lawyers do not seem to have relied upon the European Convention in their submissions and the only reference to it by the Court of Appeal concerns the recognition by the European Court in *Ireland v. United Kingdom*[20] that the terrorist threat in Northern Ireland did indeed raise a public emergency and hence, in the Court of Appeal's eyes, was a matter of national security.[21]

A related case is *R. v. Dermot Quinn*,[22] where the Crown applied for three witness statements to be admitted in evidence under the Criminal Justice (Evidence etc.) (NI) Order 1988, on the ground that the witnesses could not give oral evidence because of fear. Defence counsel relied on *Windisch v. Austria*,[23] where the European Court of Human Rights found a breach of Articles 6(1) and 6(3)(d) of the Convention when an Austrian criminal court had admitted the statements of two anonymous witnesses who did not then give oral evidence at the trial. But Hutton L.C.J. had little difficulty in dealing with that case: he said that the central issue there was whether the accused had had a fair trial and that "the provisions of Articles 5 and 6 of the 1988 Order are clearly designed to ensure that the accused receives a fair trial." This is a further example of the most senior judge in Northern Ireland adopting a norm of the European Convention and satisfying himself that it has been met in the case before him; unfortunately one cannot deduce from this that the result in the case would have been different if he had not been so satisfied.

Finally, in *R. v. Thompson*[24] one of the grounds of appeal was that when the accused

[18] (1993) 15 EHRR CD 113.
[19] [1991] 1 N.I.J.B. 68 (C.A.: Hutton L.C.J., Murray L.J. and Higgins J.).
[20] Series A, No. 25, (1979–80) 2 EHRR 25.
[21] Hutton L.C.J. repeated this reference in a third case on screening of witnesses, *R. v. H.M. Coroner for Greater Belfast, ex p. Ministry of Defence* (Lexis transcript, June 17, 1994). For further examination of how judges have reacted to the "national security" claim, see B. Dickson, "Judicial Review", above.
[22] [1993] 10 N.I.J.B. 70.
[23] (1990) 13 EHRR 281.
[24] Lexis transcript, May 5, 1994 (C.A.).

was being tried the Crown had wrongly admitted in evidence the previous convictions of his alleged accomplices, under Article 72 of the Police and Criminal Evidence (NI) Order 1989.[25] This was alleged to be a breach of Article 6(3)(d) of the European Convention, which stipulates that everyone charged with a criminal offence has the right "to examine or have examined witnesses against him." Hutton L.C.J. was able to defeat this argument with the simple rejoinder that here the prosecution had called no witness in respect of the convictions—"as no witness was called, there was no breach of the requirement that the accused should have the right to examine a witness against him." As if to underline that the Convention could in any event be used by Northern Irish judges only in limited circumstances, the Lord Chief Justice added that that "there is no ambiguity in Article 72 and no uncertainty in our law as to whether the convictions could be put in evidence." It is interesting that again he did not say that use of the Convention is limited to cases where there is an ambiguity in legislation.

Looking at the Northern Irish cases in the round, one can safely say that the views of the Northern Irish judiciary as to the applicability of the European Convention in Northern Irish law are very restrictive. While Lowry L.C.J. may have been more than willing to entertain arguments based on the Convention, and while Hutton L.C.J. has been careful not to close the door completely on future applications of the Convention, the predominant view, epitomised in the judgments of Carswell L.J. (the new Lord Chief Justice), and more recently of Kerr J., is that the Convention can be prayed in aid only when there is undeniably an ambiguity in a piece of primary legislation. As far as using the Convention to supplement the common law is concerned, there appears to be a difference of opinion: it has been referred to in that context in several cases but on other occasions the judges have poured scorn on such an approach. On balance it appears that the judges are most reluctant to achieve indirectly what they are refusing to do directly. Northern Ireland awaits a more progressive bench in this context, or at any rate an individual judge who is prepared to swim against the tide.

Conclusion

The range of cases surveyed in this chapter indicates that the European Convention on Human Rights is very much a living document in Northern Ireland. Individual litigants as well as lawyers seem well aware of its existence and are prepared to invoke it without hesitation. There have been cases not connected with the civil unrest in addition to the many which do have that connection. Among the latter there has been as strong a willingness on the part of Protestants and Unionists to resort to the Convention as on the part of Catholics and Nationalists, though the arguments raised have differed. On very few occasions, however, has the Convention provided an effective remedy; it has usually simply served as a vehicle for giving the applicant's grievance more publicity. There have been a few instances of administrative procedures or substantive rules being changed as a result of reliance on the Convention, but in the majority of cases an application to Strasbourg has proved fruitless, especially as far

---

[25] Equivalent to s. 74 of the Police and Criminal Evidence Act 1984.

as obtaining compensation is concerned. The Convention's protections have in most instances been unavailable either because of the qualifications set out in the Articles themselves or because the Commission or Court has allowed the United Kingdom Government a substantial margin of appreciation. The right to derogate from the Convention is another obvious reason for its lack of effectiveness.

In many respects, moreover, the Convention contains no provision guaranteeing protection of rights which have been under threat in Northern Ireland. The rights of families and dependants at inquests, the right to trial by jury, the right to equality under the law, the right not to be convicted on uncorroborated confession evidence, the right to have a documented miscarriage of justice investigated and corrected, the right not to be extradited to a legal system which is violating internationally recognised human rights standards, the right to exercise one's culture, the right not to be discriminated against in the spheres of employment, education, health care or housing, and the right to have proper legislative procedures for enacting laws in one's own Parliament[26]—all of these have been contentious issues in Northern Ireland but none of them can be directly dealt with under any part of the Convention.[27] The Convention's overall weakness in the context of group rights is also evident.

Nevertheless, the Convention still tends to be viewed in some quarters in Northern Ireland as a potential panacea for all injustices. Applying to Strasbourg is frequently portrayed as an automatic next step for parties who have lost on appeal in the domestic courts. At the moment decisions are pending on the admissibility of an array of applications connected, in the main, with emergency arrest powers, pre-trial and trial procedures and the use of lethal force by members of the security forces. Realistically, few of these applications have much chance of ultimate success.

---

[26] Since "direct rule" from London was imposed on Northern Ireland in 1972 there have been very inadequate Parliamentary procedures for dealing with specifically Northern Irish legislation. See generally B. Hadfield, *The Constitution of Northern Ireland* (1989), Chap. 5.

[27] There is relevant Strasbourg jurisprudence on some of these issues, but the Convention itself is unspecific in relation to them. See, for example, the discussion on extradition in P. van Dijk and G. J. H. van Hoof, *Theory and Practice of the European Convention on Human Rights* (1990), pp. 235–240.

CHAPTER 6

IRELAND AND THE EUROPEAN CONVENTION

Introduction

Ireland was one of the ten original parties to the European Convention on Human Rights.[1] On becoming a party, it entered a reservation stating that it did not interpret Article 6(3)(c) of the Convention as requiring the provision of free legal assistance to any wider extent than was provided at the time in Ireland.[2] It also made a declaration recognising the jurisdiction of the Court and another recognising the competence of the Commission to receive individual petitions. Both declarations were made *sine die*. It has subsequently become party to all but the Seventh Protocol.[3]

In the early days individual petitions or applications against Ireland were few, and in fact for very many years they remained low in number. While the first ever application to be referred to the Court for a binding decision was an individual complaint against Ireland, that of *Lawless*,[4-5] it was to be a further eighteen years before the Court was seised of another complaint against Ireland.[6] The number of complaints has risen somewhat in more recent years, and the Court has already had to consider three

---

[1] Ireland signed the Convention on November 4, 1950 and ratified it on February 25, 1953. In accordance with Article 29.5.1° of the Irish Constitution, the Convention was laid before Dáil Éireann (the House of Representatives) on March 29, 1954. On Ireland and the Convention see, *e.g.* A. Connelly, "Ireland and the European Convention on Human Rights: An Overview", in Liz Heffernan, ed., *Human Rights: A European Perspective* (1994), p. 34; P. Dillon-Malone, "Individual Remedies and the Strasbourg System in an Irish Context", *ibid.*, p. 48; L. Flynn, "The significance of the European Convention on Human Rights in the Irish legal order" [1994] *Irish Journal of European Law* 4; J. Gleeson, "The European Convention on Human Rights: Its Practical Relevance" [1993] *Irish Journal of European Law* 248; J. Jaconelli, "The European Convention on Human Rights as Irish Municipal Law" (1987) 22 I.J. (n.s.) 13; and G. Whyte, "Application of the European Convention on Human Rights Before the Irish Courts" (1982) 31 I.C.L.Q. 856.

[2] "[T]he Government of Ireland do hereby confirm and ratify the aforesaid Convention and undertake faithfully to perform and carry out all the stipulations therein contained, subject to the reservation that they do not interpret Article 6(3)(c) of the Convention as requiring the provision of free legal assistance to any wider extent than is now provided in Ireland."

[3] Ireland ratified Protocol No. 1 on February 25, 1953, Nos. 2 & 3 on September 12, 1963, No. 4 on October 29, 1968, No. 6 on June 24, 1994, No. 8 on March 21, 1988 and No. 11 on December 16, 1996. It signed without reservation as to ratification Protocol No. 5 on February 18, 1966, and Nos. 9 & 10 on June 24, 1994. It signed Protocol No. 7 on December 11, 1984 subject to ratification, but as of January 1, 1997 had not ratified this Protocol. As of June 1, 1997, Protocol No. 11 had not entered into force.

[4-5] Application No. 332/57, declared admissible by the Commission August 30, 1958, 2 YBECHR 308.

[6] *Airey*, Application No. 6289/73, declared admissible by the Commission July 7, 1977, (1977) 8 DR 42.

185

applications against Ireland in the 1990s.[7] This gradual increase in the number of individual applications is not unique to Ireland, but is a feature of the complaints procedure in general.

Where gross violations of human rights have occurred, as in Greece in the late 1960s and early 1970s and later in Turkey, Ireland has opted not to act as collective enforcer of the rights guaranteed by the Convention and Protocols, leaving this role to be played by other Contracting States.[8] It did, however, bring two applications against the United Kingdom in the early 1970s in respect of the British response to the outbreak of violence in Northern Ireland. The second application was not pursued, but the first was eventually referred to the Court, and is the only inter-State case to date to have been decided by the Court.[9] No application has ever been brought against Ireland by another State party.

Applications

The Inter-State Application

The events in Northern Ireland which triggered the interstate application was the introduction of internment without trial, on August 9, 1971, and the subsequent ill-treatment of detainees. Before the Court of Human Rights, Ireland challenged internment without trial as a violation of the personal liberty and fair trial guarantees under Articles 5 and 6 of the Convention. It also alleged that the ill-treatment of detainees infringed the guarantee in Article 3 of freedom from torture and inhuman or degrading treatment or punishment. It further contended that the fact that the extrajudicial powers were used mainly against those suspected of involvement in IRA terrorism and less against suspected Loyalist terrorists constituted prohibited discrimination contrary to Article 14.

Before deciding upon the merits of these allegations, the Court had to rule on a number of preliminary questions, including an argument put forward by the British Government that the contested instances of ill-treatment did not constitute an administrative practice on the part of the British authorities but individual cases for which effective domestic remedies were available to the persons concerned. The Court's ruling on this argument is important in relation to the operation of the exhaustion of domestic remedies rule and state responsibility for the acts of lower officials where a practice occurs. It affirmed that the domestic remedies rule applies to State applications as it does to individual applications "when the applicant State does no more than denounce a violation or violations allegedly suffered by 'individuals' whose place, as

---

[7] *Pine Valley Developments Ltd and Others*, Application No. 12742/87, declared admissible by the Commission May 3, 1989, 61 DR 206; *Open Door Counselling and Dublin Well Woman Centre Ltd and Others*, Application Nos. 14234/88 and 14235/88, declared admissible May 15, 1990; and *Keegan*, Application No. 16969/90, declared admissible February 13, 1992.

[8] Denmark, The Netherlands, Norway and Sweden lodged applications against Greece in 1967. A further joint application against Greece was lodged by Denmark, Norway and Sweden in 1970. In 1982, Denmark, France, the Netherlands, Norway and Sweden lodged applications against Turkey.

[9] Judgment of January 18, 1978, Series A, No. 25; (1979–80) 2 EHRR 25.

it were, is taken by the State."[10] However, "the rule does not apply where the applicant State complains of a practice as such, with the aim of preventing its continuation or recurrence, but does not ask the Commission or the Court to give a decision on each of the cases put forward as proof or illustrations of that practice."[11]

The Court also gave its understanding of a practice. A practice "consists of an accumulation of identical or analogous breaches which are sufficiently numerous and inter-connected to amount not merely to isolated incidents or exceptions but to a pattern or system."[12]

On the issue of state responsibility for a practice, it commented, "It is inconceivable that the higher authorities of a State should be, or at least should be entitled to be, unaware of the existence of such a practice . . . under the Convention those authorities are strictly liable for the conduct of their subordinates; they are under a duty to impose their will on subordinates and cannot shelter behind their inability to ensure that it is respected."[13]

The Court then addressed the merits of the case. The ill-treatment complained of ranged from the required performance by detainees of certain exercises to the infliction of severe injury. Complaints were also made about the use of disorientation or sensory deprivation techniques in the questioning of some detainees. These comprised spread-eagling a detainee against a wall in a stressful position for a number of hours, hooding, subjection to a continuous loud and hissing noise, deprivation of sleep and deprivation of food and drink. The Court found that, for a period, detainees at the Palace Barracks, a military camp in Hollywood, County Down, had been repeatedly subjected to violence constituting inhuman treatment. At other detention centres, such as the army camp at Ballykinler, also in County Down, where detainees were held in extreme discomfort and were made to perform irksome and painful exercises, no inhuman or degrading treatment had, however, occurred. Although the behaviour of the RUC and the army had been "discreditable and reprehensible",[14] it did not infringe Article 3. As to the interrogation techniques, the Court held that their combined use amounted to inhuman treatment because of the intense pain and suffering inflicted thereby on the persons subjected to them. The combined use of these techniques also constituted degrading treatment "since they were such as to arouse in their victims feelings of fear, anguish and inferiority capable of humiliating and debasing them and possibly breaking their physical and moral resistance."[15] It did not, however, constitute torture since "it did not occasion suffering of the particular intensity and cruelty implied by [this] word."[16]

As to internment without trial, the Court held that it ran counter to the guarantee

---

[10] *ibid.* p. 78, para. 159.
[11] *ibid.*
[12] *ibid.* p. 77, para. 159.
[13] *ibid.* pp. 77–78, para. 159.
[14] *ibid.* p. 83, para. 181.
[15] *ibid.* p. 80, para. 167.
[16] *ibid.* The Court held, by 16 votes to one, that the use of the techniques constituted a practice of inhuman and degrading treatment, and by 13 votes to four, that their use did not constitute a practice of torture. *Cf.* the opinion of the Commission, which, in its Report of February 9, 1976, was unanimously of the view that the combined use of the techniques constituted a practice of inhuman treatment and of torture in breach of Article 3.

of personal liberty in Article 5 and also, assuming Article 6 to apply, that of a fair trial, but that, given the circumstances prevailing in Northern Ireland at the time, it was justified under Article 15 of the Convention, which allows a state to derogate from some of its human rights obligations in time of public emergency threatening the life of the nation. Ireland did not contest the existence of such an emergency and the Court considered it "perfectly clear from the facts".[17] As to the need for resort to special powers of detention to deal with the situation, the Court found that, "being confronted with a massive wave of violence and intimidation",[18] the British authorities "were reasonably entitled to consider that normal legislation offered insufficient resources for the campaign against terrorism and that recourse to measures outside the scope of the ordinary law, in the shape of extrajudicial deprivation of liberty, was called for."[19]

The difference in the use of the special powers against suspected IRA and Loyalist terrorists was found not to be discriminatory, *inter alia*, because the IRA was a far more structured and well-organised paramilitary group, because of the scale of the IRA's activities and because it was, in general, easier to institute criminal proceedings against suspected Loyalist than against IRA terrorists.

Individual Applications

Individual applications against Ireland reveal a wide range of complaints. People have complained, *inter alia*, about the conditions under which they were being detained,[20] about the refusal of leave to appeal against conviction,[21] about the composition of a court,[22] about being photographed against their will at home,[23] about censorship,[24] and about the failure of the State to protect the life of an individual.[25]

Many applications have been ruled inadmissible by the Commission for failure to exhaust domestic remedies or as being manifestly ill-founded. An example of the former was a case in which the applicant argued that photographic evidence admitted by the High Court in a personal injuries action infringed her right to respect for her private and family life.[26] The evidence included photographs taken from the street of her in the living room of her home. Given that the Irish Constitution guarantees a right to privacy, the Commission held that she should have appealed the High Court's ruling on the admissibility of the evidence to the Supreme Court. An example of the

---

[17] (1979–80) 2 EHRR 25 at 91, para. 25.

[18] *ibid.* p. 93, para. 212.

[19] *ibid.* pp. 93–94, para. 212.

[20] See *X and Y v. Ireland*, Application No. 8299/78, admissibility decision, October 10, 1980, 22 DR 51.

[21] *X v. Ireland*, Application No. 9136/80, admissibility decision, July 10, 1981, 26 DR 242. See also *Eccles, McPhillips and McShane v. Ireland*, admissibility decision, December 9, 1988, 59 DR 212.

[22] See *D v. Ireland*, Application No. 11489/85, admissibility decision, December 3, 1986, 51 DR 117.

[23] *X v. Ireland*, Application No. 18670/91, December 1, 1993, unpublished.

[24] *Purcell and Others v. Ireland*, Application No. 15404/89, admissibility decision, April 16, 1991, 70 DR 262, (1991) 12 HRLJ 254.

[25] See *H v. United Kingdom and Ireland*, Application No. 9833/82, admissibility decision, March 7, 1985, 42 DR 53; and *M v. United Kingdom and Ireland*, Application No. 9837/82, admissibility decision, March 14, 1986, 47 DR 27. For applications up to 1990, see in general Donncha O'Connell, *Digest of the Applications Made Against Ireland under the ECHR* (1990).

[26] *X v. Ireland*, Application No. 18670/91.

latter was a case challenging a broadcasting ban on Sinn Fein.[27] It was argued by a number of journalists and other persons involved in broadcasting that the ban infringed their right to freedom of expression. In the Commission's view, however, the restrictions on their freedom of expression could be considered necessary to ensure that the spokespersons of certain organisations did not use the opportunity of live interviews and other broadcasts for promoting illegal activities. An early application against Ireland was rejected on the less commonly cited ground of anonymity.[28] The complaint was signed "lover of tranquillity" and postmarked "Dublin".

Of the applications which have been ruled admissible by the Commission, two have been settled without any pronouncement on the merits by either the Commission or the Court. The first application concerned the succession rights of a person born outside marriage. At the time, Irish law discriminated in several respects against persons born outside marriage.[29] The applicant's parents had lived together for almost forty years but had never married. When her father died without making a will, she complained that she had no inheritance rights over his estate. She also complained of her position under Irish law whereby she likewise had no inheritance rights over the estates of relatives on either her mother's or her father's side. Had her parents been married to one another, she would have had. The Commission admitted her complaints as raising issues under Article 14 of the Convention in conjunction with Article 8, and held a hearing on her complaints in October 1986. That year a Bill was introduced into the Irish Parliament to abolish the distinction between children born out of wedlock and those born within wedlock.[30] During the passage of the Bill, negotiations between the applicant and the Irish Government had continued with a view to the conclusion of a friendly settlement, and an agreement was reached in November 1987 whereby the applicant was prepared to accept an *ex gratia* payment of IR£10,000 from the Government in settlement of her case. The Commission endorsed this agreement, and held that, in view of the impending legislation, "a friendly settlement of the application had been secured on the basis of respect for human rights as defined in the Convention."[31]

The second application concerned the involuntary committal of a woman to a mental hospital and raised issues under Article 5 in relation to the deprivation of her liberty. In December 1996 the Commission approved a settlement whereby the Government would pay her IR£14,000 in compensation and approximately IR£50,000 in costs and expenses.[31a]

By the end of 1996, the Court had decided seven individual applications against Ireland. As already indicated, the first was that of *Lawless*. The Court rendered three

---

[27] *Purcell v. Ireland*, Application No. 15404/89.
[28] Application No. 361/58.
[29] *Stoutt v. Ireland*, Application No. 10978/84, report of the Commission, December 17, 1987, 54 DR 43. In the case of *Patrick O'Reilly v. Ireland* the Commission reported in February 1995 that there had been a violation of Art. 6(1) arising from the length of criminal proceedings. The case was not referred to the Court, and in November 1995 the Committee of Ministers decided that there had been a violation of this provision.
[30] Status of Children Bill, which was enacted in 1987.
[31] Commission report, para. 20, 54 DR 43 at 47.
[31a] *O'Reilly v. Ireland*, Application No. 24196/94, report of the Commission, December 3, 1996.

judgments in this case, the first in 1960 on questions of procedure, [32] the second in 1961 on the standing of the applicant before the Court,[33] and the third, also in 1961, on the merits.[34] The first two judgments were of considerable importance for the role of the individual in proceedings before the Court given that, prior to the entry into force of Protocol No. 9, an applicant had no formal standing in these proceedings. The Court's decision on the merits is important for its understanding of a public emergency threatening the life of the nation and for the standard of review it applied to the necessity of measures taken by the State to deal with the emergency.

In its first judgment, the Court upheld the right of the Commission, once a case was referred to the Court, to communicate documents, including its own Report, to the persons or bodies directly concerned, with the proviso that the documents should not be published. In the second, it held that the Commission, in its observations to the Court, was entitled to take into account the views of the applicant and, at its discretion, to invite the applicant to place some person at the disposal of the delegates of the Commission.

Lawless had been detained without trial in a military detention camp for almost five months in pursuance of an order made by the Minister for Justice in the exercise of special powers of arrest and detention under the Offences Against the State (Amendment) Act, 1940. He was suspected of being a member of the IRA and of involvement in activities prejudicial to the security of the State. The Court rejected his complaints under Articles 6 (right to a fair trial) and 7 (freedom from retroactive criminal offences and penalties). In its view, these provisions were not applicable since Lawless had not been charged with, or found guilty of, any criminal offences. His detention did however infringe the personal liberty guarantees of Article 5(1) and (3) which should be read as a whole. These provisions permit the arrest and detention of a person on suspicion of having committed an offence or of being about to commit an offence, provided the person is arrested or detained for the purpose of being brought before a judge who will examine the lawfulness of the detention or decide on the merits of the case, and the person should be brought promptly before a judge. Lawless was not detained for this purpose nor was he brought promptly before a judge. His detention was nevertheless permitted by Article 15. A public emergency within the meaning of this Article referred, said the Court, to "an exceptional situation of crisis or emergency which affects the whole population and constitutes a threat to the organized life of the community of which the State is composed."[35] The existence of such a situation in Ireland had been reasonably deduced by the Irish Government from a combination of several factors, namely: there existed a secret army (the IRA) engaged in unconstitutional activities and using violence to attain its purposes; this army was also operating outside the territory of the State, thus seriously jeopardising relations between Ireland and the United Kingdom; and there had been a steady and alarming increase in terrorist activities from the autumn of 1956 throughout the first half of 1957. Moreover, Lawless' detention could be regarded as "strictly required by the

---

[32] Judgment of November 14, 1960, Series A, No. 1; (1979–80) 1 EHRR 1.
[33] Judgment of April 7, 1961, Series A, No. 2; (1979–80) 1 EHRR 13.
[34] Judgment of July 1, 1961, Series A, No. 3; (1979–80) 1 EHRR 15.
[35] Para. 28, (1979–80) 1 EHRR 15 at 31.

exigencies of the situation''. Other measures such as the institution of special criminal or military courts would not have sufficed to restore peace and order, and the sealing of the border between the Republic of Ireland and Northern Ireland would have had extremely serious repercussions on the population as a whole, beyond the extent required by the exigencies of the emergency. Also, the system of administrative detention was subject to a number of safeguards designed to prevent abuses in its operation. Among these were the fact that Parliament kept the application of the 1940 Act under constant supervision and that the Act itself provided for the establishment of a Detention Commission to which any person detained under the Act could refer his case and whose opinion, if favourable to the release of the person concerned, was binding upon the Government.

The second application, *Airey*, raised very different issues.[36] Mrs Johanna Airey had tried to obtain a decree of judicial separation from her husband on the grounds of his alleged physical and mental cruelty to her and their children, such a decree only being available at the time from the High Court. She had approached several solicitors to act for her, but without success because she lacked the financial means to meet the costs involved. She alleged denial of access to the courts in breach of her rights under Article 6(1), infringement of her right to respect for her family life under Article 8 because of the absence of an effective and accessible remedy for marriage breakdown under Irish law, discrimination on the ground of property contrary to Article 14 by virtue of the exorbitantly high cost of obtaining a decree of judicial separation, and breach of Article 13 in that she lacked an effective remedy under Irish law in respect of her marriage breakdown.

The Irish Government sought to block any decision by the Court on the merits of her case by pleading, *inter alia*, that she had not exhausted domestic remedies. She could, for example, have appeared before the High Court herself without the assistance of a lawyer. Whether this possibility could be regarded as a sufficient domestic remedy was, said the Court, a question it would not be able to decide without at the same time ruling on the merits of her complaint under Article 6(1) that she did not enjoy effective access to the High Court.

As to this complaint, the Court accepted that paragraph 1 of Article 6 guaranteed Mrs Airey a right of access to the High Court in order to petition for judicial separation. It did not accept the argument of the Government that the right of access was satisfied simply by the possibility that she could appear before the High Court without the assistance of a lawyer. The Convention it said, ''is intended to guarantee not rights that are theoretical or illusory but rights that are practical and effective.''[37] What this meant was that it had to decide whether Mrs Airey would be able to present her case for judicial separation ''properly and satisfactorily''[38] before the High Court, without the assistance of a lawyer. The Court remarked on the complexity of the legal issues and procedure involved and that ''marital disputes often entail an emotional involvement that is scarcely compatible with the objectivity required by advocacy in court''.[39]

---

[36] Application No. 6289/73, decided by the Court October 9, 1979, Series A, No. 32; (1979–80) 2 EHRR 305.
[37] *ibid*. p. 314, para. 24.
[38] *ibid*. p. 315, para. 24.
[39] *ibid*.

It further noted that Mrs Airey would be at a disadvantage if her husband were represented by a lawyer and she were not, and that in all such proceedings in the previous seven years the petitioner had been represented by a lawyer. In view of these considerations, it thought it most improbable that Mrs Airey could effectively present her own case. As a result there had been a breach of Article 6(1). Since the protection of private and family life may sometimes necessitate that husband and wife be relieved from the duty to live together, and Mrs Airey had been unable to seek recognition in law of her *de facto* separation from her husband, she had also been the victim of a violation of Article 8. Having found violations of Mrs Airey's rights under Articles 6 and 8, the Court did not deem it necessary also to examine her complaints of discrimination under Article 14. Similarly, since Articles 13 and 6(1) overlapped in her case, the Court did not examine whether there had been a failure to observe the requirements of the former Article, these requirements being less strict than those of Article 6.

Airey is one of the first cases in which the Court began to recognise that compliance with its obligations under the Convention requires of a State not only that it refrain from unjustifiably interfering with individual liberty but also that at times it take some positive action to ensure respect for the guaranteed rights. In its view, the obligation to secure an effective right of access to the courts falls into this category of positive duty. In response to the Irish Government's argument that the Court should not interpret the Convention in such a way as to achieve any social or economic development in a Contracting State, the Court stated that, although the Convention essentially sets forth civil and political rights, many of these rights have implications of a social or economic nature. The mere fact, therefore, that an interpretation of the Convention might extend into these fields was not a decisive factor against such an interpretation. It was not dictating to Ireland what it should do to remedy the situation. The State has "a free choice of the means to be used"[40] to secure to litigants an effective right of access to the courts. While the introduction of a scheme of civil legal aid is one of the means of ensuring such access for those without the means to hire a lawyer, there are others, such as simplification of the legal procedures involved.

Family matters also featured in the third application, *Johnston and Others*.[41] In this case the Court had to consider the compatibility with Ireland's obligations under the Convention of the position in Irish law of an unmarried couple and their daughter. The couple had been living in a stable relationship for years but, owing to the constitutional ban on divorce,[42] could not marry, the man still being the husband of a woman he had married some thirty years earlier and from whom he had amicably separated some years before.

The couple alleged that the non-availability of divorce infringed their right to marry under Article 12, their right to respect for their family life under Article 8, and their freedom of thought, conscience and religion under Article 9. The Court rejected these allegations. It held that the right to marry guaranteed by Article 12 covers the formation of marriage, not its dissolution, and that a prohibition on divorce does not injure the substance of that right. As to Article 8, although the applicants constituted a family

---

[40] *ibid.* p. 317, para. 26.
[41] Application No. 9697/82, judgment of December 18, 1986, Series A, No. 112; (1987) 9 EHRR 203.
[42] See the related discussion in the last paragraph of this chapter.

within the meaning of this Article and were entitled to its protection, this protection could not be interpreted as extending to the introduction of measures permitting divorce and remarriage. Nor was Article 9 to be regarded as applying to the non-availability of divorce. The couple further argued that their lack of certain rights *vis-à-vis* one another, including maintenance and succession rights, constituted a violation of Article 8. The Court held however that the positive obligations flowing from this Article did not require a State to accord to unmarried couples a status analogous to that of married couples or to establish a special régime for a particular category of unmarried couples, that is, those who wished to marry but who were legally barred from doing so. The couple also alleged discrimination on the ground of financial means in that certain persons resident in Ireland with the necessary financial means could obtain a divorce elsewhere which would be recognised in Ireland. The Court noted that under the general Irish rules of private international law foreign divorces would be recognised in Ireland only if they had been obtained by persons domiciled abroad. It did not accept that the situation of the applicants was analogous to that of such other persons.

Lastly, the applicants complained of the legal status of their daughter. This, the Court found, infringed their rights under Article 8. Respect for family life entails an obligation for the State to allow ties between near relatives to develop normally. In the Court's view, Article 8 thus requires that a child born of an unmarried couple "be placed, legally and socially, in a position akin to that of a legitimate child."[43] Since the legal régime in Ireland did not reflect the child's natural family ties, there was a failure to respect the family life of all three applicants. The Court reiterated that it was not its function to indicate what measures Ireland should take to remedy the situation. Ireland was free to choose the means to be utilised in its domestic law to comply with its obligations under the Convention. In making its choice, Ireland should "ensure that the requisite fair balance is struck between the demands of the general interest of the community and the interests of the individual."[44] In view of its finding on this point, the Court was of the opinion that it was not necessary for it to give a separate ruling on the differential succession rights of legitimate and illegitimate children under Irish law. Consideration of these matters had been included in its general examination under Article 8 of the child's legal situation.

Issues under Article 8 were again to the fore in the next case of *Norris*.[45] The complaints in this case closely resembled those brought in the earlier Northern Ireland case of *Dudgeon*,[46] and in the course of its Judgment in *Norris* the Court quoted extensively from its decision in this earlier case. Norris, an active homosexual, complained of legislation which penalised male homosexual activity. Since he had at no time been charged with an offence under the legislation, the Court had first to consider the Government's argument that he could not claim to be a victim of a violation within the meaning of Article 25(1) of the Convention and that he therefore lacked standing to bring an application. The Government argued that he was seeking to bring an *actio*

---

[43] (1987) 9 EHRR 203 at 225, para. 74.
[44] *ibid.* p. 226, para. 77.
[45] Application No. 10581/83, judgment of October 26, 1988, Series A, No. 142; (1991) 13 EHRR 186.
[46] Application No. 7525/76, judgment of September 23, 1981, Series A, No. 45; (1982) 4 EHRR 149.

popularis and to get a review *in abstracto* of the contested legislation in the light of the Convention. The Court rejected the argument by a slim majority.[47] It cited previous case law to the effect that Article 25 entitles individuals to contend that a law violates their rights by itself, in the absence of an individual measure of implementation, if they run the risk of being directly affected by it. Norris did run such a risk. Moreover, one of the effects of criminal sanctions against homosexual acts was to increase the anxiety and guilt feelings of homosexuals. Turning to the issues under Article 8, the Court held that the maintenance in force of the legislation constituted a continuing interference with the applicant's right to respect for his private life. It reiterated what it had said in *Dudgeon*, that the matter before it concerned "a most intimate aspect of private life",[48] and that therefore "there must exist particularly serious reasons"[49] before interferences on the part of public authorities in this area of private life will be regarded as acceptable under the Convention. The Government had adduced no evidence pointing to the existence of factors justifying the retention of the legislation which were additional to or of greater weight than those present in the *Dudgeon* case. There was therefore a breach of Norris' right under Article 8 to respect for his private life.

The next case, *Pine Valley Developments Ltd and Others*,[50] concerned the property interests of two companies and of the managing director of one of the companies. The companies had purchased land in reliance on outline planning permission for industrial warehouse and office development on the site. The outline planning permission had however been given in material contravention of the development plan for the area and was subsequently found by the Supreme Court to be invalid. One of the consequences of this decision was a substantial reduction in the value of the property. Legislation was passed to validate permission given in contravention of the development plan but did not apply to the applicants who had initiated a court action for damages against the relevant public authorities. They alleged in Strasbourg that they had suffered a violation of their property rights under Article 1 of the First Protocol and that the remedial legislation discriminated against them in contravention of this Article taken in conjunction with Article 14 of the Convention. They further claimed that they did not have an effective remedy under Irish law in respect of their complaints as required by Article 13 of the Convention. The Court found that the company, Pine Valley Developments Ltd, in fact enjoyed no property rights under the Protocol since it had parted with ownership of the land (to one of the other applicants) prior to the Supreme Court's decision. As regards the other two applicants, the Court held that there had been an interference with their right to the peaceful enjoyment of their possessions but that the interference was justified in order to protect the environment, that is, to preserve the green belt around Dublin. Also, the annulment of their planning permission without any remedial action being taken in their favour could not be regarded as a disproportionate measure since they were engaged in a commercial venture which involved an element of risk and were aware of the development plan

---

[47] By eight votes to six.
[48] (1991)13 EHRR 186 at 200, para. 46; *Dudgeon*, (1982) 4 EHRR 149 at 165, para. 52.
[49] *ibid.*
[50] Application No. 12742/87, judgment of November 29, 1991, Series A, No. 222; (1992) 14 EHRR 319.

and of the opposition of the local planning authority to any departure from it. The Court did, however, find for these two applicants on the issue of discrimination. In fact, the Irish Government had advanced no justification before the Court for the difference in legislative treatment between the applicants and other holders of outline planning permission. Their complaint under Article 13 was rejected. The applicants had taken proceedings in the Irish courts seeking damages for their financial loss, albeit unsuccessfully. The effectiveness of a remedy under Article 13, recalled the Court, does not depend upon the certainty of success.

Alleged violations of the right to freedom of expression were the main issue in *Open Door Counselling and Dublin Well Woman Centre Ltd and Others*, decided a year later.[51] The applicants complained that an injunction restraining counselling agencies from providing information to pregnant women about specific abortion services in Great Britain infringed their freedom to impart and to receive information as guaranteed by Article 10 of the Convention. The Court upheld these complaints. It noted that it was not a criminal offence under Irish law for a pregnant woman to travel abroad in order to have an abortion and that abortion services are, in fact, lawful in other Convention States and may be crucial to a woman's health and well-being. It added that limitations on information concerning activities which had been and continued to be tolerated by national authorities call for "careful scrutiny by the Convention institutions as to their conformity with the tenets of a democratic society".[52] While accepting that the injunction pursued a legitimate aim, the protection of morals, of which the protection in Ireland of the right to life of the unborn is one aspect, the Court found that it was overly broad and had a disproportionate impact on the applicants' freedom of expression. The Court criticised the "absolute nature"[53] of the injunction. It imposed a "perpetual restraint"[54] on the provision of information to pregnant women concerning abortion facilities abroad, regardless of age or state of health or the reasons for seeking counselling on the termination of pregnancy. On this ground alone, the Court thought the injunction was disproportionate. This view was confirmed, however, by other factors. The counselling agencies had neither advocated nor encouraged abortion. They had merely explained the available options, of which abortion in Great Britain was one. Also, information about abortion facilities abroad could be obtained from other sources, such as magazines and telephone directories or persons with contacts in Great Britain. Furthermore, the injunction was largely ineffective since it did not prevent large numbers of women from continuing to obtain abortions in Great Britain. In addition, the available information suggested that the injunction had created a risk to the health of women who were seeking abortions at a later stage of pregnancy and who were not availing themselves of customary medical supervision after abortion. The injunction might also have had more adverse effects on women who were not sufficiently resourceful or had not the necessary level of education to have access to alternative sources of information. The Court made it clear that it was not called upon to examine, nor was it necessary for the purpose of the

---

[51] Application Nos 14234/88 and 14235/88, decided by the Court October 29, 1992, Series A, No. 246; (1993) 15 EHRR 244.
[52] Para. 72 of the Court's judgment, (1993) 15 EHRR 244 at 266.
[53] *ibid*. para. 73.
[54] *ibid*.

case to decide, "whether a right to abortion is guaranteed under the Convention or whether the foetus is encompassed by the right to life as contained in Article 2".[55] Having found for the applicants on Article 10, the Court did not deem it necessary also to examine whether there had been breaches of Article 8 or Articles 8 and 10 read in conjunction with Article 14.

The most recent case referred to the Court, *Keegan*, concerned the placing for adoption of a child born out of wedlock by its mother without the knowledge or consent of its natural father.[56] The latter complained about his lack of status under Irish law: that he did not enjoy even a defeasible right to be appointed guardian of his child and that he had no standing in the adoption proceedings. He alleged violations of his right to respect for family life (Article 8), his right to a fair trial (Article 6(1)), and discrimination against him as an unmarried father in comparison to a married father (Article 14).

The Court confirmed that the family protected by Article 8 is not confined to relationships based on marriage. Keegan's relationship with the mother had lasted for two years, during one of which they had cohabited. They had decided to have a child and to get married, though they in fact separated soon after their engagement to be married. The Court was therefore of the view that from the moment of his daughter's birth a bond amounting to family life existed between the applicant and his daughter. According to the principles set out by the Court in its earlier case law, where the existence of a family tie with a child had been established, the State must act in a manner calculated to enable that tie to be developed. The fact that Irish law permitted the child to be placed for adoption without the applicant's knowledge or consent, leading to the bonding of the child with the proposed adoptive parents and to the subsequent making of an adoption order, constituted an interference with his right to respect for his family life. This interference was not justified. The placing of the child with alternative carers with whom she might over time develop new bonds not only jeopardised the proper development of the applicant's ties with the child, it put him at a significant disadvantage in his contest with the prospective adopters for the custody of the child. The Irish Government had advanced no reasons relevant to the child's welfare to justify such a departure from the principles which govern respect for family ties. The Court also found that the applicant's lack of rights under Irish law to challenge the placement of the child for adoption either before the Adoption Board or before the courts violated his rights under Article 6(1). In the light of its findings on Articles 6(1) and 8, the Court did not deal also with the issue of discrimination.

The Convention and Domestic Law

In general, Ireland subscribes to the dualist view of public international law, whereby domestic law and public international law are regarded as discrete legal systems. International law will not be treated as part of domestic law unless it has been recognised

---

[55] *ibid.* p. 264, para. 66.
[56] Application No. 16969/90, decided by the Court May 26, 1994, Series A, No. 290; (1994) 18 EHRR 342.

by or incorporated into domestic law. This dualist view finds expression in relation to treaties in Article 29.6 of the Constitution, which provides: "No international agreement shall be part of the domestic law of the State save as may be determined by the Oireachtas."

Since the Oireachtas, the Irish Parliament, has not determined that the Convention and Protocols shall be part of the domestic law of the State, it would be futile to base a claim before an Irish court of violation of one's rights on these international agreements.[57] A rider, however, needs to be added to this statement of the general position. Given the primacy of European Community law over domestic law, it is possible that at some time in the future the courts will give effect indirectly to the Convention as part of Community law.[58]

In 1995 the High Court was presented with an argument that in applying the constitutional guarantee of equality before the law, account should be taken of Ireland's obligations under the European Convention on Human Rights, especially in relation to Article 6 (the right to a fair trial) and Article 14 (the prohibition on discrimination in the enjoyment of rights).[59] It was contended that the Convention is now part of domestic law by virtue of Article 29.4.4° of the Constitution and Article F of Title I of the Treaty on European Union. Article 29.4.4° of the Constitution provides: "The State may ratify the Treaty on European Union signed at Maastricht on the 7th day of February, 1992, and may become a member of that Union." Paragraph 2 of Article F of Title I of the Treaty on European Union reads: "The Union shall respect fundamental rights, as guaranteed by the European Convention for the Protection of Human Rights and Fundamental Freedoms signed in Rome on 4 November 1950 and as they result from the constitutional traditions common to the Member States, as general principles of Community law." The Court did not find it necessary to rule on this submission because it considered that the applicant had not established that his trial before the Special Criminal Court as opposed to before the ordinary courts amounted to prohibited discrimination under either the Constitution or the Convention.[60]

---

[57] See, generally, C. Lysaght, "The Status of Irish Agreements in Irish Domestic Law" (1994) 12 *Irish Law Times* 171.

[58] As regards the primacy to be afforded Community law *as a matter of domestic law*, see, in particular, Article 29.4.5° of the Constitution and the decision of the Supreme Court in *Campus Oil Ltd v. Minister for Industry and Energy and Others* [1983] I.R. 82 at 86–87. Article 29.4.5° of the Constitution provides:

> "No provision of this Constitution invalidates laws enacted, acts done or measures adopted by the State which are necessitated by the obligations of membership of the European Union or of the Communities, or prevents laws enacted, acts done or measures adopted by the European Union or by the Communities or by institutions thereof, or by bodies competent under the Treaties establishing the Communities, from having the force of law in the State."

For criticism of the Supreme Court view in *Campus Oil* that the right of appeal to the Supreme Court under Article 34 of the Constitution is subject to the primacy of Article 177 of the Treaty of Rome by virtue of Article 29.4.3° (now Article 29.4.5°) of the Constitution, see J. M. Kelly, *The Irish Constitution* (3rd ed., 1994), pp. 284–285.

[59] *Kavanagh v. Government of Ireland and Others* [1996] 1 ILRM 133.

[60] At pp. 151–152. This case was appealed to the Supreme Court, but no specific reference was made in the decision of that Court to the argument based on Articles 6 and 14 of the Convention: [1997] 1 ILRM 321.

The Convention and the Courts

Basing itself on Article 29.6 of the Constitution, the Supreme Court has generally taken a narrow view not only of the status of the Convention and its associated texts under Irish law but also of judgments of the European Court. Three Supreme Court decisions are of particular importance in this regard: *Re Ó Laighléis,*[61] *Norris v. Attorney General*[62] and *O'B. v. S.*[63]

In all three cases the applicants, having been unsuccessful before the Irish courts, took applications to the European Commission. Two of them (*Ó Laighléis* or *Lawless* and *Norris*) were eventually referred to the Court, while one (*O'B. v. S.*) resulted in a friendly settlement.

In the first case, counsel for Ó Laighléis relied on Articles 1, 5 and 6 of the Convention. Given the terms of Article 29.6 of the Constitution, he sought to base an argument on two other provisions of the Constitution dealing with international relations, sections 1 and 3 of Article 29. These provisions read,

"1. Ireland affirms its devotion to the ideal of peace and friendly co-operation amongst nations founded on international justice and morality.

. . .

3. Ireland accepts the generally recognised principles of international law as its rule of conduct in its relations with other States."

Citing English authorities, he submitted that these provisions reproduced the pre-existing common law and that, by the common law, those principles which were commonly accepted as binding by civilised nations became part of domestic law unless they could be shown to be contrary to it. Since, as the Court pointed out, he was in fact arguing that provisions of the Offences Against the State (Amendment) Act, 1940 were inconsistent with the Constitution, the submission was ill-conceived. Moreover, in the Court's view, the case law established that inconsistency with domestic law is a ground upon which the common law rejects the principles of international law. Also, the principle of incorporation upon which he was relying "applies to such parts of international law as are based on universally recognised custom and not to such parts as depend upon convention."[64] It continued:

"The insuperable obstacle to importing the provisions of the Convention for the Protection of Human Rights and Fundamental Freedoms into the domestic law of Ireland—if they be at variance with that law—is, however, the terms of the

[61] [1960] I.R. 93.
[62] [1984] I.R. 36.
[63] [1984] I.R. 316.
[64] [1960] I.R. 93 at 124. *Cf.* a number of recent cases in which the courts have indicated that they are prepared to give some effect in domestic law to customary international law in reliance on Article 29.3 of the Constitution: see *Government of Canada v. Employment Appeals Tribunal and Burke* [1992] 2 I.R. 484, [1992] ILRM 325; *ACW v. Ireland* [1993] 3 I.R. 232; and *ACT Shipping Ltd v. Minister for the Marine* [1995] 2 ILRM 30.

Constitution of Ireland. By Article 15.2.1°, of the Constitution it is provided that 'the sole and exclusive power of making laws for the State is hereby vested in the Oireachtas: no other legislative authority has power to make laws for the State.' Moreover, Article 29, the Article dealing with international relations, provides at section 6 that 'no international agreement shall be part of the domestic law of the State save as may be determined by the Oireachtas.'

The Oireachtas has not determined that the Convention of Human Rights and Fundamental Freedoms is to be part of the domestic law of the State, and accordingly this Court cannot give effect to the Convention if it be contrary to domestic law or purports to grant rights or impose obligations additional to those of domestic law.

No argument can prevail against the express command of section 6 of Article 29 of the Constitution before judges whose declared duty is to uphold the Constitution and the laws.

The Court cannot accordingly accept the idea that the primacy of domestic legislation is displaced by the State becoming a party to the Convention for the Protection of Human Rights and Fundamental Freedoms. Nor can the Court accede to the view that in the domestic forum the Executive is in any way estopped from relying on the domestic law.''[65]

The Court also rejected an argument that the 1940 Act should be construed in such a way as to conform with the State's obligations under the Convention. The ground on which it did so was that the 1940 Act had to be interpreted in the light of the conditions which existed when it became law, that is, some ten years before the State accepted the Convention.

In *Norris*, counsel for the plaintiff invoked Article 8 of the Convention and the judgment of the European Court in the *Dudgeon* case. She contended that, since Ireland is party to the Convention, there arose a presumption that the Constitution is compatible with the Convention and that in deciding whether pre-Constitution legislation has or has not been carried over by the Constitution as the law of the State,[66] regard should be had to whether the legislation was compatible with the Convention. The nineteenth century legislation challenged in this case was the same as that which had been found by the European Court to violate Dudgeon's rights under the Convention. The Court rejected this contention. In its view,

"... acceptance of [counsel's] submission would be contrary to the provisions of the Constitution itself and would accord to the Government the power, by an executive act, to change both the Constitution and the law. The Convention is an international agreement to which Ireland is a subscribing party. As such, however, it does not and cannot form part of our domestic law, nor affect in any way

---

[65] At pp. 124–125.
[66] See Article 50.1 of the Irish Constitution. The Constitution was adopted in 1937.

questions which arise thereunder. This is made quite clear by Article 29, s.6 of the Constitution. . . ."[67]

Therefore, it concluded, neither the Convention nor the decision of the European Court in the *Dudgeon* case was "in any way relevant"[68] to the question it had to consider in the case before it. One judge, while agreeing that the Convention does not form part of domestic law and that "the constitutional question that called for resolution was unaffected by the fact that the precise statutory provisions in question were held by the European Court of Human Rights in *Dudgeon* to be in breach of Article 8 of the Convention",[69] added the qualification: "That does not mean that this Court is not open to the persuasive influence that may be drawn from decisions of other courts, such as the European Court of Human Rights, which deal with problems similar or analogous to that now before us."[70]

O'B. v. S. concerned the succession rights of a person born outside marriage to the estate of her father who had died intestate.[71] Counsel for the plaintiff sought to rely in part on the decision of the European Court in the *Marckx* case in which that Court had considered the status under Belgian law of a child so born and had found, *inter alia*, that the position with respect to the child's succession rights contravened Article 8 taken in conjunction with Article 14. That case, said the Court, "can have no bearing on the question of whether any provision of the [relevant Irish statute] of 1965 is invalid having regard to the provisions of the Constitution. In so far as that case may be in conflict with the provisions of the Act of 1965, this Court is obliged to follow the provisions of the Act of 1965: see Article 29, s. 6 of the Constitution."[72] After drawing some distinctions between the case before it and the *Marckx* case, the Court further stated that "there is no object to be served by this Court entering into any examination of what conflict, if any, exists between the decision in the *Marckx* case and the provision of the Act of 1965."[73]

These decisions of the Supreme Court establish that a person may not rely upon the Convention and judgments of the European Court as the basis of a legal right which will be enforced by the courts. Furthermore, in case of conflict between an Act passed by the Oireachtas and any provision of the Convention, an Irish court will give effect to the domestic statute, whether enacted before or after Ireland became party to the Convention. Also, a person may not rely on the Convention to challenge the validity of statutory provisions passed prior to the enactment of the Constitution in 1937. Nor is there a presumption that the Constitution is compatible with the Convention. Despite the broad wording of some of the statements of the Supreme Court in *Norris*, it would nonetheless seem that the Convention and judgments of the European Court may be of some persuasive authority in interpreting the Constitution; and

[67] [1984] I.R. 36 at 66 (O'Higgins C.J., with whom Finlay P. and Griffin J. concurred).
[68] [1984] I.R. 26 at 67.
[69] Henchy J., [1984] I.R. 36 at 68–69.
[70] [1984] I.R. 36 at 69. He also pointed out that Article 8 has no counterpart in the Irish Constitution and stated that, in his view, the statutory provisions in question "seemed doomed to extinction" and would have to be replaced: see p. 78.
[71] This case was the subject of a friendly settlement in Strasbourg.
[72] [1984] I.R. 316 at 338.
[73] At p. 339.

although statutes should be interpreted in the light of the conditions which existed when they became law, the Convention may be of some relevance in interpreting post-1950 legislation, that is, legislation enacted after Ireland's signature of the Convention. In addition, it may be of relevance in interpreting the common law.

Certainly both the Convention and case law have been cited with approval by members of the judiciary in other cases, although in no case to date has such reference been determinative of the interpretation of the relevant Irish law or of the outcome of a case.

In 1976, Chief Justice O'Higgins cited both Article 6(3)(c) of the Convention and U.S. case law in support of his conclusion that constitutional justice requires that the State afford the opportunity of being legally represented to a person who is faced with a serious criminal charge and who, because of lack of means, cannot provide a lawyer for his or her own defence. The Convention clearly demonstrated that it was "generally recognised throughout Europe that, as one of his minimum rights, a poor person charged with a criminal offence had the right to have legal assistance provided for him without charge."[74] Other Supreme Court judges have also on several occasions referred to the Convention in a positive way. In stressing the need to observe the elementary requirements of justice in dealing with a charge of contempt of court, Henchy J. stated, "There is a presumption that our law in this respect is in conformity with the European Convention on Human Rights particularly Articles 5 and 10(2) thereof."[75] He also identified as a rule of statutory interpretation the assumption that, in the absence of evidence of any contrary intention, a statute was enacted subject to the postulate that it would be construed and applied in consonance with the State's obligations under international law, including under treaty. In his opinion, where a statute was enacted after ratification by the State of the Convention, the statute should be deemed to be in conformity with the Convention and should be construed and applied accordingly—provided no contrary intention was shown.[76] As evidence of the fundamental principle that justice should be administered in public, Walsh J. cited a number of international human rights provisions, including Article 6(1) of the Convention.[77] And, in the context of extradition, he stated that the Irish courts should not "ignore the answerability of the State to the organs of the European Convention of Human Rights and Fundamental Freedoms if a particular fugitive offender is handed over to any other state, whether a member of the Council of Europe or not, where the courts are not satisfied that his treatment there would not be in breach of the rights protected by the Convention."[78] Judge McCarthy was somewhat more cautious in affording weight to the Convention. He was unwilling to subscribe to the view that a statute passed four years after the ratification of the Convention should be limited by the terms of the Convention.[79] However, he did allow that "in appropriate cases",[80]

---

[74] *State (Healy) v. Donoghue* [1976] I.R. 325 at 351.
[75] *State (D.P.P.) v. Walsh and Conneely* [1981] I.R. 412 at 440.
[76] *O'Domhnaill v. Merrick* [1984] I.R. 151 at 159. See also *D.P.P. v. Gaffney* [1988] ILRM 39 at 44.
[77] *Re R. Ltd* [1989] I.R. 126 at 135.
[78] *Finucane v. McMahon* [1990] ILRM 505 at 522; [1990] 1 I.R. 165 at 217.
[79] *O'Domhnaill v. Merrick* [1984] I.R. 151 at 166.
[80] *ibid.*

a statute should be construed, if possible, so as to conform to international law "when the nature of that international law is established."[81]

Similarly, judges of the High Court have at times referred to the Convention and the case law of the Convention organs in a way which suggests that they are not totally irrelevant to the determination of the applicable Irish law. These references have usually been by the way or in conjunction with other authority to support a conclusion or opinion otherwise arrived at. Thus, in *Kearney v. Minister for Justice*,[82] Costello J., after citing Canadian and U.S. case law on the censorship of prisoners' correspondence, mentioned two judgments of the European Court[83] as indicating that some interference with prisoners' correspondence is permitted under the Convention and that in assessing the permissibility of interference regard may be had to the ordinary and reasonable requirements of imprisonment.[84] Likewise, in construing the Constitution as conferring on every accused in every criminal trial a constitutionally protected right to the presumption of innocence, the same judge commented that this right is now universally recognised, and as evidence of such recognition mentioned a number of international provisions, including Article 6(2) of the Convention.[85] Interestingly, he also referred in this case not to a judgment of the European Court but to a decision of the Commission in support of his ruling that exercise of the right to the presumption of innocence may be restricted in certain circumstances by the Oireachtas.[86]

Occasionally a High Court judge has been prepared to attach greater weight to the Convention as an aid to the interpretation of Irish law. In dealing with the law on contempt of court in Ireland, O'Hanlon J. considered what weight should be afforded the House of Lords decision in *Attorney General v. Times Newspapers Ltd.*[87] While regarding the "very exhaustive examination of the law of contempt of court by the House of Lords in the *Times Newspaper* case"[88] as a "persuasive authority of considerable importance",[89] he was also of the opinion "that the decision of the Court of Human Rights in relation to the same case is also of significance when considering whether the stringent rules adopted by the Law Lords should be accepted as a correct statement of the law of contempt of court applied in this jurisdiction."[90] He further stated that:

"As Ireland has ratified the convention and is a party to it, and as the law of contempt of court is based . . . on public policy, I think it is legitimate to assume that our public policy is in accord with the convention or at least that the provi-

---

[81] *ibid.* See also *Norris v. Attorney General* [1984] I.R. 36 at 104.

[82] [1986] I.R. 116.

[83] *Golder v. United Kingdom*, judgment of the Court, February 21, 1975, Series A, No. 18; (1979–80) 1 EHRR 524; and *Silver v. United Kingdom*, judgment of the Court, March 25, 1983, Series A, No. 61; (1983) 5 EHRR 347.

[84] [1986] I.R. 116 at 121.

[85] *O'Leary v. Attorney General* [1993] I.R. 102 at 107.

[86] [1993] I.R. 102 at 110, referring to Application No. 5124/71, *X v. United Kingdom*.

[87] [1974] A.C. 273.

[88] *Desmond v. Glackin* [1992] ILRM 490 at 512.

[89] *ibid.*

[90] *ibid.*

sions of the convention can be considered when determining issues of public policy. The convention itself is not a code of legal principles which are enforceable in the domestic courts, as was made clear in *In re Ó Laighléis. . .*, but his does not prevent the judgment of the European Court from having a persuasive effect when considering the common law regarding contempt of court in the light of the constitutional guarantees of freedom of expression contained in our Constitution of 1937.'[91]

Most recently Budd J., when considering the lawfulness of the detention of a person in a psychiatric hospital,[92] explicitly referred to two judgments of the European Court of Human Rights on the detention of persons of unsound mind,[93] and reviewed much of the previous case law with regard to the status of the Convention in Irish law. He stated that he agreed with O'Hanlon J. that a court is entitled to look at the Convention as a guide on matters of public policy, indeed as "influential guidelines with regard to matters of public policy".[94] Nevertheless, on the basis of the existing case law, he thought it clear that the Convention is a code of legal principles which are not as yet enforceable in the Irish courts and that where, as in the case before him, there was a challenge to the constitutionality of statutory provisions, a court could not have reference to the Convention "as a touchstone with regard to constitutionality".[95]

The Convention and Legislation

Most of the rights guaranteed by the Convention and Protocols are also secured by the Irish Constitution. That this protection will not, however, always be coterminous and that legislation may be needed "to secure the rights to everyone within the jurisdiction"[96] is shown by the judgments of the European Court in *Johnston and Others*

---

[91] At p. 513. He also referred to the view of Henchy J. in *State (D.P.P.) v. Walsh and Conneely* [1981] I.R. 412 at 440 that there is a presumption that the Irish law on contempt is in conformity with the Convention, particularly Articles 5 and 10(2). See also *E v. E* [1982] ILRM 497 at 499–500, where, in response to an argument that the Judgment of the European Court in *Airey* to which Ireland was a party bound the State for the future and could be given effect to in later proceedings brought against the State in domestic proceedings, he said:

> "I am unable to accept that this contention is correct. It appears to me that the defendant in the present proceedings is claiming that the State in setting up the Scheme of Civil Legal Aid and Advice did not go far enough in complying with the requirements of the European Convention, as interpreted by the Court of Human Rights in the *Airey* case, and that as a result the defendant in the present action is in danger of finding himself without any legal representation in continuing proceedings of a nature and complexity comparable to those which obtained in the *Airey* case. As this contention is strongly disputed by the Attorney General, it appears to me to be a dispute which should properly be determined by the procedure provided for in the European Convention, involving a reference of the matter to the European Commission initially, with the possibility of a later determination by the Court of Human Rights."

[92] *Croke v. Smith and Others*, unreported, July 31, 1995.
[93] *Winterwerp v. the Netherlands*, October 24, 1979, Series A, No. 33; (1979–80) 2 EHRR 387; *X v. United Kingdom*, November 5, 1981, Series A, No. 46; (1982) 4 EHRR 188.
[94] At p. 34 of the transcript of the Court's judgment.
[95] At p. 35 of the transcript.
[96] See Art. 1 of the Convention.

v. Ireland,[97] *Norris v. Ireland,*[98] and *Keegan v. Ireland.*[99] Indeed, the Court explicitly recognised in *Norris* that its decision would have effects extending beyond the confines of the particular case, and stated that it was for Ireland to take the necessary measures in its domestic legal system to ensure the performance of its obligation to abide by the decision of the Court.[1]

Of none of these cases would it be true to say that the judgment of the European Court was on its own responsible for particular legislation. Reform was already being promoted by other bodies. But it is clear that reform was well in train and the need for it more generally accepted in the case of the legal status of children born outside marriage than in the areas of homosexual activity and the parental rights of an unmarried father. Indeed, by the time the Court delivered its judgment in *Johnston and Others*, the Status of Children Bill was before Parliament, the stated purpose of this Bill being to remove as far as possible legal provisions which discriminated against children born outside marriage. In contrast, it was five years before the Government gave effect to the judgment in *Norris* by introducing legislation to decriminalise homosexual activity between adult men, despite pressure from the Committee of Ministers to do so.[2] In a follow-up to *Keegan*, the Adoption (No. 2) Bill 1996 would have introduced a procedure whereby the father of a child born outside marriage may be consulted before his child is placed for adoption, but the Bill had not passed into law before the Dail (House of Representatives) was dissolved on June 13, 1997 pending a general election.

The Judgment of the European Court in *Airey* also clearly required some improvement in the access of litigants of limited financial means to the courts. At the time the Government chose to introduce a Scheme of Civil Legal Aid and Advice[3] administratively rather than by statute. The Scheme was laid before each House of the Oireachtas by the Minister for Justice in December 1979. As might be expected, the Scheme went beyond the requirements of the *Airey* case in that it provided for legal aid in a range of civil proceedings in addition to proceedings for judicial separation.[4] In 1995 the Scheme was put on a statutory footing.[5]

In two of the cases, *Johnston and Others* and *Norris*, the need for legislative reform had been signalled in advance of the applications to the Commission by judgments of the European Court in cases involving other Contracting States. The legal rights of an unmarried mother and her child had been reviewed for compatibility with the Convention in *Marckx v. Belgium.*[6] In that case, the Court had found that the inferior rights of a child born outside marriage compared to those of a child born within marriage violated both the mother's and the child's right to respect for their family life and were discriminatory. The parallels between *Norris* and the earlier case of *Dudgeon v.*

---

[97] December 18, 1986, Series A, No. 112; (1987) 9 EHRR 203.
[98] October 26, 1988, Series A, No. 142; (1991) 13 EHRR 186.
[99] Series A, No. 290; (1994) 18 EHRR 342.
[1] At para. 50 of its judgment, (1990) 12 EHRR 342.
[2] Criminal Law (Sexual Offences) Act, 1993. See in particular ss. 2 and 14 and the Sched. to the Act.
[3] Prl 8543.
[4] These included proceedings in relation to defamation, conveyancing, disputes over rights and interests in or over land and arbitration under landlord and tenant legislation: see Sched. A to the Scheme.
[5] See the Civil Legal Aid Act, 1995.
[6] Judgment of June 13, 1979, Series A, No. 31; (1979–80) 2 EHRR 330.

United Kingdom[7] were even closer, given that the same legislative provisions were in issue.

Although there is some screening of proposed legislation for compatibility with Ireland's international obligations,[8] judgments of the European Court in cases involving other Contracting States do not appear to be rigorously examined at official level with a view to identifying any possible inconsistency between Irish law and the State's obligations under the Convention. Occasionally the Government has acted to reform the law in the light of the case law without awaiting an application against Ireland itself. On such occasions, however, the case law of the European Court has only been one element contributing to acceptance of the need for change. Domestic considerations have predominated.

An example is the Interception of Postal Packets and Telecommunications Messages (Regulation) Act, 1993.[9] It had been stated by the European Court in the cases of *Klass and Others v. Federal Republic of Germany*[10] and *Malone v. United Kingdom*[11] that state interception of communications should have a clear legal basis and that domestic law should contain "adequate and effective guarantees against abuse"[12] of the power of interception. Interception had taken place in Ireland for years on the basis of warrants issued as a matter of administrative practice by the Minister for Justice. The purpose of the 1993 Act was to place this practice on a statutory basis and to introduce new review procedures to control any abuse of the system of interception. Judicial control of such interception, while not required, had been preferred by the Court in *Klass and Others*, the Court stating that "an interference by the executive authorities with an individual's rights should be subject to an effective control which should normally be assured by the judiciary, at least in the last resort, judicial control offering the best guarantees of independence, impartiality and a proper procedure."[13]

The Act of 1993 did not provide for control through the normal judicial process, but it did introduce two safeguards of a judicial kind. First, a judge of the High Court has been entrusted with the task of keeping the operation of the Act under review and of ascertaining whether its provisions are being complied with.[14] Secondly, the Act provides that persons who suspect that their post has been intercepted or their telephone tapped may apply to a Complaints Referee, who shall be a judge of the Circuit or District Court or a practising barrister or solicitor of not less than ten years' standing, for an investigation of the matter. The first person to be appointed Referee is in fact a judge of the Circuit Court.[15] Although the judgments of the European Court impacted on the provisions of the legislative reform, they were probably less

---

[7] Judgment of September 23, 1981, Series A, No. 45; (1982) 4 EHRR 149.
[8] See E. J. Donelan, "The Role of the Parliamentary Draftsman in the Preparation of Legislation in Ireland" (1992) 14 DULJ 1 at 5.
[9] See also Health (Mental Services) Act, 1981, and *cf. Winterwerp*, judgment of the Court, October 24, 1979, Series A, No. 33; (1979–80) 2 EHRR 387.
[10] Judgment of September 6, 1978, Series A, No. 28; (1979–80) 2 EHRR 214.
[11] Judgment of August 2, 1984, Series A, No. 82; (1985) 7 EHRR 14.
[12] Para. 50 of *Klass* (1979–80) 2 EHRR 214 at 234. See also para. 81 of *Malone* (1985) 7 EHRR 14 at 45.
[13] Para. 55, (1979–80) 2 EHRR 214 at 235.
[14] Judge Declan Costello.
[15] Judge Esmonde Smyth. The Referee has the power, in appropriate cases, to quash the authorisation for an interception, to order the destruction of any copy of the intercepted information, and to recommend the payment of compensation.

influential in securing the reform itself than public disquiet resulting from a well-publicised case in which journalists' phones had been unlawfully tapped at the request of the Minister for Justice.[16]

Conclusion

The principal significance of the Convention in Ireland, as in other Contracting States, is that it provides an avenue of potential redress for individuals with a human rights grievance. While a domestic remedy will exist for most such grievances,[17] and will afford adequate redress when merited, in those few cases in which there is no domestic remedy or redress is not obtained, an extra layer of human rights protection is available which may be invoked by aggrieved individuals themselves.[18]

The redress or "just satisfaction" awarded under Article 50 to those individuals who have been successful in their applications against Ireland has varied greatly.[19] The Court awarded Mrs Airey IR£3,140 for miscellaneous expenses and mental anxiety.[20] It also endorsed as equitable an agreement between her and the Irish Government whereby the latter undertook to underwrite her reasonable costs of retaining a solicitor and counsel in proceedings for judicial separation. However, in *Johnston and Others*, the Court considered that its findings of violations on the issue of the child's status constituted sufficient just satisfaction for emotional strain and worry suffered by the applicants by reason of the child's legal situation.[21] Similarly, in *Norris*, because compliance by Ireland with the Court's Judgment would entail legislative reform, it held that its finding of a breach of Article 8 constituted adequate just satisfaction.[22] In stark contrast to these earlier decisions, in *Pine Valley*, the Court awarded both applicants the global sum of IR£1,200,000 for the pecuniary damage they had sustained by reason of the fall in the value of their property.[23] In addition, it determined that the Government should pay one of the applicants the sum of IR£50,000 for the effects the violation had had on his personal circumstances.[24] IN the *Open Door* case, only one of the clinics claimed compensation for damage, the Dublin Well Woman Centre Ltd, and it was awarded IR£25,000 in respect of the loss of income due to the discontinuance of its pregnancy counselling service.[25] Keegan, on the other hand, received only IR£10,000 for trauma, anxiety and feelings of injustice which he "must have experienced as a result of the procedure leading to the adoption of his daughter as well as the guardianship and custody proceedings."[26] These decisions suggest that quantifiable

---

[16] *Kennedy and Arnold v. Ireland* [1987] I.R. 587, [1988] ILRM 472.
[17] Particularly under the fundamental rights provisions of the Irish Constitution: see Arts. 40–44.
[18] In reality, however, given the length of the proceedings and the uncertainty of any redress, if successful, it is only for the patient and the determined.
[19] I deal here with compensation rather than legal costs or expenses.
[20] *Airey (Art. 50)*, judgment of February 6, 1981, Series A, No. 41; (1981) 3 EHRR 592.
[21] Para. 83 of the Court's judgment, (1987) 9 EHRR 203 at 227.
[22] Paras 49–50 of the Court's judgment, (1991) 13 EHRR 186 at 201–202.
[23] Judgment of February 9, 1993 (Art. 50), paras 8–15, Series A, No. 246-B; (1993) 16 EHRR 379 at 381–384.
[24] Paras. 16–17 of the Court's judgment, (1993) 16 EHRR 379 at 384–385.
[25] Paras. 85–87 of the Court's judgment, (1992) 15 EHRR 244 at 269.
[26] Para. 68 of the Court's judgment, (1994) 18 EHRR 342 at 366.

pecuniary loss as a result of a violation of the Convention will be compensated, but the Court can hardly be described as generous in the awards it gave for less easily quantifiable non-pecuniary loss such as emotional stress and feelings of injustice.

In considering applications against Ireland, the Court has made some important statements on the interpretation of the Convention. In the inter-State case Ireland took against the United Kingdom, the Court gave its understanding of what constitutes an administrative practice, and made rulings on the operation of the exhaustion of domestic remedies rule and state responsibility in relation to such a practice. It also gave an indication of the meaning to be attributed the concepts of torture, inhuman and degrading treatment under Article 3 of the Convention. In both the inter-State case and in *Lawless* the Court examined the scope of the right of derogation by a State from its human rights obligations in time of public emergency and indicated the standard of review it would apply to the opinion of the respondent State as to the existence of an emergency and the need for particular measures to deal with it.[27] *Lawless* was also important at the time for the Court's pronouncements on the role of an individual applicant in proceedings before it. Of the other individual applications, *Airey* is of particular interest for the broad interpretation adopted by the Court of the right to a fair trial, including its assertion that at times a State must take some positive action to ensure respect for the rights guaranteed by the Convention.

Some of the successful applications have played a part in legislative and administrative reform in Ireland, but, in all cases, reform was also fuelled by domestic pressures, and, with the possible exceptions of the decriminalisation of homosexual conduct in the wake of *Norris* and the proposed improvement in the rights of unmarried fathers as a result of *Keegan*, would probably have occurred when it did irrespective of the Judgment of the European Court. The same may be said of the constitutional amendment approved by the people after the Court's Judgment in the *Open Door* case.[28]

It is noticeable that five of the seven individual applications which have been decided by the Court raised issues pertaining to family and private life, and that in all five cases the Court found one or more violations of the Convention. This prompts the question whether it is in these areas that Irish law is generally out of line with the standards espoused by most other Contracting States and by the Convention as interpreted by the Court. It is at least true that, under the Constitution, the family which is described therein as possessing 'inalienable and imprescriptible rights'',[29] is the family based on marriage, while in deciding whether or not a family relationship or life exists under the Convention, the European Court attaches as much, if not greater, weight to

---

[27] *Ireland v. United Kingdom*, paras. 202–221 of the Court's judgment, (1979–80) 2 EHRR 25 at 90–97; *Lawless (No. 3)*, paras. 20–41 of the Court's judgment, (1979–80) 1 EHRR 15 at 30–35.

[28] The amendment provides that Article 40.3.3°, which guarantees the right to life of the unborn, "shall not limit freedom to obtain or make available, in the State, subject to such conditions as may be laid down by law, information relating to services lawfully available in another state." The amendment was passed in the context of controversy about the distribution in Ireland of information relating to abortion services in the United Kingdom. It was approved in November 1992 by the people in a referendum held in accordance with Article 47.1 of the Constitution. Legislation was passed in 1995 regulating the availability of such information: Regulation of Information (Services Outside the State for Termination of Pregnancies) Act, 1995.

[29] Article 41.1.1°. The rights are also described as "antecedent and superior to all positive law".

the actuality of the situation and the intention of the persons concerned than to any formal legal status.[30]

The Irish courts, citing the Constitution, have regarded the Convention as operating essentially at the international level. It is not part of domestic law and may not be relied upon to ground a claim of human rights violations before the courts. Moreover, while several judges have been prepared to afford it some persuasive value in the interpretation of legislation, the common law and the Constitution, it has not featured prominently in the interpretation of the law or in the outcome of any case to date.

The Constitution is the fundamental law of the State overriding any conflicting legal provision. In the event of a conflict between the Constitution and the Convention, effect will be given in domestic law to the Constitution.[31] In such an eventuality, constitutional change is required if Ireland is to comply with its obligations under the Convention. Such change can only be effected by referendum of the people.[32] The possibility of conflict surfaced in the case of *Johnston and Others*. At the time there was a complete constitutional ban on divorce, and had the European Court held that Article 8 or 12 of the Convention guaranteed a right to divorce and to remarry, it is doubtful whether the people would have accepted the removal of the ban from the Constitution. A proposal to change the Constitution so as to allow for divorce in limited circumstances was put to the people in a referendum in 1986 and was defeated.[33] A conflict did occur as a result of the *Open Door* judgment. The Supreme Court had earlier held that the applicant clinics were constitutionally prohibited from giving information to their clients about abortion services in Great Britain because the giving of such information infringed the right to life of the unborn.[34] The European Court, on the other hand, held that this prohibition was an infringement of the applicants' right to freedom of expression under Article 10 of the Convention. The conflict was resolved in favour of freedom of expression soon after the European Court delivered its judgment by the adoption of a constitutional amendment in November 1992. A possible area of conflict in the future concerns the availability of abortion

---

[30] See, *e.g.*, *Marckx* judgment of June 13, 1979, para. 31, Series A, No. 31; (1979–80) 2 EHRR 330 at 341–342; *Johnston and Others*, para. 55, (1987) 9 EHRR 203 at 220; and *Berrehab*, Judgment of the Court, June 21, 1988, para. 21, Series A, No. 138; (1989) 11 EHRR 322 at 329.

[31] This would be the position even if the Oireachtas, in accordance with Article 29.6 of the Constitution, determined that the Convention was to form part of domestic law.

[32] See Arts. 46 and 47.1 of the Constitution.

[33] In November 1995, the following amendment to Article 41.3.2° of the Constitution was narrowly approved by the people in a referendum:

"A Court designated by law may grant a dissolution of marriage where, but only where, it is satisfied that:
  i. at the date of the institution of the proceedings, the spouses have lived apart from one another for a period of, or periods amounting to, at least four years during the previous five years,
  ii. there is no reasonable prospect of a reconciliation between the spouses;
  iii. such provision as the Court considers proper having regard to the circumstances, exists, or will be made for the spouses, any children of either or both of them and any other person prescribed by law, and
  iv. any further conditions prescribed by law are complied with."

Legislation was subsequently enacted in implementation of this constitutional provision: the Family Law (Divorce) Act, 1996.

[34] *Attorney General (S.P.U.C.) v. Open Door Counselling Ltd* [1988] I.R. 593.

itself in Ireland. Although it has now been accepted by the Supreme Court that the constitutional right to life of the unborn is not absolute, the permissible restrictions on it are very limited.[35] Should the European Court hold that the Convention guarantees a broader right to the termination of pregnancy than is constitutionally permitted in Ireland, it is unlikely that the Irish people would vote to change the Constitution in order to comply with the State's obligations in this regard under the Convention. Such a strong conflict of standards may never arise, but the possibility that it may demonstrates the limits of any international regime for the protection of human rights, even at the regional level among States "with a common heritage of political traditions, ideals, freedom and the rule of law."[36]

---

[35] Termination of pregnancy is only constitutional permitted when it is established as a matter of probability that there is a real and substantial risk to the life of the mother which can only be avoided by termination of the pregnancy: *Attorney General v. X and Others* [1992] ILRM 401, [1992] 1 I.R. 1.
[36] See the Preamble of the Convention.

CHAPTER 7

THE COMMON LAW AND THE EUROPEAN CONVENTION

The European Convention on Human Rights is today a high-profile document. Opinions of the Commission and judgments of the Court receive extensive press coverage within states involved in applications, and many lawyers and pressure groups throughout Europe follow the development of the jurisprudence very closely. The growth in interest in the Convention is as marked in the United Kingdom and Ireland as it is anywhere else, perhaps more so because they are the only two Convention states which have not incorporated the Convention into their domestic law. In this respect the United Kingdom is even more recalcitrant than Ireland because Ireland does have a set of fundamental rights guaranteed by Articles 40–44 of its Constitution of 1937. The United Kingdom, of course, has no single written Constitution, although it does have a number of pieces of legislation which are of constitutional significance, including a seventeenth-century Bill of Rights.[1] At present there is considerable debate over whether the United Kingdom should add to this category of legislation by passing an Act incorporating the European Convention, thereby allowing British judges to interpret and apply it in domestic courts.[2] The current Labour Government has announced that it will introduce legislation to this effect in the 1997–98 parliamentary session, though the exact form it will take has still to be revealed. In the meantime, people who think they have suffered an injustice in Britain or Ireland frequently imagine that they are bound to find a remedy if they go to Strasbourg. "I will take my complaint all the way to Europe" is the cry which many a disappointed litigant is heard to utter on the steps of a British courthouse after failing to find a remedy there.

When a more dispassionate eye is cast over the European Convention, and more particularly on the case law based on it, such as has been attempted in the foregoing chapters of this book, it is clear that anyone who places complete faith in the ability of the Convention to achieve justice in all cases is severely misguided. There have

---

[1] Anyone doubting this need only look at books such as *Constitutional and Administrative Law: Text and Materials*, by D. Pollard and D. Hughes (2nd ed., 1997).
[2] The last serious attempt to achieve this was in a Bill introduced into the House of Lords in 1994 by Lord Lester of Herne Hill, Q.C. For earlier attempts see R. Blackburn, "Draft Legislation to Incorporate the European Convention on Human Rights into United Kingdom Domestic Law", in J. P. Gardner (ed.), *Aspects of Incorporation of the European Convention of Human Rights into Domestic Law* (1993), Chap. 5.

indeed been notable victories for applicants in Strasbourg, but there have been numerous failures too. The impact of the Convention within the domestic legal systems of these islands to date remains limited, and this may not change much even if the Convention is incorporated.[3] In this concluding chapter an attempt is made to draw up a balance sheet setting out the good and not so good points about the Convention and its enforcement bodies. The prospects for the future are then briefly considered.

Criticisms of the Convention

The European Convention is now nearly 50 years old, and some would say that its age is beginning to show. While it may have been a modern document in 1950, embracing all the human rights and fundamental freedoms then thought to be deserving of protection, today it lags behind other international and national documents both in the range of rights covered and in the degree of protection afforded to them.[4] This is despite the add-ons contained in several Protocols,[5] for by and large the Convention still does not protect economic, social and cultural rights, except indirectly through such provisions as those on freedom of expression and religion.[6] Nor does it mention the "new age" rights such as the right to a healthy environment, to sustainable development[7] and to peace. The rights that are conferred, moreover, are hedged around with qualifications, exemplified in Article 10(2) which, coming immediately after a provision which grants everyone the right to freedom of expression and freedom to receive information and ideas, states that:

"The exercise of these freedoms, since it carries with it duties and responsibilities, may be subject to such formalities, conditions, restrictions or penalties as are prescribed by law and are necessary in a democratic society, in the interests of national security, territorial integrity or public safety, for the prevention of disorder or crime, for the protection of health or morals, for the protection of the reputation or rights of others, for preventing the disclosure of information

---

[3] See A. Clapham, *Human Rights in the Private Sphere* (1993), where in Chaps. 1 and 2 he deals with seven situations in which the European Convention may be relevant in U.K. courts. See also J. Gleason, "The ECHR: Its Practical Relevance" (1993) 2 *Irish Journal of European Law* 248, and C. Gearty, Chap. 2 in C. Gearty (ed.), *European Civil Liberties and the ECHR* (1997). For a more pessimistic view, see Sir Nicholas Lyell, "Whither Strasbourg? Why Britain Should Think Long and Hard Before Incorporating the European Convention on Human Rights" [1997] 2 EHRLR 132.

[4] *cf.* C. McCrudden and G. Chambers (eds), *Individual Rights and the Law in Britain* (1994), pp. 575–579; D. Harris and S. Joseph (eds.), *The International Covenant on Civil and Political Rights and U.K. Law* (1995). For a recent example of the European Court's conservative approach to human rights, see *X v. United Kingdom, The Guardian*, April, 23, 1997, where by 14 votes to six it rejected a man's claim to the right to be registered as the father of four children born to his long-term partner by donor insemination; the fact that he was born a woman but later changed to be a man was held against him. The Commission of Human Rights had previously held in his favour, by 13 votes to five.

[5] Protocol Nos 1, 4, 7 and 11; see Chap. 1 above.

[6] See A. Berenstein, "Economic and Social Rights: Their Inclusion in the European Convention on Human Rights: Problems of Formulation and Interpretation" (1981) 2 HRLJ 257.

[7] See, *e.g.* D. McGoldrick, "Sustainable Development and Human Rights: An Integrated Conception" (1996) 45 I.C.L.Q. 796.

received in confidence, or for maintaining the authority and impartiality of the judiciary.''

The width of such a clause does seem to undermine considerably the protection granted to the freedoms in the preceding clause. It almost makes one wonder whether there was any point in conferring the right in the first place.

Of course, there are simple answers to these points. Just because other rights are *not* protected by the Convention does not mean that those which *are* protected are any less deserving of that status. It could also be said that life in European countries is today such a complex business that there is no other way of regulating civil and political rights in general terms than through conferring them with the one hand and qualifying them with the other. A Convention on Rights cannot do everything, unless we want it to be an enormous codification. The European Convention, so the defence would continue, is as succinct and practicable a human rights document as is capable of being devised.

Both sides of the argument are right, in part. Which side one favours depends mostly on how large and complicated a document one wants to have in this field. There is, though, room for compromise. A more modern and slightly more detailed European Convention *can* be envisaged, without having to sacrifice the merits of brevity and comprehensibility. Any attempt to achieve such a new document could usefully borrow from other human rights documents around the world, many of which are just as readable as the Convention but significantly more protective of rights.[8] But any new Convention would still need to rely considerably upon complementary human rights legislation in each of the ratifying states: the role of an international document is to provide a framework of shared principles and values which states can then tailor to meet the needs of their own legal and political culture. A good example relates to anti-discrimination law: while a Convention can be expected to lay down the basic rules, it should be left to each state to work out for itself how best to complement those rules with more detailed provisions which give them real force domestically.

The European Convention has also been criticised for having too cumbersome an enforcement procedure. Having to satisfy the Commission of Human Rights not only that an application is admissible but also that it is justifiable on the merits, and then having to convince the Court of Human Rights as well that a violation of the Convention has occurred, must all seem a long obstacle race for an applicant setting out on the path to Strasbourg. The time that elapses between the various stages can amount to years[9] and there is some irony in the fact that the Commission and Court are sometimes asked to condemn a member state for tolerating over-lengthy legal proceedings yet they themselves allow the judicial process as Strasbourg to be so protracted. If we take the judgments issued by the Court of Human Rights in 1994, we find that the average length of the proceedings before the Court was 14 months.[10] The average length of time elapsing between the date on which the application was first lodged in

---

[8] A good model to follow might be Chapter 2 of the Constitution of South Africa 1996.

[9] *E.g.* Mr Silver had been dead for four years by the time the Court of Human Rights upheld his petition in *Silver v. United Kingdom* (1983) 5 EHRR 347.

[10] Calculated from the figures supplied in the European Court's ''Survey: 35 Years of Activity 1959–1994'' (Strasbourg, 1995), pp. 103–109.

Strasbourg and the date of the Court's judgment was more than four years and eight months.[11] These delays are unacceptable at any level. The fact that one of the parties to the dispute is a government should be a reason for expediting the matter, not for putting it back, and as most of the deliberations both at the Commission and at the Court are based on written documents rather than oral testimony there is even less excuse for prevarication.

The part-time nature of the Commission and the Court has a lot to do with the delays. If and when Protocol No. 11 comes into force, leading to the merger of the Commission and Court into one full-time permanent Court, the opportunities for dealing with cases more quickly will be there to be grasped. The practice of using smaller chambers of the Court to screen out cases has already proved effective under Protocol No. 9, which allows individual applicants to refer their cases to the Court if the Commission and the state concerned have refused to do so. The same mechanism may prove useful under Protocol No. 11. But even if these procedural reforms do result in a net reduction in the time taken for a case to go all the way through the Strasbourg system, this is likely to be more than offset by the increase in the number of applications lodged with the Court in the first place. As we noted in Chapter 1, there has been a steady rise in recent years in the number of applications registered, an increase which maintains the trend from the day the Commission started functioning. Although the number of Convention states has also increased, the rise has not been proportionate to that in registered applications. It is a safe bet that as residents in new Convention states become more aware of the possibilities of taking their grievances to Strasbourg, the number of applications registered in the foreseeable future will rise just as dramatically as in the past few years.

Coupled with disquiet at the duration of Commission and Court proceedings, dissatisfaction is often expressed with the modalities of those proceedings. Neither body, for example, can insist that a member state must take interim measures to safeguard the position of an applicant prior to the case being dealt with in Strasbourg: when it wishes to do so a state can ignore such a request with impunity.[12] Nor can the Commission or Court oblige a person to attend an oral hearing, provide security for costs or disclose documents that are in his or her possession. They cannot punish anyone for contempt and they do not have a set of evidential rules to guard against the admission of inappropriate evidence.

In all of these respects the proceedings in Strasbourg are very different from those which occur in the tribunals and courts of the United Kingdom and Ireland. Indeed, they are not recognised there as amounting to judicial proceedings at all.[13] Yet despite this relative lack of procedural power, even perhaps because of it, the Commission

---

[11] Calculated from the figures supplied in *Judgments of the European Court of Human Rights—Reference Charts* by Donna Gomien (1995), pp. 169–176.

[12] See *Cruz Varas v. Sweden*, Series A, No. 201; (1992) 14 EHRR 1; (1991) 12 HRLJ 142. In *Amekrane v. United Kingdom* (1973) 16 Ybk of the ECHR 356, a man was deported to Morocco from the United Kingdom despite an application pending in Strasbourg; he was shot by firing squad there and his widow was paid £37,000 by the U.K. government in a friendly settlement of her claim that the deportation might have violated the Convention.

[13] *Guilfoyle v. Home Office* [1981] 2 W.L.R. 223, where the Court of Appeal held that just because a prisoner has lodged an application in Strasbourg this does not mean that he is "a party to legal proceedings" for the purposes of the Prison Rules.

and Court do seem to operate to the general satisfaction of the vast majority of people coming before them. To litigants and lawyers from the United Kingdom or Ireland the proceedings must seem fairly informal, not to mention cheap and simple. The infrequency and brevity of oral hearings is surely a plus, as there is little that can be said in person that cannot be said just as well, if not better, on paper. The unavailability of compulsory attendance orders and of discovery procedures has not led to any noticeable problems, even in applications starting life in these islands, and in the bulk of situations where an interim measure has been asked for the request has been acceded to by the state concerned—in any event there is nothing to stop a case proceeding even though, for instance, the applicant has in the meantime been deported to a non-Convention state.

Possibly the most attractive aspect of the Strasbourg procedure is that it is so easy to initiate. A brief letter to the Secretary of the Commission is all that is required. No fee and no official documents have to be lodged. The path for a petitioner is in this respect an easy one to travel and may not even require a lawyer as a guide, at least in the early stages. Applicants who cannot afford to pay their own legal fees can apply to the Commission for legal aid, though sometimes applicants can obtain legal aid through their own national schemes.[14] Although the expenses allowed under the Commission's scheme are not usually as generous as those allowed in the United Kingdom and Ireland, they are high enough not to act as a disincentive to legal representatives. The great accessibility of the Commission more than offsets the strictness of the rules on standing, which confine applicants to "victims" or the next-of-kin of victims. The Convention was always intended to be first and foremost a means of redressing an individual's particular grievance, not an instrument with which to denounce states. To refuse access, therefore, to representative organisations or pressure groups, which often want to litigate on behalf of nameless individuals who are or may not be directly affected by a state's actions, is on this basis not a serious flaw in the Convention. There is very little disincentive to an individual against lodging a personal petition and he or she has little to do to keep the wheels of the Strasbourg procedure turning once the petition has been lodged. Besides, pressure groups are now regularly given an opportunity to submit *amici curiae* briefs; these can provide the Court of Human Rights with a broader picture against which to assess the details of an individual's claim.

There are, however, defects in the way in which the Commission and Court come to their conclusions on applications. The net result is that the jurisprudence those bodies create is not always as helpful as it might be. In the first place, the Commission and Court will not rule *in abstracto*, except rarely.[15] They will not, in other words, answer hypothetical questions. This not only rules out applications being dealt with from potential, as opposed to actual, victims of human rights abuses; it also means that the applications lodged from actual victims have to focus very much on the

---

[14] In 1995 approximately £60,000 was spent on legal aid in Commission cases; it was granted in 120 applications, just 4 per cent of all the applications disposed of in that year. See the Commission's "Survey of Activities and Statistics—1995", pp. 2 and 20. Between 1964, when it first became available in the Commission, and the end of 1995, more than 900 applicants were granted legal aid: Information Note by the Secretary to the European Commission, January 1996.

[15] An example of this rarity is *Dudgeon v. United Kingdom*, Series A, No. 45; (1982) 4 EHRR 149.

particular facts of the victim's personal experience. This militates against the issue of general rules of interpretation by the Commission or Court.[16] More than this, if the Commission and Court are faced with claims under Articles 13 and 14 of the Convention (the right to an effective remedy and the right to enjoy Convention rights without discrimination), they will often not deal with them if they have already held that there has been no breach of any other substantive Article in the Convention. It is almost as if the Commission and Court will seek to escape having to pronounce upon whether these two Articles have been violated if they can possibly do so. As has been pointed out, breaches of Article 13 are usually considered to be remedied once the other breaches of the Convention which have given rise to the breach of Article 13 have been remedied, but this is to make Article 13 largely redundant.[17] As far as the United Kingdom is concerned, it would seem that the limited nature of judicial review proceedings (where only the procedure adopted in the making of a decision can be challenged, not the merits of the decision) inevitably entails a breach of Article 13 whether or not any other Article in the Convention has been breached. Regrettably, the European Court has not adopted a consistent position on this point, sometimes holding that the British law on judicial review is adequate[18] and at other times that it is not.[19] This adds to the precariousness of an applicant's situation and leaves a large gap in judicial protection. As has been rightly observed:

"Unless the scope of judicial review is developed so as to include the possibility of a challenge for unlawfulness (with respect not only to domestic law but also to Convention law), judicial review cases will continue to be decided in a way which ignores the Convention, and applicants will be forced to seek their remedy in Strasbourg."[20]

When the Commission or Court do issue an opinion or judgment on whether a violation of an Article has occurred, they tend to do so in as limited a manner as possible. The opinions and judgments are frequently constructed in such a way as not to be particularly useful guides for the resolution of further disputes. After stating the facts and the relevant legal rules, the opinions and judgments will outline the arguments put by both sides and then, in relatively brief paragraphs, draw conclusions. The reasoning is largely inductive, not deductive as in a common law system, and the actual outcome is therefore not always easy to link with what has gone before in the document: the Commissioners' and judges' argumentation

---

[16] See J. P. Gardner, "Procedural Incorporation: The Right to Remedies", Chap. 8 in J. P. Gardner (ed.), *Aspects of Incorporation of the European Convention on Human Rights into Domestic Law* (1993), p. 93. For a discussion of the activism of the Commission and Court during their early years, see C. C. Morrison, *The Dynamics of Development in the European Human Rights Convention System* (1981), especially Chaps. 1 and 2. He identifies Judge Fitzmaurice as one of the two most self-restrained of the judges.

[17] R. Churchill, "Aspects of Compliance with Findings of the Committee of Ministers and Judgments of the Court with Reference to the United Kingdom", Chap. 9 in J. P. Gardner (ed.), *Aspects of Incorporation of the European Convention of Human Rights into Domestic Law* (1993), pp. 110–111.

[18] *E.g.* in *Soering v. United Kingdom* (1989) 11 EHRR 439.

[19] *E.g. Weeks v. United Kingdom* (1988) 10 EHRR 293.

[20] A. Clapham, *Human Rights in the Private Sphere* (1993), p. 50.

is at time elliptical. In common law terms, it is often difficult to pinpoint the *ratio decidendi* of a case. The crux of the decision may well be just a sentence or two in the opinion or judgment and they are not detailed enough to serve as a useful indicator as to how the case would have been resolved had the facts and relevant legal rules been slightly different. While the Commission and Court are increasingly making references to their own previous opinions and judgments, this is sometimes done rather perfunctorily, with the very same words being repeated time and time again with no further elucidation.

Perhaps the best illustration of this opacity is the Commission's customary resort, when deciding whether an application is admissible, to the phrase "manifestly ill-founded", which was inserted into Article 27(2) at a comparatively late stage in the Convention's drafting history.[21] The Convention itself does not expand upon this ground of inadmissibility and the Commission has not been very systematic in devising its own taxonomy of cases in this regard. In general terms one can identify just two classes of application that are rejected on this criterion. One is where the application, though otherwise satisfying the conditions of admissibility, is simply not supported by credible evidence. The other is where the alleged violation of a right can be justified under the limitation clauses adjoined to most Articles of the Convention: what has happened may, for example, be justifiable because of the need to protect public order. The difficulty is that Article 27(2) talks of applications being inadmissible if they are *manifestly* ill-founded, which should mean that if there is any substantial doubt about an application's lack of foundation it should nevertheless be declared admissible so that it can then be considered on the merits. In fact the Commission's practice is to avoid having to consider the merits by ruling the application inadmissible at an early stage.

One way of ensuring that no sense of real injustice arises out of this is for the Commission to look at the admissibility question and the merits question simultaneously, which it invariably does if an oral hearing is ordered for the application. It would still be better if, in any revamped Convention, this ground for declaring an application inadmissible were to be dropped altogether and the admissibility hurdle made instead into a purely procedural one (to be looked at by a small committee of Commissioners); more opinions on the merits would therefore have to be issued, with more detailed reasons given. The initial impact might be an increase in the average length of time required for each application to be fully processed, but gradually the more nuanced jurisprudence ought to make admissibility decisions easier and quicker.

When Protocol No. 11 takes effect, causing the Commission and the Court to merge, the admissibility question will be one which a three-member panel of judges will first consider.[22] If they unanimously declare the application inadmissible that will be the end of the matter—there will be no possibility of an appeal against the decision—but the panel must only make this declaration "where such a decision can be taken without further examination",[23] that is, in a clear case. If the panel does not take a decision on admissibility the responsibility for doing so passes to a seven-judge Chamber of

---

[21] R. Beddard, *Human Rights and Europe* (3rd ed., 1993), p. 222.
[22] Art. 28 of the Convention, as amended by Protocol No. 11.
[23] *ibid.*

217

the Court. The criteria to be applied by the panel and Chamber when deciding upon admissibility will remain the same as at present:[24] the opportunity was not taken, when Protocol No. 11 was being negotiated, to expand upon the phrase "manifestly ill-founded" or to replace it with a series of more precise criteria.

Allied to the reluctance of the Commission to articulate more precisely its reasons for refusing to allow an application to proceed to the merits is the Court's unwillingness to develop a jurisprudence on what constitutes just satisfaction to an applicant once his or her case has resulted in a judgment that a violation of the Convention has occurred. The Court has not been keen to establish a set of rules on damages in particular or remedies in general in the way that most domestic legal systems of the member states have done, primarily because the Court has seen its main role as being the identification of Convention breaches rather than the granting of redress to victims.[25] The original intent of the framers of the Convention was that it was the member states that should be left to pick up the pieces after a decision by the European Court. The Court still largely endorses that attitude today, relying upon the general statement in Article 53 of the Convention that "The High Contracting Parties undertake to abide by the decision of the Court in any case to which they are parties".[26] The Committee of Ministers, likewise, is fairly indifferent as to whether a member state has so acted in response to a finding of violation that both the actual victim and future potential victims are assured of full justice. In this regard the practice concerning friendly settlements is particularly under-developed: at the moment these settlements are not even widely notified, let alone systematically monitored to ensure that respect for human rights is being upheld. Some such settlements have resulted in changes to U.K. law and practice, but too often this has been achieved through Government circular rather than by legislation.[27]

There is, moreover, a more general problem concerning the relationship between the European Convention and domestic legislation in the U.K. or Ireland, countries which have not incorporated the Convention. This is that the Court of Human Rights has no direct power, no more so than the European Court of Justice in Luxembourg, to strike down national legislation. All it can do is to declare the legislation's incompatibility with the Convention, leaving it to the member state to decide what to do with the legislation. The state may decide to amend the legislation or allow it to fall into disuse. If it continues to apply the legislation there will be likely to be further applications to Strasbourg. However, what seems to be clear is that other people, apart from the successful applicant in the case in question, cannot rely upon the judgment

---

[24] Art. 35 of the Convention, as amended by Protocol No. 11.
[25] See, for example, *Findlay v. United Kingdom* (February 25, 1997), where the Court held the United Kingdom's court martial system to be in breach of Article 6 of the Convention. Mr Findlay's claim for £440,000 for his distress, lost earnings and pension was rejected entirely, but he was awarded his legal costs, estimated at £23,000.
[26] See *Marckx v. Belgium* (1979–80) 2 EHRR 330.
[27] See A. Clapham, *Human Rights in the Private Sphere* (1993), pp. 65–66. He cites *Hodgson v. United Kingdom*, Application No. 11553/85 as leading to s. 159 of the Criminal Justice Act 1988 (allowing a right of appeal against a judge's order that the press or public be excluded from a trial) and *X v. United Kingdom* (1979) 14 DR 205 as resulting in a Government circular to all educational authorities warning that corporal punishment in schools might be inhuman or degrading treatment under Art. 3 of the Convention.

of the Court of Human Rights in a domestic court, for unless the legislation has been repealed it must still be obeyed by that court. In this regard the Convention procedures are not as mature as those now existing within the European Community legal order. After the *Factortame* decision[28] we now know that a domestic court can "suspend" a piece of national legislation on the ground that it does not comply with the requirements of that order. This judicial power can be interpreted as flowing from the European Communities Act 1972 but in fact there is little to stop a domestic court from according under the common law just as great a significance to decisions of the European Court of Human Rights: now that the doctrine of Parliamentary sovereignty has been breached at at least one point,[29] there is no reason why it should not be breached elsewhere. All it requires is for the judges to hold that the decisions of the European Court of Human Rights, because of the eminence of that Court and its role as an international arbiter of legal standards, must be deemed to be a "higher" source of law than an Act of Parliament which, whether passed before or after the United Kingdom's accession to the Convention in 1951, cannot have been enacted with the intention of contravening international norms to which the United Kingdom now agrees to adhere—especially as the United Kingdom's compliance (or attempted compliance) with all of the Court's judgments issued against it to date can be viewed as a recognition of the binding nature of the Convention within customary international law. However heretical such a thesis may appear, it is one that leading British judges have themselves come close to espousing in extra-judicial writings.[30] Others have mooted a "reference" procedure comparable to that available under Article 177 of the Treaty of Rome[31] or, especially if the Convention were to be incorporated into domestic law, a Human Rights Division of the High Court or a Human Rights Tribunal.[32]

It can be argued, finally, that the Commission, Court and Committee have not been very successful at devising a proactive strategy to deal with human rights abuses. Through not always issuing opinions, judgments or findings that provide lessons for other member states, or even perhaps for the particular member state in question, opportunities are often lost to prevent applications having to be lodged in the future. There is, moreover, no satisfactory mechanism for ensuring that member stages of the Council of Europe take steps to comply with standards laid down by the Council of Europe's own bodies. When an analysis is conducted of the United Kingdom's reaction to judgments of the Court identifying a violation, it becomes clear that the record

[28] *Factortame Ltd v. Secretary of State for Transport* [1991] AC 603. See also *R. v. Secretary of State for Employment, ex p. the Equal Opportunities Commission* [1995] 1 A.C. 1, where the House of Lords refused to apply a provision in an Act of Parliament even without first referring the matter to the European Court of Justice.

[29] Some may see the House of Lords' decision in *Pepper v. Hart*, where it was held that statutes may at times be interpreted with the aid of what was said by individual Members of Parliament, as another relaxation of the principle of Parliamentary sovereignty.

[30] Sir John Laws, "Law and Democracy" [1995] P.L. 72; Sir Stephen Sedley, "Human Rights: A Twenty-First Century Agenda" [1995] P.L. 386; Lord Browne-Wilkinson, "The Infiltration of a Bill of Rights" [1992] P.L. 397. For a more reserved view, see Lord Irvine, "Judges and Decision-Makers: The Theory and Practice of *Wednesbury* Review" [1996] P.L. 59.

[31] J. P. Gardner, "Procedural Incorporation: The Right to Remedies," Chap. 8 in J. P. Gardner, (ed.), *Aspects of Incorporation of the European Convention on Human Rights into Domestic Law* (1993), p. 101.

[32] G. Bindman, "Bringing Rights Home" (1997) 147 New L.J. 284, 286.

of compliance is patchy.[33] To some extent this is due to the difficulties inherent in knowing what legal reforms would satisfy the Convention's rather vague standards, as is the case with the Interception of Communications Act 1985 which the United Kingdom enacted in purported compliance with the judgment of the Court of Human Rights in *Malone v. United Kingdom*,[34] but on many occasions the reason for non-compliance is simple procrastination. Even when the United Kingdom lost a case in the Court of Human Rights[35] because it had failed to change its law in compliance with a decision of that Court in an earlier case,[36] this led to no adverse consequences for the member state concerned. At the time of writing the United Kingdom Government has still not altered any law in order to comply with the judgment of the Court more than a year earlier in *John Murray v. United Kingdom*.[37] The Committee of Ministers, because of course it is a political body, is very reluctant to chastise a government for such blatant flouting of the Convention.

In this context it is worth citing Article 57 of the Convention on Human Rights, which on its face provides a suitable tool for monitoring, if not enforcing, judgments: "On receipt of a request from the Secretary General of the Council of Europe any High Contracting Party shall furnish an explanation of the manner in which its internal law ensures the effective implementation of any of the provisions of this Convention." Regrettably, very little use has been made of the Secretary General's power in this Article. When it has been used it has been in order to canvas the views of all member states as to how they are complying with a particular provision in the Convention. No country-specific inquiry has yet been ordered. If such were to occur it might contribute significantly to a diminution in the number of applications being brought against particular countries for particular types of breaches. It would also save a great deal of time and trouble for those applicants who would otherwise be taking test cases.

Achievements of the Convention

Although it is not common to admit as much, perhaps because it runs counter to the accusation that the Convention is showing its age, the single most welcome achievement of the European Convention on Human Rights is probably that it has survived so long. To do so it has had to earn the respect of member states of the Council of Europe and it has done this so successfully that becoming a signatory to the Convention is now a precondition to admittance to the Council. Respect for the Convention has no doubt flowed from the fact that it has not become *too* invasive of the legal and political culture of the various member states: they can tolerate the occasional rebuke in the Court so long as they can be assured that on matters about which they feel very deeply they can maintain their own standards. The doctrine devised by the Court to

---

[33] R. Churchill, "Aspects of Compliance with Findings of the Committee of Ministers and Judgments of the Court with Reference to the United Kingdom," in J. P. Gardner (ed.), *Aspects of Incorporation of the European Convention of Human Rights into Domestic Law* (1993), Chap. 9.

[34] (1985) 7 EHRR 14; see Churchill, *ibid.*, pp. 107–109.

[35] *Thynne, Wilson and Gunnell v. United Kingdom* (1995) 19 EHRR 333.

[36] *Weeks v. United Kingdom* (1988) 10 EHRR 293.

[37] (1996) 22 EHRR 29.

accommodate this desire for a reasonable amount of national autonomy is that of the margin of appreciation.[38]

Significantly, the Court has tended to grant a wider margin of appreciation in matters concerning national security and crime control than in matters concerning private morality.[39] The right to express one's sexuality as a gay man or lesbian woman is a right which has been upheld in the teeth of popular opposition in both Northern Ireland and the Republic of Ireland, yet the British and Irish governments have been permitted to devise laws which considerably restrict freedom of movement and the right to free speech because that is a tactic which they, as independent sovereign nations, deem essential in the fight against terrorism. Ardent civil libertarians will argue that the Commission and Court have been more tolerant than they should have been of anti-terrorist laws and practices which violate human rights standards, but it would be a brave set of unelected judges who, sitting so far away from the location of terrorist atrocities, would choose to override the wishes of an elected Parliament in a member state on such vital issues, especially if the laws in question are regularly reviewed by supposedly independent legal experts. A careful dissection of the reasoning processes employed by the Strasbourg Commissioners and judges in cases involving emergency laws in Northern Ireland shows that every effort has been made to strike a balance that is both humane for the individual and safe for society.[40] In *Brogan v. United Kingdom* the Court of Human Rights did take a stand against violations of rights that had not been properly justified under the Convention: this prompted the United Kingdom Government to issue a notice of derogation which, when subsequently challenged, was later adjudged by the Court to be in compliance with Article 15 of the Convention.[41] Although this sequence of events has been characterised by some as illustrating the United Kingdom's cavalier attitude towards the Convention, in fact the issuing of a notice of derogation could be viewed as a vindication of the Convention's obligatory status. It is perhaps not the United Kingdom Government that should be criticised so much as the wording of Article 15.

On a different level, the Convention has also worked well as an accommodator of both civil law and common law systems. Despite the great differences between the United Kingdom and Ireland on the one hand and Continental European jurisdictions on the other, the Commission and Court have apparently experienced no difficulty at all in reconciling the variations. This was illustrated most clearly in the recent cases of *SW v. United Kingdom* and *CR v. United Kingdom*, where English judges retroactively removed a husband's immunity for the rape of his wife.[42] Surprising though the results in those cases might have been to lawyers trained in a civil law system, who have always had difficulty with the notion that judges can make law, including law that operates retrospectively to make people guilty of crimes, it must have come as a great

---

[38] See J. G. Merrills, *The Development of International Law by the European Court of Human Rights* (2nd ed., 1993), Chap. 7.

[39] Although the Court's decision in *Laskey, Jaggard and Brown v. United Kingdom* (1997) 24 EHRR 39, holding that the U.K. authorities were perfectly entitled to prosecute men for indulging in consensual sado-masochistic practices, bucks the trend somewhat.

[40] See Chap. 5 above.

[41] *Brannigan and McBride v. United Kingdom*, Series A, No. 258-B; (1994) 17 EHRR 539.

[42] (1996) 21 EHRR 363. See P. R. Gandhi and J. A. James (1997) 9 Child & Family L.Q. 17.

relief to the British and Irish legal establishments that judicial creativity, even in the field of criminal law, was not ruled to be a violation of Article 7. If it had been, the whole basis of the common law system applying in the United Kingdom and Ireland would have been undermined. Even the House of Lords' Practice Statement in 1966 could have come under question. It has to be remarked, though, that in at least two respects the European Court's reasoning in these cases is open to criticism. First, the Court stated that the applicants could have reasonably foreseen the change in law; second, it suggested that the offence of rape is such a heinous wrong that a person ought to be tried for it even if it was not a crime at the time. The former point is just unrealistic, the latter positively dangerous. In the field of human rights the role of judges should surely be to limit the power of official authorities, not to extend it. Nobody would seriously argue today that marital rape ought not to be a crime, but to convict somebody of the offence retrospectively (remembering that a charge of assault could still have lain) seems unprincipled.

Where the Convention could be used more proactively is within the member states themselves. Administrators, law enforcers, Parliamentarians, judges, lawyers—all of them could usefully keep the Convention further to the forefront of their minds when they are considering what new laws to devise, how to implement them and how to reform them. In the United Kingdom and Ireland, although officials and draftspersons do apparently have regard to the Convention's requirements,[43] there seems to be no *systematic* scrutiny of proposed laws in order to check whether they do or do not comply with the European Convention's standards,[44] nor, in general, are lawyers and judges familiar enough with those standards to be able to relate them immediately to the cases they handle. Ireland does benefit from a system of constitutional preview, whereby the President can refer proposed legislation to the Supreme Court for a ruling on its constitutionality,[45] but even this does not guarantee obedience to the Convention's standards because these are not identical to the Constitution's standards. Official British and Irish legal circles pay little regard to the European Court's judgments in cases involving their own governments—they are not, for example, reported in the official series of law reports—let alone to the judgments issued in cases involving other European states. The excuse is often heard that these latter cases are of limited relevance to the United Kingdom and Ireland because the common law systems are so different from the civil law systems. In fact, because the same problems often arise in both types of system, judgments in every case are very relevant throughout all the member states.

The Convention can also claim considerable success as an export good, and ironically one of the chief agents of this has been the U.K. government. Nearly every country which has gained independence from the British Empire since 1950 has had a version of the European Convention incorporated into its new Constitution. We

---

[43] See C. Symmons, "The Effect of the European Convention on Human Rights on the Preparation and Amendment of Legislation, Delegated Legislation and Administrative Rules in the United Kingdom" in M. Furmston, R. Kerridge and B. Surfin (eds), Chap. 12 in *The Effect on English Domestic Law of Membership of the European Communities and of Ratification of the European Convention on Human Rights* (1983).

[44] This could be a role for a new Human Rights Commission in either country.

[45] Art. 26 of the Constitution, 1937.

therefore find its phrases recurring in places as far afield as Latin America, West Africa and South East Asia. When an important case was brought to the European Court involving an incident in Gibraltar it came as no surprise to discover that the Constitution of Gibraltar has imported part of the European Convention virtually word for word into its opening section.[46] Some of the courts in these countries do refer to the Strasbourg jurisprudence when interpreting the equivalent words in their own Constitutions, but as yet it is not possible for the governments of those countries to adhere to the Convention directly unless they are first able to join the Council of Europe. The Organisation for Security and Co-operation in Europe has non-European members (Canada and the USA), so in principle there is nothing to stop such expansion. In any event some of the former Republics of the USSR are more Asian than European but no-one suggests that they should be ineligible for membership of the Council of Europe on that ground alone.

Countries in the developing world often find it difficult to keep up with Strasbourg developments simply because the Commission' opinions and Court's judgments are not always readily accessible. Even within Europe, despite the general distribution policy of the Secretariat in Strasbourg, finding the relevant documents in law libraries, particularly those dealing with applications prior to 1980, is not always easy. There has also been an inordinate delay in ensuring that Convention material is available electronically, but plans are supposedly in hand within the Court's library to put matters right in this regard.[47]

Prospects for the Future

It is clear that a sea-change will occur in the Strasbourg system within the next few years, given the imminence of the entry into force of Protocol No. 11. It is also predictable that the number of applications lodged each year will continue to rise. No doubt the proportion of applications submitted against governments in Eastern Europe will dramatically increase as residents there become more aware of their entitlements under the Convention. It is a safe bet, therefore, that we have not yet witnessed the high-water mark of the Convention's success.

Yet care must be taken not to instill too great a feeling of confidence in what the Convention can achieve. It is by no means a panacea for social injustice. It does not create a Constitutional Court of Europe, despite intimations to that effect in addresses delivered by its current President.[48] Applicants who ultimately "win" their case will

---

[46] Though in fact there was a vital difference in the wording concerning the right to life: see the discussion of *McCann and Others v. United Kingdom* in Chap. 5 above.

[47] There appears to be no adequate Web site reproducing Commission opinions and Court judgments on a regular basis. The Lexis database does include Court judgments in its European Law library.

[48] See the speeches by Rolv Ryssdal in London (March 22, 1990), "The Future of the European Court of Human Rights", Council of Europe document Cour (90) 296; in Strasbourg (September 18–19, 1990), "Europe: The Roads to Democracy. The Council of Europe and the 'Architecture of Europe' ", Council of Europe document Cour (90) 223; in Vienna (January 18, 1991), "Forty Years of the European Convention on Human Rights", Council of Europe document Cour (91) 61; and in Potsdam (June 3–5, 1992), "European Human Rights Protection in the Year 2000", Council of Europe document Cour (92) 173. Also his "On the Road to a European Constitutional Court" in *Collected Courses of the Academy of European Law*, Vol. II, Book 2 (1993).

continue to be a small fraction of those who set out on the road to Strasbourg. Nevertheless the Convention has tremendous present and potential value even as a symbol. The very knowledge that a supra-national court exists which can address some cases of alleged abuses of human rights should itself be a factor contributing to a reduction in the number and severity of such abuses. In this sense the Convention may well have a preventive impact that is every bit as effective as its remedial one. For this reason, as well as for others such as the innate conservatism of our judiciary and the variety of let-outs in the Convention itself, incorporation of the Convention into British or Irish law may not significantly alter its impact in those countries except at the law-making stage.[49]

What might render incorporation of the Convention more palatable for certain politicians is if the enforcement machinery were to be altered in some way so as to make it more difficult for a member state to be held to have violated the Convention. In 1996 Lord Mackay L.C. personally visited Strasbourg to urge reforms.[50] He wanted new procedures to be introduced for vetting candidates nominated as judges: the present procedures, he thought, did not discriminate enough in favour of persons who already had judicial experience, making it too easy for academics or administrators to be appointed. He also wanted the new Court that is to be established under Protocol No. 11 to have more effective fact-finding procedures so that governments would know as early as possible exactly what allegations they had to defend: at present the Commission and Court can be accused of roving too widely in their search for issues to put before impugned governments. Most controversially of all, Lord Mackay wanted the Court to adopt a more flexible margin of appreciation doctrine. It is clear that his Government has been perplexed at losing some important test cases in Strasbourg concerning issues such as the confiscation of the assets of a convicted drug dealer,[51] the Home Secretary's power to have the final say over when a person should be released from an indefinite jail sentence,[52] and a judge's power to order a journalist to disclose his or her sources.[53] These are the sorts of matters which Lord Mackay believes should be retained under the control of a state's own Parliament.

There is some irony in the fact that on the very day when Lord Mackay was making these recommendations in Strasbourg the Court of Human Rights ruled in favour of the U.K. government in a case where an applicant had complained that a film he had

---

[49] cf. R. Churchill, "Aspects of Compliance with Findings of the Committee of Ministers and Judgments of the Court with reference to the United Kingdom", in J. P. Gardner (ed.), Aspects of Incorporation of the European Convention of Human Rights into Domestic Law (1993), p. 113: "While incorporating the Convention into British law would be unlikely to make a major impact in improving the United Kingdom's record of complying with decisions of the Court and Committee finding it to have violated the Convention, it is likely that it would nevertheless lead to some improvement in this matter." For a further evaluation of the likely effects of incorporation, see A. Clapham, Human Rights in the Private Sphere (1993), Chap. 3 ("[A] Bill of Rights would not transfer vital political questions to an unelected body of judges, but could operate to prevent some violations of civil liberties, and at the same time perform an important educative function": p. 67). See also Lord Lester, "First Steps Towards a Constitutional Bill of Rights" (1997) 2 EHRLR 124.

[50] The Times, November 25, 1996, p. 10. The Home Secretary has apparently spoken to Council of Europe officials in less diplomatic language: The Guardian, January 17, 1997, p. 2.

[51] Welch v. United Kingdom (1995) 20 EHRR 247.

[52] Hussain v. United Kingdom (1996) 22 EHRR 1.

[53] Goodwin v. United Kingdom (1996) 22 EHRR 123.

made had been unjustly banned as blasphemous.[54] The United Kingdom Government does not seem to complain about Strasbourg whenever decisions go in its favour. What it does object to, in a way that seems not to be mirrored in Ireland or in any other Council of Europe state, is "interference" in its legal system by a European body. Of course a similar campaign has been waged by the United Kingdom Government against the allegedly exorbitant powers of the European Court of Justice in Luxembourg. Whether such sabre-rattling is just that, or something more serious, remains to be seen. In this field the attitudes adopted by new governments elected in both Britain and Ireland during 1997 are certain to come under intense scrutiny in the years ahead.

[54] *Wingrove v. United Kingdom* (1997) 24 EHRR 1.

APPENDICES

APPENDIX A

THE 1950 EUROPEAN CONVENTION FOR THE PROTECTION OF HUMAN RIGHTS AND FUNDAMENTAL FREEDOMS

The governments signatory hereto, being Members of the Council of Europe,

Considering the Universal Declaration of Human Rights proclaimed by the General Assembly of the United Nations on 10th December 1948;

Considering that this Declaration aims at securing the universal and effective recognition and observance of the rights therein declared;

Considering that the aim of the Council of Europe is the achievement of greater unity between its Members and that one of the methods by which that aim is to be pursued is the maintenance and further realisation of human rights and fundamental freedoms;

Reaffirming their profound belief in those fundamental freedoms which are the foundation of justice and peace in the world and are best maintained on the one hand by an effective political democracy and on the other by a common understanding and observance of the Human Rights upon which they depend;

Being resolved, as the governments of European countries which are like-minded and have a common heritage of political traditions, ideals, freedom and the rule of law, to take the first steps for the collective enforcement of certain of the rights stated in the Universal Declaration;

Have agreed as follows:

Article 1

The High Contracting Parties shall secure to everyone within their jurisdiction the rights and freedoms defined in Section 1 of this Convention.

SECTION 1

Article 2

1. Everyone's right to life shall be protected by law. No one shall be deprived of his life intentionally save in the execution of a sentence of a court following his conviction of a crime for which this penalty is provided by law.

2. Deprivation of life shall not be regarded as inflicted in contravention of this Article when it results from the use of force which is no more than absolutely necessary:

   a. in defence of any person from unlawful violence;

   b. in order to effect a lawful arrest or to prevent the escape of a person lawfully detained;

   c. in action lawfully taken for the purpose of quelling a riot or insurrection.

Article 3

No one shall be subjected to torture or to inhuman or degrading treatment or punishment.

Article 4

1. No one shall be held in slavery or servitude.

2. No one shall be required to perform forced or compulsory labour.

3. For the purpose of this Article the term "forced or compulsory labour" shall not include:

   a. any work required to be done in the ordinary course of detention imposed according to the provisions of Article 5 of this Convention or during conditional release from such detention;

   b. any service of a military character or, in case of conscientious objectors in countries where they are recognised, service exacted instead of compulsory military service;

   c. any service exacted in case of an emergency or calamity threatening the life or well-being of the community;

   d. any work or service which forms part of normal civic obligations.

Article 5

1. Everyone has the right to liberty and security of person. No one shall be deprived of his liberty save in the following cases and in accordance with a procedure prescribed by law:

a. the lawful detention of a person after conviction by a competent court;

b. the lawful arrest or detention of a person for non-compliance with the lawful order of a court or in order to secure the fulfilment of any obligation prescribed by law;

c. the lawful arrest or detention of a person effected for the purpose of bringing him before the competent legal authority on reasonable suspicion of having committed an offence or when it is reasonably considered necessary to prevent his committing an offence or fleeing after having done so;

d. the detention of a minor by lawful order for the purpose of educational supervision or his lawful detention for the purpose of bringing him before the competent legal authority;

e. the lawful detention of persons for the prevention of the spreading of infectious diseases, of persons of unsound mind, alcoholics or drug addicts or vagrants;

f. the lawful arrest or detention of a person to prevent his effecting an unauthorised entry into the country or of a person against whom action is being taken with a view to deportation or extradition.

2. Everyone who is arrested shall be informed promptly, in a language which he understands, of the reasons for his arrest and of any charge against him.

3. Everyone arrested or detained in accordance with the provisions of paragraph 1.*c* of this Article shall be brought promptly before a judge or other officer authorised by law to exercise judicial power and shall be entitled to trial within a reasonable time or to release pending trial. Release may be conditioned by guarantees to appear for trial.

4. Everyone who is deprived of his liberty by arrest or detention shall be entitled to take proceedings by which the lawfulness of his detention shall be decided speedily by a court and his release ordered if the detention is not lawful.

5. Everyone who has been the victim of arrest or detention in contravention of the provisions of this Article shall have an enforceable right to compensation.

Article 6

1. In the determination of his civil rights and obligations or of any criminal charge against him, everyone is entitled to a fair and public hearing within a reasonable time by an independent and impartial tribunal established by law. Judgment shall be pronounced publicly but the press and public may be excluded from all or part of the trial in the interest of morals, public order or national security in a democratic society, where the interests of juveniles or the protection of the private life of the parties so require, or to the extent strictly necessary in the opinion of the court in special circumstances where publicity would prejudice the interests of justice.

2. Everyone charged with a criminal offence shall be presumed innocent until proved guilty according to law.

3. Everyone charged with a criminal offence has the following minimum rights:

   a. to be informed promptly, in a language which he understands and in detail, of the nature and cause of the accusation against him;

   b. to have adequate time and facilities for the preparation of his defence;

   c. to defend himself in person or through legal assistance of his own choosing or, if he has not sufficient means to pay for legal assistance, to be given it free when the interests of justice so require;

   d. to examine or have examined witnesses against him and to obtain the attendance and examination of witnesses on his behalf under the same conditions as witnesses against him;

   e. to have the free assistance of an interpreter if he cannot understand or speak the language used in court.

Article 7

1. No one shall be held guilty of any criminal offence on account of any act or omission which did not constitute a criminal offence under national or international law at the time when it was committed. Nor shall a heavier penalty be imposed than the one that was applicable at the time the criminal offence was committed.

2. This Article shall not prejudice the trial and punishment of any person for any act or omission which, at the time when it was committed, was criminal according to the general principles of law recognised by civilised nations.

Article 8

1. Everyone has the right to respect for his private and family life, his home and his correspondence.

2. There shall be no interference by a public authority with the exercise of this right except such as is in accordance with the law and is necessary in a democratic society in the interests of national security, public safety or the economic well-being of the country, for the prevention of disorder or crime, for the protection of health or morals, or for the protection of the rights and freedoms of others.

Article 9

1. Everyone has the right to freedom of thought, conscience and religion; this right includes freedom to change his religion or belief and freedom, either alone or in community with others and in public or private, to manifest his religion or belief, in worship, teaching, practice and observance.

2. Freedom to manifest one's religion or beliefs shall be subject only to such limitations as are prescribed by law and are necessary in a democratic society in the interests of public safety, for the protection of public order, health or morals, or for the protection of the rights and freedoms of others.

Article 10

1. Everyone has the right to freedom of expression. This right shall include freedom to hold opinions and to receive and impart information and ideas without interference by public authority and regardless of frontiers. This Article shall not prevent States from requiring the licensing of broadcasting, television or cinema enterprises.

2. The exercise of these freedoms, since it carries with it duties and responsibilities, may be subject to such formalities, conditions, restrictions or penalties as are prescribed by law and are necessary in a democratic society, in the interests of national security, territorial integrity or public safety, for the prevention of disorder or crime, for the protection of health or morals, for the protection of the reputation or rights of others, for preventing the disclosure of information received in confidence, or for maintaining the authority and impartiality of the judiciary.

Article 11

1. Everyone has the right to freedom of peaceful assembly and to freedom of association with others, including the right to form and to join trade unions for the protection of his interests.

2. No restrictions shall be placed on the exercise of these rights other than such as are prescribed by law and are necessary in a democratic society in the interests of national security or public safety, for the prevention of disorder or crime, for the protection of health or morals or for the protection of the rights and freedoms of others. This Article shall not prevent the imposition of lawful restrictions on the exercise of these rights by members of the armed forces, of the police or of the administration of the State.

Article 12

Men and women of marriageable age have the right to marry and to found a family, according to the national laws governing the exercise of this right.

Article 13

Everyone whose rights and freedoms as set forth in this Convention are violated shall have an effective remedy before a national authority notwithstanding that the violation has been committed by persons acting in an official capacity.

Article 14

The enjoyment of the rights and freedoms set forth in this Convention shall be secured without discrimination on any ground such as sex, race, colour, language, religion, political or other opinion, national or social origin, association with a national minority, property, birth or other status.

Article 15

1. In time of war or other public emergency threatening the life of the nation any High Contracting Party may take measures derogating from its obligations under this Convention to the extent strictly required by the exigencies of the situation, provided that such measures are not inconsistent with its other obligations under international law.

2. No derogation from Article 2, except in respect of deaths resulting from lawful acts of war, or from Articles 3, 4 (paragraph 1) and 7 shall be made under this provision.

3. Any High Contracting Party availing itself of this right of derogation shall keep the Secretary General of the Council of Europe fully informed of the measures which it has taken and the reasons therefor. It shall also inform the Secretary General of the Council of Europe when such measures have ceased to operate and the provisions of the Convention are again being fully executed.

Article 16

Noting in Articles 10, 11, and 14 shall be regarded as preventing the High Contracting Parties from imposing restrictions on the political activity of aliens.

Article 17

Nothing in this Convention may be interpreted as implying for any State, group or person any right to engage in any activity or perform any act aimed at the destruction of any of the rights and freedoms set forth herein or at their limitation to a greater extent than is provided for in the Convention.

Article 18

The restrictions permitted under this Convention to the said rights and freedoms shall not be applied for any purpose other than those for which they have been prescribed.

APPENDIX B

THE SUBSTANTIVE PROTOCOLS TO THE CONVENTION

PROTOCOL NO. 1
20 MARCH 1952

The Governments signatory hereto, being Members of the Council of Europe,

Being resolved to take steps to ensure the collective enforcement of certain rights and freedoms other than those already included in Section I of the Convention for the Protection of Human Rights and Fundamental Freedoms signed at Rome on 4th November, 1950 (hereinafter referred to as "the Convention"),

Have agreed as follows:

Article 1

Every natural or legal person is entitled to the peaceful enjoyment of his possessions. No one shall be deprived of his possessions except in the public interest and subject to the conditions provided for by law and by the general principles of international law.

The preceding provisions shall not, however, in any way impair the right of a State to enforce such laws as it deems necessary to control the use of property in accordance with the general interest or to secure the payment of taxes or other contributions or penalties.

Article 2

No person shall be denied the right to education. In the exercise of any functions which it assumes in relation to education and to teaching, the State shall respect the right of parents to ensure such education and teaching in conformity with their own religious and philosophical convictions.

Article 3

The High Contracting Parties undertake to hold free elections at reasonable intervals by secret ballot, under conditions which will ensure the free expression of the opinion of the people in the choice of the legislature.

Article 4

Any High Contracting Party may at the time of signature or ratification or at any time thereafter communicate to the Secretary General of the Council of Europe a declaration stating the extent to which it undertakes that the provisions of the present Protocol shall apply to such of the territories for the international relations of which it is responsible as are named therein.

PROTOCOL NO. 4
16 SEPTEMBER 1963

The Governments signatory hereto, being Members of the Council of Europe,

Being resolved to take steps to ensure the collective enforcement of certain rights and freedoms other than those already included in Section I of the Convention for the Protection of Human Rights and Fundamental Freedoms signed at Rome on 4th November 1950 (hereinafter referred to as "the Convention") and in Articles 1 to 3 of the First Protocol to the Convention, signed at Paris on 20th March 1952,

Have agreed as follows:

Article 1

No one shall be deprived of his liberty merely on the ground of inability to fulfil a contractual obligation.

Article 2

1. Everyone lawfully within the territory of a State shall, within that territory, have the right to liberty of movement and freedom to choose his residence.

2. Everyone shall be free to leave any country, including his own.

3. No restrictions shall be placed on the exercise of these rights other than such as are in accordance with law and are necessary in a democratic society in the interests of national security or public safety, for the maintenance of *ordre public*, for the prevention of crime, for the protection of health or morals, or for the protection of the rights and freedoms of others.

4. The rights set forth in paragraph 1 may also be subject, in particular areas, to restrictions imposed in accordance with law and justified by the public interest in a democratic society.

Article 3

1. No one shall be expelled, by means either of an individual or of a collective measure, from the territory of the State of which he is a national.

2. No one shall be deprived of the right to enter the territory of the State of which he is a national.

Article 4

Collective expulsion of aliens is prohibited.

Article 5

1. Any High Contracting Party may, at the time of signature or ratification of this Protocol, or at any time thereafter, communicate to the Secretary General of the Council of Europe a declaration stating the extent to which it undertakes that the provisions of this Protocol shall apply to such of the territories for the international relations of which it is responsible as are named therein.

2. Any High Contracting Party which has communicated a declaration in virtue of the preceding paragraph may, from time to time, communicate a further declaration modifying the terms of any former declaration or terminating the application of the provisions of this Protocol in respect of any territory.

3. A declaration made in accordance with this Article shall be deemed to have been made in accordance with paragraph 1 of Article 63 of the Convention.

4. The territory of any State to which this Protocol applies by virtue of ratification or acceptance by that State, and each territory to which this Protocol is applied by virtue of a declaration by that State under this Article, shall be treated as separate territories for the purpose of the references in Articles 2 and 3 to the territory of a State.

Article 6

1. As between the High Contracting Parties the provisions of Articles 1 to 5 of this Protocol shall be regarded as additional Articles to the Convention, and all the provisions of the Convention shall apply accordingly.

2. Nevertheless, the right of individual recourse recognised by a declaration made under Article 25 of the Convention, or the acceptance of the compulsory jurisdiction of the Court by a declaration made under Article 46 of the Convention, shall not be

effective in relation to this Protocol unless the High Contracting Party concerned has made a statement recognising such right, or accepting such jurisdiction, in respect of all or any of Articles 1 to 4 of the Protocol.

Article 7

1. This Protocol shall be open for signature by the Members of the Council of Europe who are the signatories of the Convention; it shall be ratified at the same time as or after the ratification of the Convention. It shall enter into force after the deposit of five instruments of ratification. As regards any signatory ratifying subsequently, the Protocol shall enter into force at the date of the deposit of its instrument of ratification.

2. The instruments of ratification shall be deposited with the Secretary General of the Council of Europe, who will notify all Members of the names of those who have ratified.

PROTOCOL NO. 6
28 APRIL 1983

The member States of the Council of Europe, signatory to this Protocol to the Convention for the Protection of Human Rights and Fundamental Freedoms, signed at Rome on 4 November 1950 (hereinafter referred to as "the Convention"),

Considering that the evolution that has occurred in several member States of the Council of Europe expresses a general tendency in favour of abolition of the death penalty,

Have agreed as follows:

Article 1

The death penalty shall be abolished. No one shall be condemned to such penalty or executed.

Article 2

A State may make provision in its law for the death penalty in respect of acts committed in time of war or of imminent threat of war; such penalty shall be applied only in the instances laid down in the law and in accordance with its provisions. The State shall communicate to the Secretary General of the Council of Europe the relevant provisions of that law.

Article 3

No derogation from the provisions of this Protocol shall be made under Article 15 of the Convention.

Article 4

No reservation may be made under Article 64 of the Convention in respect of the provisions of this Protocol.

Article 5

1. Any State may, at the time of signature or when depositing its instrument of ratification, acceptance or approval, specify the territory or territories to which this Protocol shall apply.

2. Any State may at any later date, by a declaration addressed to the Secretary General of the Council of Europe, extend the application of this Protocol to any other territory specified in the declaration. In respect of such territory the Protocol shall enter into force on the first day of the month following the date of receipt of such declaration by the Secretary General.

3. Any declaration made under the two preceding paragraphs may, in respect of any territory specified in such declaration, be withdrawn by a notification addressed to the Secretary General. The withdrawal shall become effective on the first day of the month following the date of receipt of such notification by the Secretary General.

Article 6

As between the States Parties the provisions of Articles 1 to 5 of this Protocol shall be regarded as additional Articles to the Convention and all the provisions of the Convention shall apply accordingly.

Article 7

This Protocol shall be open for signature by the member States of the Council of Europe, signatories to the Convention. It shall be subject to ratification, acceptance or approval. A member State of the Council of Europe may not ratify, accept or approve this Protocol unless it has, simultaneously or previously, ratified the Convention. Instruments of ratification, acceptance or approval shall be deposited with the Secretary General of the Council of Europe.

Article 8

1. This Protocol shall enter into force on the first day of the month following the date on which five member States of the Council of Europe have expressed their consent to be bound by the Protocol in accordance with the provisions of Article 7.

2. In respect of any member State which subsequently expresses its consent to be bound by it, the Protocol shall enter into force on the first day of the month following the date of the deposit of the instrument of ratification, acceptance or approval.

Article 9

The Secretary General of the Council of Europe shall notify the member States of the Council of:

a. any signature;

b. the deposit of any instrument of ratification, acceptance or approval;

c. any date of entry into force of this Protocol in accordance with Articles 5 and 8;

d. any other act, notification or communication relating to this Protocol.

PROTOCOL NO. 7
22 NOVEMBER 1984

The member States of the Council of Europe signatory hereto,

Being resolved to take further steps to ensure the collective enforcement of certain rights and freedoms by means of the Convention for the Protection of Human Rights and Fundamental Freedoms signed at Rome on 4 November 1950 (hereinafter referred to as "the Convention"),

Have agreed as follows:

Article 1

1. An alien lawfully resident in the territory of a State shall not be expelled therefrom except in pursuance of a decision reached in accordance with law and shall be allowed:

a. to submit reasons against his expulsion,

b. to have his case reviewed, and

c. to be represented for these purposes before the competent authority or a person or persons designated by that authority.

2. An alien may be expelled before the exercise of his rights under paragraph 1.*a*, *b* and *c* of this Article, when such expulsion is necessary in the interests of public order or is grounded on reasons of national security.

Article 2

1. Everyone convicted of a criminal offence by a tribunal shall have the right to have his conviction or sentence reviewed by a higher tribunal. The exercise of this right, including the grounds on which it may be exercised, shall be governed by law.

2. This right may be subject to exceptions in regard to offences of a minor character, as prescribed by law, or in cases in which the person concerned was tried in the first instance by the highest tribunal or was convicted following an appeal against acquittal.

Article 3

When a person has by a final decision been convicted of a criminal offence and when subsequently his conviction has been reversed, or he has been pardoned, on the ground that a new or newly discovered fact shows conclusively that there has been a miscarriage of justice, the person who has suffered punishment as a result of such conviction shall be compensated according to the law or the practice of the State concerned, unless it is proved that the non-disclosure of the unknown fact in time is wholly or partly attributable to him.

Article 4

1. No one shall be liable to be tried or punished again in criminal proceedings under the jurisdiction of the same State for an offence for which he has already been finally acquitted or convicted in accordance with the law and penal procedure of that State.

2. The provisions of the preceding paragraph shall not prevent the reopening of the case in accordance with the law and penal procedure of the State concerned, if there is evidence of new or newly discovered facts, or if there has been a fundamental defect in the previous proceedings, which could affect the outcome of the case.

3. No derogation from this Article shall be made under Article 15 of the Convention.

Article 5

Spouses shall enjoy equality of rights and responsibilities of a private law character between them, and in their relations with their children, as to marriage, during marriage and in the event of its dissolution. This Article shall not prevent States from taking such measures as are necessary in the interests of the children.

Article 6

1. Any State may at the time of signature or when depositing its instrument of ratification, acceptance or approval, specify the territory or territories to which this Protocol shall apply and state the extent to which it undertakes that the provisions of this Protocol shall apply to such territory or territories.

2. Any State may at any later date, by a declaration addressed to the Secretary General of the Council of Europe, extend the application of this Protocol to any other territory specified in the declaration. In respect of such territory the Protocol shall enter into force on the first day of the month following the expiration of a period of two months after the date of receipt by the Secretary General of such declaration.

3. Any declaration made under the two preceding paragraphs may, in respect of any territory specified in such declaration, be withdrawn or modified by a notification addressed to the Secretary General. The withdrawal or modification shall become

effective on the first day of the month following the expiration of a period of two months after the date of receipt of such notification by the Secretary General.

4. A declaration made in accordance with this Article shall be deemed to have been made in accordance with paragraph 1 of Article 63 of the Convention.

5. The territory of any State to which this Protocol applies by virtue of ratification, acceptance or approval by that State, and each territory to which this Protocol is applied by virtue of a declaration by that State under this Article, may be treated as separate territories for the purpose of the reference in Article 1 to the territory of a State.

Article 7

1. As between the States Parties, the provisions of Articles 1 to 6 of this Protocol shall be regarded as additional Articles to the Convention, and all the provisions of the Convention shall apply accordingly.

2. Nevertheless, the right of individual recourse recognised by a declaration made under Article 25 of the Convention, or the acceptance of the compulsory jurisdiction of the Court by a declaration made under Article 46 of the Convention, shall not be effective in relation to this Protocol unless the State concerned has made a statement recognising such right, or accepting such jurisdiction in respect of Articles 1 to 5 of this Protocol.

Article 8

This Protocol shall be open for signature by member States of the Council of Europe which have signed the Convention. It is subject to ratification, acceptance or approval. A member State of the Council of Europe may not ratify, accept or approve this Protocol without previously or simultaneously ratifying the Convention. Instruments of ratification, acceptance or approval shall be deposited with the Secretary General of the Council of Europe.

Article 9

1. This Protocol shall enter into force on the first day of the month following the expiration of a period of two months after the date on which seven member States of the Council of Europe have expressed their consent to be bound by the Protocol in accordance with the provisions of Article 8.

2. In respect of any member State which subsequently expresses its consent to be bound by it, the Protocol shall enter into force on the first day of the month following the expiration of a period of two months after the date of the deposit of the instrument of ratification, acceptance or approval.

Article 10

The Secretary General of the Council of Europe shall notify all the member States of the Council of Europe of:

a. any signature;

b. the deposit of any instrument of ratification, acceptance or approval;

c. any date of entry into force of this Protocol in accordance with Articles 6 and 9;

d. any other act, notification or declaration relating to this Protocol.

INDEX

(All references are to page numbers)

245